Family Law in Practice

REFERENCE

Family Law in Practice

The City Law School
CITY UNIVERSITY LONDON

Authors
Maryam Akhavan-Tabib, Barrister, Coram Chambers
Simon Barry, Barrister, former Lecturer, The City Law School
Susan Blake, Barrister, Reader, The City Law School
His Honour Judge Glenn Brasse
Emma Burgess, Barrister, former Senior Lecturer, The City Law School
Ros Carne, Barrister, former Senior Lecturer, The City Law School
Virginia Dunn, Barrister, Visiting Lecturer, The City Law School
Deirdre Fottrell, Barrister, Coram Chambers
Veronica Lachkovic, Barrister, Senior Lecturer, The City Law School
Elpha Lecointe, Barrister, Coram Chambers
Lisa Parkinson, Mediator, Co-Founder of Family Mediators Association
Yvonne Snape, Advice Worker, Gingerbread
Archna Thaman, Barrister

Editors
Virginia Dunn, Barrister, Visiting Lecturer, The City Law School
Veronica Lachkovic, Barrister, Senior Lecturer, The City Law School

Series editor
Julie Browne, Barrister, Senior Lecturer, The City Law School

OXFORD
UNIVERSITY PRESS

OXFORD

UNIVERSITY PRESS

Great Clarendon Street, Oxford OX2 6DP

Oxford University Press is a department of the University of Oxford.
It furthers the University's objective of excellence in research, scholarship,
and education by publishing worldwide in

Oxford New York

Auckland Cape Town Dar es Salaam Hong Kong Karachi
Kuala Lumpur Madrid Melbourne Mexico City Nairobi
New Delhi Shanghai Taipei Toronto

With offices in

Argentina Austria Brazil Chile Czech Republic France Greece
Guatemala Hungary Italy Japan Poland Portugal Singapore
South Korea Switzerland Thailand Turkey Ukraine Vietnam

Oxford is a registered trade mark of Oxford University Press
in the UK and in certain other countries

Published in the United States
by Oxford University Press Inc., New York

7th Edition published 2006
8th Edition published 2008
9th Edition published 2010

British Library Cataloguing in Publication Data
Data available

Typeset by Laserwords Private Ltd, Chennai, India
Printed in Great Britain on acid-free paper by
CPI Group (UK) Ltd, Croydon, CRO 4YY

ISBN 978–0–19–964150–5

10 9 8 7 6 5 4 3 2 1

FOREWORD

I am delighted to write this foreword to the manuals. They are written by a combination of practitioners and members of staff of The City Law School, formerly the Inns of Court School of Law, and are designed primarily to support training on the Bar Professional Training Course (BPTC), wherever it is taught. They embrace both compulsory and optional subjects and provide an outstandingly useful resource for all those involved in the teaching and acquisition of the skills and knowledge that practising barristers need. Originally designed for the Bar Vocational Course, they have been comprehensively revised to meet the requirements of the new BPTC. They are updated regularly and, in addition, the publishers maintain a complementary website for the series, an Online Resource Centre, which can be used by readers to keep up-to-date throughout the academic year.

The manuals, together with the Online Resource Centre, exemplify the practical and professional approach that is central to the BPTC. I congratulate the authors on the excellent standard of the series and I am grateful to Oxford University Press for its ongoing enthusiastic support. The manuals are not only invaluable to all prospective barristers, but also reflect an ongoing commitment to raise standards in the public interest.

Professor Adrian Keane
Barrister
Director of Professional Programmes
The City Law School
City University, London
2012

GUIDE TO USING THIS BOOK

The Bar Manuals series includes a range of tools and features to aid your learning. This guide will outline the approach to using this book, and help you to make the most out of each of the features within.

Where to start

This is a very easy Manual to use. Begin with a careful read of Chapter 1, which will give you a feel both for this area of practice and for the layout of the book as a whole. It also alerts you to recent changes in the law since the last edition.

Practical-based approach

The rest of the Manual is divided into the areas within family practice which lawyers typically have to contend with. These are easily discerned from the Table of Contents. For example, issues in relation to children are dealt with in Chapters 8, 9 and 10. Typically the approach is practical and court-based, so that explanations about the law are always accompanied (either within a chapter or in an accompanying chapter) by practical information and guidance, in the form of a case study, sample drafts, suggested lines of cross-examination and so on.

Features to aid your analysis

To assist understanding, there are also various flow charts, checklists and the like. To deepen or widen your understanding, further reading in the form of relevant case law, interesting articles or pertinent practitioner texts is suggested in each chapter.

As appropriate there is clear cross-referencing (in **bold**) within and between chapters.

Online Resource Centre updates

Family law is a field which evolves and changes. For further material and updates to selected Manuals in this series please visit the Online Resource Centre at www.oxfordtextbooks.co.uk/orc/barmanuals

OUTLINE CONTENTS

DETAILED CONTENTS

LIST OF ABBREVIATIONS

2000 Act	Child Support, Pensions and Social Security Act 2000
2008 Act	Child Maintenance and Other Payments Act 2008
ABWOR	Assistance By Way Of Representation
ACA 2002	Adoption and Children Act 2002
ADR	Alternative dispute resolution
AE	Additional element
BE	Basic element
CA 1989	Children Act 1989
CAA 2006	Children and Adoption Act 2006
Cafcass	Children and Family Court Advisory and Support Service
CALM	Comprehensive Accredited Lawyer Mediators
CAO	Child assessment order
CCR	County Court Rules
CEV	Cash equivalent value
CGT	Capital gains tax
CMC	Case Management Conference
CMEC	Child Maintenance and Enforcement Commission
CO	Contact order
CPA 2004	Civil Partnership Act 2004
CPR	Civil Procedure Rules
CPS	Crown Prosecution Service
CSA	Child Support Agency
CSA 1991	Child Support Act 1991
DLSA 1971	Divorces and Legal Separations Act 1971
DPMCA 1978	Domestic Proceedings and Magistrates' Courts Act 1978
DVCVA 2004	Domestic Violence, Crime and Victims Act 2004
DVMPA 1976	Domestic Violence and Matrimonial Proceedings Act 1976
ECHR	European Court of Human Rights
EPO	Emergency protection order
FA	First appointment
FA 1988	Finance Act 1988
FAO	Family assistance order
FHDRA	First Hearing Dispute Resolution Appointment
FDR	Financial Dispute Resolution
FJC	Family Justice Council
FLA 1996	Family Law Act 1996
FLBA	Family Law Bar Association
FMA	Family Mediators Association
FMC	Family Mediation Council

FMS	Family Mediation Scotland
FPC	Family Proceedings Court
FPC(MP)R 1991	Family Proceedings Courts (Matrimonial Proceedings etc) Rules 1991
FPCR 1991	Family Proceedings Courts (Children Act 1989) Rules 1991
FPR 2010	Family Procedure Rules 2010
HASC	Home Affairs Select Committee
HMCS	Her Majesty's Court Service
HRA 1998	Human Rights Act 1998
ICO	Interim care order
ICTA 1988	Income and Corporation Taxes Act 1988
IRH	Issue Resolutions Hearing
ITA 1984	Inheritance Tax Act 1984
LSC	Legal Services Commission
MCA 1973	Matrimonial Causes Act 1973
MCA 1980	Magistrates' Courts Act 1980
MEA 1991	Maintenance Enforcement Act 1991
MFPA 1984	Matrimonial and Family Proceedings Act 1984
MHA 1983	Matrimonial Homes Act 1983
MLR 2007	Money Laundering Regulations 2007
NAO	National Audit Office
NFM	National Family Mediation
NRP	Non-resident parent
PD	Practice Direction
PET	Potentially exempt transfer
PHA 1997	Protection from Harassment Act 1997
PLO	Public Law Outline
POCA 2002	Proceeds of Crime Act 2002
PPF	Pension Protection Fund
PR	Parental responsibility
PRFD	Principal Registry of the Family Division
PSO	Prohibited steps order
PWC	Parent with care
REMO	Reciprocal Enforcement Maintenance Order
RO	Residence order
SFLA	Solicitors Family Law Association
SGO	Special Guardianship Order
SIO	Specific issue order
SOCA	Serious Organised Crime Agency
TCGA 1992	Taxation of Chargeable Gains

TABLE OF CASES

TABLE OF PRIMARY LEGISLATION

TABLE OF SECONDARY LEGISLATION

Treaties and Conventions

Introduction

1.1 The family courts

Family law is a unique and largely self-contained area of practice at the Bar. Although it is civil law, it has its own rules of proceedings—the new Family Procedure Rules 2010 (FPR 2010)—and to a large extent its own courts. At the magistrates' level, family cases are heard in the Family Proceedings Courts (FPCs), where magistrates with specialist competence in family law sit and no other types of proceedings are heard. In the High Court, there is a Family Division with its own team of specialist family senior judges, headed by the President of the Family Division, currently Sir Nicholas Wall. In the county courts, you are most likely to find circuit judges and district judges who mix the hearing of family cases with other areas of civil practice, although some judges and courts specialise in family law matters. There is also the Principal Registry of the Family Division (PRFD), a unique court (in High Holborn, after a long time at Somerset House), which is staffed by a team of district judges of the High Court who specialise solely in family law and by circuit judges allocated to hear family proceedings, who all bring a high level of expertise and experience to their daily lists. Unlike the majority of court proceedings, family cases (other than committal proceedings) are heard in private, but there is now a right of access by the media.

1.2 The Family Bar

Despite its specialist qualities, most barristers who enter non-commercial practice will do some family cases in their early years, so a working knowledge of how this area of law operates, and how to research within it, is useful even to those who are not intending to pursue it as an area of specialisation. Almost all common law chambers and most sets that do some criminal or civil work will also have some family work passing through the clerks' room. There are specialist family sets, all of whose members are solely family practitioners. Moreover, some of those sets, and certainly many practitioners, specialise in one particular facet of family practice. The Family Law Bar Association (FLBA) is the specialist Bar association for family barristers and has over 2,300 members. It produces *At A Glance*, an excellent and widely used ready reckoner for use in financial cases. It also produces an interesting newsletter, *Family Affairs*, which is well worth reading in order to pick up the working practitioner's perspective on issues in family practice.

1.3 The ethos

As an area of practice, family law has a distinctive feel that can take a while to pick up and become familiar with. The issues involved are often highly emotive and even distressing and the parties involved can be extremely hostile to each other. Yet in terms of end results, this is one of the least adversarial areas of practice—most private law cases settle by consent. In most family cases, the processes are all about finding a solution, which for the parties and the advocates will involve building bridges, accepting compromise, letting matters go, seeing things from all sides, getting people to focus on the future instead of the past—all with a view to finding a way forward that the parties can live with and which will enable them to get on with their lives. Most cases involve a sequence of hearings, usually for directions, that head towards a final contested hearing. Every hearing is an opportunity to negotiate and, through a combination of such negotiations, solicitor correspondence and indications and guidance from judges, most cases wend their way towards an order made by consent without the need for that final contest.

Although consensus is often the outcome in family cases, the process of getting there can involve some very tough bargaining and extremely adversarial positioning. Family practitioners are under the same duty as any other barrister to do the best for their client and the negotiating at court at the interim stages can be very tough indeed. Advocates at court will usually test the resolve and confidence of their opponents very directly, while retaining at the back of the mind a sense of ultimate compromise. At court, the advocate often feels that he or she is wearing two faces while involved in a kind of shuttle diplomacy: one explaining to the client why he or she needs to consider compromise and try to move on; the other telling the opponent why compromise is not possible and why your client's issues are still so relevant.

1.4 The discretionary legislation

Another feature of family practice that gives it its distinct feel is the legislation itself. Family statutes tend to follow a pattern of governing situations by directing the court to have regard to all the circumstances and then providing a list of features or factors to which the court is to pay particular regard (see, eg, Family Law Act 1996 (FLA 1996), s 33(6), Children Act 1989 (CA 1989), s1(3), Matrimonial Causes Act 1973 (MCA 1973), s 25). The court will almost always have discretion in how to exercise its powers. The approach is designed for the complex and personal situations that family law governs; every effort is made to avoid there being a sense of 'winners' and 'losers' and it would be inappropriate for outcomes to be achieved and the judge's hands tied by legal positioning, rather than by consideration of practical outcomes. So, usually the court must consider a set of factors or a checklist, which gives focus and consistency, but ultimately has a discretion in how to apply and balance those factors and to consider other circumstances, which gives flexibility and adaptability. Although intellectual ability is always an asset, it is probably true to say that family cases are often better argued by an approach that is fundamentally sensible rather than cerebral.

1.5 Overview of the Manual

This Manual aims to underpin and complement the experience of a pupillage that includes family work and to prepare the newly qualified advocate for his or her first steps as a practitioner in the family courts. The three biggest areas of practice within family law are orders under s 8 of the Children Act 1989, financial remedies and care proceedings. These areas are dealt with here in detail, as is the law relating to domestic violence and occupation of the family home. The divorce process and other elements of financial provision are covered in less detail. There is a comprehensive checklist for committal proceedings, these being the ultimate sanction of the family courts for non-compliance. Other less common areas of family practice, which are not covered in this Manual, include adoption, child abduction, probate, issues under the Human Fertilisation and Embryology Act 1990 and matters relating to foreign divorce. There is a chapter on mediation, an increasingly important tool in the resolution of some family matters and also a continuing opportunity for practitioners to diversify their skills and their practices.

The first types of work in which new practitioners are likely to be instructed are applications for non-molestation orders and occupation orders and also directions hearings in other practitioners' cases. The former are a good way of taking responsibility for a simple, but entire, application and of impressing on instructing solicitors your ability to handle lay clients and achieve the desired result with a minimum of fuss. Conducting other practitioners' directions hearings is a good way of getting exposed to more complicated briefs with minimal risk. Even if the directions are simple and the hearing a formality, you are well advised to take the opportunity to read and master the brief as if you were taking it through its course and to discuss the issues at court as much as you can with the other practitioners you meet. In this way, when you do have conduct of a more significant brief for the first time, in possibly more adversarial circumstances, you are less likely to be overwhelmed by a feeling of being there for the first time. This continues to be true for many years; even as you establish yourself with full conduct of simpler matters, you will always want to be getting exposure to more complex cases. Depending on the type of work that the chambers or firm does, the new practitioner can typically expect to be instructed in straightforward s 8 matters, simple claims for financial remedies (which used to be called ancillary relief) and perhaps early/interim applications by a local authority. Care cases, weightier claims for financial provision and contact or residence cases involving complex issues are not usually taken on by inexperienced advocates.

This Manual takes a practical approach and includes within the text relevant case law, legislation, rules of procedure and practice directions. Examples of commonly drafted documents are included. The relevant procedures are described along with observations and guidance on commonly occurring situations, interpretation and practical issues. Family practice involves the use of the full range of legal skills; the ability to negotiate and draft consent orders freehand at court are particularly prominent.

1.6 Skills of the family lawyer

Social skills and understanding are also very important. It is not just a case of getting on well with a client—parties to cases are usually in circumstances of breakdown and change, involving personal issues, strong feelings, the need to confront uncertainty and allegations of personal shortcomings, as well as the loss of fundamental elements of their lives which may have been taken for granted for many years. Dealing with such clients requires sensitivity and maturity. Younger advocates who have been straight through university may be dealing with situations of which they have no direct life experience—this will not be a problem as long as they have the humility and self-confidence to listen to and learn from their clients and take the advice of their colleagues.

In financial cases, numerical skills are at a premium. You will need to be able to prepare and present detailed breakdowns and summaries of incomes, assets and out-goings and to have a working knowledge of the more common financial products, mortgages, pensions and benefits. It is common at a financial dispute hearing for figures to be argued over and for the advocates and the judge to be tapping away together at calculators comparing results and looking for an agreed basis on which to proceed.

This is a time of significant change in family law. You will need to be particularly alert to proposals for reform and their progress. Some have already been introduced and others are currently being debated and considered.

1.7 The new Family Procedure Rules 2010 (FPR 2010)

In April 2011 a whole new procedural code came into force for family proceedings. These rules apply to all family proceedings, whether they are in the magistrates' court, county court or High Court. A significant change in ethos introduces the overriding objective to all proceedings with obligatory proactive case management powers. Alternative dispute resolution (ADR) must be considered at all stages and a pre-application protocol provides for the parties, subject to certain exceptions, to attend a mediation information and assessment meeting before they can issue court proceedings in private children matters and for a financial remedy (FPR 2010, Part 3 and see **Chapter 11**). There has been some modernisation of language (to make the system accessible to litigants in person) and the introduction of new forms, but not to the extent that had originally been hoped by the Committee which has steered through the changes. Those of you familiar with the mainstream Civil Procedure Rules (CPR) will find the FPR 2010 very familiar, both in tone and layout. Indeed, harmonisation with the CPR was one of the aims behind the new rules. There are thirty-six parts to the FPR and most also have a Practice Direction (PD), although it does not follow immediately after like the CPR. The idea is the same, however: the rule will tell you what to do and the PD will tell you how to do it. The new rules and such changes as they introduce are referred to at the relevant points throughout this Manual, and you should assume that any reference to the FPR in this Manual refers to the new rules. For ease of reference, the overriding objective is summarised here, to avoid it being repeated at regular intervals throughout. It is important to be able to access these new rules: they and all accompanying Practice Directions can be viewed on the free Family Law website at www.familylaw.co.uk/articles/FPRPDs-FullList-16022011.

You will be familiar with the overriding objective from civil procedure, but the emphasis and objectives are adapted to family law. Under the FPR 2010, the overriding objective applies in all family proceedings and is set out in Part 1, which closely resembles Part 1 of the CPR. Like the CPR, the FPR 2010 are stated to be a new procedural code to enable the court 'to deal with cases justly', but 'having regard to any welfare issues involved'. Dealing with a case justly includes dealing with it:

- expeditiously and fairly;
- in a proportionate manner;
- so as to save expense;
- by allotting it an appropriate share of the court's resources.

There is a positive duty on the parties to help the court to further the overriding objective (r 1.3) and the court must further it by active case management. The definition of case management (r 1.4) is virtually identical to that in r 1.4 of the CPR, but the family courts are also involved in identifying the appropriate parties to the proceedings, which issues in the case do not need full investigation and deciding the appropriate procedure. Expert evidence and the court's powers to control evidence generally are considered in **Chapter 10**.

1.8 Proposals for legal aid reform

On 21 June 2011 the government published its Response to the consultation process on proposed changes in legal aid (*Reform of Legal Aid in England and Wales Government Response*). It can be found on the Ministry of Justice website, in the consultations section. The Ministerial Foreword makes the rationale behind the proposals clear and it is not the purpose of this Manual to debate this. The aims of the proposed reform are expressed to be: 'to target legal aid to those who need it most; to make substantial savings to the cost of the scheme; and to deliver better value for money for the taxpayer'. The two most significant proposals for family practitioners are: the removal of financial remedies and private family law matters (other than cases where domestic violence or child abuse is present) from the scope of legal aid; and the commitment to reduce family fees by 10 per cent. Where there is evidence of domestic violence or child abuse, legal aid will be available to the victim for financial remedies or private law family and children cases. Paragraph 30(i) to (iii) of the Government Response defines these. The FLBA and many other interested bodies continue to press the government to amend these proposals as they go through Parliament and there is continuing debate in the media on the possible consequences, including the fear of a huge increase in litigants in person. In her speech to the Law Society on 27 June 2011, 'Equal Access to Justice in the Big Society', Lady Hale, one of the justices of the Supreme Court, expressed concern that they would have 'a disproportionate effect upon the poorest and most vulnerable in society'.

1.9 Family Justice Review

In March 2011 the Interim Report of the Family Justice Review was published. It makes proposals for significant changes to the family justice system, to both public and private law children cases and also proposes that divorce itself should be an on-line administrative process in the majority of cases. If you are interested in family law and are considering practising in this field, you should at least familiarise yourself with the bare bones of the proposals. The full report and its executive summary and recommendations can be found on the Ministry of Justice website, in the independent reviews section. There is further discussion of the proposals in **Chapter 11** and the final report was expected in autumn 2011 but had not been produced at the time of writing. The key points are probably these:

- The creation of a Family Justice Service which should, over time, take responsibility for legal aid, court social work (ie, the work currently performed by the Children and Family Court Advisory and Support Service (Cafcass)) and publicly funded mediation.
- The creation of a single family court with one point of entry.
- In private law children matters:
  - The assumption that parents will work together to reach agreement on issues in relation to their children—a Parenting Agreement
  - Compulsory assessment for mediation, followed by access to Separated Parents Information Programmes
  - Residence and contact orders will no longer be used, but issues that have not been agreed will be dealt with by a specific issue order
  - A statement in the legislation that there is an assumption that children need both parents.
- In public law children matters:
  - A reduction in the role of the court (the focus to move away from scrutinising the care plan and to concentrate on whether the threshold has been crossed)
  - A reduction in the use of experts
  - A target of six months in which cases should be completed.

1.10 Other current issues in family practice

These include:

- The tension between the civil and criminal methods of enforcing domestic violence injunctions.
- The pilot of the new police powers to make 'Go' orders.
- The increasing importance of shared care as a solution in private law children cases.
- The principles to be applied by the court when permission is sought to remove children permanently from the jurisdiction in emigration cases and the new Court of Appeal authority of *Re K* [2011] EWCA Civ 793.
- The continuing growth of mediation and ADR, both as a means of resolving disputes and as an area of practice and diversification for family lawyers; how the new Mediation Protocol will work in practice.
- Continued significant concerns about the adequacy of fees for publicly funded work and the worry that those most vulnerable will be unrepresented in family proceedings.
- Concern in the profession about the ability of the courts and practitioners to meet the increased volume of care cases.
- The government's proposals to implement the reforms to the child protection system recommended by the Munro Review, the detail of which is expected at the end of 2011.

- The effectiveness of the child support system and the uncertainty surrounding the proposed support to be given to parents to help them make their own agreements.

- Continued debate about whether there should be amendments to the law on pre-nuptial agreements; what will the Law Commission recommend when it reports in 2012?

1.11 Useful sources

The monthly journal, *Family Law*, is an excellent source of comment and analysis, up-to-the-minute case law and practical information. It has a website at www.familylaw. co.uk (where you can also find the FPR 2010 and its Practice Directions). Another very helpful website which is particularly quick at disseminating recent authorities is www. familylawweek.co.uk. The Family Law Reports are the dedicated law reports in universal use. So far as practitioner texts are concerned, it is generally better to use the readily updated loose-leaf binder publications; for financial matters, *Duckworth* is widely used; and for children's matters, *Hershman and McFarlane* is the best-known text. The FLBA publication, *At A Glance*, is very useful and is published every year. Resolution (formerly the Solicitors' Family Law Association) produces a useful booklet of precedents, *Precedents for Consent Orders*, and other interesting publications, with details contained on its website at www.resolution.org.uk.

The law and procedure is stated as at 31 August 2011.

2

Domestic violence and occupation of the family home

2.1 Introduction

Modern living brings with it benefits, but at the price of increasing insecurity for many people—especially during times of economic instability. Sadly, this has an impact on family life and one manifestation is the persistent prevalence of domestic violence, which accounts for nearly 25 per cent of recorded crime, despite the fact that only about one-third of such incidents are ever brought to the attention of the police. On average, two women die at the hands of an abusive partner each week. Although procedurally the law in this area is coherent and rational, if not entirely straightforward, nevertheless it remains an aspect of family practice requiring great care and skill. Whether domestic violence is a cause or a by-product of family breakdown, it remains a traumatic occurrence.

Domestic violence is perhaps easier to identify than define precisely. The 1993 Home Affairs Select Committee (HASC) Report on Domestic Violence described it as 'any form of physical, sexual or emotional abuse which takes place within the context of a close relationship. In most cases, the relationship will be between partners (married, cohabiting, or otherwise) or ex-partners.' Although, typically, abusers are male and the abused, female, men in heterosexual relationships can be victims, as can same-sex partners. Children are also often affected—directly, or indirectly by witnessing the abuse of a parent. Thus recent local authority guidance characterised domestic violence as including 'threatening behaviour, violence or abuse (psychological, physical, sexual, financial or emotional) between persons who are, or have been, intimate partners, family members or members of the same household, regardless of gender or sexuality' (as cited in *Yemshaw v Hounslow LBC* [2011] UKSC 3, at p 10). Some think 'domestic abuse' is a better description.

Family law's main civil response to the problem is found in a legislative framework which is by now tried and tested. It is found in Part 4 of the Family Law Act 1996 (FLA 1996) which provides injunctive remedies in family proceedings to victims of domestic violence. Unlike the criminal law, which punishes past behaviour, remedies under the FLA 1996 are directed towards the *future* by regulating the conduct of perpetrators. This legislation was long overdue when it was passed, and replaced what had been a piecemeal approach to this area of practice with a comprehensive body of statute law. In many respects the FLA 1996 gave effect to the Law Commission's recommendations which preceded it ('Family Law: Domestic Violence and Occupation of the Family Home': Law Commission Report No 207, May 1992). It thus sought to extend its remit to a wide range of relationships in which domestic abuse can take place, and attempted to give the courts very real powers to protect victims.

There was, however, an in-built bias towards heterosexual couples, which was eventually removed by the combined effects of the Domestic Violence, Crime and Victims Act 2004 (DVCVA 2004) and the Civil Partnership Act 2004 (CPA 2004). The latter gives same-sex couples who enter 'civil partnerships' equality of treatment with married couples and broadens the definition of 'cohabitant' to include same-sex couples. The former widens access to protection under the FLA 1996 and enlists the help of the criminal law for purposes of control and enforcement. Unless otherwise indicated, all provisions referred to below have been brought into force.

This chapter will largely be devoted to explaining the somewhat intricate workings of the FLA 1996, as amended, including related and recent initiatives in the criminal justice system. Bear in mind, however, that domestic violence is not usually an isolated issue and may well have relevance to and an impact on other aspects of family practice, especially contact between separated parents and their children (see **Chapter 8**) and, increasingly, financial provision after divorce (see **Chapters 4** and **5**). It is not at all uncommon that what begins as a domestic abuse case evolves into a divorce and 'contest' over the children, and you need to keep alive to the implications for these other matters.

Remember, too, that understanding the law and procedure is only half the battle in this area of practice; it is important also to appreciate (but not identify too closely with) the personal anxieties involved. Legal redress, while contributing what it can to the cause of tackling the disease of domestic abuse, is not a panacea and cannot by itself remove the distress suffered by its victims. Underlying causes abound. When you are advising and representing lay clients, always try to remember that, more often than not, they will be in a highly volatile and emotional state. Decisions on how to proceed in a way which best protects the interests of your client usually means giving careful consideration not only to that person's individual needs, but to the overall family situation as well.

2.2 The remedies

The FLA 1996 creates a single set of remedies, available from all courts having civil jurisdiction in family matters, to give personal protection from domestic violence and to regulate the occupation of the family home. A person seeking a remedy under the Act is called the 'applicant'; the person against whom the order is sought is called the 'respondent'.

There are two kinds of remedy—a **non-molestation order** and an **occupation order**—each with its own criteria, but capable of combination with one another and other family remedies. Both types of order may be made in relation to 'associated persons' (see **2.3**) and 'relevant child(ren)' (see **2.4**). An occupation order relates to persons who have lived or are living together under one roof and so has additional criteria making it available to a very limited subclass of associated persons.

2.3 Associated persons

This is the entrée into the legislation and the initial prerequisite for those seeking assistance under it. If the applicant and respondent are *not* 'associated', there is no scope for protection under this piece of legislation.

The FLA 1996 thus applies to 'associated persons', which from the outset was defined widely so as to encompass those living in almost any family or domestic living arrangement. The intention was to include many categories of people who had previously been excluded and so increase the availability of protection against domestic abuse, especially non-molestation orders. The DVCVA 2004 and CPA 2004 extended the reach of the legislation further by giving same-sex couples who have formed a civil partnership ('civil partners') equal status to spouses and by widening the class of associated persons generally.

Associated persons is defined by s 62(3), as amended, to include: spouses or former spouses; cohabitants (now defined by s 62(1)(a) as 'two persons who are neither married to each other nor civil partners of each other but are living together as husband and wife or as if they were civil partners') or former cohabitants; couples who have agreed to marry or enter into a civil partnership, so long as the agreement was not terminated more than three years previously (s 42); parties to the same family proceedings (other than under the FLA 1996 itself); and a variety of relatives (including in-laws). In *Re H (A Minor) (Occupation Order: Power of Arrest)* [2001] FCR 370, for example, a father obtained a non-molestation and occupation order against his 17-year-old son. Also included are people who live or have lived *in the same household* other than as a mere employee, tenant, lodger or boarder (ie, a domestic rather than business relationship).

The DVCVA 2004 added another category of 'associated person', namely persons 'who have or have had an intimate personal relationship with each other which is or was of significant duration'. The purpose behind this extension is to give protection from abuse to those who meet the test of intimacy, but who are or were not living together (stereotypically, perhaps, a man and a mistress set up in separate accommodation). As originally drafted, the FLA 1996 was very focused on households, so that a cohabiting gay couple would have been 'associated', but a girlfriend and boyfriend who never lived (and had no children) together would not. This new category of associated person would now cover some such couples, although the point at which dating becomes an intimate relationship of 'significant duration' awaits judicial interpretation. The description would seem to exclude one-night stands or longstanding platonic friendships, but just as a relationship can be sexual without being intimate, presumably it can be intimate without also being sexual (see explanatory note to DVCVA 2004, para 24).

Also 'associated' are the parents of the same child; individuals (not, eg, a local authority) who have or have had parental responsibility for the same child; and persons connected by virtue of the adoption process: s 62(5).

2.4 Relevant child

Children are a common feature of family life. Predictably, they also frequently figure in matters of family strife. The 'relevant child' is therefore a recurring concept in the legislation, and one which is very widely drawn, in effect including any child who needs protection from domestic abuse.

By s 62(2), a 'relevant child' in relation to any proceedings under the FLA 1996 includes:

(a) any child living with, or who might reasonably be expected to live with, either party to the proceedings;

(b) a child involved in existing children proceedings; and

(c) any other child whose interest the court considers relevant.

2.5 The non-molestation order

A non-molestation order is a form of injunction containing either or both of the following:

(a) a provision prohibiting the respondent from molesting another person who is associated with the respondent;

(b) a provision prohibiting the respondent from molesting a relevant child: s 42(1).

A great deal of thought was given to whether there should be a statutory definition of 'molestation'—a curiously archaic term used in previous legislation and which seemed incapable of simple, yet accurate modernisation. In the absence of any evidence of problems caused in the past by lack of a definition, and given the possibility that any delineation might be over-restrictive, it was decided to leave the term undefined in the FLA 1996. Thus the courts continue to be guided by the old case law which established that 'violence is a form of molestation but molestation may take place without the threat or use of violence and still be serious and inimical to mental or physical health' (*per* Viscount Dilhorne in *Davis v Johnson* [1979] AC 264). Lack of a statutory definition keeps the remedy flexible and able to adapt to novel circumstances.

In *Horner v Horner* [1982] 2 All ER 495 sending threatening letters and intercepting the applicant on the streets were regarded as molestation. In *Johnson v Walton* [1990] 1 FLR 350 it was suggested that sending partially nude photographs of the applicant to the press so as to cause her distress would amount to molestation. Thus, any serious form of pestering, intimidation or harassment is included in the concept.

There are, however, limits and the need for direct contact between perpetrator and victim was stressed in *C v C* [1998] 1 FLR 554. In that case, a husband and wife were in the process of divorcing. Newspaper articles, critical of the husband's marital conduct, were published with the assistance of information provided by his wife. The husband claimed the articles were harmful to him and sought an order restraining his wife from speaking to the press so as to procure further such articles. The issue on appeal was whether the wife's behaviour amounted to molestation. Sir Stephen Brown, then President of the Family Division, confirmed that molestation 'implies some quite deliberate conduct which is aimed at a high degree of harassment of the other party, so as to justify the intervention of the court'. But he held that the wife's revelations of her marital past 'come nowhere near molestation as envisaged by s 42'. He found the lack of direct communication between the parties relevant and concluded that the (by then ex-) husband was concerned with damage to his reputation rather than molestation as such. This case seems to confirm that molestation needs to be of a direct and personally troublesome nature, which excludes invasions of privacy which may be said only to damage one's reputation. The remedy for the latter lies in defamation.

The court may make a non-molestation order either:

- *on application* by a person who is 'associated with the respondent' whether or not other family proceedings have been initiated (thus it can be, and usually is, a 'stand-alone' application, often in conjunction with an application for an occupation order, see **2.6**): s 42(2)(a); or

- *on its own initiative*, in any family proceedings to which the respondent is a party if it considers that the order should be made for the benefit of any other party to the proceedings or any relevant child: s 42(2)(b). More specifically, whenever the court is considering making an occupation order (see **2.6**), it must also consider whether to make, on its own initiative, a non-molestation order: s 42 (4A) and (4B), inserted by DVCVA 2004, Sch 10, para 36. This is intended to give the court all options to deal with abuse in its many contexts.

In deciding whether to grant a non-molestation order, the court by virtue of s 42(5) shall have regard to *all of the circumstances* of the case, *including* the 'need to secure the health, safety and well-being' of the applicant (or, where applicable, the person for whose benefit the order is made) and of any relevant child. Note the emphasis on the *protection* of the victim.

General molestation is restrained by 'forbidding' the respondent (or anyone acting on behalf of the respondent) from 'using or threatening violence against, harassing, intimidating or pestering' the victim (notice that the word 'molestation' does not appear in the actual order). But applications are usually provoked by particular behaviour and so *specific* acts (eg, communications of certain kinds, damaging property belonging to the applicant) can and should be restrained by precise wording.

It is also possible to forbid a perpetrator invading the victim's space, as it were. This is done by means of a so-called 'zonal' order, which forbids the respondent entering or approaching named places or property, typically the applicant's place of work or a property to which an applicant has moved. These latter can resemble, but should not be confused with, occupation orders (see **2.6**). Specificity is important, both for the respondent (to whom it should be clear what he is not allowed to do) and for those responsible for enforcing such orders (see **2.14**). It is particularly important to word zonal prohibitions carefully where the respondent needs, for example, to have contact with other family members—typically the parties' children (which can be formulated as an exception to the general restraint).

Non-molestation orders may last for a specified period or until further order: s 42(7). This gives the court total flexibility. In general, non-molestation orders are intended as a temporary ameliorating measure to last only until a long-term solution is found (eg, reconciliation or separation), but every case is different and there will be occasions when a long-term or indefinite order is justified: see *Re B-J (A Child)*, *sub nom Re B-J (Power of Arrest)* [2001] 2 WLR 1660 where an indefinite non-molestation order, granted for the benefit of a child, was upheld by the Court of Appeal.

Note, however, that a non-molestation order made in the course of other family proceedings will cease if those proceedings are dismissed or withdrawn: s 42(8).

One of the vexed problems with domestic violence is that it straddles the civil and criminal law, but victims (and perpetrators) too easily fall between these two different stools. In an attempt to engage in 'joined-up' solutions and signal the seriousness with which the law views domestic violence, a major change wrought by the DVCVA 2004 was to make breach of a non-molestation order a criminal offence: FLA 1996, s 42A. This innovation, which is discussed in more detail below at **2.14**, has so far received mixed reviews from the professionals.

2.6 Occupation orders: the general scheme

Known colloquially as 'ouster orders', these regulate the occupation of the family home to protect those remaining in it. Typically, they exclude a perpetrator of domestic violence from the family home altogether or from some defined part of it. They may even preclude an abuser coming within a specified distance of the property. An abuser who has left the home can be prevented from returning.

Occupation orders are, in their nature, more limited in their scope than non-molestation orders. They come in various, if essentially standard, permutations and their availability depends on the rights and/or relationship of *both* parties to the application. *The greatest protection is given to those with property rights in the home in question and to people who have (or had) formalised their relationship (ie, as married persons or civil partners).*

The FLA 1996 distinguishes, in the first instance, between applicants who are legally entitled to occupy the family home ('entitled applicants') and those who are not. Occupation orders, which effectively force people to leave their own homes, are draconian in their nature, and are therefore easiest to justify in the case of an applicant who is independently entitled to occupy the property. Conversely, they are most difficult to justify where the applicant has no such right but the respondent does. Therefore, an applicant who is, first, 'associated' with the respondent (see **2.3**) and also 'entitled' to occupy the family home can get access to the fullest protection that is available under the Act, *irrespective* of the specific nature of her relationship to the respondent (although often it is this relationship which is the source of the entitlement—see **2.8.1**).

Non-entitled applicants, on the other hand, may *only get orders against a former spouse, former civil partner, cohabitant or former cohabitant* (now redefined to include same-sex couples who are not civil partners) and are, to a degree, discriminated against in terms of the possible duration of such orders. In addition, a further distinction is made between those who have formalised their relationship and those who have not. Cohabitants are specifically deprived of the mandatory aspects of the so-called 'balance of harm' test (see **2.8.4**), which in certain circumstances *compels* the court, when dealing with spouses/civil partners or former spouses/civil partners, to make an order in favour of the applicant.

These various permutations are reflected in the five separate, but subtly unequal sections, as amended, under which applications under the FLA 1996 are made. These are explained in detail below. In a nutshell the amendments effected by the CPA 2004 mean that civil partners are treated in the same way as married couples. Given that the parties must in any event be 'associated persons', which section is appropriate then depends on the status of the parties as follows:

- if the applicant is '*entitled*': apply under s 33 (whatever the respondent's status) (see **2.8**);

- if the applicant is *not entitled*, but the respondent *is*: apply under s 35 if the parties are *former* spouses/civil partners (see **2.9.1**), or apply under s 36 if the parties are existing or former cohabitants (see **2.9.2**);

- if *neither* applicant nor respondent is entitled: apply under s 37 if the parties are spouses/civil partners or former spouses/civil partners (see **2.10.1**), or apply under s 38 if the parties are existing or former cohabitants (see **2.10.2**).

In all cases, when deciding whether to make an occupation order, the court should also consider its powers to make a non-molestation order (see **2.5**): s 42(4A), as added by DVCVA 2004.

2.7 Two types of occupation order

There are two types of occupation order: declaratory and regulatory. The latter, as the name suggests, regulates the occupation of the family house. The former declares, extends or creates rights and is a necessary prerequisite to a regulatory order where the respondent is already entitled to occupy the home, but the applicant is not.

Declaratory orders are possible in respect of any dwelling that is, has been or was intended to be a family home. They are not, however, applicable where neither party is 'entitled' (see **2.10**).

2.8 Entitled applicant: s 33

Under s 33(1)(a) (i) and (ii), an applicant is an 'entitled applicant' if he or she is entitled to occupy the dwelling-home by virtue of:

- a beneficial estate or interest (eg, resulting trust);
- a contract (eg, tenancy agreement);
- any enactment giving the right to remain in occupation; or
- 'home rights' in relation to the dwelling-house (see **2.8.1**).

2.8.1 Home rights

Both spouses and civil partners can acquire 'home rights'. Where one spouse has legal or other rights of occupation in the matrimonial home, and the other spouse does not, the latter is given equal occupation rights, or what the FLA 1996 originally called 'matrimonial home rights'. These have now been extended to civil partners in just the same way, and therefore renamed 'home rights': FLA 1996, s 30(1) as amended by CPA 2004, Sch 9. Home rights in effect give both parties to a marriage or civil partnership equal rights to occupy the family home.

Home rights are defined in s 30(2) as being—

(a) *if in occupation*: a right not to be evicted or excluded from the dwelling-house or any part of it by the other spouse or civil partner except with the leave of the court given by an order under s 33;

(b) *if not in occupation*: a right with the leave of the court to enter into and occupy the dwelling-house.

Home rights (like the court's power to regulate the exercise of those rights) apply to any dwelling-house which is, has been or *was intended* to be the family residence: s 30(7)— not, for example, a property bought for investment purposes. In the normal course, such rights expire on divorce, termination of the civil partnership or the death of either spouse/partner, but can be extended by the court: s 33(5).

In practice, most applications under the FLA 1996 fall within s 33.

2.8.2 Possible s 33 orders

On application under s 33, the court may make any one or combination of the following 'regulatory' orders (s 33(3)):

(a) enforcing the applicant's entitlement to remain in occupation as against the respondent;

(b) requiring the respondent to permit the applicant to enter and remain in the dwelling-house or part of the dwelling-house;

(c) regulating the occupation of the dwelling-house by either or both parties;

(d) prohibiting, suspending or restricting the exercise by the respondent of his right to occupy the dwelling-house;

(e) restricting or terminating the respondent's home rights;

(f) requiring the respondent to leave the dwelling-house or part of the dwelling-house;

(g) excluding the respondent from a defined area in which the dwelling-house is included.

This menu of possibilities is designed to deal with all eventualities. Thus, for example, there could be an order preventing the locks being changed by one party who is trying to stop the other from entering the premises; or an order requiring either party to vacate the premises at specific times. Orders can even be made preventing a respondent from entering a named part of the home, either at all (eg, the main bedroom) or at certain times (eg, the kitchen), although such orders can sometimes cause as much aggravation as they seek to avoid, unless the premises are very large.

There is usually no need for a declaratory order under s 33, because the applicant, by definition, already has full entitlement to occupy the property.

2.8.3 The core criteria

The factors lying at the heart of the need (or not) for an occupation order are set out in s 33(6). In deciding whether, and in what terms, to make a regulatory order, the court must have regard to *all the circumstances* of the case, and *in particular* the:

- housing needs and resources of the parties and children;
- financial resources of the parties;
- likely effect of an order (or lack of one) on the health, safety and well-being of the parties or any relevant child; and
- conduct of the parties in relation to each other and otherwise.

These factors, which are essentially a matter of common sense, might usefully be described as the '*core criteria*' to be considered by the court. **They are common to *all* applications for occupation orders under the Act.**

2.8.4 The 'balance of harm' test

In addition, the court must apply the so-called 'balance of harm' test. This says the court *must* make a regulatory order *if* it appears that the applicant (or any relevant child) is likely to suffer *significant harm* (attributable to the respondent) if an order is not made *unless* it appears that the respondent (or relevant child) is likely to suffer equal or greater harm if the order is made (whether attributable to the applicant or not): see s 33(7).

Harm is defined in s 63. In relation to a child it means ill-treatment (specifically including sexual abuse) or the impairment of health or development. In relation to an adult it means ill-treatment (but, curiously, no mention of sexual abuse) or the impairment of health (but not development—apparently adults do not develop any further after a certain age!). Note that although the significant harm to the applicant referred to in s 33(7) must be 'attributable' to the respondent, it need not be intentional: see *G v G* (occupation order: conduct) [2000] 2 FLR 36 (CA).

Although the core criteria are obviously relevant when weighing the balance of harm, subsections (6) and (7) are distinct stages of the decision making process. In particular, the mandatory nature of subsection (7) *only* comes into play if the applicant or relevant child is likely to suffer 'significant harm'. The dictionary definition of 'significant' (ie, 'considerable, noteworthy or important')—accepted by Booth J in *Humberside County Council v Second Defendants* [1993] 1 FLR 257 (a Children Act case)—is taken as applying equally in this context (see s 63). In *Chalmers v Johns* [1999] 1 FLR 392, the Court of Appeal allowed a husband's appeal against the making of an occupation order because the judge had wrongly applied the balance of harm test in a case where the harm which the applicant and child might suffer if the order were not made was, given the history, too slight to be considered 'significant'. Confirming both the draconian nature of ouster orders generally and the fact that subsection (7) is 'designed to cater for (the) more extreme situations', Thorpe LJ went on to say at p 396:

> The court has first to consider whether the evidence establishes that the applicant or any relevant child is likely to suffer significant harm attributable to the conduct of the respondent if the order is not made. If the court answers that question in the affirmative, then it must make the order unless balancing one harm against the other, the harm to the respondent or the child is likely to be as great. If, however, the court answers the question in the negative, then it enters the discretionary regime provided by sub-section (6).

One might have said 'returns to' rather than 'enters' the discretionary regime of sub-section (6), since aspects of the core criteria set out there are obviously relevant to the question of risk of significant harm. The point is that where the court finds there is *not* a risk to the applicant of significant harm, it is *not bound* by the mandatory requirements of subsection (7) so that it has the *power* to make an order, taking into account the core criteria (ie, housing needs, conduct, etc), but is under *no obligation* to do so. See, eg, the interesting case of *Grubb v Grubb* [2009] EWCA Civ 976, now reported as *G v G (Occupation order)* [2011] 1 FLR 687.

In the sad case of *Banks v Banks* [1999] 1 FLR 726, a husband, aged 75, applied for non-molestation and occupation orders against his wife, aged 79, who suffered from senile dementia. The wife could be both verbally and physically aggressive, but had never physically injured the husband. After a spell in hospital, her doctors thought it was in her best interests to be at home in familiar surroundings. Her husband, however, felt too frail, in body as well as spirit, to cope and sought an occupation order under the FLA 1996—in effect to force her return to hospital. Although sympathetic to the husband, the court dismissed his application on the basis that there was no risk to him of significant injury if the order were not made, and so no compulsion to make an order arose. The judge also suggested that even had there been a risk of significant harm to the husband, the balance of harm in any event would have favoured the wife. A non-molestation order was also refused, principally because the wife would have been mentally incapable of understanding, much less abiding by it.

In the all too prevalent cases, however, where the court does find that there is a likelihood of significant harm, the discretion becomes a duty and the court *must* make an order if, after weighing the harm likely to be suffered by both parties and by any relevant children, the 'balance of harm' favours the applicant (or relevant child). If the applicant is unable to show risk of the *greater* harm, then the court still has the *power,* but again is under *no duty*, to make an order. See, for example, *B v B (Occupation Order)* [1999] 1 FLR 715. In that case, after suffering substantial violence at the hands of her husband, a wife moved out of the family home with the couple's 2-year-old daughter. They were temporarily housed in bed and breakfast accommodation by the local authority while the husband remained in the family house with his 6-year-old son by a previous relationship. Both children were 'relevant' children. The wife obtained an occupation order against the husband. The husband appealed.

The Court of Appeal allowed the appeal against the order because the judge had wrongly applied subsection (7), in part due to his mistaken belief that the local authority would be obliged, were the husband excluded from his home, to provide him and his son with permanent housing. In fact, a husband (albeit with a child) removed from the family home on account of his own violence is considered 'intentionally homeless', requiring the local authority only to give advice and temporary shelter. By contrast, if the mother and daughter were made homeless on account of the husband's violence, the local authority was obliged to provide them with suitable permanent accommodation. The Court of Appeal thus held that:

- the judge had been perfectly correct to decide that the wife and daughter would suffer significant harm were an order not made; but
- he had erred in balancing the risks of harm. In weighing the risk as regards the two children, the balance came down not in the favour of the applicant and her daughter, as the judge had supposed, but in favour of the husband's child, who would be very precariously housed were an occupation order made. Therefore, the judge had not been *required* by subsection (7) to make the order and in the circumstances, had he realised he had a choice, it was unlikely that he would have exercised his discretion to do so.

This case also confirms the fact that where there are significant risks to children, their interests are likely to become paramount in weighing up the balance of harm. Indeed, the Court of Appeal was at pains to ensure that the outcome of this case, which turned on a very particular set of facts, should not be viewed as condoning what had been very serious domestic violence.

2.8.5 Duration

Section 33(10) provides that orders under s 33 may be for a specified period, until the occurrence of a specified event, or until further order. In other words, these orders can be of unlimited duration.

The rest of the legislation follows the above pattern, with adaptations as appropriate to the circumstances, and to produce the result that the further away one gets from property rights or a formalised marital or civil partnership, the more notionally dilute is the protection given under the FLA 1996.

2.9 Unentitled applicant and entitled respondent

2.9.1 Former spouses/civil partners: s 35

2.9.1.1 Possible orders

Possible regulatory orders under s 35(5) are an adaptation of those available under s 33. Because the applicant is (as yet) 'unentitled', those regulatory orders included in the s 33(3) list (see **2.8.2**), but excluded from the s 35(5) list, are orders (a), (b) and (e), which in this context need to be dealt with by way of declaratory order. The court cannot make a regulatory order under s 35 without first making the relevant declaratory order, in effect giving the applicant the same rights of occupation as the respondent before any regulation of those rights is then imposed. The declaratory order is, in essence, an equalising exercise.

Thus, where the court makes a regulatory order under s 35, it *must* also include a declaratory order giving the applicant relevant occupation rights, ie:

- *if the applicant is already in occupation of the property:* there must be a provision giving the applicant the right not to be evicted or excluded from the dwelling-house or any part of it by the respondent for the period specified in the order, plus a provision prohibiting the respondent from evicting the applicant during this period (s 35(3));
- *if the applicant is not in occupation:* there must be a provision giving the applicant the right to enter into and occupy the dwelling-house for the period specified, plus a provision requiring the respondent to permit the exercise of that right (s 35(4)).

It is possible (but uncommon) for a court to make a declaratory order without going on to make further regulatory orders.

2.9.1.2   Criteria for s 35 orders

In deciding whether, and in what terms, to make a s 35 declaratory order the court is to have regard to the *core criteria* (see **2.8.3**), plus certain additional matters relating to the circumstances; namely the length of time that has elapsed since the parties ceased living together, the length of time since the marriage or civil partnership was terminated and the existence of any relevant pending family proceedings (regarding property or children). These last might be viewed as relevant to the issue of how justified a declaratory order would be, given the applicant's lack of property rights vis-à-vis the respondent.

As to whether to go on to make further regulatory orders (which the court may, usually will, but need not necessarily do), the court shall have regard to the *core criteria*, plus the length of time which has elapsed since the parties ceased living together. In addition, the court *must* make a regulatory order under s 35(5) if the balance of harm test is satisfied (see **2.8.4**).

2.9.1.3   Duration

The duration of any order granted under FLA 1996, s 35 must, on the first occasion, not exceed six months, but may be extended on subsequent occasions for no more than six months at any one time: s 35(10).

2.9.2   Cohabitants and former cohabitants: s 36

2.9.2.1   Possible orders

The same menu of order possibilities applies for s 36 FLA 1996 as for s 35 (see **2.9.1**). Thus, if the court is to make a regulatory order under s 36, it must first make the relevant declaratory order: s 36(3) and (4). Declaratory orders can stand alone, but almost inevitably will be followed by a further regulatory order (s 36(5)).

The differences, and remaining discrimination against cohabitants (albeit that this term has been extended), arise in the following aspects of the legislation and are indicated below in bold italics.

2.9.2.2   'Commitment criteria' for cohabitants

In deciding whether, and in what terms, to make a s 36 declaratory order the court is to have regard to the *core criteria* (see **2.8.3**), plus certain additional matters, again relating to the circumstances and the issue of whether such an order is justified; namely the length of time that the parties lived together, whether there are or were any children, the length of time which has elapsed since the parties ceased living together and the existence of any relevant pending family proceedings (regarding property or children). *In addition the court must have regard to the 'nature of the party's relationship, and in particular the level of commitment involved in it'* (s 36(6)(e) as amended by DVCVA 2004). This latter requirement replaces a more judgemental (and rarely invoked) provision in the original legislation (inserted at the behest of the 'family values' lobby in the dying days of the last Tory government), by which the court was to have regard to the fact that the parties had 'not given each other the commitment of marriage'. This of course is legally impossible for gay couples and in any event accentuated the negative rather than the positive. Time, and the legislation, have moved on (although not as far as some would like).

2.9.2.3   Balance of harm: *no duty*

As to whether to go on to make further regulatory orders (which the court may, usually will, but again need not necessarily do), the court shall, in addition to the *core criteria*, have regard to:

- whether the applicant or any relevant child is likely to suffer significant harm attributable to the conduct of the respondent if a regulatory order is not included in the order; and
- whether the harm likely to be suffered by the respondent or child if the provision is included is as great or greater than the harm (attributable to the conduct of the respondent) which the applicant or child is likely to suffer if the provision is not made.

Note that in the s 36 context, these are merely additional factors to be taken into account and impose no duty. *There is thus no obligation on the court to make a s 36 order, even where it is the case that the applicant will suffer significant and the greater harm if an order is not made* (although in such circumstances the court would usually exercise its discretion to do so).

2.9.2.4   Duration

Like s 35, orders under s 36 are limited in the first instance to a specified period, not exceeding six months. *However, s 36 orders may only be extended on one occasion.*

2.10   Both applicant and respondent unentitled

In most cases, at least one of the parties will be entitled to occupy the property in question, so applications under this head will be relatively rare. Situations where both parties are unentitled include squatters and bare licensees (eg, a couple living with one of the party's parents).

2.10.1   Existing/former spouses/civil partners: s 37

2.10.1.1   Possible orders

Only regulatory orders are possible, ie from the list set out in FLA 1996, s 33(3) (see **2.8.2**), but excluding those, namely (a), (d) and (e), which enforce or restrict what, in this context, are non-existent rights. As *neither* party has any rights of occupation, equality between the parties already exists in this regard—there is thus *no scope* for an equalising declaratory order. In addition, s 37 orders *cannot* apply to *intended* family homes.

2.10.1.2   Criteria for s 37 orders

In deciding whether and in what terms to make a regulatory order under s 37, the court shall have regard to the *core criteria* (see **2.8.3**). In addition, the court **must** make a regulatory order if the balance of harm test (see **2.8.4**) is satisfied: s 37(4).

2.10.1.3   Duration

As under FLA 1996, s 35—see **2.9.1.3**.

2.10.2   Cohabitants/former cohabitants: s 38

2.10.2.1   Possible orders

The possibilities are the same here as under s 37 (see **2.10.1**).

2.10.2.2   Criteria for s 38 orders

In deciding whether and in what terms to make an order under s 38, the court shall have regard to the *core criteria* (see **2.8.3**). In addition, the court shall have regard to the risk of significant harm as set out above at **2.9.2.3**. As with s 36, the court has a discretion but **no duty** to make an order were the balance of harm to favour the applicant or any relevant children.

2.10.2.3   Duration

As under s 36—see **2.9.2.4**.

2.11   Ancillary orders

When an occupation order has been made under either ss 33, 35 or 36 FLA 1996 (ie, where at least one of the parties is entitled to occupy), the court has power to make appropriate orders regarding the property in question: s 40 FLA 1996. These may impose obligations relating to repair and maintenance, discharge of rent, mortgage repayments or other outgoings, as well as the use and care of furniture and other household equipment (which can be the target of revengeful perpetrators). Such ancillary orders, as they are called, may be particularly useful where the occupation order is to last for any length of time or where an order for financial provision following divorce is awaited (see **Chapters 4** and **5**). Meaningful enforcement (especially of orders requiring money payments to third parties) can be problematic, however.

2.12   Without notice applications

These are applications heard without having notified the respondent and therefore in his absence (and so without hearing, from him, his version of events). They used to be known as '*ex parte*' applications, and you may find this expression still being used sometimes. It is, as a matter of principle, very serious to seek and gain redress without giving the other side a chance to have his say, and so such applications are only appropriate in *emergencies*.

Therefore, where the situation is not urgent, applications must be made giving all parties notice of the date, place and time of the hearing. Formerly known as '*inter partes*' applications, these are now called on (or with) notice applications.

Unfortunately, emergencies are all too common in domestic violence cases. The FLA 1996 therefore empowers the court to grant both occupation and non-molestation orders on an application without notice. However, in this context the approach to these two orders is very different. Orders to vacate the family home can interfere with the respondent's legal rights and so such orders are rarely granted until both sides have been given an opportunity to tell their stories, unless the case is clearly made out or the risks extremely serious. The courts are less anxious about granting non-molestation orders without notice, since it is not such an infringement of a person's rights that he be prevented from doing something he should not be doing in the first place (although it would undoubtedly be an affront were the complaint unjustified).

Section 45(1) says that the court should only exercise its discretion to make a without notice order where it is 'just and convenient to do so'. In determining whether to grant the order or not the court must have regard to *all the circumstances* (s 45(2)), including:

(a) any risk of significant harm to the applicant or a relevant child, attributable to conduct of the respondent if the order is not made immediately;

(b) whether it is likely that the applicant will be deterred or prevented from pursuing the application if an order is not made immediately; and

(c) whether there is reason to believe that the respondent is aware of the proceedings, but is deliberately evading service and that the applicant or a relevant child will be seriously prejudiced by the delay involved in effecting service of the proceedings (where the court is a magistrates' court) or (in any other case) in effecting substituted service (now known as service by an alternative method, or alternative service).

These provisions encompass both the notion of urgency and the need for secrecy. Section 45(2)(b) represents a useful recognition of the fact that some applicants may be so terrified of the respondent that the secrecy afforded a without notice application is needed to gain meaningful protection under the Act.

It is *imperative* that the application and supporting evidence explain *why* an application is being made without giving the respondent notice, since it should be the *exception*, not the rule to grant injunctive relief in such circumstances. This is a matter of common sense, but also required by the rules: Family Procedure Rules 2010 (FPR 2010), r 10.2(4).

Section 45(3) provides that where the court does make an order on a without notice application it must give the respondent an opportunity to make representations as soon as 'just and convenient' at a full hearing, of which notice has been given to all the parties in accordance with rules of court. This suggests, and is taken by many district judges to mean, that an order made in these circumstances should specifically state an early 'return date' when the court will revisit the order and hear both sides. If no fixed date is given, the order will make clear to the respondent that he can trigger a hearing date. Not all respondents take advantage of these opportunities.

Similarly, where a without notice application is refused, the court will usually ensure that a hearing where both parties can be present takes place quickly, again often within a week.

2.13   Undertakings and power of arrest

2.13.1   Applications on notice

Undertakings and powers of arrest have both played a role in the resolution of domestic abuse cases which come before the courts. But it is important to appreciate that they are *very different*. An **undertaking** is not an admission of guilt, but a *promise* made by the respondent to the court to do, or not do, certain things, which is given voluntarily to *avoid* a hearing and the making of a court order. Undertakings must now be signed by the parties in court (FPR 2010, PD 33A, para 1.4) and should be as specifically worded as an order might have been. Since some people give as good as they get, undertakings can be given by both parties in respect of their behaviour towards each other ('cross undertakings'), if the situation warrants it.

A **power of arrest**, by contrast, is used as an aid to *enforcing* an order which the court *has made* at the end of an FLA 1996 hearing. Before that legislation, it was exceptional for the court to attach a power of arrest to orders it made in domestic violence cases; over time it became the norm. It allows the police to arrest, *without a warrant*, a person whom they have reasonable cause to suspect of being in breach of the order, who will then be quickly brought back before the *civil* court which made it and dealt with (for alleged contempt of court). Where a power of arrest is warranted, it should *only* be attached to that part of the order to which it relates, ie, the terms excluding the respondent from the family home, and not, for example, an ancillary order (see **2.11**). This should be clear on the face of the order.

There is an obvious tension between these two contrasting approaches to abuse cases, which has sometimes proved difficult to reconcile. Historically, the acceptance by the court of undertakings has been a useful, and often used, device in such applications. In appropriate circumstances, they can defuse fraught situations in that they avoid a court hearing which can be traumatic for victims, thereby saving time, saving tempers—and saving face (by allowing a party to avoid the stigma of the imposition of a court order). They can have calming properties and are thus given statutory recognition in FLA 1996, s 46(1), which enables the court to accept an undertaking from any party where it has the power to make an occupation or a non-molestation order.

However, the legislation also seeks to give real protection to victims of domestic abuse and to that end requires that where it 'appears' to the court that the respondent has *used or threatened violence* against the applicant or a relevant child, then it *must* ensure that any order it makes can be enforced by arrest without warrant, unless it is satisfied that in the circumstances the applicant or the child in question will be adequately protected without this. In the case of occupation orders, this is achieved by attaching a power of arrest to the order (s 47(2) FLA 1996).

The same was true of non-molestation orders until very recently, but the DVCVA 2004 went one critical step further and made breach of a non-molestation order itself a criminal offence. It inserted s 42A into the FLA 1996, which provides that 'a person who without reasonable excuse does anything that he is prohibited from doing by a non-molestation order is guilty of an offence'. It was thought that this significant change rendered the power of arrest redundant as far as non-molestation orders are concerned, and so it was abolished for such purposes (DVCVA 2004, Sch 10, para 38). However, arrest on suspicion of commission of a crime can leave a victim exposed while bail and prosecution decisions are made, or worse, a mere caution given, and there have been some calls to resurrect the civil courts' previous capacity to deal promptly with breach of non-molestation orders by means of the court ordered power of arrest (see generally **2.14**).

It is important to note that arrests without warrant are used to enforce court *orders*. They are *not* possible where a respondent is in breach of an *undertaking* (which are otherwise enforceable like court orders: **see 2.14**). Because an undertaking is given voluntarily, and not imposed by the court, a power of arrest *cannot* be attached to it: s 46(2) FLA 1996. Furthermore, the court is expressly *forbidden* from accepting an undertaking in those cases where it would be required to ensure that any order it were to make is enforceable by arrest without warrant: FLA 1996's 46(3) and (3A) (as added by DVCVA 2004). The combined effect of these provisions restricts the court's ability to accept undertakings and has been the object of some criticism for tying judges' hands. Having said that, it appears that a reasonable number manage to circumvent the legislation's constraints (eg, by not making relevant findings of fact about violence) if the recent evidence from the President of the Family Division, Sir Nicholas Wall, to the House of Commons on the government's proposed reduction in civil legal aid is any guide. He referred to domestic abuse cases often being dealt with by way of undertakings and expressed concern about the latter's future. He said that if funding is only to be retained in the range of private family law cases where domestic violence is also an issue, as has been suggested, this could create a 'perverse incentive' to litigate to get an injunction, as a passport to public funding for other matters in dispute, when the giving of undertakings might have been a possible solution. He felt it important not only to ensure that the term 'domestic violence' was not viewed narrowly for funding purposes, but also that undertakings as to future conduct (and not merely court orders) should be sufficient to confer eligibility for legal aid (Justice Select Committee's Third Report: Government's Proposed Reform of Legal Aid, Published 15 March 2011, Part 5, paras 85–87). These suggestions, however, did not find favour with the government in its 'Response To Reform of Legal Aid' of June 2011.

2.13.2 Applications without notice

A power of arrest (which has been abolished for non-molestation orders) may be attached to an occupation order made without notice where it is shown that the respondent has used or threatened violence against the applicant (or relevant child) *and* that there is a risk of significant harm to the applicant (or the child) from the respondent if the power of arrest is not attached immediately: s 47(3). This reflects the fact that attaching a power of arrest to an order when the respondent has not had the opportunity to be heard should be treated with some caution. However, where there has been actual or threatened violence and there is additionally a risk of significant harm to the applicant or child, a power of arrest will be attached to an emergency occupation order.

Rather obviously, the acceptance of undertakings in lieu of a court order is not applicable to applications where the respondent is not present, since he is not there to offer any.

2.14 Enforcement

The new offence of breach of a non-molestation order is an arrestable offence, triable either way. Arrested persons are processed through *criminal*, not civil channels. Upon conviction on indictment, the maximum custodial sentence is five years; on summary conviction, the defendant may face up to 12 months' imprisonment. Other options open to the criminal courts include fines, community sentences and various treatment orders, the latter of which may attempt to tackle the underlying causes of the offending behaviour, including so-called 'perpetrator programmes'. Sentencing Guidelines speak of the seriousness of the offence, but also the importance of securing compliance with the order and the protection of the victim (Sentencing Guidelines Council (2006b), para 2.2). And see s 42A(5) FLA 1996.

Copies of the non-molestation order should be delivered to the applicant's local police station once it has been served on the respondent, who may then be arrested on the spot if there are reasonable grounds to believe he is in breach (and it needn't necessarily be the applicant who alerts the police). Where a non-molestation order has been obtained without notice, a person can only be guilty of an offence in respect of 'conduct engaged in at a time when he was aware of the existence of the order': s 42A(2). This is somewhat lax wording since a respondent may be aware of the 'existence' of an order, but not its content. However, the rules now make clear that the respondent must be served 'with the order or informed of its terms…' (FPR 2010, r 10.10). A respondent can be 'informed' of the terms of an order by various means (having been in court at the time, by telephone, etc), but even so, service of the order is always desirable. Solicitors should organise this with the safety of the applicant in mind.

As regards occupation orders, where (and to the extent that) a power of arrest has been attached, a police officer may arrest without warrant where he or she has reasonable cause to suspect the respondent of being in breach of the relevant provisions of the order. The order and power of arrest form must be delivered to the local police station and state clearly to which parts of the order the power relates and when it expires. As with the non-molestation order, the benefit to the applicant is that it is not necessary to make a separate application to court for a warrant of arrest to be issued. All she needs do is alert the police. In this case, however, if arrested, the respondent must be brought before the *civil* court which made the order within 24 hours of the arrest; either the respondent is dealt with then or released on bail (with appropriate conditions) until a later hearing (FLA 1996, s 47).

Where there is no power of arrest attached to any (or the relevant) part of an occupation order and the respondent (having been properly served, and so on) breaches the order—or indeed any undertaking given to the court in the FLA 1996 proceedings—the applicant has two choices. She can apply for a warrant for the respondent's arrest, to be brought before the civil court which made the order: FLA 1996, s 47. Such an application is *without notice* and must be supported by evidence *on oath* to satisfy the court that there are reasonable grounds for believing that the respondent has failed to comply with the order/undertaking. If granted, the warrant for arrest is sent to the officer in charge at the relevant police station for it to be executed. Once before the court, if there is sufficient evidence to deal with the respondent for his contempt of court (eg, if he admits the breach), then the court may do so then and there. If not, it will adjourn for a fully fledged committal hearing: FPR 2010, r 10.11. Alternatively, the applicant could skip option one and go straight to option two: an application *on notice* for an order to commit the respondent to prison for contempt of court.

Committal proceedings (to determine if the respondent should be 'committed' to prison) are the oldest form of enforcement and so, not surprisingly, the most cumbersome. Atypically in the family courts, they are normally heard in public and so (somewhat unusually for family practitioners) require the wearing of robes. Because the respondent's liberty is at stake, committal proceedings are in many respects treated more like a criminal than civil matter. Thus, the burden of proof is on the person alleging breach of the court's order, and the standard of proof is the criminal standard. If the contempt is established, then it is for the respondent to 'show cause' as to why he should not be sent to prison. It is relatively unusual for a respondent not to be given at least one more chance to comply before the most serious punishment is handed down, but much depends on the circumstances. The Court of Appeal in *Hale v Tanner* [2000] 1 WLR 2377, in giving detailed sentencing guidance in such cases, observed that 'there are two objectives always in contempt of court proceedings. One is to mark the court's disapproval of the disobedience to its order. The other is to secure compliance with that order in future.' Although the sentencing possibilities for civil contempt are more limited than in criminal cases, full use of them should be made, bearing in mind always the domestic context and ultimate objectives (*per* Hale LJ).

Enforcement options requiring further applications by the victim are obviously more drawn-out processes than simply calling the police, but at present they are the only possibilities for breach of non-molestation orders if the criminal route is not appealing to the victim (and she has a choice, since she needn't be the one to alert the police). They are also the only option for alleged breaches of occupation orders which carry no power of arrest.

In any case, *all* orders and undertaking forms must include what is known as a 'penal notice', ie, a warning to the respondent that a breach of the order amounts (at the very least, in the case of a non-molestation order) to a contempt of court which may be punishable by imprisonment. Without the warning, the civil penalty cannot follow. (See **Chapter 13** for a detailed guide to committal proceedings in the enforcement context.)

Note that as regards non-molestation orders, it is not possible for a person both to be *convicted* of the new offence under s 42A and also be punished for contempt by the civil courts. Having said that, there is no bar to parallel proceedings (until one comes to fruition) and contempt proceedings remain an alternative if criminal proceedings either are not brought or result in an acquittal, although given that the standard of proof is the same for contempt as for criminal prosecutions, it might be a rare case where an acquittal in the criminal courts could be followed by successful contempt proceedings.

Despite the best intentions of law and policy makers, enforcement of orders made under the FLA 1996 is fraught with difficulties. In particular, there is (and probably always will be) a tension between due process and the safety of victims; between state and individual action; between protection and punishment. Enlisting the criminal law to enforce non-molestation orders adds gravitas, and sends an important message, but it also inserts complexities and quandaries into the mix. A victim may not want the matter played out in the open criminal courts (as opposed to the private family courts). What happens if the police merely caution and leave? What happens following an acquittal? What role does the abused have in prosecution decisions? Meanwhile, civil enforcement of non-molestation orders is time-consuming and costly as public funding diminishes. Most people just want the abuse to stop and it is not clear that the criminal route is preferable to the civil in achieving this for victims, whose circumstances can vary widely, which makes it all the more important for there to be a true choice. As far as non-molestation orders are concerned, this may require the return of the court ordered power of arrest (see also **2.24**).

2.15 Variation of occupation and non-molestation orders

Either the applicant or respondent can apply to vary or discharge any order made under FLA 1996. If the court has made an order of its own motion, then it can vary or discharge it: s 49.

2.16   Applications by children under the age of 16 years

A child under the age of 16 years may make an application for a non-molestation order or an occupation order but only with the permission of the court: s 43(1). Such applications should be made in a county court and the child in question will need to act through a litigation friend, who should be the Official Solicitor if another choice would effectively pit one parent against the other.

The test that the court applies in deciding whether to give permission is whether the court is 'satisfied that the child has sufficient understanding to make the proposed application': s 43(2). There should be evidence in front of the court on this issue. In the case of *Gillick v West Norfolk & Wisbech Area Health Authority* [1986] AC 112, Lord Scarman suggested that sufficiency of understanding came with 'the attainment by a child of an age of sufficient discretion to enable him or her to exercise a wise choice in his or her own interests'. Like the *Gillick* case itself, s 43 opens up some uncomfortable possibilities, but has yet to generate much controversy. It seems more common for parents to be obtaining such orders against their teenage children, rather than the other way round. See, eg, *JH v RH* [2001] 1 FLR 641.

Having said that, it is worth looking at the interesting case of *Re A (Non-Molestation Proceedings by a Child)* [2010] 1 FLR 1363, in which many of the points set out above were made. In that case a 12-year-old child applied, by his father as litigation friend, for permission to commence proceedings for non-molestation and occupation orders against his mother. The child alleged he had been the victim of numerous physical and verbal assaults by the mother at the family home where they all lived, none of which the father had witnessed. The child had special educational needs and although the boy's solicitor told the court he had met his client and deemed him to be *Gillick* competent, no basis for this assessment was given. In saying (which must have been fairly obvious) that the father was not a good choice of litigation friend when proceedings were brought against the mother, the court noted that had the Official Solicitor been involved, other litigation options, including the father making the application in his own right, for the benefit of a 'relevant child', could have been considered. This was especially true of the occupation order application, since the child himself was not in that limited class of associated person who could make the application. In fact, very few under-16s would be.

2.17   Jurisdiction: family courts

One great benefit of the FLA 1996, when it was passed, was that it rationalised what had until then been a fractured system jurisdictionally. It did this by giving the same powers to the High Court, county courts and the family proceedings/magistrates' courts. Although some slight procedural variations remained, the effect of the FLA 1996 was to create a single *civil* jurisdiction between all levels of *family* court, enabling choice as well as equality of access and speed for all parties seeking a remedy under the Act. In *practice*, however, the county courts deal with most domestic abuse cases.

Despite the unitary jurisdiction of the family courts, the increasing role of the criminal justice system in such cases has tended to pull in the opposite direction, militating against an integrated approach to the problem. Jurisdictions become blurred when, for example, breach of the civil non-molestation order becomes a criminal offence, which re-introduces an element of fragmentation. As the Court of Appeal observed in 2005, there remains a somewhat 'unsatisfactory ... interface between the criminal and family courts ... It is expensive, wasteful of resources and time-consuming. It is stressful for the victim to move from court to court in order to obtain redress and protection from the perpetrator': *Lomas v Parle* [2005] 1 WLR 1643, para 51.

The logical answer seemed to be to integrate the family, civil and criminal jurisdictions within one 'Domestic Abuse Court', on a model familiar in the US, so that one judge can deal (so far as possible) with all aspects of a case. At present this holistic ideal remains just that—an ideal. A recent pilot project of just such an integrated court in Croydon had a very disappointing outcome, mainly because so few cases were put through the system. As a result, the government has, for the time being at least, dropped the idea.

2.18 Procedure: rules for FLA 1996 cases

There may not be a Domestic Abuse Court, but there is now procedurally one Family Court in England and Wales. In the spirit of unification, family court *procedure* has recently been completely overhauled and rationalised. The new rules, FPR 2010, which came into force on 6 April 2011, effectively create a single code of practice for all family courts. They completely supplant their predecessor (see **1.7**, which includes instructions on accessing the rules).

The procedure for applications for non-molestation or occupation orders is governed by FPR, Part 10 and not much has changed from the previous rules. Applications are made in Form FL 401, whether the application is freestanding or in other proceedings, supported by evidence in the form of a witness statement verified by a statement of truth. This evidence should convey, as economically as possible, a clear and complete picture of why and on what grounds the order is sought. (See example at **2.23**.) The application will be heard in private ('in chambers') unless the court otherwise directs (but see **2.21** regarding media access).

2.19 Amendments to the Children Act 1989

2.19.1 Temporary Exclusion order

Section 52 and Sch 6 of the FLA 1996 amended the Children Act 1989 (CA 1989), creating ss 38A, 38B, 39(3B), 44A, 44B, 45(8A) and 45(8B) and enabling the court to make an ouster order for the protection of children when making an interim care order (CA 1989, s 38) or an emergency protection order (CA 1989, s 44), but not an interim supervision order—see generally **Chapter 9** and **9.8** in particular. These changes produced welcome improvements in the *emergency* protection of children by permitting the removal, albeit as a *temporary short-term measure*, of a suspected abuser from the family home rather than the removal of the child from the source of the suspected abuse. This power is intended to supplement the emergency protection order or interim care order, rather than provide a long-term alternative to a care order. To reinforce this supplemental aspect, the expression 'exclusion requirement' is used instead of 'ouster' or 'occupation order'.

2.19.2   The conditions

The conditions for attaching an exclusion requirement, as set out in the CA 1989, ss 38A(2) and 44(A) are:

(a) that there is reasonable cause to believe that, if a person ('the relevant person') is excluded from a dwelling-house in which the child lives, the child will cease to suffer, or cease to be likely to suffer significant harm; *and*

(b) that another person living in the dwelling-house (whether a parent of the child or some other person):

  (i)   is able and willing to give to the child the care which it would be reasonable to expect a parent to give him; *and*

  (ii) consents to the inclusion of the exclusion requirement.

These provisions do not seem to be utilised very much—presumably because of the difficulty of obtaining the necessary cooperation and consent from the child's other parent or carer. It is an unhappy feature of domestic child abuse that very often the relationship of that person with the suspected abuser is such that the former assumes the role, if not of co-abuser, then of colluder. Even if the collusion is the result of incompetence, rather than malice, it can still be difficult to be assured of the required level of responsibility from the remaining adult to give the child the necessary protection.

2.19.3   The nature of the exclusion requirement

The exclusion requirement provisions are set out in the CA 1989, s 38A(3)–(10). The requirement can be to leave a dwelling-house in which the child lives, not to enter a dwelling-house in which the child lives, or to be excluded from a defined area in which the dwelling-house where the child lives is situated. As to the evidential and procedural requirements, see *Re W (Exclusion: Statement of Evidence)* [2000] 2 FLR 666 and FPR 2010, r 12.28.

The court can attach a power of arrest to an exclusion requirement to last for the period of the main order or a shorter period. Enforcement procedure is the same as for any order with a power of arrest (see **2.13–14**). See also FPR 2010, PD 12K.

An exclusion requirement ceases to have effect at the same time as the interim care order or emergency protection order comes to an end. The 'package' is thus intended as a temporary solution.

The court may accept an undertaking from a relevant person in lieu of attaching an exclusion requirement: CA 1989, ss 38B and 44B.

A person excluded can apply to vary or discharge the exclusion requirement whether or not he or she is entitled to make any application in relation to the main order itself: CA 1989, s 39(3A). If a power of arrest is attached, an application can be made for it to be discharged.

2.20   Protection from Harassment Act 1997

The range of people who can apply under the FLA 1996 for protection from domestic abuse is now very wide, but there will still be those who fall outside the class of 'associated person' who will need to look elsewhere for assistance. The criminal law has always been one source of help, of course, because often such abuse amounts to a crime (eg, assault, GBH, false imprisonment etc), although the criminal justice system is not without its drawbacks, including the different standard of proof, a relatively slow process more orientated to football hooligans than emergency protection, and the concern of many victims about criminalising members of their own family. Moreover, historically, police officers did not uniformly consider a 'domestic' to be real crime. The point of the DVCVA 2004 was to dispel this latter notion and give the criminal law a more prominent role in tackling domestic violence. Common assault was made an arrestable offence and a new offence of causing or allowing the death of a child or vulnerable adult was created (see, eg, 'Victim or Criminal?: the Interplay Between 'Failure to Protect' Offences and Domestic Violence' by Georgina Vallance-Webb, *Family Law*, May 2008, p 453). And of course, as discussed above, in an attempt to bring together the forces of the civil and criminal law to both protect and punish, breach of a non-molestation order is now a crime in itself.

This 'marriage' of the criminal and civil law in common cause is novel, but not unique. The model is the Protection from Harassment Act 1997 (PHA 1997), passed shortly after the FLA 1996. The latter was implemented after a long public debate; by contrast, the former seemed to slip onto the statute books almost unnoticed. It was introduced principally to deal with stalking by strangers, but was soon found to have greater potential (and thus more pitfalls) than the legislators anticipated and has come to be used for a range of antisocial behaviour. It can have particular relevance to family cases, particularly those where stalking and other forms of harassment follow the breakdown of an intimate relationship.

The innovative hallmark of the PHA 1997 was the hybrid nature of the legislation in that in certain circumstances breach of a civil injunction against harassment became a crime, and criminal courts were themselves given the ability to grant injunctive relief ('restraining orders') by way of sentence (as in, eg, the case of *R v Hammond* [2011] EWCA Crim 606). This mixing and matching of the civil and criminal law is not without its difficulties and detractors, but it was perpetuated in the DVCVA 2004, which, besides amending the FLA 1996, also made some significant amendments to the PHA 1997. Two of the more radical came into force in September 2009, when ss 12 and 13 of the DVCVA 2004 were implemented: it is now possible for the judge to impose a restraining order following the conviction of *any* offence, not simply behaviour associated with harassment. Even more controversially, the court now has the power to grant restraining orders against defendants who have been *acquitted* of an offence where it is thought 'necessary to do so to protect a person from harassment'.

There are obvious overlaps between the FLA 1996 and the PHA 1997, both of which deal with, and are capable of criminalising, harassment, but the focus of the two pieces of legislation is still rather different. For example: applications under the former are family proceedings, whereas applications under the latter are mainstream civil proceedings; only 'associated persons' can apply under the FLA 1996 whereas anyone can apply under the PHA 1997; occupation orders are not a remedy available under the PHA 1997; damages, which can be awarded under the PHA 1997, are not available under the FLA 1996; emergency orders are specifically catered for in the FLA 1996 but not in the PHA 1997. Practitioners need to be well aware of both statutes, and able to make a meaningful choice in the circumstances (as, eg, in *Singh v Bhakar* [2007] 1 FLR 880, where the claimant won significant damages from her former mother-in-law after a clear campaign of harassment). But often if there is a choice, it would still seem that the FLA 1996 will more usually be invoked to protect (rather than compensate) victims of abuse arising in the many domestic situations catered for in the legislation, as now enhanced by recent amendments.

2.21 The Human Rights aspect

The effect of the Human Rights Act 1998 (HRA 1998), which came into force on 2 October 2000, is to make rights under the European Convention for the Protection of Human Rights and Freedoms 'directly enforceable' against 'public authorities' (which is defined to include the courts), thus obviating the need for individuals to apply to the European Court of Human Rights (ECHR). Under s 3, the courts must minimise interference with the Convention and interpret legislation so as to be compatible with it. In addition, domestic law must be enacted, amended and interpreted so as to be compatible with the Convention. The higher courts can make declarations that legislation is 'incompatible' with a Convention right, although they cannot directly strike down primary legislation.

2.21.1 Rights of the respondent

Because an occupation order usually has the effect of precluding the respondent exercising a legal right to occupy his or her home, it necessarily interferes with the right to 'private and family life' (European Convention, Art 8). But this right is qualified and the state is entitled to infringe it in certain circumstances, including to 'protect health or morals' or to 'protect the rights and freedom of others'. The FLA 1996 was drafted so as to comply with the Convention, and it seems that the balance which the latter strikes between the rights of the individual and the rights of others has been adequately reflected in the legislation.

The ability to obtain non-molestation and/or occupation orders on applications which have been made without giving the respondent notice raises a possible conflict with Art 6 (the right to a fair trial). However, it seems that the latter is complied with so long as the need to apply without notice is made out (eg, urgency) and such orders can be reviewed or last only for so long as it takes to hear the respondent's representations at a with notice hearing. In addition, the new rules say that if an order is made on a without notice application, the terms of that order and the person to whom it is addressed should be announced in open court at the earliest opportunity: FPR 2010, PD 10, para 3.1.

2.21.2 Rights of the victim

Until relatively recently, human rights concerns tended to focus on procedural fairness to the alleged perpetrator of abuse. Increasingly, however, it has been the rights of victims which have dominated the conversation—and the time of the ECHR. The notorious case of *Opux v Turkey* (App No 33401/02, ECHR)(2009) made clear the positive obligation of states to be proactive in protecting victims of domestic violence. Turkey made rather an easy target (the husband was sentenced only to pay a fine having been convicted of stabbing the applicant multiple times, and he was released pending an appeal after having killed the applicant's mother for reasons, he said, 'of honour'), but the applicant successfully argued that indifferent policing, prosecution and sentencing of domestic violence not only infringed the right to life (Art 2) and the right not to be subjected to degrading treatment (Art 3), but also amounted to unlawful discrimination (Art 13). As the court put it (at para 198): 'the applicant has been able to show ... the existence of a prima facie indication that the domestic violence affected mainly women and that the general and discriminatory judicial passivity in Turkey created a climate that was conducive to domestic violence'.

This case, and others like it, have been one of the motivating factors behind recent initiatives to enhance the criminal justice system's role and response to domestic violence, both in supporting victims (witness support, etc) and dealing seriously with perpetrators. The most recent is a pilot scheme testing (in certain police authorities) a procedure which allows the police to ban suspected abusers from their homes temporarily—a sort of police version of a without notice ouster (occupation) order, known as 'Go' orders. This is discussed further at **2.23**.

2.21.3   Privacy, the media and justice

The general requirement under ECHR, Art 6 for open justice and public hearings nevertheless recognises the need for privacy in several circumstances, including the protection of the private life of the parties and the interests of children. It has long been assumed here that holding family law hearings in private (except proceedings for contempt of court, where the liberty of the respondent is at stake) was the best way to protect families dealing with the legal and personal fallout from domestic trauma. Over time, however, this came to be seen as a rather blanket approach, which, among other things, conflicted with the importance and benefits of ensuring that justice is not only done, but also seen to be done. The widespread perception, for example, that non-resident parents (often fathers) are treated unfairly by the courts is in part perpetuated by a lack of transparency. But navigating competing human rights in the context of family proceedings is tricky, to say the least.

There have, for many years, been strict restrictions on the *reporting* of information from family proceedings to protect children and families, although the courts do have power in some circumstances to lift these to an extent (to enlist the public's help, for example, in finding a child, who would otherwise be referred to by anonymising initials). A first step towards greater openness, taken in 2009, had a different focus. The Family Proceedings (Amendment) (No 2) Rules 2009 introduced provision for the *attendance* of accredited journalists and similar parties (but not the general public) at private hearings, subject to a contrary court direction. The idea is that the media (as representatives of the public) can see, and thus report on, how the system works (ie, justice being seen to be done), and thereby hold the courts to account. The existing statutory reporting restrictions remained unchanged, however, thus continuing to limit what documents journalists can see and the details on which they can report (which does not mean that the fear of public disclosure might not be used to some tactical advantage). This continued to be a source of journalistic frustration and so the Children, Schools and Families Act 2010 contains provisions (in Part 2) allowing greater media access to documents and the reporting of the 'substance' of cases (with safeguards). These, however, have been the subject of much apprehension amongst family practitioners and other professionals (see, eg, Wall LJ's comments in 'Justice For Children: Welfare or Farewell?' [2010] *Family Law* 29) and at the time of writing have *not* been brought into force.

It is, in any case, unclear the extent to which greater access to the courts (and/or fewer reporting restrictions) will advance the cause of public confidence in the family court system, especially as the administration of justice often does not make good copy. Opportunities to attend hearings may not be taken, even in a case which is the subject of media coverage, as noted in *Re L (A Child: Media Reporting)* [2011] EWHC B8 (Family), paras 185–193. This was a challenging child care case, which required the judge to make findings of fact about the alleged mistreatment of a 6-week-old baby by its parents, having heard evidence from both lay and expert witnesses. In his judgment, HHJ Bellamy (sitting as a High Court judge) berated a crusading *Telegraph* journalist who, without having attended any of the hearings (the dates of which he knew), published inaccurate stories based only on one-sided information (provided by the mother, who the judge decided had been responsible for breaking the baby's arm). The judge said that this highlighted the 'dangers inherent in journalists relying on partisan and invariably tendentious reporting by family members and their supporters rather than being present in court to hear the evidence which the court hears'. The press, he continued, have a right to highlight and criticise shortcomings in the family justice system, but 'should not lose sight of the fact that journalistic freedom brings with it responsibility, not least the responsibility to ensure fair, balanced and accurate reporting'.

The balance between transparency and openness, on the one hand, and safeguarding sensitive material in the interest of children and families, on the other, is a very delicate one. The dispensing of justice tends to be slow and deliberate; journalists often need a quick, fast-paced fix. If HHJ Bellamy's experience is anything to go by, public understanding of and confidence in the family justice system may not be improved any time soon.

2.22 The Forced Marriage (Civil Protection) Act 2007

There is an obvious overlap between forced (as opposed to arranged) marriage and domestic violence. The hallmark of a forced marriage is the absence of valid consent on the part of both parties, and the presence of abuse or duress, whether physical, financial, emotion or otherwise. In *NS v MI* [2007] 1 FLR 66, Munby J (as he then was) said that 'the court must not hesitate to use every weapon in its protective arsenal if faced with what is, or appears to be, a case of forced marriage'. Until the Forced Marriage (Civil Protection) Act 2007 (FM(CP)A 2007), those weapons included care proceedings (if children were involved) or the (domestic) criminal law (assuming a victim would be willing to give evidence, which might well expose her to more violence), the FLA 1996 as it then stood or the inherent jurisdiction of the High Court (eg, to grant annulments, thus avoiding the cultural stigma of divorce, which would otherwise be time barred, as in *B v I (Forced Marriage)* [2010] 1 FLR 1721). There were, however, limits to what the court could do. For example, one of the great challenges of forced marriage is its extra-jurisdictional nature; young people are often taken abroad for such purposes, and it is difficult for the arm of the law to reach that far.

The FM(CP)A 2007 widened the ambit of the FLA 1996 in an attempt to accommodate the complexities of forced marriage. It adds a new Part 4A to the FLA 1996, providing protection from having been or being 'forced into a marriage or from any attempt to be forced into a marriage'. The terms of a Forced Marriage Protection Order (FMPO) made under Part 4A may relate to conduct within *or outside* the jurisdiction of England and Wales and can be directed at a wide range of persons, whose identity may or may not be known to the court, who is involved, however peripherally, with forcing an individual into marriage. An FMPO may not only contain the usual prohibitions (such as non-molestation orders, etc), but also 'restrictions, requirements or other terms', including, for example, an order that a respondent surrender the victim's passport (so as to prevent the latter being taken abroad against her will). In an attempt to bolster the effectiveness of the forced marriages legislation, in 2008 the government raised the minimum age limit for those applying for visas as partners or spouses of British nationals from 18 to 21 years of age (the British national must be 21 as well). Although problematic for genuine marriages involving younger people requiring visas, the courts have upheld the policy as a reasonable and justified response to a 'pernicious' problem (*Quilla v Secretary of State for the Home Department* [2009] EWHC 3189 (Admin)).

An application for a FMPO may be made by the person to be protected or by a 'relevant third party' (which now includes local authorities: Family Law Act 1996 (Forced Marriage) (Relevant Third Party) Order 2009). Any other person may make an application with the court's permission. The court is required to take into account the 'ascertainable' wishes and feelings of the victim when considering whether to make the order. Often such feelings can be mixed, to say the least. Victims often perceive legal intervention as a stark choice between the 'security' of a home and having no home or standing in their community whatsoever.

FMPOs can be made in the county court or High Court, on notice or without notice, and a power of arrest can be attached in much the same way as occupation orders. To this extent Part 4A mimics Part 4 of the FLA 1996 (the relevant procedure is found in FPR 2010, Part 11). When this new legislation was brought into force in late 2008, the hope was that with proper training and understanding, and sufficient support from frontline services (eg, social services, schools, doctors), it would become more than 'a symbolic outlawing' of forced marriage and make a real contribution to its eradication. Two years on reviews are mixed, in part because the problem is in reality more social than legal. Nearly 300 orders have been made in that time, mostly (but not exclusively) in anticipated geographic and cultural clusters. Interestingly, some 14 per cent of those who sought assistance were male (gay men are particularly vulnerable because they can be targeted to avoid 'shame' being brought on their cultural community). There are few reported cases (which is frustrating for practitioners but not necessarily a bad thing) and these have focused on procedural issues, in particular arguments for withholding sensitive information from disclosure (eg, evidence from informants who may be family members and also at risk). It seems that local authorities themselves have been more apt to issue care proceedings than apply for FMPOs (there is an obvious overlap between the two) and, predictably, potential victims themselves are reluctant to come forward. We know that most one-on-one domestic abuse cases go unreported and unrecorded; forced marriage involves whole families against a victim, and invokes cultural notions of 'shame' and 'honour' which run very deep. Some headway has been made, as noted in a recent review in a House of Commons Home Affairs Committee report on *Forced Marriage* (HC 880), published in May 2011 (which recommended criminalising forced marriage which is now government policy); but as the report concluded, and the President of the Family Division put it when speaking of the cases which had been through the High Court (December [2010] Fam Law 1335): 'we still have a mountain to climb'. It seems that it is still progress at the grassroots which, if anything, will make the difference.

2.23 Latest initiatives: police pilot scheme

In November 2010 the coalition government announced specific funding for specialist services and initiatives designed to assist in the struggle against domestic abuse, including education and early intervention strategies, training of frontline staff and support for vulnerable women. Among these is a pilot scheme, now to be operated by three police forces (Greater Manchester, Wiltshire and West Mercia), giving officers on the ground power to issue civil orders to protect victims following suspected abuse. So-called 'Go' orders will prohibit alleged abusers from having contact with the victim or returning to the victim's home for an initial period of 48 hours (on service of a Domestic Violence Protection Notice), which a court can extend for a period of 14 to 28 days (with Domestic Violence Protection Order). This pilot is said to be modelled on similar schemes operating abroad, such as in Germany, Poland and Switzerland. These pilots are intended to operate for one year from the summer of 2011 (although the number of participating police forces has already been reduced from four to three for reasons of cost).

'Go' orders are in effect mini ouster and non-molestation orders handed out initially by the police, rather than the courts. They continue the trend of giving the police and criminal courts a greater role in responding to abuse situations, thereby reducing a victim's need for a solicitor. It is perhaps no accident that they also come at a time when funding for civil legal aid is under great strain. Given that domestic violence may come to be seen as something of a passport to funding in family cases, it will be interesting to see what impact 'Go' orders have on the number of domestic abuse incidents reported to the police as compared to the number of applications in the family courts under the FLA 1996 in the pilot scheme areas. Practitioners will watch the developing law with interest.

2.24 Criminal v civil proceedings?

Although this chapter necessarily focuses on the family court's procedures for responding to domestic abuse, the increasing role of the criminal justice system is an important element of the equation. It is important for family practitioners to be aware of this, as well as the choices it offers and complexities it introduces. The dynamics of domestic violence are uniquely difficult, because as a social ill it straddles the public and private domain, social and legal contexts, the civil and criminal law. The line between these last two may have become blurred over the last 10 years, but it has not disappeared. At present the situation is less a seamless transition than a pick-and-mix where at times other people are making the selections for you.

The choice between criminal and civil (family) proceedings raises several issues: the range of sanctions available, degree of victim involvement, timing, evidential rules, costs and public funding. There are at present pros and cons about both jurisdictions, but sometimes choice is illusory. Criminalisation sends out a clear social message, increases sentencing options, and makes it more difficult for perpetrators to blame victims for their judicial fate. Appropriate bail conditions can fill the gap between arrest and trial. Giving the criminal courts the ability to grant 'restraining orders' by way of sentence avoids victims having to go back to the family courts for a civil order. The value of 'Go' orders remains to be tested.

There is a risk, however, that victims' wishes, although taken into consideration, can become marginalised in the criminal courts, along with their control over how to deal with what has happened to them. After all, prosecutors represent the public, not the complainant. Moreover, the trial can be an ordeal since criminal courts do not typically have access to the evidence on which the original non-molestation order was based (even for sentencing purposes—see, eg, comments in *R v Briscoe* [2010] EWCA Crim 373), which can mean a victim has to rehearse much of this all over again, in open court (although with the help of witness support, etc). Furthermore, giving a perpetrator a criminal record can, paradoxically, be counter-productive by inflaming a situation when family members still need to maintain some contact with each other (eg, because of children)—especially where so-called family 'honour' is concerned. The public forum and stigma of the criminal courts can be a disincentive for those seeking protection.

Where breach of a non-molestation order is concerned, theoretically a victim who does not wish to involve the police and/or wishes to stay in control of proceedings has the option of seeking civil enforcement (see **2.14**). The matter is then dealt with by a court with relevant expertise and full knowledge of the family history. But this route raises questions of delay (while the arrest warrant is sought), costs and lack of public funding. Furthermore, the choice may be effectively removed by the police (if they are called) who respond to the alleged breach. If the perpetrator is arrested, the case will be sent to the Crown Prosecution Service (CPS), which will consider the evidence (usually without a clear picture of the family history) and decide whether or not a conviction is likely to be secured. If charges are brought, there may be an election for trial by jury. The criminal standard of proof can pose difficulties for crimes typically committed in private, and cross-examination of the victim by criminal practitioners can be gruelling. Following an acquittal, a victim could feel very aggrieved—and vulnerable—at the end of what may have been a very long process. Concurrent proceedings are possible, but the interaction needs to be watched.

Victims vary enormously in their needs and priorities, and there are no easy answers. Practitioners must be aware of the nuances of the approaches of both the civil and criminal systems to domestic abuse: how they relate to each other, what choices they offer, what combinations may be needed to best protect the client. It has been suggested by some commentators and judges that in order to give victims real choice between civil and criminal remedies, the family court's ability to deal with breach of non-molestation orders by means of the family court ordered power of arrest should be revived, and the sentencing capabilities following proceedings for civil contempt enlarged (see, eg, DJ Edwina Millward's comments in 'More Harm Than Good', *Law Society Gazette*, April 2008). The more revolutionary solution of creating a truly unitary Domestic Violence Court structure (a one-stop shop, where the civil and criminal jurisdictions can be dispensed by the same judges who know the case history) would still seem to be a long way off.

OCCUPATION ORDERS

[of home which is, was, or was intended to be a common home]
Family Law Act 1996, as amended

Assuming R is 'associated' (now includes almost every domestic/enduringly intimate
relationship) with A:

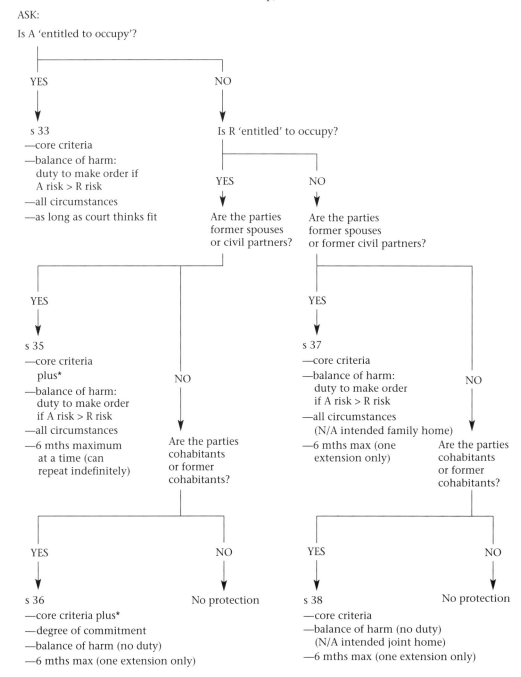

ASK:

Is A 'entitled to occupy'?

YES

s 33
—core criteria
—balance of harm:
  duty to make order if
  A risk > R risk
—all circumstances
—as long as court thinks fit

NO

Is R 'entitled' to occupy?

YES

Are the parties
former spouses
or civil partners?

YES

s 35
—core criteria
  plus*
—balance of harm:
  duty to make order
  if A risk > R risk
—all circumstances
—6 mths maximum
  at a time (can
  repeat indefinitely)

NO

Are the parties
cohabitants
or former
cohabitants?

YES

s 36
—core criteria plus*
—degree of commitment
—balance of harm (no duty)
—6 mths max (one extension only)

NO

No protection

NO

Are the parties
former spouses
or former civil partners?

YES

s 37
—core criteria
—balance of harm:
  duty to make order
  if A risk > R risk
—all circumstances
  (N/A intended family home)
—6 mths max (one
  extension only)

NO

Are the parties
cohabitants
or former
cohabitants?

YES

s 38
—core criteria
—balance of harm (no duty)
  (N/A intended joint home)
—6 mths max (one extension only)

NO

No protection

* ie, additional factors relevant to status, eg, how long together, etc

2.25 An example of domestic violence proceedings in the county court

Instructions to counsel

IN THE CLERKENWELL AND SHOREDITCH COUNTY COURT   Case No 12/162

IN THE MATTER OF THE FAMILY LAW ACT 1996

BETWEEN

MS EMMA JANE BROWN   Applicant

and

MR DAVID MITCHELL BROWN   Respondent

INSTRUCTIONS TO COUNSEL

Counsel has herewith:

1. Copy application dated 9.1.2012

2. Copy sworn statement of the Applicant sworn on 9.1.2012

3. Statement of Mr Brown

Counsel acts for the Respondent, Mr Brown. On 9 January 2012 his wife, Mrs Brown, obtained without notice a non-molestation injunction. The return day is 16 January 2012. Counsel is referred to the application and statement of Mrs Brown.

Counsel is instructed to draft the witness statement of Mr Brown of 9A Haliday Road, London N1 in reply to the application of Mrs Brown to exclude him from the matrimonial home at the above address and to renew the non-molestation injunction. Counsel will note from the statement of Mr Brown that he disputes the recent allegation of violence but makes some admissions to the older allegations.

Mr Brown says that he cannot go and stay with his brother James Brown because he now has a lodger and there would be no room for him to move in. Instructing solicitors are of the view that there is a chance of Mr Brown being excluded from the property despite not having anywhere to live. Instructing solicitors spoke with Mr Brown this morning, who says that yesterday his wife returned to the property when he was there and things were fine, although she did go back to sleep at her friend's flat.

Application for:
a Non-Molestation Order
an Occupation Order

Family Law Act 1996 (Part IV)

The Court

Clerkenwell and Shoreditch County Court

To be completed by the Court

Date issued   *9 January 2012*

Case number   *12/162*

Please read the accompanying notes as you complete this form.

1. About you (the Applicant)

State your title (Mr, Mrs etc), full name, address, telephone number and date of birth (if under 18):

Mrs Emma Jane Brown
9A Halliday Road
London N1 OJE

0795 234 1799

State your solicitor's name, address, reference, telephone, FAX and DX numbers:

Messrs Ling & Ton
2 Upper Street
London N1 2LT
Tel: 0207 226 4175
Fax: 0207 226 4299

2. About the Respondent

State the Respondent's name, address and date of birth (if known):

David Mitchell Brown
9A Halliday Road
London N1 OJE

(dob: 16.05.1986)

3. The Order(s) for which you are applying

This application is for:

[✓] a non-molestation order

[✓] an occupation order

[✓] Tick this box if you wish the Court to hear your application without notice being given to the
     Respondent. The reasons relied on for an application being heard without notice must be stated
     in the statement in support.   **[P.T.O.**

FL401   Application for: a Non-Molestation Order/an Occupation Order (09.09)   1   FL401/1

4. Your relationship to the Respondent (the person to be served with this application)

Your relationship to the Respondent is:

(Please tick only one of the following)

1 [✓] Married

2 [ ] Civil partners

3 [ ] Were married

4 [ ] Former civil partners

5 [ ] Cohabiting

6 [ ] Were cohabiting

7 [ ] Both of you live or have lived in the same household

8 [ ] Relative.
        State how related:

9 [ ] Agreed to marry.
        Give the date the agreement was made. If the agreement has ended, state when.

10 [ ] Agreed to form a civil partnership.
        Give the date the agreement was made. If the agreement has ended, state when.

11 [ ] Both of you are parents of, or have parental responsibility for, a child.

12 [ ] One of you is a parent of a child and the other has parental responsibility for that child.

13 [ ] One of you is the natural parent or grandparent of a child adopted, placed or freed for adoption, and the
        other is:
            (i) the adoptive parent
        or (ii) a person who has applied for an adoption order for the child
        or (iii) a person with whom the child has been placed for adoption
        or (iv) the child who has been adopted, placed or freed for adoption.
        State whether (i), (ii), (iii) or (iv):

14 [ ] Both of you are the parties to the same family proceedings (see also Section 11 below).

[P.T.O.

FL401/2

5. Application for a non-molestation order

If you wish to apply for a non-molestation order, state briefly in this section the order you want. Give full details in support of your application in your supporting evidence.

Respondent to be forbidden to use/threaten violence, intimidate, harass or pester the Applicant, enter the Applicant's place of work, instruct or encourage any other person to do any of the above.

6. Application for an occupation order

If you do not wish to apply for an occupation order, please go to section 9 of this form.

(A)   State the address of the dwelling-house to which your application relates:

9A Halliday Road
London N1 OJE

(B)   State whether it is occupied by you or the Respondent now or in the past, or whether it was intended to be occupied by you or the Respondent:

Both the Applicant and the Respondent

(C)   State whether you are entitled to occupy the dwelling-house: ☑ Yes   ☐ No

If yes, explain why:
Provided by Applicant's employer

(D)   State whether the Respondent is entitled to occupy the dwelling-house: ☑ Yes   ☐ No

If yes, explain why:
Home Rights

[P.T.O.

On the basis of your answers to (C) and (D) above, tick one of the boxes 1 to 6 below to show the category into which you fit:

1 ☑ a spouse or civil partner who has home rights in the dwelling-house, or a person who is entitled to occupy it by virtue of a beneficial estate or interest or contract or by virtue of any enactment giving him or her the right to remain in occupation.

If you tick box 1, state whether there is a dispute or pending proceedings between you and the Respondent about your right to occupy the dwelling-house.

2 ☐ a former spouse or former civil partner with no existing right to occupy, where the Respondent spouse or civil partner is so entitled.

3 ☐ a cohabitant or former cohabitant with no existing right to occupy, where the Respondent cohabitant or former cohabitant is so entitled.

4 ☐ a spouse or former spouse who is not entitled to occupy, where the Respondent spouse or former spouse is also not entitled.

5 ☐ a civil partner or former civil partner who is not entitled to occupy, where the Respondent civil partner or former civil partner is also not entitled.

6 ☐ a cohabitant or former cohabitant who is not entitled to occupy, where the Respondent cohabitant or former cohabitant is also not entitled.

Home Rights.
If you do have home rights please:
State whether the title to the land is registered or unregistered (if known):
unknown

If registered, state the Land Registry title number (if known):
unknown

If you wish to apply for an occupation order, state briefly here the order you want. Give full details in support of your application in your supporting evidence.

An order excluding the Respondent from the property known as 9A Halliday Road London N1 OJE

[P.T.O.

FL401/4

7.   Application for additional order(s) about the dwelling-house

If you want to apply for any of the orders listed in the notes to this section, state what order you would like the Court to make:

8.   Mortgage and rent

Is the dwelling-house subject to a mortgage?   ☐ Yes   ☐ No

If yes, please provide the name and address of the mortgagee:
unknown

Is the dwelling-house rented?   ☑ Yes   ☐ No

If yes, please provide the name and address of the landlord:
No details (I rent from my employers)

9. At the Court

Will you need an interpreter at Court?   ☐ Yes   ☑ No

If yes, specify the language:

If you require an interpreter, you must notify the Court immediately so that one can be arranged.

If you have a disability for which you require special assistance or special facilities, please state what your needs are. The Court staff will get in touch with you about your requirements.

[P.T.O.

FL401/5

10. Other information

State the name and date of birth of any child living with or staying with, or likely to live with or stay with, you or the Respondent:

N/A

State the name of any other person living in the same household as you and the Respondent, and say why they live there:

N/A

11. Other Proceedings and Orders

If there are any other current family proceedings or orders in force involving you and the Respondent, state the type of proceedings or orders, the court and the case number. This includes any application for an occupation order or non-molestation order against you by the Respondent.

NONE

This application is to be served upon the Respondent.

Signed: *Emma Jane Brown*   Date: 9 January 2012

                    2009 Edition 9.2009

No. of Witness Statement	1
On behalf of	Applicant
Date:	9.1.12
No. of Exhibits:	0
Case No	12/162

IN THE CLERKENWELL AND SHOREDITCH COUNTY COURT

IN THE MATTER OF AN APPLICATION UNDER PART IV OF
THE FAMILY LAW ACT 1996

BETWEEN:-

MS EMMA JANE BROWN

Applicant

and

MR DAVID MITCHELL BROWN

Respondent

FIRST WITNESS STATEMENT OF APPLICANT

Status

1. I, EMMA JANE BROWN, am employed as a waitress and live at 9A Haliday Road, London N1 0JE.

2. The Respondent, DAVID MITCHELL BROWN, and I are associated persons within Section 62(3) of the Family Law Act 1996 because we are husband and wife.

3. I am making this witness statement in support of my application, made without notice to the Respondent, for a non-molestation order forbidding the Respondent from using violence against me or from threatening, intimidating, harassing or pestering me. I especially do not want him coming to my place of work. I also seek an order requiring the Respondent to vacate the matrimonial home at 9A Haliday Road, London N1 0JE, supported by a power of arrest. I make this witness statement from matters within my own knowledge, except where otherwise stated.

Background

4. I met the Respondent in November 2010 and we got married on 16 April 2011. He moved into my one-bedroomed flat, which is located around the corner from the cafe where I work. My work address is 24 Bishops Road, London N1 0JD.

Conduct

5. I did not know of the Respondent's serious drink problem until after we were married. Very shortly after our honeymoon he began to drink to excess on a regular basis. When he gets drunk he becomes abusive and violent but particularly his drunkenness manifests itself in an uncontrollable paranoia that I am engaging in affairs with different men.

6. The Respondent began visiting the cafe where I work, usually without warning, and sometimes many times in the day, to see if I had any men hidden behind the serving area or in the store room. He was also rude to the male customers telling them to 'keep their hands off his missus' and not to 'eye me up'. This was extremely distressing for me and embarrassing for both me and my customers.

7. One day in July 2011 the Respondent and I were walking down the street when we met a married couple who are friends of mine. After we chatted for a few minutes the Respondent shouted at the man to 'stop imagining that you are having sex with my wife'. I did not know what to do or say so I just kept quiet.

8. On 6 August 2011 the Respondent and I went to a party where we met one of his friends. The friend complimented me in front of the Respondent who immediately lost his temper. He punched

his friend in the face, broke his nose and there was blood everywhere. I was very embarrassed and frightened and did not dare say anything to the Respondent about this outburst.

9.   The next day the Respondent noticed that I was wearing some silver earrings. I bought these before we were married and have worn them many times. However, he was convinced that they were a present from one of my customers. He grabbed me by the wrists, pulled the earrings out of my ears and tore my lobes as he did so.

10.   Since then, the Respondent has assaulted me on more occasions than I can remember. He began going to the pub more and more and would often come home and beat me or kick me or bend back my fingers. I felt too ashamed to go to the doctor for help. I wore trousers and long sleeved tops so that nobody noticed the bruises.

Significant harm

11.   Two nights ago the Respondent and I decided to hold a party with a Mexican theme for about twenty of the Respondent's friends and a couple of my girlfriends. I spent the whole day preparing the food whilst the Respondent provided the alcohol. Unfortunately he drank a glass of tequila with each guest as they arrived and got very drunk. He then got jealous of everyone complimenting me on the food, how pretty I looked in the Spanish dress that I was wearing and the attention that I was receiving. He got hold of a bowl of dip and threw it at me causing the dip to run down my dress. He shouted at me to 'stop behaving like a tart' and said 'now you will want to strip off your dress you slapper'. He then grabbed me by the wrists and dragged me to the bedroom trying to rip off my dress. He slapped me around the face and told me to change clothes. I felt humiliated because everyone was watching so I stayed in the bedroom and waited for everyone to go.

12.   About an hour later the Respondent staggered into the bedroom and hurled an empty bottle at me narrowly missing me and hitting the wall behind. He jumped on top of me on the bed and twisted back my arms. I received a large bruise on my left upper arm. Then he pulled my hair right back, slapped my face and then started to hit my head against the headboard. He only stopped when I poked his eyes with my fingers. He then rolled over and fell off the bed. I quickly ran to the bathroom and locked the door and stayed there all night.

13.   Last night I slept on the sofa of Janice Ham, a work colleague who lives close to the Angel. She has a small flat and I cannot stay there for more than a few days. I have nowhere else to go. My flat is provided by my employers, as part of my wages. Otherwise, I only earn £80 per week net and I cannot afford to rent any other accommodation. The Respondent can stay with his brother in Finchley where he lived prior to the marriage. His brother has a two bedroom house and it is not far for him to commute to work in his car. He is a garage mechanic working at Highbury Corner.

Emergency application

14.   I am too frightened to return to my flat. The Respondent behaves irrationally and I believe that he will continue to assault me if he is allowed to remain in the flat. I am frightened by how the Respondent will react to my applying for this injunction and I therefore seek an order without notice in the terms as set out in paragraph 3 of this statement and/or in such terms as the Court sees fit.

I believe the facts stated in this witness statement are true.

Emma Jane Brown
Dated 9 January 2012

In the Clerkenwell and Shoreditch County Court

Non-molestation Order under Section 42 of the Family Law Act 1996   Case No 12/162

	Applicant	Emma Jane BROWN
	Ref:	
	Respondent	David Mitchell BROWN
	Ref:	

To DAVID MITCHELL BROWN of 9A Haliday Road
London N1 0JE

IMPORTANT NOTICE

You must obey this order. You should read it carefully. If you do not understand anything in this order you should go to a solicitor, Legal Advice Centre or Citizens Advice Bureau. You have a right to apply to the court to change or cancel this order.

If, without reasonable excuse, you do anything which you are forbidden from doing by this order, you will be committing a criminal offence and liable on conviction to a term of imprisonment not exceeding five years or to a fine or to both.

Alternatively, if you do not obey this order, you will be guilty of contempt of court and may be fined or sent to prison.

This order has been made without notice to the Respondent under sections 42 and 45 of the Family Law Act 1996.

On 9th January 2012, District Judge Linda Swanson considered an application for an order and Upon Hearing the Solicitor for the Applicant;

THE COURT ORDERED THAT :

From and after the time when the respondent is made aware of the terms of this order whether by personal service or telephone or otherwise the respondent whether by himself or acting jointly with any other person is forbidden to:

1. use or threaten any unlawful violence towards the applicant;

2. enter or come within 50 metres of 24 Bishops Road, London N1 0JD, the applicant's place of work;

3. harass, pester or intimidate the applicant;

4. instruct or encourage any other person to do anything which he is forbidden to do by this order.

This order shall remain in force until **9 July 2012**.

Costs reserved

AND the Court FURTHER ORDERED that

1. The court will re-consider the application and whether the order should continue at a further hearing at Clerkenwell and Shoreditch County Court on Monday, 16 January 2012 at 10:30 am (time estimate 15 minutes).

   If you do not attend at the time shown the court may make an order in your absence.

2. You the respondent must file any sworn evidence on which you intend to rely at the court office and serve copies on the applicant's solicitor (or if unrepresented then on the applicant) no later than Thursday, 12 January 2012.

IMPORTANT NOTICE TO THE RESPONDENT

This order has been made after a hearing of which no notice was given to you. A date for reconsideration of the order has already been fixed by the court but in case of real urgency you have the right to apply for the order to be reconsidered before that date. Your application must be supported by a sworn statement of evidence which should explain why your case is urgent. You must also inform the applicant or the applicant's solicitors that you are making an urgent application for the order to be reconsidered.

Note to the Arresting Officer

Under Section 42A of the Family Law Act 1996 breach of a Non-Molestation Order is a criminal offence punishable by up to five years' imprisonment. It is not necessary to obtain a warrant.

Family Law Act 1996, Section 42A(1):
A person who without reasonable excuse does anything that he/she is prohibited from doing by a Non-Molestation Order is guilty of an offence.

STATEMENT OF MR BROWN

I can't believe what she is saying. Whilst it is true that I used to go and visit her at work a lot, that was only because we had just got married and I missed her when we came back from our honeymoon. It was out of affection and not out of jealousy. I did accuse Emma of receiving the earrings from a customer but it is very difficult because she gets lots of builders and the like coming into her cafe and they are always being sweet on her. I asked her to take them off because it upset me seeing her wearing them and she refused. She just smiled and said nothing. She refused to answer my questions so I did take them off her. Maybe I was a bit heavy handed but they are very tricky things to remove. Anyway, she never complained about it at the time.

I admit that I did accuse Dave Canker of imagining that he was having sex with my wife when we met them in the street but that is because he has a reputation of having affairs and started chatting up Emma in front of Amy, his wife, who was getting all upset and crying and Emma was laughing at her and I wanted to help Amy because Dave is so thoughtless and would not stop.

I admit that I got drunk on the 6 of August last year and punched Frank Lee, but he asked for it. He has always been going on at me about how pretty Emma is and how he fancied her and so when he met her for the first time at that party and started coming on strong I was furious. I don't trust him an inch. He is a letch and if he could get his hands on Emma he would.

Emma is very aware of the effect she has on men. She can switch on the charm and sex appeal when she wants to and she does it to tease me. It is true that I have hit her a couple of times in the past but that is only because she was trying to get my attention by chatting up other men. She knows that I get jealous and she does it on purpose. I have never kicked her. I have bent back her fingers but that is to stop her poking out my eyes. It is true that I go to the pub most evenings and some lunchtimes but that is because most of my mates go down there. As I have said, I do not get drunk and beat up Emma; rather, she teases me to get me jealous.

How Emma has described the Mexican party is a pack of lies. I did not drink a glass of tequila with every guest on their arrival. How would she know because she was not standing by the door greeting guests as they came in. Rather she was doing provocative dances with some of my mates from work. That is why I threw the food at her. It was the only way I could stop her dancing those close up Latin American dances. She was trying to attract my attention and to get me jealous. She stormed into the bedroom. When I came in later to see if she was alright she attacked me. She was screaming and kicking and when I tried to defend myself she tried to poke my eyes out.

I cannot stay with my brother in Finchley. He has rented out his spare room to a lodger and my car is not reliable enough to travel the distance to work. I cannot afford to be late for work because I already have a warning at work over my time-keeping. There is nobody else who has the room to put me up and I can't afford to rent because I am trying to pay off my credit card. I owe about £4,300 and I make payments of £200 a month. This comes out of my take home pay of £255 a week.

2.26 *Brown v Brown*: drafting the witness statement

The witness statement is the party's evidence before the court and is an absolutely crucial document. It takes a high degree of skill—and lots of practice—to draft such statements effectively. Barristers are not often called upon to do this, but solicitors and other advocates will be.

When drafting a witness statement, which must be verified by a statement of truth, you want to put forward the relevant facts as convincingly as possible. In effect your job is to present the evidence so that it has the best chance of achieving its purpose. Remember that judges often have to sit and read such statements all day long. If yours can be that much more compelling, clear and to the point, you will be doing yourself and your client a valuable service.

See generally FPR 2010, Part 17 and City Law School's *Drafting Manual* (Oxford University Press) for the rules of presentation of witness statements.

2.26.1 Content

It is imperative that the story you tell is the *client's* story—not your story or a story you think you would rather be telling. Obviously, you should never invent evidence.

In the statement, your client should set out the relief or outcome sought and the eligibility for such relief, eg, the category of associated person and rights of occupation in the property. If the application is without notice, then the statement *must* include an explanation of why this is the case.

The statement should contain the relevant facts available to show why the party needs the court's protection or on what basis he or she resists the injunction(s) sought. It should focus on the main incidents said to justify the making (or not) of the order(s). The statement does not recite the law, but it needs to be drafted with the law clearly in mind. What it must do is set out the facts material to the criteria which the court will apply under the relevant section of the FLA 1996. If it is a statement in reply, it should show why the criteria are not satisfied and/or why the court's discretion should be exercised in favour of the respondent and not the applicant.

2.26.2 Structure

It is important to tell your client's story well. The facts should be presented logically, setting out clearly the incidents of violence (or replying to each allegation of violence). A chronological telling is often easiest to follow. It may also help (but is not strictly necessary) to use subheadings relating to the relevant legal provisions.

Try to develop a 'theory of the case' and draft accordingly. Describing a steady escalation of violence will require a different presentation from the portrayal of an out-of-the-blue series of attacks. Always set the scene carefully and think in terms of a 'strong finish'. Tailor the structure to meet the needs of your case; never use 'off-the-peg' statements.

Be as specific as you can. In Mrs Brown's statement she asserts that she has been assaulted on 'more occasions than she can remember'. Unless she really has been attacked so many times it has affected her short-term memory, she will be challenged on this telling lack of detail.

A witness statement in reply would normally adopt the order of the applicant's statement and should always respond to *every* allegation.

2.26.3 Language

The statement is the witness's evidence and it is important to set out the facts so that his or her 'voice' comes through. Having said this, it is also important to express the statement in a grammatically and readily comprehensible way. The aim is not to make the statement unnecessarily formal but to make it clear and compelling. If it is appropriate to include the actual words spoken by a person, this should be done in the normal way using quotation marks.

2.26.4   Persuasiveness

The aim of the statement is to persuade the court to make the order applied for or to resist the making of the order. Your 'theory of the case' must be an effective one; you must set out the facts in such a way that the inference you wish the judge to draw is credible and one which will achieve your goal. For example, Mrs Brown's theme might be that her husband is of a jealous disposition which especially manifests itself when he is drunk. He misinterprets situations, is increasingly violent towards her and will continue to do this unless she obtains protection from the court. She gives examples of his behaviour: he pesters her at work; he accuses her of having affairs; he tore out her earrings; he has developed a habit of getting drunk and using violence towards her. When there is a history of violence, an applicant is more likely to get the additional protection of an occupation order if he or she can show that it has escalated.

In reply, Mr Brown's theme might be that he does not misinterpret situations, but rather that his wife deliberately taunts him and behaves in an alluring manner towards other men so as to make him jealous. While he does admit to, and regret, the occasions when he has lost his temper in response to such behaviour, eg, throwing the dip, he asserts that the allegations greatly exaggerate the situation and that his wife, who has voluntarily returned to the flat since her application, is herself capable of violence.

2.27   *Brown v Brown*: at the without notice hearing

This hearing, of which Mr Brown is not given notice, is brought in the county court and heard in chambers (ie, in private, but see **2.21**)—usually by a district judge or a circuit judge. Mrs Brown's counsel (or solicitor advocate) will introduce himself or herself, explain that the application is for a non-molestation order and an order excluding Mr Brown from the matrimonial home situated at 9A Haliday Road, London, the latter to be supported by a power of arrest. Counsel will then briefly give some background facts—the very short courtship; the date of the marriage; the immediacy of Mr Brown's unfounded suspicions and pestering which has escalated into violence first towards others and then his wife.

The judge should then be given an opportunity to read the statement if he or she has not done so already. Counsel will then get into the heart of the application. The essence of the case is that Mr Brown is of a jealous disposition which especially manifests itself when he is drunk and he uses violence towards his wife. He particularly seeks her out at her place of work. Counsel will refer to the paragraphs in Mrs Brown's witness statement to support this theory and the fact that Mr Brown's conduct towards his wife has got worse, culminating in the Mexican party when he threw a bowl and bottle at her, grabbed her by the wrists, jumped on top of her and twisted her arms back; pulled her hair back; slapped her face and started to hit her against the headboard. Highlight relevant facts and repeat useful detail, but do not merely recite whole paragraphs which the court has already read.

Counsel will then seek to persuade the judge that Mrs Brown needs proper protection and, importantly, draw attention to her reasons for applying without notice. Much will be made of the fact that Mrs Brown sought refuge in the bathroom and sanctuary at her friend's and that she cannot stay for long at Janice Ham's on the sofa whereas her husband could stay with his brother in Finchley and drive to work. In the absence of Mr Brown, Mrs Brown's counsel must be mindful of the need for full and frank disclosure (which is sometimes difficult to achieve given the emotions involved in such family crises). In any case, you should always be aware of and be prepared to deal with weakness in the case (eg, a lack of medical evidence, her return to the flat).

The outcome will likely be based on Mrs Brown's statement and it is most unlikely that she will be called to give evidence unless, for example, the judge wishes to hear evidence of her injuries because there is no medical evidence to support her case (if possible, you should always get such evidence). Also, if there have been other incidents since the statement was made, then Mrs Brown could be called to give evidence of these, in exceptional circumstances, but it is more likely that her advocate will inform the judge of them. The FPR 2010 provide that evidence at interim hearings should be by evidence in writing: r 22.2(2)(b). For this reason, witness statements should be carefully drafted.

Alternatively, it might well be that the judge has had an opportunity to read the papers before the case is called into court. The judge is then likely simply to seek any clarification from the advocate on any matter that concerns him or her. Here, for example, the question is likely to be whether Mrs Brown is proceeding with her application for an exclusion order at this without notice hearing.

This is because the judge is unlikely to make an occupation order excluding Mr Brown because these are not exceptional circumstances (see **2.12**). He or she would, however, be likely to grant a non-molestation injunction, including a zonal order prohibiting Mr Brown going to Mrs Brown's place of work. This can no longer be supported by a power of arrest, since its breach would be a criminal offence.

The judge would then fix a return day for the with notice hearing which is usually about seven days later. Both parties will have the opportunity to put their case at this time. The without notice order itself is now usually made for a reasonable period, usually at least six months. At the return date, the court will consider whether the order should be amended or terminated; the benefit of making the order for six months initially is that a fresh order does not have to be made and served after the subsequent hearing. This is particularly useful if the respondent does not turn up to that hearing.

Costs are usually reserved. If Mrs Brown is publicly funded (which would be indicated on the front page of the brief to her counsel), an order for the assessment of her costs should be sought at the last hearing conducted in relation to her application.

The without notice hearing is likely to last only five to ten minutes. It is vital to present a focused and succinct application. Not only is this apt to be more persuasive, but the courts are very busy and will have a number of matters listed for the day.

Mrs Brown should have been advised before the hearing that she was unlikely to get the occupation order at this stage, and so should not be unduly surprised if she has not. She may, however, still have concerns so, after the hearing, counsel should explain the outcome, and especially the effect and added protection of the fact that it is a criminal offence to break a non-molestation order.

The order will only take effect once it has been drawn up and served upon Mr Brown personally—if appropriate, by an enquiry agent. Mrs Brown should be advised when the order has been served and what, in practical terms, to do if her husband is in breach of the terms.

2.28   Brown v Brown: at the with notice hearing

Again, the hearing is in private (but see **2.21.3**). This time, however, *both* parties are able to put their case, Mr Brown having by now made and served his witness statement in reply to Mrs Brown's. His statement, too, should be verified by a statement of truth.

Counsel for Mrs Brown will introduce the case (and both parties' advocates) and remind the court that a non-molestation injunction was ordered at the earlier hearing on 9 January 2012 and that this is the return day for the applications. As this hearing has been listed for 15 minutes, it is likely to be treated as a directions hearing, since Mr Brown wishes to contest the making of the exclusion order and the court is unlikely to have time to hear a contested hearing on this return date. A date will be fixed for the contested hearing.

At the contested hearing, having briefly opened the case, Counsel will refer the judge to the two witness statements in the matter and then call Mrs Brown as a witness. Having taken the oath, she will be asked to identify herself and then to confirm that she did make her statement on 9 January 2012 and that its contents contain her account of events to the date of its being made. If there are no other matters which need to come out, then generally Mrs Brown should not be asked questions-in-chief, but be tendered for cross-examination. As for the without notice hearing, if you want to get a power of arrest attached to the occupation order, you need the court to make a finding that there has been the use of or threat of violence. You may feel better able to show this if Mrs Brown tells her side of the story by relating the serious incidences of violence prior to cross-examination, but do not simply rehash what is in her statement (which otherwise stands as her evidence-in-chief). Some judges like to hear some oral evidence-in-chief in order to assess credibility. But others will stop you. You need to be flexible and learn to know your tribunal. If in conference before the hearing, Mrs Brown tells counsel of new matters since the statement was made, eg, new details of violence, accommodation and financial matters, then she can be asked questions-in-chief to elicit this information. Strictly speaking, the permission of the court is required to adduce further evidence-in-chief, in the same way as in general civil hearings: r 22.6(3) FPR 2010.

Counsel for Mr Brown will then cross-examine Mrs Brown. He or she will question her on all the disputes of fact, putting Mr Brown's case to her. Counsel will seek to advance Mr Brown's theory of the case and to discredit hers. For example, he or she will seek to obtain from Mrs Brown admissions that she has behaved in an alluring manner to other men knowing that her husband would be provoked by this. Counsel would point out omissions and contradictions in her evidence. For example, she cannot recall details of the other incidents, which might indicate that they are invented; or the fact that in her statement she says her husband bent her fingers back but she omits to say that this was to avoid her poking out his eyes. There may be a suggestive lack of medical evidence.

Mrs Brown will be re-examined if necessary. Assuming there are no other witnesses, that concludes the case for the applicant. Remember to avoid surprise witnesses; if there are other people who can speak to relevant matters, ensure that their statements are available.

Counsel for the respondent then calls Mr Brown. The same points concerning examination-in-chief apply here and if Mr Brown is willing to give relevant undertakings, tell the court and make the appropriate forms available. Then, counsel for Mrs Brown will cross-examine him with any necessary re-examination to follow.

Finally, the closing speeches. The respondent goes first, giving the applicant the last word. The most effective submissions will take the judge through the s 33 'core criteria' and balance of harm test (see **2.8.3** and **2.8.4**), applying them to the facts. You are more likely to be successful if you relate each part of the test to the relevant facts and articulate your arguments fully while at the same time being concise and focused on matters likely to influence the decision.

The judge is well familiar with the legislation, so concentrate on persuading him or her that, *on the facts of this case*, your client is entitled to the remedy/outcome he or she seeks. As regards the occupation order, be aware of how s 33(6) and (7) relate to one another (see **2.8.4**). Apply the s 33(6) criteria to each party, relying on your own version of the events (as adapted through any concessions made in cross-examination), and compare and contrast with the version of events put forward by the other side.

When dealing with the balance of harm test contained in s 33(7), think in terms of both whether the test applies (ie, whether there is a risk of 'significant harm') and whether the balance favours your client. Set out the facts that support your submission on these points and contrast with any argument your opponent can make or has made. Deal with the mandatory/discretionary parts of s 33 in such a way that it advances your own case. Even if the court is not required to make the order in the applicant's favour, this does not mean it will not, in its discretion, do so.

If he is present, the respondent will know the terms of any order made, but it should also be drawn up and served personally on him. Copies of any non-molestation order (and any occupation order to which a power of arrest is attached) should be sent to the local police. In addition, if an occupation order is made under ss 33, 35 or 36, the applicant must serve a copy of the order on the mortgagee or landlord (as the case may be) of the property in question. Remember that breach of a non-molestation order is now a criminal offence and so arguments on accepting undertakings in lieu of such an order will focus on the applicant's need for the protection that the order thus brings by way of enforcement (or lack of it). Costs will be apt to follow the event, although if both parties are publicly funded, the court will make no order as to costs. Counsel should ask for a certificate for counsel.

Again, after the hearing, counsel should spend a moment explaining the outcome of the case and its practical implications to the applicant, and deal with any questions or concerns which he or she might still have.

2.29 Further reading

Chokowry, K. and Skinner, K., 'The Forced Marriage (Civil Protection) Act 2007: Two Years On', *Family Law (In Practice)*, January 2011.

'Compensation for Domestic Abuse after *Singh v Bhakar*' [2008] *Family Law Week*, 25 September; www.familylawweek.co.uk.

James, B., 'Prosecuting Domestic Violence', *Family Law*, May 2008, p 456.

Millward, E., DJ, 'More Harm Than Good' *Law Society Gazette*, 3 April 2008.

Platt, J., HHJ, 'The Domestic Violence, Crime and Victims Act 2004 Part I: Is it Working?' [2008] *Family Law*, July, 642.

Re L (A Child: Media Reporting) [2011] EWHC 1285 (Fam), case notes [2011] *Family Law*, 764 (July).

Segal, M., DJ, 'The Ouster Dilemma' [2009] *Family Law*, April, 295.

Whitehead, L., 'Non-Molestation Orders: The New Provisions of the DVCVA 2004' [2010] *Family Law*, December, 1299.

3 The divorce process

This chapter provides a basic, practical outline of grounds upon which a divorce may be obtained, the procedure for getting a divorce and examples of relevant drafting. Irretrievable breakdown is the sole basis upon which a divorce may be sought, but this must be shown by alleging and proving one of five facts, three of which are entirely fault based.

The procedure has been subject to significant criticism for a variety of reasons. Fault-based divorce has the potential to encourage recrimination rather than resolution, it can put the emphasis on ending a marriage rather than on reconciliation, and it can permit a relatively quick divorce which might leave important matters relating to children and money unresolved for some considerable time. There are also concerns about the cost of divorce.

A comprehensive attempt to address these problems was made in the Family Law Act 1996 (FLA 1996), which proposed the introduction of a wholly new procedure which was not based on fault, sought to support marriages that could be saved, encouraged mediation rather than litigation, and provided for the resolution of matters relating to children and money before a divorce was finalised. However, pilot projects highlighted difficulties with some of the proposed changes and, in January 2001, the government announced that it no longer intended to put the legislation into effect. Some elements of these proposed changes are currently being revived with changes made in the Family Procedure Rules 2010 (FPR 2010), including new requirements to promote the use of mediation, and with the likely cuts in entitlement to public funding to finance divorce proceedings proposed in the Legal Aid Bill 2011 (see **1.8**). Some of these changes are controversial, and their extent and effect remains to be seen.

3.1 Getting married

It is a prerequisite of divorce that the couple be validly married. The law on the validity of marriage is not within the scope of this Manual, save where the marriage is void or voidable, see **3.6**. The rules governing capacity to marry can be found in the Matrimonial Causes Act 1973 (MCA 1973), s 11. In effect, they allow persons who are not closely related, who are of the opposite sex to one another, not already married and who are aged over 18, or over 16 with parental consent, to marry. Special rules allow those who are not domiciled in England or Wales to marry polygamously outside England or Wales.

Even where the parties have the capacity to marry, the validity of the marriage may be questioned if the formalities have not been complied with (MCA 1973, s 11), or if the marriage has not been consummated or one of the parties either did not consent to it or had not the capacity to consent to it, or married a person who was pregnant by another or suffering from venereal disease at the time of the marriage (MCA 1973, s 12). Note that MCA 1973, s 13 provides defences to some of these grounds. See also **2.22** on forced marriage.

When s 12 applies, a decree annulling the marriage must be obtained; whereas when s 11 applies, a declaration from the court should be obtained.

Formalities for the marriage service are governed primarily by the Marriage Act 1949. The Act allows a marriage to take place in any approved building, and many hotels and locations such as football stadia and London Zoo have been approved. There are some requirements as to the content of the ceremony; see, for example, the Marriage Ceremony (Prescribed Words) Act 1996. While rules on the formalities of marriage are well established, they can cause some difficulties. For example, a marriage that follows the rites of a religion will not necessarily be formally valid if there is not also a civil ceremony in a Registry Office.

Since 5 December 2005 it has been possible for two people of the same sex to enter a civil partnership under the Civil Partnership Act 2004 (CPA 2004). The ceremony must be performed in an approved building and registered. Civil partners have many of the same rights as a married couple in terms of maintenance, benefits, inheritance, etc. Similarly, the divorce process is the same, although the vocabulary differs slightly (civil partnerships are 'dissolved').

3.2 The ground for divorce/dissolution

If a person decides that his or her marriage is over, a divorce is available under the MCA 1973, s 1, only on the ground that the marriage has broken down irretrievably. This irretrievable breakdown may be shown in one of five ways:

(a) That the respondent has committed adultery and the petitioner finds it intolerable to live with the respondent.

(b) That the respondent has behaved in such a way that the petitioner cannot reasonably be expected to live with the respondent.

(c) That the respondent has deserted the petitioner for a continuous period of at least two years immediately preceding the presentation of the petition.

(d) That the parties to the marriage have lived apart for a continuous period of at least two years immediately preceding the presentation of the petition and the respondent consents to the decree being granted.

(e) That the parties to the marriage have lived apart for a continuous period of at least five years immediately preceding the presentation of the petition.

Only the first two involve no interval of time and can be used immediately, and therefore tend to be the most popular. However, both are based on the fault of the other spouse and are therefore to some extent antagonistic. The fourth ground is the only one which is consensual and makes no allegation of fault, but this requires two years of separation before a divorce can be granted.

There may be important considerations in deciding which basis for divorce to allege if there is any choice on the information provided by the client. Of course, the basis must be legally sound and supported by available evidence, but if there is a choice it should be carefully made. Adultery and 'behaviour' are most commonly used for speed, whereas the alternatives require a wait of at least two years. Two years' separation and consent has the advantage of a parting by agreement. If more than one basis for divorce may be alleged, the choice may be based on the strength of available evidence, or on tactics. To give an example, an allegation of behaviour may be useful if it lays a foundation for claims to be made in financial or children hearings, but may be unwise if it upsets a spouse with whom it is hoped a good financial settlement can be negotiated.

3.3 The procedure for obtaining a divorce

The court must have jurisdiction to hear the divorce. This depends on the residence and domicile of the parties, and if there is an international element to the case it can be a complex issue. The details are beyond the scope of this Manual but should be researched if necessary. A spouse may wish to apply for a divorce in a particular country where he or she feels that financial provision rules may be more advantageous. In recent years there has been a perception that English rules may favour wives where a husband has substantial assets.

The great majority of divorce petitions are not defended and, in the case of an undefended divorce, r 7.20 of the FPR 2010 allows the divorce to be granted without a hearing; this will be the procedure that applies in the vast majority of cases. A divorce can be defended on the basis that the facts alleged are not true or do not justify the grant of a decree. In the case of five years' separation there is a statutory defence if it can be shown that a divorce would result in grave financial or other hardship for the respondent (MCA 1973, s 5). This is rarely used, and may be avoided if it is possible to find some way of making financial provision.

Divorce is a two-stage process, consisting of an interim decree (or 'decree nisi') and a final decree (or 'decree absolute'), and the parties are only free to remarry once the latter has been obtained. Applications for a decree nisi are made using FPR Form D84 (see **3.4**); for a decree nisi to be made absolute, application is made using FPR Form D36. Generally, it is the petitioner who will apply for the decree absolute six weeks after the decree nisi has been granted by the court, but the respondent can apply once a further three months have elapsed if the petitioner has not done so. When the court grants a decree absolute, it now uses the suitably unromantic sounding FPR Form D37D.

The hearing of applications relating to financial matters, and ancillary matters relating to children is normally adjourned to be heard in private. Since 6 April 2011 it has been a requirement that a person initiating an application should follow a Pre Action Protocol, which requires that (except in limited circumstances) the potential applicant should consider with a mediator whether the dispute may be capable of being solved by mediation: FPR 2010,, PD3A, Pre Application Protocol for Mediation Information and Assessment (see **11.17** and **11.18**). There are a range of concerns about how effective this requirement will be, and this remains to be seen.

There may be a delay in the issue of the decree absolute if the judge feels it is necessary to use the court's powers with relation to the children (MCA 1973, s 41). Arrangements need not be detailed and final, but the judge must feel confident that there are no serious potential problems. A decision is taken on the basis of a written 'statement of arrangements', FPR 2010, Form D8A. If the judge is satisfied with these, the divorce will proceed under the special procedure. If the judge is not, he or she can ask for further evidence and if necessary there can be a hearing relating to the arrangements. The divorce can be delayed under s 41 if there are exceptional circumstances and it is felt that this would be in the interests of the children.

Under the current law, there are a variety of tactical and practical considerations that may be relevant in bringing or defending a divorce. Although it is possible to allege more than one basis in a petition, it is common, for costs reasons if no other, to plead only one basis, and a decision should be taken not only on the strength of the evidence but also on the likely reaction of the other side. The precise legal interpretation of each possible basis for divorce should be checked. For example, the test for behaviour is partly objective, but is also subjective; in *Birch v Birch* [1992] *Family Law* 290, the court allowed a wife to divorce a dogmatic and chauvinistic husband.

3.4   Application for a divorce or dissolution of a civil partnership

A divorce must be originated by petition. From 6 April 2011, the previous approach of a petition drafted by a lawyer has been replaced by FPR Form D8, Divorce/dissolution/ (judicial) separation petition. The form is in most respects relatively straightforward, though it will still need advice from a lawyer to be completed properly, especially as regards Part 6 ('Statement of Case'). A wide range of other forms for specific purposes are provided in FPR 2010, PD 5A.

3.4.1   The application form

Guidance on completion of FPR Form D8 is provided in FPR Form D8 Notes.

The petition form to commence the divorce or dissolution proceedings is filed in the local divorce county court or in the Divorce Registry in London, as appropriate. The form needs to be completed with a signed statement of truth: FPR, Part 17. With it are filed:

(a) A statement of arrangements for children (if there are 'any children under 16 or over 16 but under 18 who are at school or college or are training for a trade, profession or vocation' (FPR Form D8A)).

(b) The marriage certificate.

(c) A solicitor's certificate that reconciliation has been attempted (FPR Form D6).

Other provisions relating to the procedure for applications in matrimonial and civil partnership proceedings are included in FPR 2010, Part 7.

3.4.2   Completing the form/petition

Generally, most parts of the form are formal and simply recount practical matters. Part 1 asks for details of the parties, such as address and age. The petitioner may get permission to withhold his or her address if there is a real threat of danger from the respondent. Part 2 asks for details of the marriage or civil partnership, such as where and when it took place. Part 3 asks for the facts giving jurisdiction to the court. Part 4 asks whether there are any other proceedings in respect of the marriage. This will include domestic violence proceedings, existing maintenance orders, etc. Part 5 requires the petitioner to specify the ground of divorce/dissolution. Part 6 asks the petitioner to state briefly the facts relied on (MCA 1973, ss 1 and 2). In many cases, the facts can be alleged briefly and concisely, as is often the case for adultery or desertion, but all appropriate details must be given, including, for example, any periods of resumed cohabitation after separation that could be relevant under the MCA 1973.

More details are likely to be required where behaviour is relied on. It is important to organise allegations to produce a clear and strong but concise draft. The court can if necessary order that information given be clarified or added to: FPR 2010, r 7.15.

In general terms, when raising behaviour, the following is good advice:

(a) Use an overall structure, whether it be chronological or putting the worst allegations first and then lesser allegations (or vice versa).

(b) Draft each allegation concisely and clearly.

(c) If there are many allegations, choose the strongest.

(d) Allege facts, not evidence.

(e) Try to include specific actions, rather than generalisations and emotions.

(f) Use appropriate vocabulary, and if necessary put the lay client's words into a suitable form for presentation to the court. The tone should be measured, not pompous.

While it is technically possible to petition relying on more than one basis in the alternative, Form 8 does not realistically allow for this, and it should be avoided as it is only likely to increase costs, which would not be in keeping with the overriding objective.

Part 7 asks for details of any children who are either children of the family, or who are relevant to the application even though they are not children of both spouses. Parts 8 and 9 deal with access to court and details for service. Part 10 encapsulates the prayer where the petitioner should list all forms of relief sought, including financial remedies, residence order, costs, etc. Financial remedies sought should be checked with the client, but it is generally thought wise to claim widely at this early stage, thus keeping all options open.

3.4.3   Samples for completion of Part 6 of Form D8

<u>Sample where behaviour is alleged</u>

Note that allegations of any complexity or detail will need to be put on a separate sheet of paper, since the space allotted in Part 6 of the form is very small.

(i) Since about January 2008 the Respondent has become increasingly cold and neglectful towards the Petitioner, and unjustifiably critical of her abilities as a housewife and mother.

(ii) From March 2008 the Respondent began working late, often not returning home until the late evening. When the Petitioner asked about the reason for this the Respondent merely said that he liked his work, and the Petitioner would not understand anything about it.

(iii) In May 2008 the Respondent refused to take the Petitioner to an important social function connected with his employment, saying that the function was only for those who supported their spouses in their work, and falsely claiming that she gave him no support at all.

(iv) On several occasions over the summer of 2008 the Petitioner suggested that the Respondent should take her out for the evening, but he always refused, saying that he was too tired, and that in any event he found the Petitioner's company boring, and she should be spending more time keeping the house clean and learning to cook.

(v) In December 2008 the Respondent invited several business associates to the matrimonial home, giving the Petitioner little notice of their arrival. When they left, the Respondent flew into a temper, throwing crockery at the Petitioner, and breaking several items from a dinner service that had been a wedding present from the Petitioner's parents.

(vi)   From March to September 2009 the Respondent insisted on attending a course which took him away from home most weekends, although the Petitioner had asked him to spend more time with her and the children. When the Respondent was at home, he spent most of his time in his study, becoming angry with the children whenever he heard them playing. On one occasion in August 2009 he falsely accused the Petitioner of being an incompetent mother who could not control her own children. On completion of the course, the Respondent continued to spend many weekends away from the home, despite the requests of the Petitioner to stay at home.

(vii) Since July 2010 the Respondent has consumed alcohol in excessive quantities. The Petitioner has pleaded with him on several occasions, but the Respondent refuses to accept that he drinks too much, saying only that he needs a drink to help him to relax. The Petitioner has become most concerned for the welfare of the children of the family when the Respondent is drunk.

(viii) In November 2010 the Petitioner returned home early one evening to find the Respondent in a drunken stupor, although he had promised to look after the children for the day, thereby putting their welfare at risk.

(ix)   In May 2011 the Petitioner asked for an explanation from the Respondent on finding several empty whisky bottles secreted about the matrimonial home. The Respondent became extremely angry and struck the Petitioner, causing her injury which required hospital treatment and the insertion of five stitches on the side of her head. It was as a result of this incident that the Petitioner was granted the order referred to in Part 4 above. The Respondent left the matrimonial home as a result of this order and has not returned since.

Sample where adultery is alleged

Note that the person with whom adultery is alleged to have been committed, if made a party, will be the co-respondent. However, the divorcing parties are discouraged from citing others in this formal way, unless such persons have an interest in the outcome of the proceedings: FPR 2010, PD7A.

1.   The Respondent committed adultery with Mary Mopp on 16 October 2010 at the Grand Hotel, Station Road, London SW40.

2.   The Respondent also committed adultery with another woman the Petitioner could identify if required to do so.

3.   The Respondent has since 1 July 2011 lived, cohabited and committed adultery with Mary Mopp at 26 Wild Street, Dorchester, Dorset.

Sample where desertion is alleged

The Respondent informed the Petitioner on 17 December 2009 while she was in hospital that he was leaving the matrimonial home. On 20 December 2009 the Petitioner returned to the matrimonial home to find that the Respondent had indeed left. Since that day the parties have lived separate and apart.

Sample where two years' separation and consent is alleged

The parties separated by agreement on 25 December 2008 since which day they have lived apart except that cohabitation was resumed from 1 April 2009 to 1 June 2009 at 6 The High Street, Birkenhead, which period amounted to less than six months in all.

Sample where five years' separation is alleged

On 28 February 2006 the Petitioner ejected the Respondent from the matrimonial home, since which day the parties have lived separate and apart.

3.5 Defending an application

3.5.1 The decision to defend

Form D8 is served on the respondent with a form for acknowledgement of service (FPR Form D 10A), and a notice informing the respondent what courses he or she can take. Respondents who wish to defend the case should give notice of intention to defend within seven days.

It is not now common to defend a divorce petition. Even if there are disputes about money or children, many couples agree in advance what the basis for the divorce should be, and which spouse should be the petitioner. According to FPR 2010, r 7.12, an answer is only required, within 21 days of the date for filing the notice of intention to defend, if a respondent (or co-respondent):

- wishes to defend the petition, or dispute any facts alleged in it;
- wishes to cross-petition, that is, to seek a divorce on an alternative basis; or
- wishes to oppose the grant of divorce under the MCA 1973, s 5 (petition alleging five years' separation and there is a defence of grave financial or other hardship).

It is not necessary to file an answer simply to be heard on ancillary matters relating to finance or the children. The decision whether to file an answer may involve practical considerations, bearing in mind that the majority of divorces are undefended and that defending will normally have the effect of making the divorce procedure longer and more expensive. This may require some discussion with the client, whose emotions may not immediately suggest the wisest course. In practical terms, an answer will be required:

- if the respondent does not want a divorce at all, and has some basis for defending the allegation in the petition;
- if the respondent really cannot accept the basis on which a divorce is sought in the petition, and has good reason for alleging an alternative basis; or
- if the petition makes allegations that may prejudice the respondent in the financial hearings or those concerned with children.

3.5.2 Form D8B

An Answer effectively fulfils the role of a Defence, and should thus generally deal with those allegations in the petition application form which are disputed and add any further relevant points. The Answer remains an important document, which can require careful drafting, although relatively few cases are defended (*Lawlor v Lawlor* [1995] 1 FLR 269).

FPR Form D8B is the set format for the Answer. Part 1 asks whether or not it is agreed that the marriage has broken down. It should of course be admitted that the marriage has broken down if the respondent wants a divorce, even if he or she wishes to rely on a different basis. Part 2 asks about an allegation of grave financial hardship if five years' separation is the ground for divorce, as this can provide a statutory defence.

Part 3 asks the respondent to deal with the basis for divorce relied on in the petition, pleading both to the fact alleged, and to any details provided. A bare denial is permissible (*Haque v Haque* [1977] 1 WLR 888) but it is a better policy to respond in more detail, especially as regards allegations of behaviour (*Andrews v Andrews* [1974] 3 All ER 643). Indeed, there may be good reason for responding to behaviour allegations in some detail, especially to confess and avoid, ie, to give further information to explain, or to put a different interpretation on facts alleged.

Part 4 asks for information on any orders sought by the defendant, which effectively includes what was formerly known as a cross-petition. Parts 5–7 ask about costs, facilities potentially needed in court and service.

3.5.3 Sample for completing Part 3 of Form D8B

1   Except as is expressly admitted, the Respondent denies each and every allegation contained in the petition.

2   The Respondent denies that he became cold or neglectful towards the Petitioner as alleged or at all. He worked long hours, especially once he set up his own business, of which the Petitioner was unsupportive. Meanwhile, the matrimonial home was rarely cleaned, the Petitioner (who did not work outside the home) failed to discipline the children properly, and rarely presented proper meals, normally resorting to pre-packed dishes.

3   The Respondent admits that he frequently worked late. This was necessary as the joint bank account held by the Petitioner and the Respondent was frequently overdrawn, largely due to the sums spent by the Petitioner. The Respondent did not try to discuss his work with the Petitioner, as she frequently said that she did not understand how computers worked. The function in May 2008 was only open to employees of the Respondent's employer.

4   The Petitioner herself asked the Respondent to invite some of his colleagues from work to the matrimonial home. Having stated that she would cook a meal, the Petitioner merely provided light snacks, thereby causing the Respondent embarrassment.

5   The Respondent admits that he attended a course between March and September 2009. He did so hoping to gain promotion at work as a result. The Petitioner failed to support him in this enterprise, and indeed started an affair in Spring 2010, causing the Respondent distress.

6   The Respondent denies that he has ever consumed alcohol in excessive quantities as alleged or at all. As to the incident referred to in November 2010, the Respondent in fact had a bad cold and had simply taken a cold remedy.

7   The Respondent admits that he did strike the Petitioner in May 2011, but this was an isolated incident and borne out of his frustration at the Petitioner's continuing affair. The Respondent is not a violent man. The injury to the Petitioner was accidental in that she hit her head on a table as she fell.

(*Note that on these facts the Respondent could go on to cross-petition on the basis of his wife's adultery.*)

3.6 Void and voidable marriages

It should be kept in mind that divorce is not the only option if a client wishes to end a marriage. It is possible that the marriage may be void (MCA 1973, s 11) or voidable (MCA 1973, s 12). If either spouse is not domiciled in England and Wales, or was not so domiciled at the time of the marriage, then conflict of law points should be considered.

The grounds on which a marriage may be void are:

(a) That the parties are within a prohibited degree of relationship.

(b) That either party is under the age of 16.

(c) That vital formalities relating to the marriage were disregarded.

(d) That at the time of the marriage either party was already lawfully married.

(e) That the parties are not respectively male and female.

(f) That in the case of a polygamous marriage entered into outside England and Wales, either party was at the time of the marriage domiciled in England and Wales.

The grounds on which a marriage may be voidable are:

(a) That the marriage has not been consummated owing to the incapacity of either party.

(b) That the marriage has not been consummated owing to the wilful refusal of the respondent.

(c) That either party to the marriage did not validly consent to it, whether in consequence of duress, mistake, unsoundness of mind or otherwise.

(d) That at the time of the marriage either party was suffering from mental disorder of such a kind or to such an extent as to be unfitted for marriage.

(e) That at the time of the marriage the respondent was suffering from venereal disease in a communicable form, and the petitioner did not know this.

(f) That at the time of the marriage the respondent was pregnant by some person other than the petitioner, and the petitioner did not know this.

The last four of these may only be used within three years of the marriage. In the case of either a void or a voidable marriage, it is possible for the court to order financial provision and to make orders for the care of children. FPR Form D8N is used for a nullity petition.

3.7 Judicial separation

A final alternative is judicial separation (MCA 1973, s 17). This does not end the marriage, but is appropriate where the client does not want this for emotional, religious or cultural reasons. A decree of judicial separation may be granted where one of the bases for a divorce is made out, and it is possible for the court to make orders for financial provision, and orders regarding the care of children when making an order that the parties live apart. The procedure for seeking a judicial separation is similar to that for seeking a divorce.

Financial provision—financial remedies: law and practice

4.1 Introduction

Chapters 4 to **7** deal with the principles and practice involved in applications for financial provision. This chapter is intended to provide a broad framework on which to base the very practical work involved in applications for financial provision where couples are divorcing. Until the new Family Procedure Rules 2010 (FPR 2010) came into force on 6 April 2011, this was known as ancillary relief (or more colloquially 'AR'), that is to say, applications for financial relief ancillary to divorce. The term ancillary relief has been replaced by 'financial remedies', which is the term that will be used in this Manual, although do not be surprised if you still hear the term ancillary relief. Financial remedies are covered by Part 9 of the FPR 2010, which provides a unified procedure for most financial applications; this is considered in detail in **Chapter 5**. Financial remedies are by far the most common type of money-related applications that occur in family practice.

Also important in practice are financial applications relating to children. These mainly comprise applications under the Children Act 1989 (CA 1989), Sch 1 or applications to the Child Support Agency (CSA). Applications relating to children are dealt with in **Chapter 7**. It is important to note from the outset that the financial remedies regime does not apply to separating unmarried couples or cohabitants. It is possible, though rare, for applications for financial provision to be made between partners to a marriage who are not divorcing—this uncommon situation is dealt with in **Chapter 6**.

In dealing with applications for financial remedies, the importance of thorough and detailed fact management cannot be over emphasised. Obviously, it is essential to be fully conversant with the legal principles and factors that are applied to such applications and the procedure involved. As in other areas of family law, it can take the newcomer a while to get a feel for how practitioners and courts tend to interpret and use the checklist of factors that they are required by statute to take into account. However, unless you have a brief with an unusual feature, the biggest variables affecting the outcome of an application are the facts relating to the financial resources and needs of the parties. Most of the work in a typical financial remedies brief revolves around acquiring, managing, updating and formulating arguments based on this factual information. The importance of numerical skills will become obvious.

There are several useful texts designed to assist the practitioner. The best known is *Matrimonial Property and Finance* by Peter Duckworth. Other well-known texts include Roger Bird and Andy King's very up-to-date *Ancillary Relief and Financial Orders Handbook*, Jordans, 2011 ('Bird and King'), *Butterworths Family Law Service, Family Court Practice, Practical Matrimonial Precedents* and the Family Law Bar Association (FLBA) publication *At A Glance*.

4.1.1 The legal framework

Broad powers to order financial provision are provided by statute, primarily in the Matrimonial Causes Act 1973 (MCA 1973), as amended. Procedure is set out in Part 9 of the FPR 2010. The powers of the court with regard to maintenance for children are limited by the Child Support Act 1991 (CSA 1991) (as amended) (see **Chapter 7**). You must read and refer to the relevant law. The best place to start is always the more comprehensive practitioner texts, such as those set out above.

Because every case will involve different assets and different problems, the powers provided by statute are very wide to allow orders to be tailored to fit each individual case. For this reason, the statutory provisions themselves include only general guidance as to how the powers should be exercised. The MCA 1973, s 25 contains a list of matters to which the court must have regard when deciding how to exercise its powers. This list is widely referred to in practice as the 's 25 factors' and these factors govern all applications for financial remedies. The words of the statute are plain and are designed to give judges latitude and discretion; practitioners will always seek to base their arguments, and judges their conclusions, on the words of the statute itself. Each case turns on its own facts and decided cases will rarely be persuasive or relevant, even when they have similar features. However, on occasion, decided cases can assist with interpretation and general guidance on how the s 25 factors should be understood and applied in practice.

The court's powers under the statute and their application are dealt with in detail below at **4.2** to **4.4**.

4.1.1.1 The Civil Partnership Act 2004

The Civil Partnership Act 2004 (CPA 2004) came into force on 5 December 2005 and allowed same-sex couples to gain the rights and responsibilities of marriage, including the same sort of access to financial remedies upon the dissolution of their partnership as married couples do upon divorce. The statutory provisions for civil partnership are virtually identical to those for marriage—the CPA 2004, Sch 5 mirrors the MCA 1973, Part II; and the FPR 2010 apply.

Although the legal provisions are the same it remains to be seen whether civil partnerships bring additional considerations to the field of financial remedies and, in particular, in respect to the application of the s 25 factors to same-sex relationships. Differences potentially include the absence of gender discrimination and the view of roles within the relationship and the significance of cohabitation prior to the partnership. At the time of writing there have been no significant reported cases.

4.1.2 Procedure

As indicated above, the FPR 2010 were introduced in April 2011; in relation to financial remedies, they are largely consolidatory and Part 9 contains the rules which were previously found at rr 2.51A–2.70 of the 1991 Rules, which had been introduced in June 2000. The 2000 changes brought much greater efficiency into the decision making process. The *powers* of the court to make financial orders were the same as before, but the *procedure* was changed.

The pre-2000 procedure was based on sworn statements (affidavits) and was very adversarial. In practice, it was found to be inefficient in terms of defining issues and collecting information, and proved to be time-consuming and costly. Although this old procedure has now gone, you may see it referred to in older reported cases.

Modern procedure places greater emphasis on the completion and use of standard forms and involves tight timetables, a greater emphasis on defining issues and reaching agreements, and more court control. The procedure was extensively piloted in various courts around the country and resulted in much cross-fertilisation with the reforms then being planned in civil practice generally. You will be familiar with the overriding objective from civil procedure, but the emphasis and objectives are slightly different in family law. Under the FPR 2010, the overriding objective now applies in all family proceedings and is set out in Part 1, and it closely resembles Part 1 of the CPR (see **1.7**).

The main elements of the procedure in Part 9 are:

(a) Once there has been an application for financial remedies, there will be a first appointment (FA) within 12 to 16 weeks.

(b) Not less than 35 days before that appointment, there will be a simultaneous exchange of statements of the financial position of both spouses, containing specified information in a common format (Form E). Full supporting documentation will be attached.

(c) No other disclosure is allowed prior to the first appointment.

(d) Not less than 14 days before that appointment, both parties will file a concise statement of the issues between the parties, a chronology and a questionnaire, seeking further information and specifying relevant documents to be produced.

(e) The parties also decide at this stage whether they wish to use all/part of the FA as a Financial Dispute Resolution hearing (FDR) (they notify the court by way of Form G, a 'Notice of Response re First Appointment').

(f) At the FA, the district judge (DJ) will review the case with a view to defining and limiting the issues and saving costs. The DJ will see if the FA can become an FDR; if not, he will set a date for an FDR. Exceptionally, he may, if he considers an FDR inappropriate, set a date for a final hearing. He will give directions as to disclosure, documentation, valuations, evidence and any other case management directions necessary to prepare for the FDR.

(g) The FDR is to be treated as an opportunity for open discussion and negotiation. The DJ will facilitate and assist in this process. They are without prejudice meetings and the rules of confidentiality which flow from that apply. If appropriate, the DJ may adjourn and fix a date for a further FDR and give further directions or the DJ may fix a date for the final hearing, which must be before a different DJ. Before a final hearing, both parties must file a concise statement of the nature and amounts of the orders they will be inviting the court to make.

(h) Both sides must have an updated estimate of current costs available at each hearing (Form H).

The procedure, including issues relating to costs, is dealt with in detail in **Chapter 5**.

4.1.3 The practical approach

Statute provides general powers and a checklist of considerations. Case law, at best, merely provides examples of their application. So there is rarely a single, obvious answer as to the correct financial provision in any particular case. Although there is a defined set of factors, there is no set formula on how to apply them. Indeed, trying to apply the same formula to different circumstances would almost certainly be unjust. Instead, there are usually a variety of perspectives and approaches (from the facts, the instructions, the law, common sense and the advocate's own experience of practice) from which a case can be built, and an overall basis for provision proposed.

It is important to appreciate this. This is not an area where legal principles can simply be applied to calculate an outcome. Everything depends on a complete and thorough *factual* analysis of the individual case, and an intelligent development of arguments, in the light of the law. This makes a really practical approach vital—applying the s 25 factors to the unique facts and landscape of each situation and accompanying instructions. Although the powers of the courts are wide, advocates cannot make waffly arguments or general proposals. In each case, the facts must be carefully gathered and analysed, the detailed arithmetic done (and done properly, by you, so do get used to it), and specific and practical arguments and proposals formulated. Throughout, the client's objectives must be kept clearly in view.

This broad and non-linear approach can make it difficult for the newcomer to know where to start. Here are some tips for things to consider in order to get going with a brief:

(a) What sort of provision does the client want? In terms of capital? In terms of income?

(b) What assets do your client and the other side have?

(c) What income do your client and the other side have?

(d) What are the fundamental needs of your client and the other side? In particular: are there children? Who will be caring for them? Where will they live?

(e) What are the income needs of your client and the other side? Be realistic—what do they really need to live? How much will it really cost?

(f) How can these needs be met? Can the parties realistically be expected to work? Are there other sources of funds or support?

(g) What is the position in relation to pensions?

(h) What are the s 25 factors which seem most relevant to this case?

(i) What are the s 25 factors which strengthen/weaken your client's claims?

(j) Is a clean break possible?

(k) What then is the appropriate overall basis for provision? Are there any options?

(l) Work out full details for the proposal you are making. Do full arithmetic to show the position which each spouse will be left in if that provision is ordered, taking into account tax, etc. You should be aiming to devise a package that works for both parties.

(m) Check that the detailed proposals are practical, realistic and meet your client's objectives as far as possible.

(n) Check your proposal against the yardstick of equality. If your proposal does not amount to an equal division of resources, how can this be justified by reference to the s 25 factors?

(o) Remember that lawyers representing parties in a case have a duty to investigate figures fully and to advise their clients properly about their options. All parties have a duty to further the overriding objective.

(p) Use your common sense and maturity. They are indispensable tools.

4.2 Court powers to make orders

It is important to note from the very outset that the court does not exercise any of its powers in isolation from each other. After considering everything it is required to consider under the MCA 1973, s 25, the court will decide what result it wants to achieve and, choosing from among the powers available to it, will design a package of interrelating orders that best achieve its objectives. The most commonly used of these powers are found in the MCA Part II, especially ss 21–25C.

4.2.1 Overview and terminology

The court has the jurisdiction to make orders for financial remedies on the grant of a decree of divorce, nullity or judicial separation. The FPR 2010 define 'financial order' as any of the following:

- an avoidance of disposition order;
- an order for maintenance pending suit;
- an order for maintenance pending outcome of proceedings;
- an order for periodical payments or lump sum provision both in respect of divorce and civil partnership;
- a property adjustment order;
- a variation order;
- a pension-sharing order;
- a pension-sharing compensation order.

A variation order is defined as an order under the MCA 1973, s 31 or under Part 11 of Schedule 5 of the CPA 2004. Maintenance pending suit, which is an interim application for maintenance, is dealt with at **4.5**. Financial remedies include all financial orders and a variety of other orders, including an application in respect of children under Sch 1 of the Children Act 1989 (CA 1989) (see the interpretation section at r 2.3). Sch 1 applications are dealt with at **7.5**. The most significant of the other orders are as follows.

4.2.2 Financial provision orders: MCA 1973, s 23

4.2.2.1 Order for periodical payments to a party to the marriage or to/for a child of the family (s 23)

Periodical payments are an ongoing obligation to pay a sum at regular intervals, usually weekly or monthly. This type of order used to be called, and is still commonly referred to as, maintenance. Orders for periodical payments may be varied on further application, and may run for a set term or until the death of either of the parties or the remarriage of the person in whose favour the order is made. In considering an order for periodical payments, the court must weigh its obligation under the MCA 1973, s 25A to consider a clean break (see **4.4.3**).

4.2.2.2 Order for secured periodical payments to a party to the marriage or to/for a child of the family (s 23)

This is an order for periodical payments with an additional order that some kind of secure capital fund or asset be provided out of which the payments can be made or guaranteed.

The main advantage of such an order is that the payments are protected against the death, insolvency or disappearance of the payer. Orders for secured periodical payments may be varied on further application, and may run for a set term or until the death or the remarriage of the person in whose favour the order is made. Again, the court must consider a clean break. Orders for secured periodical payments are comparatively rare.

4.2.2.3   Order that a lump sum be paid to a party to the marriage or to/for a child of the family (s 23)

A lump sum order is intended to be a final order and, with limited exception, may only be made once. A lump sum order is essentially a means of adjusting the balance of capital resources between the parties. However, within the final package of orders that a court makes it may serve a more specific purpose. Examples of such a purpose include enabling a party to purchase property, or compensating a party for exiting a jointly run business, or providing a fund to cover all purposes in big money cases, or as a way of capitalising maintenance (known as a *Duxbury* fund). The statute refers to 'lump sum or sums'. This still means that only one order may be made, but it may provide for the payment of more than one lump sum, or for instalments, or for payment to be deferred along with the payment of interest: see, for example, *V v V (Financial Relief)* [2010] 2 FLR 516, where the jurisdiction to make a series of lump sum orders was doubted, but an order was made for the payment of a lump sum of £2.4 million by instalments over four and a half years.

4.2.3   Property adjustment orders: MCA 1973, ss 24–24A

4.2.3.1   Transfer of property order, ie, an order that one party to the marriage transfer property to the other party or to/for the benefit of a child of the family (s 24)

This can be any kind of property but is usually concerned with houses and land. Usually, the housing needs of the parties and children are a high priority and in many cases the former matrimonial home will be the sole or principal asset. The court may not make more than one order but it may provide for the transfer of more than one item of property in the same order. The property may be transferred outright, or it may be transferred subject to a charge in favour of the transferor. This charge could be realisable on a fixed date or on the occurring of a certain trigger event (eg, the youngest child reaching 18).

4.2.3.2   Settlement of property order (s 24)

When used, these orders perform much the same function as transfer of property orders, described above. Generally, courts use transfer of property orders and other orders available under the statute to achieve the desired outcome and, as a result, settlement orders are less frequently used nowadays.

4.2.3.3   An order varying the effect of any ante- or postnuptial settlement (s 24)

Traditional marriage settlements are less common than they were; however, the use of postnuptial settlements seems perhaps to be increasing. The powers to vary a settlement are wide and include the power to give the capital or income in a settlement to either party or the children, to extinguish the interest of a party under the settlement and to terminate the settlement itself.

4.2.3.4   Order for sale (s 24A)

This is not strictly speaking a property adjustment order but it is conveniently dealt with here. The court may only make an order for sale when it has made a secured periodical payments order or a lump sum order or a property adjustment order. The purpose of the order for sale is to facilitate the capital order to which it relates.

4.2.4   Orders relating to pensions

It is generally the wife who is in a more vulnerable position in relation to her pension provision as she may, for example, have had time away from the employment market to care for children. Clearly, it could equally be the husband and references in this section to the wife should be read as applying equally to the husband in an appropriate case.

4.2.4.1   Pension-sharing orders: MCA 1973, ss 21A, 24B

Pension-sharing orders are available in respect of petitions for divorce or nullity (not judicial separation) filed after 1 December 2000. The order provides that one party's shareable pension rights (or state scheme rights) are subject to pension sharing for the benefit of another party. The order specifies the percentage value of the shareable pension rights to be transferred to the benefiting party. This must be expressed as a simple percentage, not as a sum converted into a percentage: *H v H* [2010] 2 FLR 173. The pension arrangement as a whole is valued and the actual amount to be transferred is the percentage of that value. The actual amount received by the person in whose favour the order is made is known as the 'pension credit'. In effect, the relevant pension fund is split and a portion hived off to be used by the person for whose benefit the order is made. After the order is made, the 'person responsible' for the pension arrangement (ie, the trustees or managers) must within four months transfer the pension credit to a suitable pension scheme or an arrangement of the transferee's choice. For possible problems with pension-sharing orders, especially in relation to valuation, see the articles referred to at the end of **4.3.3.11**.

4.2.4.2   Other orders relating to pensions

The court has a range of orders available to it to deal with the complicated issues of pensions. Pension-sharing orders are the preferred way of dealing with most situations, but other orders are used in some circumstances. The orders made in a given case will depend on what the court is trying to achieve in relation to the issue of pension provision and on the other factors and considerations in the case (see **4.3.3.11**).

4.2.4.2.1   *Offsetting*

Offsetting is a way of compensating a wife for the loss of pension benefits by providing her with some additional capital, usually in the form of a lump sum or an enlargement of a lump sum already being considered. It is a useful tool, but requires there to be sufficient funds available from which the lump sum, or increased lump sum, can be paid.

4.2.4.2.2   *Attachment orders*

Attachment orders (formerly known as 'earmarking') are orders that oblige the persons responsible for a pension arrangement to pay to someone who is not a member of the pension fund sums that would normally have gone to the member. All attachment orders are liable to applications for variation (which means that they may be varied before they are ever realised). They are also at risk from a change in the circumstances of the pension holder, such as bankruptcy. See *Re Nunn (Bankruptcy: Divorce: Pension Rights)* [2004] 1 FLR 1123, where an order that a husband pay his wife one-half of his pension lump sum was not enforceable after the bankruptcy of the husband, the whole pension fund going into the husband's estate in bankruptcy.

Attachment for income purposes (s 25B) This order will provide periodical payments to the person in whose favour the order is made, paid out of the pension fund. It is, in effect, an attachment of earnings order against the pension fund. It would cease to have effect on the death of either party.

Attachment for a capital sum (s 25B) This would be appropriate where the wife was to receive a deferred lump sum from the husband's pension entitlement, usually because there was insufficient capital to provide her with the appropriate amount at the time of the making of the order. A weakness of this order is that the court has no power to order the pension holder to take his pension at any particular time.

Attachment of death-in-service benefits (s 25C) This order would be appropriate where the wife continues to be dependent on the husband. If he died before retirement, any lump sum, or part of it, would be payable to the wife. The court has the power to force the husband to nominate his ex-wife to be the person to receive some or all of the benefits (most pension schemes require the pension holder to nominate the person who will receive death-in-service benefits and the persons responsible for the scheme must follow this nomination).

Pension Protection Fund Compensation (s 21B, s 21F) Since 6 April 2011 the court has jurisdiction to make a pension-sharing or attachment order in relation to Pension Protection Fund (PPF) compensation. These new sections of the MCA were inserted by the Pensions Act 2008: see 'PPF Compensation and Financial Provision Following a Matrimonial or Civil Partnership Order' April [2011] *Family Law*.

4.2.5 Avoidance of disposition orders and other injunctions: MCA 1973, s 37

Section 37 gives the court the power, in financial remedies proceedings, to prevent or set aside a disposition of property by one of the parties to the proceedings. This type of order is applied for and made when there is a suspicion that one of the parties is about to dispose, transfer or otherwise deal with property with a view to defeating or avoiding all or part of a claim for financial remedies, or one of the parties has already done so.

So there are essentially two powers under this section. The first is pre-emptive and is an order to one of the parties not to deal with certain assets in certain ways. Copies of this order can be served on banks and any relevant institutions and the order usually has the effect of freezing or barring transactions concerning the asset. The second is the power to set aside any disposition that has already been made. Such an order will require the person to whom the assets were transferred to transfer them back so that they will form part of the funds being considered in the proceedings for financial remedies.

The burden is on the person applying for a s 37 order to prove that the disposition will be or has been made 'with the intention of defeating the claim for financial relief'. It is for the judge, however, to decide whether or not he is 'satisfied' that the condition is met and it has been held that further qualification of the standard of proof is not helpful (*K v K* (*Avoidance of Reviewable Disposition*) [1983] FLR 31). Although the intention can be inferred from conduct, the court must be careful in situations where there could be more than one reason for the disposition, most typically in situations where a party's livelihood or business activity depends on the movement of such assets as are under consideration. The court must be satisfied that the intention to defeat the claim exists.

There is no general power under s 37 to freeze assets as a holding or precautionary measure pending the outcome of a claim, although the court has jurisdiction to do this under the Civil Procedure Rules (CPR) and under its powers to grant a freezing injunction (see below). There are two further significant considerations relating to the power to set aside a disposition that has already been made. First, it must be a 'reviewable disposition' as defined in s 37(4). This essentially protects the bona fide purchaser for value without notice (in this case, without notice of the respondent's intention to defeat the applicant's claim). Unless the respondent can satisfy the court that the conditions in s 37(4) are met, it is presumed that the disposition is reviewable. Secondly, s 37(5) provides that in some situations there is a presumption of intention to defeat the claim. Essentially, the presumption applies where the disposition was made within three years before the date of the application and where the court is satisfied that the disposition has, or would have, the consequence of defeating the applicant's claim for financial remedies.

Applications for s 37 injunctions should, if practicable, be heard at the same time as any related application for financial remedies (FPR 2010, rr 9.6 and 9.7). Where there is urgency, the application can be made without notice and, if it grants the application, the court will fix an on notice return hearing at the earliest date.

Practitioners need to keep in mind the court's powers under s 37 and be prepared to exercise their judgement as to whether the circumstances warrant such an application. If so, then the application should be made without delay.

Three further types of injunctive relief are on occasion used by the family courts. They are used far less frequently than the s 37 order discussed above and so are dealt with in overview here.

In situations where the conditions of s 37 have not been made out but doing justice in the case requires the use of injunctive powers, the court can invoke its inherent jurisdiction. This means it can make such order as it sees fit in order to preserve the status quo, or achieve whatever end is required: see *Shipman v Shipman* [1991] 1 FLR 250 and *Poon v Poon* [1994] 2 FLR 857. It is doubted that the county court has such an inherent jurisdiction; the practice in the Principal Registry is to transfer to the High Court an application to invoke the inherent jurisdiction. The Court of Appeal in *Wicks v Wicks* [1998] 1 FLR 470 considered the limits of the inherent jurisdiction.

Freezing injunctions (formerly *Mareva* injunctions) are available to the civil courts generally. Essentially, a freezing order forbids, until trial, the respondent from removing funds or assets from the jurisdiction of the court, or otherwise dissipating or dealing with assets so as to thwart the court's judgment. Such an injunction can be worldwide. The county court can grant an injunction in a family matter but under normal circumstances should transfer such applications to the High Court. The statutory basis is the Senior Courts Act 1981, s 37 and the procedural basis is dealt with in the CPR, Part 25.

Search orders (formerly *Anton Piller* orders) may be made where it appears that the respondent has in his possession documents or materials which should have been disclosed and that he may destroy or tamper with them, if not imminently then when he is given notice of the intention to seek a court order for their disclosure. Thus, it is a without notice order. It empowers the applicant to enter the respondent's premises and seize and remove materials of the class(es) specified. In the past, such orders have rarely been made and if their execution does not turn up materials of the class sought, the applicant may be severely penalised in costs. Its statutory basis is the Civil Procedure Act 1997, s 7 and the procedure is also dealt with in CPR, Part 25.

The Court of Appeal in *Immerman v Immerman* [2010] 2 FLR 814 recently suggested that both search orders and freezing injunctions are suitable tools to be used in family cases where there is a concern about the concealing of evidence and/or the threatened dissipation of assets. It recommended greater use of these interim remedies rather than the methods of self-help known as the *Hildebrand* rules which had previously been used and which are roundly criticised. Under the *Hildebrand* rules, a party to a marriage could rely in financial remedies proceedings on documents illegally obtained, if they had been so obtained due to a fear that the other party was seeking to hide assets and therefore not complying with the duty of full and frank disclosure required by the FPR 2010.

4.2.6 Limitations on and duration of orders

Most of the significant features of the orders available to the court have been set out above. There are three further points to note:

(a) An application for financial remedies may be made at the same time as the application for a matrimonial order or at any time after that application has been made: FPR 2010, r 9.4. The court has no power to make orders until decree nisi has been granted (usually a formality done at the outset of proceedings). The orders of the court will not take effect until decree absolute has been granted; that is, they will take effect at the same time as the marriage is officially and finally dissolved.

(b) The MCA 1973, s 28 makes provisions relating to continuing financial provision orders. Periodical payments orders (secured or otherwise) may not be expressed to begin before the date of the application (ie, the court can 'backdate' an order to that point, but no earlier).

(c) The MCA 1973, s 29 makes provisions relating to continuing financial provision orders made in relation to children. Save in appropriate circumstances (eg, education beyond 18 or special need), no financial provision may be made in respect of a child who has reached 18 years of age. Further, orders for periodical payments to or for a child (which may begin from the date of application) shall not extend, in the first instance, beyond school-leaving age and in any event not beyond the date of the child's eighteenth birthday. Periodical payments orders to or for a child shall cease upon the death of the payer (save for any arrears).

4.2.7 Powers of the court relating to overseas divorce

This subject is not dealt with in detail in this Manual. Most of the relevant legislation is found in the Matrimonial and Family Proceedings Act 1984 (MFPA 1984) and in the Recognition of Divorces and Legal Separations Act 1971 (RDLSA 1971). For the court to have jurisdiction, the separation must be recognised as valid under the RDLSA 1971, ss 2–6 and the applicant must show a connection with England and Wales in accordance with the MFPA 1984, s 15. The applicant must then apply for permission to make the application. If granted, the court will hear the application—the powers and considerations of the court are very similar to those applicable to a domestic divorce and are contained in the MFPA 1984, ss 14 and 17–26.

4.3 The s 25 factors

4.3.1 The factors

On an application to court for financial remedies, there is, as has been said, no standard formula for calculating appropriate provision. If it were that simple, there would be little role for the courts in considering the case. Although there may be similarities between cases, and there may be broad categories into which some cases will fall, the details of each are unique in terms of available assets and the needs of both parties. The system for determining provision has to be sufficiently flexible to allow for this, and therefore, rather than a single rule, the statute provides a list of relevant factors, to be taken into account by the court when deciding how to exercise its powers.

The factors are listed in the MCA 1973, s 25(1)(2) and are widely referred to as 'the s 25 factors'. The court must also take into account the provisions of s 25A, which direct the court to try to achieve a 'clean break' between the parties, if this is practicable (see **4.4.3**). It is worth emphasising from the outset the central role that the s 25 factors play in determining applications for financial remedies. All the analysis and evaluation of the facts of the situation must be carried out by reference to the s 25 factors. All arguments and proposals made in the case must be framed in terms of the factors. All the orders that the court could make must be considered and justified in the light of s 25.

It is worth setting s 25(1) and (2) out in full:

(1) It shall be the duty of the court in deciding whether to exercise its powers under sections 23 or 24 or 24A or 24B above and, if so, in what manner, to have regard to all the circumstances of the case, first consideration being given to the welfare while a minor of any child of the family who has not attained the age of eighteen.

(2) As regards the exercise of the powers of the court under section 23(1)(a) (b) or (c), 24, 24A or 24B in relation to a party to the marriage, the court shall in particular have regard to the following matters—

(a) the income, earning capacity, property and other financial resources which each of the parties to the marriage has or is likely to have in the foreseeable future, including in the case of earning capacity any increase in that capacity which it would in the opinion of the court be reasonable to expect a party to the marriage to take steps to acquire;

(b) the financial needs, obligations and responsibilities which each of the parties to the marriage has or is likely to have in the foreseeable future;

(c) the standard of living enjoyed by the family before the breakdown of the marriage;

(d) the age of each party to the marriage and the duration of the marriage;

(e) any physical or mental disability of either of the parties to the marriage;

(f) the contributions which each of the parties has made or is likely in the foreseeable future to make to the welfare of the family, including any contribution by looking after the home or caring for the family;

(g) the conduct of each of the parties, if that conduct is such that it would in the opinion of the court be inequitable to disregard it;

(h) in the case of proceedings for divorce or nullity of marriage, the value to each of the parties to the marriage of any benefit which, by reason of the dissolution or annulment of the marriage, that party will lose the chance of acquiring.

(3) As regards the exercise of the powers of the court under sections 23(1)(d) (e) or (f) (2) or (4), 24 or 24A above in relation to a child of the family, the court shall in particular have regard to the following matters—

(a) the financial needs of the child;

(b) the income, earning capacity (if any), property and other financial resources of the child;

(c) any physical or mental disability of the child;

(d) the manner in which he was being and in which the parties to the marriage expected him to be educated or trained;

(e) the considerations mentioned in relation to the parties to the marriage in paragraphs (a) (b) (c) and (e) of subsection (2) above.

(4) As regards the exercise of the powers of the court under section 23(1)(d) (e) or (f) (2) or (4), 24 or 24A above against a party to a marriage in favour of a child of the family who is not the child of that party, the court shall also have regard—

(a) to whether that party assumed any responsibility for the child's maintenance, and, if so, to the extent to which, and the basis upon which, that party assumed such responsibility and to the length of time for which that party discharged such responsibility;

(b) to whether in assuming and discharging such responsibility that party did so knowing that the child was not his or her own;

(c) to the liability of any other person to maintain the child.

4.3.2 Using the factors

The factors listed by statute are effectively the building blocks from which the barrister constructs an argument in an individual case. No one factor is intrinsically more important than any of the others. However, in dealing with any given case, some factors will almost certainly be more central, and occupy more of the court's time, than others. Which factors are more important than others in any given case depends entirely on the circumstances of that case. Dealing with the relevant factors in a practical and professional way can only come with practice, but as a suggested starting point in a case:

(a) Identify which factors from the general list are relevant to the particular case.

(b) Weigh up each relevant factor, deciding by reference to the facts which are central to the case and those which are less important.

(c) Remember that the factors can interrelate to each other. For example, *disability* is a factor in its own right but the fact of a disability will quite possibly relate to *earning capacity* and perhaps also to *needs*. *Age* is a factor and the older a person is, the lower their *earning capacity* is likely to be if they have been out of the labour market. Some facts may fit under more than one factor, for example, payment for music lessons could be considered a *financial obligation* and/or an issue relating to the *welfare of a child of the family*.

(d) Clearly identify the relevant factors that favour your client, which will therefore be central to your case.

(e) Clearly identify the relevant factors that undermine your client's case or favour the other side, and which you will therefore have to try to counter.

If one factor overshadows all others in the case, it may suggest an overall basis for provision (see **4.4**). If no factor is substantially more important than others, all relevant factors will go into the balance.

4.3.3 What the factors mean

The meaning of the factors should be understood primarily from the words of the statute itself. Decided cases from appellate courts can provide guidance on interpretation and establishing the broad approach of the courts to certain issues. Other than this, they are usually of little relevance in deciding how a court should exercise its discretion in a particular case. In *White v White* [1998] 2 FLR 310, CA, Butler-Sloss LJ said: 'There is a danger that practitioners in the field of family law attempt to apply too rigidly the decisions of this court and of the Family Division, without sufficiently recognising that each case involving a family has to be decided upon broad principles adapted to the facts of the individual case. It is the statutory wording and judicial reasoning in cases, not their outcome as such, which act as a guide to the meaning of the s 25 factors.'

4.3.3.1 All the circumstances (s 25(1))

The statute states: 'It shall be the duty of the court...to have regard to all the circumstances of the case ...' This means that the court must not confine itself to the listed factors but must consider any circumstance that is relevant. In practice, relevant circumstances almost always fall under one of the listed factors. However, this provision can be useful when formulating arguments and proposals, especially in a case that involves an unusual feature, so it is important to keep it in mind.

4.3.3.2 Welfare of the children of the family under 18 (s 25(1))

This consideration is limited to children of the family, which is defined as any child who has been treated by both of the parties to the marriage as a child of their family (MCA 1973, s 52(1)). This includes stepchildren. What it does not include is children conceived by one of the parties outside of the marriage, who were not part of the marital home. Such children can be considered under other factors, such as obligations, but not here. The statute says that the welfare of children of the family will be the 'first consideration'. This does not mean that it is a consideration that should take precedence over the other factors (although in the weighing of the circumstances of a case, the court usually comes to the view that it is)—it means that it is the first matter to which the court should direct its attention.

Maintenance for any children of the family was the province of the Child Support Agency (CSA), which was due to be reincarnated as the Child Maintenance and Enforcement Commission (CMEC) by legislation passed in 2008. The legislation has not wholly come into effect (see generally **Chapter 7**). CMEC's declared purpose is to maximise the number of effective child maintenance arrangements in place—whether private or statutory—for children who live apart from one or both parents. The emphasis on encouraging parents to reach private agreements for their children's maintenance is a welcome development.

The main issue in financial remedies proceedings is usually housing the children. The court will want to ensure that the children are adequately housed in a location that takes into account their needs in terms of schooling, family relationships and social networks and activities (the latter varying according to age). The main carer will, of course, be housed with the children but this will primarily be a matter of the children's welfare—it is not a right or a benefit conferred on that carer. Either parent may or may not have a financial interest in some or all of the children's home—that will depend entirely on how the court decides to divide the assets. It is quite common for the resident carer to be required to sell the home and move to a smaller property once the children have left and no longer need it.

The welfare of the child should not, however, unduly prejudice the need of the non-resident spouse for a home (*M v B (Ancillary Proceedings: Lump Sum)* [1998] 1 FLR 53). The court will, if possible, try to stretch the resources so that the latter has housing suitable for regular contact, ensuring that children can not only visit, but can also spend the night ('staying contact').

Generally, the younger a child is, the longer its needs will last, the more multifarious those needs are likely to be, and the further the court will go to try to balance available resources in order to ensure that they are adequately catered for. The closer a child is to

18, the less important its needs are likely to be in the overall balance (unless it has special needs).

4.3.3.3 Income, earning capacity, property and other financial resources (s 25(2)(a))

The importance of getting full details and figures for capital and income cannot be over emphasised. Getting a complete and open picture of all the resources of the parties is one of the central features of financial remedies procedure. Only when the court has determined what is available can it go on to determine how those assets should be allocated. The parties are under an ongoing obligation to make full and frank disclosure. There should be no partial disclosure nor should a party wait for the other side to ask for relevant information before disclosing it. The judge is required to consider penalising in costs a party who fails to disclose completely and voluntarily within the appropriate timescale. An attempt to hide assets is serious litigation misconduct, to say the least.

A party's resources can be highly relevant not only to the amount, but also to the type of provision ordered. Lump sum payments, for example, require sufficient capital and/or income to raise the funds. Equally, if there is not sufficient income available to the person wanting to remain in the matrimonial home to pay the mortgage and outgoings, there may be no realistic alternative to selling it.

Note that all financial resources are relevant, and this is widely interpreted to include benefits, for example, free or cheap accommodation available with a job. There are, however, some limits; for example, proceeds of crime that are liable to be confiscated might not be taken into account, depending on the circumstances. Neither an application for a confiscation order under the Drug Trafficking Act 1994, s 2, nor a claim for financial remedies has priority over the other. The High Court must determine the outcome according to the public interest and applicable Convention rights. For the practice in this situation, see *Re MCA; HM Customs and Excise Commissioners and Long v A and A; A v A* (*Long Intervening*) [2003] 1 FLR 164 and, for the procedural effect of the Proceeds of Crime Act 2002 (POCA 2002), *Webber v Webber* [2007] 2 FLR 116 (and see *Stodgell v Stodgell* [2009] 2 FLR 218, discussed at **4.3.3.10**).

As regards earnings, it is important to appreciate that the court will also look to a party's *earning capacity*, ie, it will take into account not only what he or she is earning, but what he or she may be reasonably expected to earn if exploiting all opportunities fully, both in the short term and the long term. Parties who choose not to work or not to maximise their resources when they could do so are likely to have adverse inferences drawn against them. The subsection specifically requires the court to consider any increase in earning capacity that it would be *reasonable* to expect a party to take steps to acquire. The court will be realistic about what it is reasonable to expect people to do in the circumstances. For example, it is not likely to expect carers of very young children to go out to work full-time. If it takes the view that an applicant may need some time to retrain and/or otherwise adjust to future financial independence, the court may allow for this by making a fixed-term periodical payments order (as an alternative to a normal open-ended order which puts the onus on the paying party to apply for a variation when circumstances change).

'Property' is widely defined. It includes all real property, all personal property, any financial stock or other business assets or interests, any beneficial interest under a trust; this list is not exhaustive.

'Other financial resources' can include expectations, ie, property or income that a party is likely to have in the foreseeable future. Note that this does not include pensions, which are considered separately (see **4.3.3.11**). Caution must be exercised in relation to an expectation—there must be evidence upon which the court can be satisfied as to the likelihood and extent of the expectation. An example of a common expectation is the prospect of being a beneficiary under a will (or an intestacy). The problems with this expectation are that it can be difficult to gauge life expectancy and to estimate the size of the potential benefit. A testator cannot be compelled to disclose his or her intentions which may change over time. The court does have the power to adjourn the lump sum element of an application for financial provision, where there is an expectation of a significant inheritance and where the court considers it necessary to take this course in order to achieve fairness in a particular set of circumstances (*Re G (Financial Provision: Liberty to Restore Application for Lump Sum)* [2004] 1 FLR 997). This is, however, an exceptional course of action.

Regular financial support from a third party could, again with caution, be viewed as a resource. The court would need to be satisfied on evidence that it was reasonable to expect this support to continue in the foreseeable future. A recoverable debt owed by a third party would normally be seen as a resource.

Resources available from a cohabitee may also be relevant, but the position of a cohabitee cannot be fully equated with that of a spouse, and the income of a party's cohabitee will not simply be added to that of the party. Where cohabitation is disputed the court must first make a finding as to its existence. If found as a fact, the financial circumstances should be investigated and a key question is what the cohabitee ought to be contributing: *Grey v Grey* [2010] 1 FLR 1764.

A court may draw inferences as to resources that are available provided there is sufficient reason to do so (*Thomas v Thomas* [1995] 2 FLR 668), especially if there is serious non-disclosure (*Baker v Baker* [1995] 2 FLR 829). A resource which is considered too remote (eg, a possible future inheritance) will be disregarded.

Although all assets and resources must be identified, not all will necessarily be available for redistribution. For example, a family business will have a net worth but it is also likely to provide essential income and so it may not be desirable to realise it as a capital asset. The situation may be different, however, if the business depended on the partnership of the divorcing couple for its efficacy, in which case it may be appropriate to order sale of the business and its assets. Specialist advice is often needed in cases involving businesses or other ventures a little out of the ordinary, such as farms or an Internet business, and case law often provides guidance on this—for example, see: *P v P (Financial Relief: Illiquid Assets)* [2005] 1 FLR 548, *D v D&B Ltd* [2007] 2 FLR 548. A pragmatic approach needs to be adopted, however, in deciding whether an expert should be instructed to value a business. Such an exercise is not an exact science; a detailed investigation is not only expensive but may not assist the court and costs must be proportional—see: *H v H* [2008] 2 FLR 2092. (See also **4.4.8.1**.)

Other assets that may or may not form part of the matrimonial pot are assets acquired prior to the marriage and/or assets acquired under an inheritance or under a family trust. It is a question of fact and judgement whether such assets become part of the matrimonial assets during the marriage, depending on how they were acquired, held and used. Since the House of Lords' decision *in Miller v Miller; McFarlane v McFarlane* [2006] 1 FLR 1186 ('*Miller; McFarlane*'), the courts have much more routinely applied themselves to the question of determining what is and is not 'matrimonial property'. Although this issue receives a lot of judicial attention, it is usually only an issue in bigger-money cases, where there is more money than is required to meet the needs of all the parties. In *Miller; McFarlane*, Lord Nicholls and Baroness Hale differed in their views as to the distinction between matrimonial and non-matrimonial property. According to Lord Nicholls, non-matrimonial property is viewed as all property which the parties bring with them into the marriage or acquire by inheritance or gift during the marriage (plus perhaps the income or fruits of that property), while matrimonial property is viewed as all other property. Baroness Hale's approach is that non-matrimonial property includes not merely: (a) property which the parties bring with them into the marriage or acquire by inheritance or gift during the marriage (plus perhaps its income or fruits); but also (b) business or investment assets generated solely or mainly by the efforts of one party during the marriage. For recent cases, see: *Rossi v Rossi* [2007] 1 FLR 790, *S v S* (*Non-Matrimonial Property; Conduct*) [2007] 1 FLR 1496. In *Charman v Charman* [2007] EWCA Civ 503, Potter P stated that the newly elevated 'sharing principle' (see **4.4.4**) applied to all property, but, to the extent that property is non-matrimonial, there is likely to be better reason for a departure from equality. He also preferred the more generous (to the payee) view of matrimonial property, despite its minority status in the House of Lords' judgment; see the recent guidance given by the Court of Appeal in *Robson v Robson* [2010] EWCA Civ 1171.

Care needs to be taken so far as wealth acquired by one party *after* the breakdown of the relationship but before the determination of the financial remedies application is concerned. Such assets are a resource available to that party and may be taken into account under the factors of need and compensation (see *Miller; McFarlane*), but in the absence of such factors, sharing ends at the point of separation: *B v B* [2010] 2 FLR 1214.

So far as pensions in particular are concerned, as a resource they are relevant no matter how far in the future the benefit might be realised. See MCA 1973, s 25B, as added by the Pensions Act 1995. For more on pensions generally, see **4.3.3.11**.

4.3.3.4   Financial needs, obligations and responsibilities (s 25(2)(b))

As regards needs, it is necessary to get accurate details of all the household expenses, such as the mortgage, gas and electricity bills, etc. The term 'needs' can be interpreted widely to include any reasonable expense of living, and this should be fully investigated—get the client to think of everything that has to be paid for. Remember that for your client you would try to include all arguable needs, whereas in relation to the other side's needs, you might be more apt to claim that they should be pruned and kept within more reasonable bounds (while being aware that their advisor will argue likewise). In low-to-average income cases, the subsistence level indicated by current state benefit levels plus housing costs is often used in practice as a yardstick for minimum needs.

The term 'obligations' can include any legal or moral obligation to meet an expense, including obligations to third parties, such as relatives, cohabitees or children who are being supported. In some cases, this may mean that the resources of one person have to be divided between their former spouse and their new spouse or cohabitee, and any children. This can be very contentious, especially when resources are overstretched. While the court will try to give precedence to the first family, it has to be realistic—for example, it is often easier for the former wife on her own to claim benefits than the new cohabitee living with a person of average income.

Where there is a purported debt that is being claimed by a third party, then the court cannot anticipate the outcome of other proceedings. The court will decide if the debt is significant and if so will either adjourn to await the outcome, or have the cases heard in tandem by the same judge (*George v George* [2004] 1 FLR 421).

It used to be that different considerations applied to 'big-money' cases and the concept of 'reasonable requirements' was used in place of needs. However, since the House of Lords' decision in *White v White* [2000] 2 FLR 981, this approach has been disapproved and it is established that, in the context of s 25(2)(b), consideration of needs is what the statute requires in all cases.

4.3.3.5   The standard of living of the family before the breakdown (s 25(2)(c))

In most cases, it will not be possible to maintain the standard of living that the parties enjoyed during the marriage. Except in big-money cases, if the money that has financed a single household has to be split to finance two, there will almost certainly have to be some drop in the standard of living.

The concern of the court will be to see that the standard of living does not slip more than is necessary and to ensure that one party does not suffer a significantly greater drop in living standards than the other.

It is worth noting that the subsection refers to the standard of living of the family, not the parties. This means that the standard of living of the children must also be considered.

4.3.3.6 The age of each party (s 25(2)(d))

The main relevance of age is in relation to earning capacity and to the importance of providing for retirement. A young wife will normally be seen as having an earning potential, whereas an older person, who has not worked for years, will have less ability to enter the labour market and less time to accrue savings or investments for the future. For an older person, it will also be more expensive to pay a mortgage as the 25-year term will not be available.

In the case of a younger person, a clean break or deferred clean break is more likely to be possible. With an older person, there is more likely to be a dependency and it will be important to investigate the pension situation.

4.3.3.7 The duration of the marriage (s 25(2)(d))

For marriages of average or greater length, the duration is not normally relevant, as the usual guidelines will apply. Duration is usually most relevant if the marriage is short. In the case of an extremely short marriage, the court may order no financial provision at all, for example where a marriage effectively lasted only two weeks (*Krystman v Krystman* [1973] 1 WLR 927). It is particularly likely that no provision will be ordered where neither spouse has suffered financially as a result of the marriage. For a marriage that has lasted more than a few weeks, it is quite possible that some provision will be ordered, even if it is at a low level, such as the award of a small lump sum or a limited term of periodical payments to allow the applicant to readjust.

In a short marriage, other s 25 factors may be less significant—there will probably have been far less by way of contribution and earning potential is likely to be higher. On the other hand, the existence of children of the marriage will be very significant. Even after a short marriage, the needs and welfare of any children must be properly catered for (see *B v B (Mesher Order)* [2003] 2 FLR 285, and see further at **4.4.7**).

In *Miller; McFarlane*, Lord Nicholls expressed clearly the view that a short marriage was no less a partnership of equals than a long marriage and disapproved the approach that a party's entitlement increased over time. The short duration of a marriage might affect the amount of matrimonial property at stake between the parties—but the entitlement of the parties would be still subject to the yardstick of equality before considering whether there was a good reason for departure. Baroness Hale differed slightly in recognising that duration was a factor that the courts are required to consider. In her view, non-matrimonial assets were more likely to be excludable from the common pot in a shorter marriage, whereas, in the normal course of events, such distinctions would be likely to fade and such assets become part of the common enterprise—in this sense a short marriage might justify a departure from equality.

What is clear is that post-*Miller; McFarlane*, the line of authorities for short-marriage cases pre-*White*, which focused on the needs of the wife, cannot now be relied upon, and the post-*White* authority of *Foster v Foster* [2003] 2 FLR 299 is approved. The principle of sharing and the yardstick of equality apply—the significance of short duration is that it may justify departure or it may diminish what is at stake.

When considering the length of the marriage, the court has traditionally taken it as lasting from the time of marriage to the time of breakdown. Cohabitation before (or after) the marriage was not normally relevant to duration (*Foley v Foley* [1980] Fam 160), unless the circumstances were exceptional—a 25-year cohabitation as a family where the husband could not marry for legal reasons (*Kokosinski v Kokosinski* [1980] Fam 72).

Recently, however, the courts have shown greater willingness to treat a period of cohabitation as being part of the effective duration of the marriage. In *GW v RW* (*Financial Provision: Departure from Equality*) [2003] 2 FLR 108, Nicholas Mostyn, QC (as he then was) included 18 months' cohabitation as part of the duration of the marriage, concluding that, 'where a marriage moves seamlessly from cohabitation to marriage without any major alteration in the way the couple live, it is unreal and artificial to treat the periods differently'. He commented that, since the decision in *Foley*, public opinion had moved on and was more willing to recognise fully committed relationships outside of marriage. He also thought it relevant to consider how the parties themselves define their period of cohabitation. In *CO v CO* (*Ancillary Relief: Pre-marriage Cohabitation*) [2004] 1 FLR 1095, Coleridge J gave full weight to eight years' cohabitation preceding a four-year marriage. He held that, contingent on the parties having eventually married, committed and settled relationships outside marriage should be treated with the same validity as relationships which had publicly recorded that same degree of commitment by marrying.

This development has been criticised in some quarters; for some strong counter-arguments see the article in [2004] *Family Law* 205. One of many arguments is that cohabiting couples should not be deprived of the ability consciously to distinguish their state from that of married couples by an erosion of the distinction between the two.

Recent cases set no precedent but it is clear that the latitude of the courts' discretion is now open to the argument, based on the intention and conduct of cohabiting parties, that a relationship period longer than the marriage itself may be the appropriate measure. See **4.4.7**.

4.3.3.8   Any physical or mental disability of either of the parties (s 25(2)(e))

This point is fairly straightforward. If either spouse has a physical or mental disability which makes it difficult or impossible to be self-supporting, then that will be a factor in its own right as well as being relevant to earning capacity and possibly to needs.

However, the fact of the disability must be put in context. If the spouse who has a disability can claim social security benefits, while the spouse against whom a claim is made has a limited income, it is possible that no order will be made (see *Ashley v Blackman* [1988] Fam 85).

4.3.3.9   Contributions to the welfare of the family (s 25(2)(f))

Contributions to the welfare of the family can take many forms. One form is financial, but this provision also puts value on non-monetary contributions by making particular reference to looking after the household. So far as it can gauge them, the court will take into account contributions in the future as well as in the past.

Financial contributions include the earnings of the spouses over the course of the marriage and any capital sums or property that they bring or acquire during the marriage. As to inheritances, windfalls, family trusts and assets acquired before the marriage, see **4.3.3.3**.

Non-monetary contributions are usually those of the spouse who does not work in order to bring up children and look after the household. From the 1970s, there has been steadily increasing recognition of the value and status of such contributions. Now, since the House of Lords' decision in *White v White* [2000] 2 FLR 981, we have arrived at a position of direct equality between financial and non-financial contributions, at least as a starting point. In that case it was held to be a principle 'of universal application' that there should be no discrimination between husband and wife in their respective roles. A marriage involves a division of labour and, however this labour is divided, there should be no bias in favour of the breadwinner at the expense of the homemaker and child-carer. (For further consideration of *White*, see **4.4.4**.) Other types of non-monetary contributions, such as caring for an elderly or sick family member, or playing a support role to the career of the main earner, should not be overlooked where they are relevant.

Consideration of future contributions includes both financial and non-financial contributions. Where one party will be caring for children, this will be a relevant factor and the longer the dependency, the greater its significance. The likelihood of making financial contributions in the form of child support over a significant period of time will also be a relevant consideration.

4.3.3.10   Conduct (s 25(2)(g))

You will almost certainly have to explain to your client at some point that this factor is not concerned with the 'normal' types of misbehaviour often associated with the breakup of a marriage. This is not an easy issue on divorce. One spouse may be very upset at the way that the other has behaved—indeed that conduct may to them personally be the most important issue in the case. However, the court is loath to go into a detailed examination of the causes and effects of marital breakdown, as this can be very expensive in terms of time and money, and is rarely relevant to deciding the best way forward for the future. In *McCartney v Mills* [2008] 1 FLR 1508, Bennett J declined to hear evidence or argument about conduct on the basis that it would make little or no difference to the final result. As a result, the court will only take the most serious misconduct into account.

The statute provides that conduct will only be taken into account if it is such that 'in the opinion of the court it would be inequitable to disregard it'. In fact, there have been relatively few reported cases where the court has held that conduct is sufficiently bad to have a substantial effect on the level of provision ordered.

A departure from this well-established approach was suggested by the Court of Appeal in the *Miller* case itself, where Thorpe LJ cited the fact that the husband was responsible (in no extreme way) for the breakdown of the marriage as a factor influencing the balancing exercise. This aspect of that judgment drew much adverse comment and when *Miller* went to the House of Lords this point was expressly overruled. Conduct can only be taken into account if it is such that it would be inequitable to disregard it.

It is clear that adultery will not be sufficiently serious to be taken into account unless there is some aggravating factor, for example, if the adultery is with a father-in-law (*Bailey v Tolliday* (1982) 4 FLR 542). Where a person's right to apply for financial remedies has been based on deceitful or criminal behaviour, such as bigamy, then it has been held that such persons should not be entitled to benefit from their deceitful act (*Whiston v Whiston* [1995] 2 FLR 268). However, bigamy is not an automatic bar to entitlement; it will depend on the circumstances, including the other spouse's degree of knowledge and complicity (*Rampal v Rampal (No 2)* [2001] 2 FLR 1179) (though see [2003] *Family Law* 415 for a trenchant criticism of this decision). Serious violence has been held to be relevant conduct. In *H v H (Financial Provisions: Conduct)* [1994] 2 FLR 801, the husband had been imprisoned for violently assaulting and raping his wife; this was held to be relevant and the court further took into account that he had put himself in a position where he could not support the family. In *Evans v Evans* [1989] 1 FLR 351, it was held that a wife's right to maintenance should end after she was convicted of inciting the murder of her husband. In *K v K* (*Financial Provision: Conduct*) [1988] 1 FLR 469, a wife's conduct in assisting her husband's suicide attempts was held to be relevant to her level of entitlement. In *H v H* (*Financial Relief: Attempted Murder as Conduct*) [2006] 1 FLR 990, a husband convicted of the attempted murder of his wife received only a small portion of the matrimonial assets. Coleridge J stated that, 'The court should not be punitive or confiscatory for its own sake. The proper way to have regard to the conduct is as a potentially magnifying factor when considering the other subsections and criteria. It places the wife's needs as a much higher priority to those of the husband because the situation the wife finds herself in is, in a very real way, his fault.' See also *K v L* [2010] EWCA Civ 125 for a recent example of a case where conduct was considered relevant and for the interplay between this and the fact that much of the wife's wealth (which she retained under the order) had been inherited by her in the early years of the marriage and so was considered non-matrimonial property (see **4.3.3.3**).

Serious financial misconduct may also be relevant. In cases where a party dissipates or fritters away family assets, or brings about financial ruin through obviously selfish and unreasonable behaviour, then the court may take the view that he or she is not entitled to claim on an equal footing with the other spouse, a part of what remains. For examples, see *Beach v Beach* [1995] 2 FLR 160 and *Le Foe v Le Foe and Woolwich plc* [2001] 2 FLR 970. The case of *Stodgell v Stodgell* [2009] 2 FLR 218 is a dramatic example of the effects of serious financial misconduct. It deals with the conflict between a criminal confiscation order (made after the husband's conviction for tax evasion and fraud) and the wife's financial remedies claim. Holman J held that neither the MCA 1973 nor the Criminal Justice Act 1988 took priority over the other and that the husband's fraudulent activities amounted to conduct it would be inequitable to disregard. However, the husband's total assessed tax liabilities were virtually identical to his whole assets (£900,000) and the confiscation order prevailed. Leave to appeal was refused ([2009] 2 FLR 244), even though it was likely that the wife would then be forced to turn to the state for assistance. A wife who has been complicit in the crime giving rise to the confiscation order is vanishingly unlikely to succeed in a claim for financial remedies to tainted property. Her prospects of success depend on her level of complicity. However, the fact that she has not been complicit is no guarantee that she will succeed in her application; it depends on the particular circumstances: see *G v G* [2010] Fam Law 572.

Misconduct in the course of the proceedings, such as misrepresentation, making false statements or wilful non-disclosure, may well be relevant to the court's considerations. In *P v P* (*Financial Relief: Non-disclosure*) [1994] 2 FLR 381, Thorpe LJ held that, though the conduct was such that it would be inequitable to disregard it, this should be reflected in the order for costs rather than in the apportioning of the assets. However, in *M v M* (*Ancillary Relief: Conduct: Disclosure*) [2006] 2 FLR 1253, the husband had gambled away a significant amount of assets and had repeatedly failed to disclose matters, leading to penal notices and eventually a subpoena. The judge took account of both elements of bad conduct in the balancing exercise, rather than just confining the litigation element to a costs penalty.

4.3.3.11   Value of any benefit the parties will lose the chance of acquiring (s 25B(1))

The Pensions Act 1995 deleted the reference to pensions that used be part of s 25(2)(h) and inserted s 25B, which is entirely concerned with pensions. Issues other than pensions that may fall for consideration under this factor might include early retirement or redundancy rights, or in some circumstances inheritance rights.

Section 25B(1) added considerations to the s 25(2) factors. It provides:

(1) The matters to which the court is to have regard under section 25(2) above include—

(a) in the case of paragraph (a), any benefits under a pension arrangement which a party to the marriage has or is likely to have, and

(b) in the case of paragraph (h), any benefits under a pension arrangement which, by reason of the dissolution or annulment of the marriage, a party to the marriage will lose the chance of acquiring, and, accordingly, in relation to benefits under a pension arrangement, section 25(2)(a) above shall have effect as if 'in the foreseeable future' were omitted.

Thus, the court is now required in every case to consider, no matter how remote these events may be, the benefits that the parties might receive from a pension scheme and the effect of the commensurate loss on a party as a result of the divorce. In most cases, there are two types of loss. The first is the loss of the ability to share with the husband the benefits of the payments he will receive on retirement. The second is the loss of the protection, most commonly the widow's pension, which the scheme will confer on the death of the husband.

Although the court is obliged to consider pension benefits, such consideration is not a separate consideration outside of the s 25 approach. The court considers whether and how pension considerations should affect the terms of the order it is considering making, just as with any other factor. Having considered pension issues, the court may give them as much or as little weight, including disregarding them altogether, as it thinks appropriate.

Considering pension rights is a process that can become very complex. It may involve, for example, detailed evaluation of intricate financial products, calculations of future worth and application of discounts for accelerated receipt and contingency. In complex cases, it may be appropriate to obtain expert actuarial advice. What is given here is an overview of the appropriate steps to take in considering pension rights. See also a very useful introductory article 'A Beginner's Guide to Pensions within Family Proceedings' [2009] *Family Law* 341.

4.3.3.11.1 *Valuation*

Regulations, made under the MCA 1973, have been made for the extent of any benefit under a pension scheme to be valued and verified for the purposes of making an order under the Act. These regulations are the Divorce etc (Pensions) Regulations 2000 (SI 2000/1123), and the Pensions on Divorce etc (Provision of Information) Regulations 2000 (SI 2000/1048), which themselves refer to the Pension Schemes Act 1993, ss 93–101. The value of the pension arrangement shall be taken as at a day to be specified by the court. The method of valuation is to calculate the cash equivalent value (CEV) (formerly cash equivalent transfer value (CETV)). The process has been complicated by the introduction of new regulations from 1 October 2008 which apply to some pensions, but not others (the Occupational Pensions Schemes (Transfer Values) (Amendment) Regulations 2008 (SI 2008/1050)). Calculating the CEV is a specialist process—essentially it calculates a present (ie, the date specified by the court) cash value for the value of the member's payments on retirement and other pension benefits. The CEV does not include death-in-service benefits nor discretionary benefits. The managers of pension schemes must provide a CEV to a party on request or within three months of being ordered to do so by the court.

The CEV is the standard method of valuation but it is not the only one and the method has its critics (see the article referred to at the end of this section). Most criticisms argue that the CEV, for various reasons, tends to undervalue the actual value of the fund that will be accrued or the benefit that will be conferred. Although the court is required to use the CEV, it can also take other methods into account, provided that it is satisfied by expert evidence that it is appropriate to do so.

4.3.3.11.2 *Weight*

The next thing to consider is what weight to attach to the value of the benefits. A helpful insight can be gained from reading Court of Appeal judgments in *Martin-Dye v Martin-Dye* [2006] 2 FLR 901. Generally, the most significant facts are the ages of the parties, the length of the marriage and the amount of time remaining until retirement. With younger couples, the prospect of retirement will be far away and courts will tend to regard any future lost benefits as being too remote to be justly considered. The duration of the marriage is likely to be shorter, so the shareable benefits will be smaller. Additionally, younger divorcees will have plenty of time to make provision for their own futures—so there will be considerably less need under this factor and considerably less dependency, if any, on any existing pension arrangement. Conversely, the older a couple is, the closer in time will be the anticipated losses and the more important it will be for the court to make provision for them. The amount of time spent together accruing benefits is likely to be longer and therefore the value and significance of shareable benefits will be higher. Most importantly, the wife may only have a short time until retirement during which she will probably not be in a strong position in the labour market. She will therefore have little time and means by which to provide for her retirement and will be dependent, perhaps heavily or even solely, on the retirement arrangements of her husband.

Another basic consideration is to decide the time over which the pension benefit was accruing. In *H v H (Financial Provision: Capital Allowance)* [1993] 2 FLR 335, Thorpe J, as he was then, set out an approach that is commonly followed. He said that the value of what was earned during the period of cohabitation was more relevant than what may be earned during the period between separation and retirement. In that case, the pension had been earned over 13 years of service but there had only been seven years of cohabitation. The CETV was divided by the number of years of service and multiplied by the number of years of cohabitation.

District judges often follow this 'straight line' fractional approach. However, there is criticism of this approach—see below.

As can be imagined, the courts are reluctant to prescribe any periods of time or specific conditions for the relevance or otherwise of pension arrangements. However, decided cases tend to follow some broad principles and considerations:

(a) Where the parties, especially the wife, are young, possibly up to early thirties, the value of the pension may have little or no relevance.

(b) Similarly, if the pension is realisable more than 20 years into the future, it may well be of little or no relevance.

(c) Taking into account the case as a whole, what are the wife's reasonable needs for income or capital after retirement? Where there is not a clean break, there is more likely to be a future dependency.

(d) It is important to consider the position the wife will be in if the husband dies.

(e) In most cases, the court will have given priority to considering the wife's and any children's housing needs and income needs—if substantial provision has been made here, this may, taking into account the overall balance, affect the weight given to the wife's retirement needs.

(f) The needs of the husband must not be forgotten, especially in limited assets cases where the balance has gone against him in terms of housing and/or income.

(g) It is most important to bear in mind that these are merely illustrative tendencies derived from decided cases—every case will turn on its own facts.

4.3.3.11.3 *The final order*

The final thing to consider is how to reflect the value and weight of pension benefits in the final order. Pension benefits constitute a consideration under the overall s 25 exercise. When considering what, if any, orders to make in relation to pensions, the overall balance of all the relevant factors and circumstances must be borne in mind. There is no need to interfere with pension entitlement unless it is justified by reference to relevant factors or to the overall yardstick of equality (see **4.4.4**).

In circumstances where there are sufficient funds to meet all the wife's income and capital needs for life, it may be appropriate to consider offsetting, ideally in the form of a *Duxbury* fund (see **4.2.2.3**). Offsetting may also be appropriate where there is a younger couple and the wife has no serious requirement justifying adjustment of the husband's pension entitlement—but it may be considered just to reflect some loss of provision in a lump sum.

In circumstances where it is foreseen that there is likely to be an ongoing dependency crossing over into retirement, an attachment order for periodical payments could meet this purpose. In some circumstances, for example where the dependency is strong, or where there are dependent children being provided for, or where the husband is significantly older than the wife, it may be appropriate to strengthen the wife's protection by providing for the possible death of the husband, which can be achieved by an order for attachment of death-in-service benefits.

If there were insufficient funds at the time of the proceedings to make such lump sum order as the court considered appropriate, an attachment order for a lump sum could be used. This is in effect a deferred lump sum order.

In cases where there is a clean break and it is desired to provide for the wife with a share of the husband's pension, a pension-sharing order will usually be appropriate. There does not have to be a clean break—a pension-sharing order can be combined with an order for periodical payments. It is not possible to combine pension sharing with an attachment order—so the less independent a wife is, the less appropriate a pension-sharing order is likely to be. An advantage of a pension-sharing order is that it gives the wife a sum that is not subject to variation, nor at risk from changes in the husband's circumstances, such as bankruptcy—once she has her pension credit it is hers for life.

For a description of these various types of order, see **4.2.4**.

4.3.3.11.4 *Criticism of current practice*

In the post-*White* era of fairness there is a greater trend towards pension-sharing orders. However, the straightforward approach adopted by many judges may not be doing justice to the complexity of pensions. Comparing cash equivalent values between different pension schemes can be very misleading in that those values can be quite unrelated to the actual income streams that the given pensions will produce. For further discussion of this and related problems, see 'Pensions and Equality' [2007] *Family Law* 310.

For further articles expressing detailed concern at the CEV valuation method and the problems with pension-sharing orders, see 'The Reality of Pension Sharing—Part One' [2003] *Family Law* 517 and 'Part Two' [2003] *Family Law* 679.

4.3.4 Keeping an open mind

Examples have been given in this section of some of the most common issues that may arise in relation to the s 25 factors and the approaches that may be adopted in relation to them.

However, it is repeated throughout this chapter, and we are constantly reminded in leading judgments, that every case is individual and must be approached with an open mind. With any brief, you must consider all the s 25 factors with a fresh perspective and be prepared to make a sensible argument supporting a realistic proposal based on them.

4.4 Bases for provision

4.4.1 Introduction

An identification and balancing of the relevant factors in the case must finally be brought into focus in deciding on an overall basis for provision using the orders available to the court. The fact that the statutory powers to make orders and to take factors into account are wide may seem to provide a bewildering array of possibilities, but for every case a coherent solution must be found. This requires the development of professional expertise.

In any case, the overall basis may suggest itself from one, or more than one, salient or dominant feature of the circumstances. Statute directs the court to consider whether a clean break is possible and also to consider the needs of any children of the family first; either of these considerations could, if appropriate, become a basis for shaping the overall package. In particular circumstances, one of the factors in the case may be so important that it overrides all others; or a combination of two or more factors may provide the basic objectives around which a package of measures can be constructed.

The following notes offer a broad summary of possibilities rather than a comprehensive study. A basic overall guide suggesting an approach for deciding on an appropriate basis can be found at **4.4.9**.

4.4.2 Consider the needs of children first

The welfare of any children is stated by statute to be a first consideration (MCA 1973, s 25(1)). However, this does not mean that the children are entitled to be given outright assets belonging to their parents, but rather that provision for the children should be taken into account in dividing the assets of the parents. The most common effect of this principle is that where there are young children, the matrimonial home will often be used to provide a home for them either by settling it (that is, by apportioning beneficial interest in the home between the parties) or by transferring it to the custodial parent.

Although stability in the life of children is important, the existence of children will not always mean that the matrimonial home is preserved. In some cases, especially where the husband too has need of rehousing, or if the house is larger than is strictly required by the children of the family and the parent with care, it will have to be sold to provide capital and smaller properties purchased.

The welfare of children is also important in terms of income, and child support liability (see **Chapter 7**) means that in practice payments of maintenance for children will need to take priority. This will inevitably have an effect on overall settlements and may make it less likely that generous capital provision will be made.

4.4.3   The clean break

The idea of the clean break is that resources should be divided once and for all between the spouses, with no further financial obligations between them, and leaving each free to start a new life. This can usually only be achieved if there are sufficient available assets to satisfy the reasonable claims of the applicant, and if both spouses have such income or earning potential that maintenance payments will not be necessary.

4.4.3.1   Legislative framework

The objective of trying to achieve a clean break between spouses on divorce was made statutory in 1984, when s 25A was inserted into the MCA 1973. There are three sub-sections to s 25A.

Subsection (1) provides that whenever the court exercises its powers under ss 22A–24A, it is under a duty to consider whether it should do so in a way that terminates the financial obligations of the parties to each other as soon after decree absolute as the court considers just and reasonable. If the court does not conclude that termination is appropriate, then subsection (2) requires the court, when it makes an order for periodical payments (secured or otherwise), to consider whether it is appropriate to set a term for the payments that lasts only as long as necessary to allow the benefiting party to adjust without undue hardship to the termination of their financial dependency on the other party. Subsection (3) provides that if the court dismisses the application for periodical payments (secured or otherwise), then it may do so with an order barring further applications in relation to that marriage. The desirability of self-sufficiency may also be read in the 1984 amendment to s 25(2)(a) directing the court to consider any increase in earning capacity that it would be reasonable to expect a party to take steps to acquire (see **4.3.3.3**).

4.4.3.2   The approach of the courts

The court must consider the possibility of achieving a clean break in every case. However, it should only do so after having regard to all the s 25 factors and not in isolation from them. Although the court is required to try to achieve a clean break, it is under no obligation to pursue one as a priority or at the expense of other considerations.

In most cases, the court will have two decisions to make: should there be an immediate clean break (*per* s 25A(1)); or should there be a clean break at some future time (a deferred clean break) (*per* s 25A(2))? When considering a deferred clean break, the court must further think about whether to make an order under s 28(1A), which prohibits the party in whose favour the order is made from making further applications for extension or variation under s 31.

In considering what is appropriate, there are three broad categories that cases might fall into: 'big money', 'no money' and 'normal money'. In 'big-money' cases, a clean break can often be achieved because, whatever the wife's short- or long-term entitlements, there is enough money to meet them for her lifetime by providing her with some form of capital fund, such as a *Duxbury* fund. All continuing claims can be dismissed because the capital fund provides real self-sufficiency. In such cases, however, the liquidity of any business assets can be a highly relevant factor—see *F v F* (*Clean Break: Balance of Fairness*) [2003] 1 FLR 847 for an example of a case where it was held to be inappropriate to order a clean break in order to preserve a significant and illiquid business that generated income for the parties. In *Miller; McFarlane*, the House of Lords confirmed the principle that periodical payments can be ordered to provide a spouse with a fair share of the matrimonial assets where there was insufficient capital to do so. This is a departure from the previous view that periodical payments could only be used to meet ongoing needs. It is probably limited to big-money cases where the payer is unusually 'capital-poor' but 'income-rich'—even here critics wonder whether a lump sum order in instalments would not fit the purpose better.

In 'no-money' cases, a clean break may be ordered on the basis that there is no possibility nor prospect of the husband paying periodical payments. In such circumstances, the clean break at least avoids ongoing uncertainty, litigation and cost. It should be said that even with no clean break, where there is no money, there is less possibility of continued uncertainty.

It is the 'normal-money' cases that present the most difficulty in considering the clean break possibilities. Often the husband does not have enough money to make payments without hardship but the wife does not have an earning capacity that would enable her to be self-supporting. The most significant fact is whether or not there are children of the family—wherever there are children, a clean break becomes very hard to achieve and is unlikely to be attempted. This is for very practical reasons including the obvious fact that, with children, the caring parent will have greater needs and diminished earning capacity. In addition, with children present, the parties are going to have a serious and long-term ongoing joint responsibility, so achieving a clean break may be less important. Remember that the clean break relates to the parents—one can never achieve a clean break for one's obligations to children.

In balancing available money against needs, it is important to consider the latter side of the balance carefully, especially with childless couples. If the needs are not great, then a clean break may still be achieved even where there is not a great deal of money. Needs may be fewer where there has been a short marriage, or the parties are young, or where they both have careers.

Authoritative guidance on how to approach the question of a clean break was given by Ward LJ in *C v C* (*Financial Relief: Short Marriage*) [1997] 2 FLR 26. Although that case involved a short marriage and the facts were very unusual, the guidance is of general application. To summarise:

(a) The first task is to consider whether an immediate clean break is appropriate. Section 25A(2) provides the test in considering a deferred clean break of the payee being able 'to adjust [to the termination of dependency] without undue hardship'. It is commonly inferred from decided cases that this same test applies to considering an immediate clean break (even though it is not written in the statute).

(b) If the court decides to order periodical payments of some sort, then it must also consider whether to set such payments for a finite term. It should only do this if satisfied that the payee will at the end of the term have adjusted to the termination of support without undue hardship. There must be evidence before the court to support such a conclusion.

(c) What is appropriate must depend on all the circumstances of the case, including the welfare of any minor child and the s 25 factors. The duration of the marriage may be of particular relevance but a short marriage does not always lead to a clean break.

(d) In considering whether and when the payee can cope with the termination of financial dependence, the question is *can* she adjust, not *should* she adjust. In answering that question, the court will pay attention not only to the duration of the marriage but to the effect of the marriage and its breakdown; the need to care for minor children and the effect of this on the earning capacity of the payee; and any difficulties she will have in entering the labour market, resuming a fractured career and making up any lost ground.

(e) If there is doubt about whether the payee will be able to adjust, then it is wrong to set a term with the onus on the payee to apply for an extension. The proper course is to set no term and leave the payer to apply for variation.

The same principles apply when considering whether to terminate an order for periodical payments on an application to vary under s 31; the test is still *can* the payee adjust? Any cohabitation by the payee is also likely be relevant. A helpful case on how the discretion is exercised at this stage can be found in Moylan J's decision *W v W (Periodical Payments: Variation)* [2010] 2 FLR 985.

4.4.3.3   The Inheritance (Provision for Family and Dependants) Act 1975

The Inheritance (Provision for Family and Dependants) Act 1975, s 1(1)(b) (I(PFD)A 1975) allows former spouses to make a claim for financial relief against the estate of a deceased person. This would not be appropriate in a case where the court had effected a clean break. Section 15(1) of the I(PFD)A 1975 provides that, on a decree of divorce, separation or nullity the court can, if it considers it just to do so, make an order that the other party shall not be entitled to apply under the I(PFD)A 1975 against the estate of the deceased party. This is commonly done in clean break cases but it is a separate consideration and will not always be appropriate, for example, in the 'no-money' cases discussed above. The court will not make this order unless asked so you should take care not to overlook it.

4.4.3.4   Extension of terms

Where there is a direction under the MCA 1973, s 28(1A) barring applications for an extension/variation of the term, that is final and the court cannot reconsider it.

According to the guidance in *C v C*, there should not be a situation where a fixed-term order for periodical payments is made without a s 28(1A) order. However, it does happen and when it does the payee may apply for an extension/variation under s 31. He or she must do so before the term expires, as once the term has expired the right to apply for an extension is lost.

4.4.3.5   Advising the client

It is vital to appreciate, and to make it clear to the client, that a clean break will, except in exceptional circumstances, bring a permanent *end* to all the client's claims for provision for herself (see *Hewitson v Hewitson* [1995] Fam 100). Contrast this with a nominal maintenance order. This is an order for periodical payments of a low or token sum, which can be varied if circumstances change. Clean break orders are not susceptible to variation. Appeals or applications for further provision will only be possible in cases of fraud or the like. This will be an advantage for the person against whom provision is sought, but it must be considered seriously by the spouse seeking provision. Sometimes clients are very keen to get a clean break even when your advice is that they would be, or might in the future be, entitled to maintenance. In such circumstances, if a client insists on instructing you to obtain a clean break, you should get them to endorse your brief to confirm that they have listened to and understood your advice.

4.4.3.6   Summary of common orders

4.4.3.6.1   *Open-ended order for maintenance*

This is appropriate where the dependency of the payee will continue for a long time or for life or where there is uncertainty. This is often the case where there are young children or where the payee is older and the court is uncertain that she will be able to become self-sufficient.

4.4.3.6.2   *Maintenance order with a term and s 28 (1A) direction*

This will most often be used where the court is satisfied that after a period of readjustment the payee will be able to achieve a state of self-sufficiency, for example, a younger wife with a large part of her working life ahead of her.

4.4.3.6.3   *Maintenance order with a term without s 28(1A) direction*

This is contrary to judicial guidance, which says that if there is uncertainty then an order without term should be made (see **4.4.3.2**). However, this may be appropriate, for example, where there are older dependent children and the wife does have the means to achieve self-sufficiency, but the future dependency of the children cannot be ascertained with certainty.

4.4.3.6.4   *Immediate clean break on income*

This will be appropriate in circumstances where the court considers that there should not be an ongoing dependency, for example, where there are no children, the marriage is short, the wife is able to become self-supporting immediately or is already self-sufficient. It may be that the wife could have been entitled to some kind of maintenance but she gave that up in return for a greater share elsewhere in the package, such as an increased share in property, which preserved the overall balance and may also have decreased her income needs.

4.4.3.6.5   *Capitalised maintenance, no periodical payments*

This is a lump sum out of which the payee can provide maintenance for herself. This kind of solution can be used where there is a dependency but there is sufficient money to provide for that dependency with a capital fund and thus make a clean break possible.

4.4.3.6.6   *Nominal maintenance order*

This is an order for periodical payments of a token sum such as five pence per year. This kind of order can be used where it is thought that a clean break is possible and/or desirable but the circumstances are such that the payee should not be left without the ability to reapply. For example, if the payee is cohabiting but not remarried, she may be supported by the cohabitant for the time being but she does not have the certainty nor the legal rights that come with remarriage. Another situation where nominal payments may be appropriate is where the husband simply cannot afford maintenance but there is a chance that his situation will improve, so it should be left open to the wife to reapply if he becomes able to afford to support her.

4.4.4   Finding a starting point—fairness, non-discrimination and equality

The s 25 factors govern the exercise of the court's discretion—but it is necessary to consider what the court, in the exercise of its discretion, is trying to achieve. Is there a fundamental basis, or starting point, for the court in deciding how to approach issues of financial relief? In decided cases, there is regular reference to the objectives of 'achieving fairness' and 'doing justice'. In the Court of Appeal in *White v White* [1998] 2 FLR 310, Butler-Sloss LJ stated: 'Sections 25 and 25A provide the guidelines and require the court to have regard to all the circumstances of the individual case and to exercise the discretion of the court to do justice between the parties.' In *Cowan v Cowan* [2001] 2 FLR 192 at 213, Thorpe LJ stated that 'the unexpressed objective of the [s 25] exercise is to arrive at a fair solution'. It is helpful to consider now what 'doing justice' and 'arriving at a fair solution' have been held to mean in more practical terms.

After the passing of the MCA 1973, the first major case to deal generally with how discretion should be exercised was *Wachtel v Wachtel* [1973] Fam 72. This case proposed the use of the 'one-third rule' as a starting point for evaluating how to apportion the assets of the marriage. Essentially, it meant that a fair division of assets in a standard situation could mean one-third going to the wife and two-thirds going to the husband. Within a few years this 'rule' became subject to regular criticism and numerous court decisions emphasised that the only proper approach was to consider the statutory factors. The 'one-third rule' is now totally extinct and is of historic interest only.

A principle that partly replaced the 'one-third rule', at least for cases where there was a significant level of income and capital, was that of seeking to meet the applicant's 'reasonable needs'. This term was developed by the courts as a way of interpreting the statutory factors and achieved widespread use, even outside of bigger-money cases. However, there are many situations where there is insufficient money to meet all 'reasonable needs', or where such a principle is inappropriate, as both spouses have built up and have good claims to income and capital.

The principle of 'reasonable needs' has now been replaced by the guidance of the House of Lords in *White v White* [2000] 2 FLR 981 and the subsequent line of authority, although not without some comment and difference of opinion. Although *White* was a case involving significant assets, which were more than sufficient to meet needs, Lord Nicholls set out some principles to be followed in future cases:

(a) It is a principle 'of universal application' that there should be no discrimination between husband and wife in their respective roles. Fairness dictates that, whatever the division of labour, this should not prejudice either party when considering the statutory factors.

(b) When considering how to give effect to the factors, the judge should check his or her provisional views against 'the yardstick of equality of division'. 'As a general guide, equality should be departed from only if, and to the extent that, there is good reason for doing so.'

(c) However, although equality is a 'yardstick' or a 'cross-check', it is not a 'starting point' nor a 'presumption'.

(d) The concept of 'reasonable needs' is a misconception. The wording of the statute is simply 'needs' and no general qualification of this is desirable.

There has been some debate about how much *White* applies outside of big-money cases. Lord Nicholls' speech makes it clear that the non-discrimination principle is 'of universal application'. The 'yardstick of equality' is a little less straightforward, being a 'yardstick' but not a 'starting point'.

In *Cowan v Cowan* [2002] 2 FLR 192 (which was a big-money case), the Court of Appeal declined to take the opportunity to provide authoritative guidance on how *White* should be applied across all types of cases, but Thorpe LJ said in his judgment: 'The decision in *White* clearly does not introduce a rule of equality. The yardstick of equality is a cross check against discrimination. Fairness is the rule.' In *Cordle v Cordle* [2002] 1 FLR 207 (which was not a big-money case), Thorpe LJ said: 'There is no rule in *White* that district judges must produce equality of outcome unless there are good reasons to justify departure.'

In *Miller; McFarlane*, the House of Lords again considered the question of fairness: 'In arriving at a fair outcome, three elements must be considered: the needs of the parties and children; compensation for any economic disadvantage arising from the marriage; and sharing the fruits of the matrimonial partnership.' Baroness Hale added this important qualification: 'The ultimate objective is to give each party an equal start on the road to independent living.' In addition, the remit of periodical payments was extended beyond maintenance to include compensation in appropriate cases (see **4.4.3.2** above).

In the High Court the new guidance was applied with a sense of restraint. In *RP v RP* [2006] EWHC 3409 (Fam), Coleridge J said care had to be taken in ensuring that the guidance in *Miller; McFarlane* was not elevated to some kind of quasi-statutory amendment—it was the commentary of the House of Lords on a well-trodden statute now in its fourth decade. He stated that it was questionable whether 'compensation', which did not appear in the statute, added anything to 'financial... obligations and responsibilities' under s 25(2)(b). In *H v H* [2007] EWHC 459 (Fam), Charles J said the fact that both parties to a marital relationship are free to bring it to an end, along with its cooperation and common goals, leads to the conclusion that by reference to the rationale of compensation or sharing, the lower-income earner is not, and should not be, entitled to long-term economic parity.

The Court of Appeal, however, pulled in a slightly different direction. In *Charman v Charman* [2007] EWCA Civ 503, Potter P stated that the 'sharing principle' (of the three strands identified by the House of Lords in *Miller; McFarlane*) is the dominant principle in big-money cases and that it should be the starting point of ancillary relief consideration—rather than come at the end of the exercise. He said that the sharing principle should come before needs, unless needs produces a bigger award. He also limited Baroness Hale's views on non-matrimonial property as applying only to short-marriage cases and as being less preferable to Lord Nicholls' more 'logical' view (see **4.3.3.3**).

Some commentators said that this marked the end of the 'yardstick of equality' and that the principle of fairness should now be understood as having a starting point of sharing. This was a little premature—it has to be remembered that this was a big-money case and that in most cases courts are mainly concerned with stretching available resources to cover adequately the needs of the parties—as Lord Nicholls put it in *Miller; McFarlane*: 'In most cases the search for fairness begins and ends at that stage.'

The yardstick of equality, involving in any given case a calculation of what equal division would be, should still be a useful cross-check against discrimination—a tool rather than an objective. In most cases, resources are limited. Various factors, such as cost of living and children and the need to house everyone, will have such weight that, after they are carefully balanced in a non-discriminatory way, they may well produce an outcome that is unequal (in terms of the allocation of resources), but fair (in terms of all the circumstances and relevant factors).

In most 'normal' cases there will be little or nothing remaining over which to have a protracted debate about the value of various types of contribution. This is often true even in 'well-off' families with well-above-average incomes, as the perceived needs and entitlements tend to be of higher value—the houses cost more, the living standard to be met is higher, there are school fees and other private outgoings—so there is still nothing remaining that is perceived as a surplus to needs. It should be said that in normal-money cases, even though contribution may not be a leading factor, it is still relevant and the non-discrimination principle will apply. It may be more important in cases where there is a small enterprise to be divided or where there are no children; see *Foster v Foster* [2003] 2 FLR 299, CA for the principle applied to a small business in a short, childless marriage.

Four years post-*Charman*, it is still true that the only overall objective that is always relevant and can never be departed from is fairness—and the starting point for achieving this is always the s 25 factors. It is well described by Thorpe LJ in *Cordle*, at 214:

> The second difficulty that needs mention is the impact the decision of their Lordships in *White* has had upon what may be described as a routine district judge case...The first point, that cannot be over emphasised, is that there is no rule that district judges must produce equality of outcome...The cross-check of equality of outcome is intended to be a safeguard against discrimination...it is the first duty of the court to apply the s 25 criteria in search of the overarching objective of fairness...in the typical...case the district judge will always look first to the housing needs of the parties...the court's first concern will be to provide a home for the primary carer and the children...where there is sufficient to go beyond that, the court's concern will be to provide the means for the absent parent to rehouse...Another factor that should be considered is buttressing the ability of one or other of the parties to work...if there be cash beyond that the judge has to look to what in his estimation is the fair result.

These considerations will apply in many standard cases, but they are, of course, not exclusive. The only universal rule is to apply the s 25(2) criteria to all the circumstances of the case (giving first consideration to the welfare of the children) and to arrive at a fair result that avoids discrimination. This approach was reiterated by the Court of Appeal in *B v B (Ancillary Relief)* [2008] 2 FLR 1627, where the court emphasised that there is no rule that equal division is the starting point in all cases, but that the financial position of the parties and s 25 factors are the starting point. The Court of Appeal emphasised that in all cases the objective was fairness and that the yardstick of equality is to be applied to every outcome and only to be departed from to the extent that there is a good reason for doing so: paras [24] and [25]. The importance of concentrating on the s 25 factors was again revisited by the Court of Appeal in *Robson v Robson* [2011] 1 FLR 751: see Ward LJ at para [43] and his useful reminder that:

> The fact is that no formula and no resort to percentages will provide the right answer. Weighing the various factors and striking the balance of fairness is, after all, an art not a science.

4.4.5 The rich couple

The application of reasonable needs has been done away with by *White*. So, too, in theory anyway, has the discrimination between wealth-creating work and 'homely management' of the house and children. In big-money cases, there has been great emphasis on the need to justify departure from the yardstick of equality. In doing this, there is often (although not exclusively) a focus on contribution. This is partly because wealth tends to render most of the other factors irrelevant; but it also shows that, while the courts are anxious to avoid discriminating with regard to the nature of the contribution made by the parties, they have still been willing to find differences in the level of contribution made and to reflect that in the division of the assets. In *Cowan*, departure from equality was justified by the fact that 'the husband's contribution...was truly exceptional'. In *Lambert v Lambert*, at first instance, departure was justified by 'the really special contribution of the husband'. However, on appeal (*Lambert v Lambert* [2003] 1 FLR 139), the Court of Appeal became much more wary of the issue of special contribution, making 'a cautious acknowledgement that special contribution remains a legitimate possibility but only in special circumstances'. Courts continued to limit the concept of special contribution and in *Miller; McFarlane* the House of Lords stated that 'the question of contributions should be approached in much the same way as conduct. Exceptional or special contributions should only be regarded as a factor pointing away from equality of division when it would be inequitable to proceed otherwise.'

It will generally be easier to achieve a clean break where there are substantial assets, but continuing maintenance may be ordered, for example, where it is not reasonable to expect the claimant spouse to go out to work or where the payer's huge salary may come to a predictable end (eg, *Parlour v Parlour* [2004] EWCA Civ 872, the footballer case). An alternative may sometimes be for a sufficiently large lump sum to be ordered to buy out the right to continuing maintenance (see **4.4.3.4**).

4.4.6   The poor couple

There are, unfortunately, many cases where the joint assets of the spouses are not sufficient to provide properly for both. Where the money that has managed to finance one household needs to be stretched to provide for two, there may simply not be enough to go around. This is, perhaps, the most obvious and frequently used reason for departing from 'the yardstick of equality'. There may not be an easy solution in such cases, and you will need a particularly practical understanding of the problems that such a couple may face, and a thorough understanding of the social security benefit system. This knowledge will need to be both detailed and up-to-date.

One spouse cannot normally expect the state to take over the expense of caring for the other spouse, as that is a legal liability of the spouse. However, it is appropriate when assessing the potential income of a party to include non-means-related state benefits. Generally, parties are expected to apply for benefits designed to assist people in their position; a commonly occurring example is the working family tax credit. Clearly, it would be unreasonable and illogical to order a spouse to pay maintenance if that would put the payer below subsistence level, as the effect would simply be that the payer would be in need of state benefit him or herself (*Stockford v Stockford* [1982] 3 FLR 58) and in such a situation a maintenance order will not normally be made. This is not an invariable rule, particularly in cases where a paying party has taken on new liabilities irresponsibly and without proper regard for his or her obligations to his or her children and/or former spouse (*Campbell v Campbell* [1998] 1 FLR 828). Generally, though, in a case where joint resources are so low that it is inevitable that one spouse will have to rely on state benefits, it may be appropriate that a nominal order or no order be made for maintenance, and the claimant spouse be left to rely on state benefits.

Where resources are limited, the 'net-effect' approach can be used in considering maintenance payments. This was first enunciated in *Stockford* by Ormrod LJ and is still a useful practice. In any case where the need for financial provision may outweigh the available resources, the best approach is to calculate as accurately as possible how much the payer can afford to pay towards the maintenance of the other spouse. Attention is centred on the sum each party will have left to live on. The object is to ensure that the payer's net income (after deductions, including the maintenance payable to the spouse) is not reduced below subsistence level (ie, the income needs of the payer's new household as indicated by the appropriate income support level and the cost of his or her accommodation).

There is no set formula for what is, basically, a common-sense exercise. It involves ascertaining the net income from all sources for each of the parties, adding to or subtracting from that according to the amount of the proposed order and allowing for any tax changes that may result. This gives the income of each party if the proposed order were made, which figures can be compared and related to their respective needs, and the hypothetical order adjusted accordingly.

Where there are children, note that a child support calculation will have to be made first. If the payer is not well off, this may well leave little or nothing for any additional maintenance for the caring spouse.

4.4.7 The short marriage

Since *Miller; McFarlane* (see **4.3.3.7** above) all pre-*White* authorities on the effect of a short marriage must be treated with caution.

Probably authorities relating to very short marriages—relationships that in effect never got off the ground—are still useful guidance. If a marriage is short, then this may be an overriding factor which dictates the whole basis for provision. After a very short marriage (lasting weeks), there may be no provision at all (although a brief marriage can be debilitating; see *C v C (Financial Relief: Short Marriage)* [1997] 2 FLR 26). After a marriage lasting months, provision is likely to be on the basis of what the applicant has lost by the marriage. Another feature may be to provide the wife with maintenance for a limited term sufficient to enable her to rejoin the labour market, although note the *dicta* of Ward LJ in *C v C* to the effect that, just because the marriage is short, it does not automatically mean that there should be a term.

However, while these may be the effects of a short marriage on the overall package of provision, it is essential to note that, as always, all the circumstances and factors must be considered. The existence of a child of the marriage will almost certainly alter the picture completely. Foreign cultural factors may also affect the court's approach to a short marriage (see **4.4.8.4**).

For marriages long enough to be measured in years the best starting point is probably *Foster v Foster* [2003] 2 FLR 299, CA, which was cited with approval in *Miller; McFarlane*. In this case, a four-year marriage without children, Hale LJ restored a DJ's order that intended to give back to the parties what they had brought into the marriage (and spent after separation) while sharing equally between them, despite different levels of financial contribution, the assets they had accumulated during the marriage. For an example of a very short marriage of less than a year where there was a child, see *B v B (Mesher Order)* [2003] 2 FLR 285, Family Division. Munby J made large (relative to the assets) orders for indefinite periodical payments and a lump sum (for housing) that left the husband short of capital. The judge said that the existence of the child meant that effectively the wife would be making a contribution to this marriage for two decades, and that her earning capacity would be severely reduced, while the husband's large earning capacity meant that he would be able to rebuild his capital. These factors meant that it was fair and necessary to make significant and long-term provision in her favour.

In cases where there is a surplus after meeting the parties' needs, short duration is a factor that might justify departure from equality, particularly in respect of non-matrimonial property (see **4.3.3.3** for the leading views in *Miller; McFarlane*). Baroness Hale takes a slightly more expansive view of the possible effect of a short marriage, noting that it is a statutory requirement to consider it. See also **4.3.3.7**.

4.4.8 Special circumstances and assets

The facts of an individual case may reveal some special circumstances in the position of either spouse, or with regard to the assets available for provision, which may inevitably have some practical bearing on the basis on which financial provision can be ordered.

4.4.8.1   A business forming part of the assets

One type of asset that may require special consideration is a business or an interest in a business. If either or both spouses is involved in the running of a business, there may be complex problems in deciding to what extent the business should be taken into account, how the business should be valued and how provision might be made from a business, as it may be difficult to extract money from it without prejudicing its chances of success. Expert assistance may well be required in dealing with accounts, taxation, the marketability of shares and future projections for business success. For examples, see *Mubarak v Mubarak* [2001] 1 FLR 673 and *A v A* [2000] *Family Law* 470. For thorough consideration of how to value a business for financial remedies purposes, see [2004] *Family Law* 187.

Historically, there has been a reluctance by the courts to 'kill the goose that lays the golden egg'. The income generated by a business is often more important than the cash that could be raised by selling it. However, if one of the parties is retiring from the business or if the business was run together by the separating parties, then it may be appropriate to realise the value of the business. After *White*, there was a trend, in big-money cases, in favour of selling business assets if necessary to reflect equality of contribution; see *Parra v Parra* [2003] 1 FLR 942 (and also discussion of *Lambert* and *Cowan* at **4.4.5**). However, there is now a greater tendency to try to find ways of preserving the business. See *F v F (Clean Break: Balance of Fairness)* [2003] 1 FLR 847, dealing with the fairly common situation of an illiquid business. Singer J preserved the business by ordering ongoing maintenance (rather than a lump sum that could only be raised by selling the business) to the wife in a situation where a clean break would otherwise have been quite appropriate. For a very creative solution to illiquidity, see *R v R (Lump Sum Repayments)* [2004] 1 FLR 928, where, without selling the family business, the husband would have been left with £448,000 and the wife with £30,000, which was obviously not an acceptable outcome. The High Court ordered the husband to make a lump sum payment by 240 monthly instalments; as a lump sum order these payments would continue if the wife remarried and also were subject to variation if there were unforeseen circumstances. In *R v R (Financial Relief: Company Valuation)* [2005] 2 FLR 365 the husband was given five years to pay a lump sum of £1 million but was incentivised by early payment discounts of up to 20 per cent.

4.4.8.2   Agreements

Parties may wish to enter into an agreement about what is to happen should their marriage come to an end (or, indeed, when it has). Such agreements can be made at one of three distinct times: before the marriage and in contemplation of it; during the marriage; or after separation. These are referred to by a variety of different names: antenuptial, prenuptial or premarital agreements for the first type; postnuptial or postmarital agreements for the second type; and separation agreements for the third. The courts have developed a clear approach to separation agreements which has withstood the test of time for over 30 years and this is dealt with below.

It is the first two categories which have resulted in differing approaches and in respect of which there have been calls for reform in recent years. It has been suggested in the media that prenuptial agreements should be made binding. The justification is, perhaps, that parties, particularly the very wealthy, should be free to determine for themselves the financial consequences of their marriage not enduring. Baroness Hale in her dissenting judgment in the leading authority, *Radmacher v Granatino* [2010] 2 FLR 1900, commented that this area of law is 'ripe for systematic review and reform' [133]. The Law Commission is conducting a review into the status and enforceability of agreements between spouses and civil partners (and those contemplating marriage or civil partnership). In January 2011, having waited for the decision of the Supreme Court in *Radmacher v Granatino*, the Law Commission published its consultation paper and its final recommendations are expected in 2012. See also Law Commissioner Professor Elizabeth Cooke's article at [2011] *Family Law* 145.

Until that review and/or the passing of any new legislation, what is clear in the meantime is that none of these types of agreement is legally binding. They do not oust the jurisdiction of the court to determine the financial consequences on divorce (or on the cessation of a civil partnership): *Hyman v Hyman* [1929] AC 601. Such an agreement falls to be considered as one of the 'circumstances of the case' that the court must take into account in exercising its discretion under s 25.

In recent years, the courts have come to attach increasingly more weight to prenuptial agreements. In *Crossley v Crossley* [2008] 1 FLR 1467, Thorpe LJ expressed the view that, on the facts of that case (short, childless marriage between two independent, wealthy individuals who had both been previously married and both consulted lawyers), the prenuptial agreement was a factor of 'magnetic' importance.

However, the Supreme Court, in *Radmacher v Granatino*, has now given clear guidance on this issue of the weight to be attached to the first two types of agreement. This guidance is relevant to both pre and postnuptial agreements, the Supreme Court holding that the Privy Council in *MacLeod v MacLeod* [2009] 1 FLR 641 was wrong to draw a distinction between them. *Radmacher* is, therefore, authority for the courts' approach to both types of agreement.

In giving the lead judgment (with which six of the Supreme Court Justices agreed), Lord Phillips held that the court should give effect to a nuptial agreement that is freely entered into by each party with a full appreciation of its implications, unless in the circumstances prevailing it would not be fair to hold the parties to their agreement [para 75]. In considering the circumstances leading up to the making of the agreement, Lord Phillips considered that the court should approach this in the same way as it has been approached in relation to post-separation agreements (see below). He said:

The first question will be whether any of the standard vitiating factors: duress, fraud or misrepresentation, is present. Even if the agreement does not have contractual force, those factors will negate any effect the agreement might otherwise have. But unconscionable conduct such as undue pressure (falling short of duress) will also be likely to eliminate the weight to be attached to the agreement, and any other unworthy conduct, such as exploitation of a dominant position to secure an unfair advantage, would reduce or eliminate it [para 71].

The court will also consider other matters: the parties' emotional state at the time of the agreement, what pressure they were under to agree (but in the context of what would have happened without such pressures), the age, maturity and experience of the parties and whether the marriage would have gone ahead without the agreement in that form. For an example of undue influence in a postnuptial agreement, see *NA v MA* [2006] EWHC 2900 (Fam), where Baron J considered the subtle and particular pressures that parties can be subject to within a marriage relationship. Here the husband had effectively threatened to end the marriage if she did not sign and such legal advice that she received was poor. The judge gave no weight to the agreement.

Dealing with fairness will be dictated by the facts of each particular case, but Lord Phillips gave some general guidance. A nuptial agreement could not be allowed to prejudice the reasonable requirements of children of the family; the court should accord respect to the decision of a married couple as to the manner in which their financial affairs should be regulated, particularly where this addresses existing circumstances; dealing with non matrimonial property in a nuptial agreement is not inherently unfair; it will be pertinent to look at the extent to which an agreement fails to provide fairly for future circumstances. Referring to the three strands of need, compensation and sharing (identified in *White* and *Miller; McFarlane* as the main principles which govern the distribution of property in a financial relief application), he suggested that the principles of need and compensation were the two crucial aspects for fairness. If these strands are satisfied, the court is more likely to uphold the nuptial agreement rather than make some other order. Lord Phillips approved the general approach of Baron J at first instance in *Radmacher,* that the agreement fell to be considered as one factor in all the circumstances of the case, but in the right sort of case it could be the most compelling factor [para 83].

Unsurprisingly, the authorities on nuptial agreements concern cases with significant assets. However, the guidance in *Radmacher* may well mean that more couples wish to enter such agreements in order to assert their own autonomy over the financial consequences flowing from the possible ending of their marriage or civil partnership. It is clear that post *Radmacher*, the courts' view will be that parties who enter such agreements will be assumed to intend that effect should be given to them. The Law Commission made this same point (see para 5.2). The drafting of such agreements is likely to be a growth area. Perhaps the key issue identified in the consultation is that in order for there to be an absolute degree of certainty through marital agreements, the court's discretion would need to excluded. Even if this were the ultimate recommendation of the Commission, one wonders whether there is sufficient interest in this rather narrow topic for it to be given room in the coalition government's legislative programme.

As for post-separation agreements, these are governed by the line of authorities following *Edgar v Edgar* [1980] 3 All ER 887. Ormrod LJ said that regard must be had to the conduct of both parties leading up to the agreement and their subsequent conduct in consequence of it. He highlighted circumstances that would be relevant: undue pressure, exploitation of a dominant position, inadequate knowledge, (possibly) bad legal advice, an unforeseen change of circumstance. He also stated the principle that formal agreements, properly and fairly arrived at, should not be displaced unless there are good and substantial grounds for believing that an injustice will otherwise be done.

The problem of poor legal advice was considered by the Court of Appeal in *Harris v Manahan* [1997] 1 FLR 205. Although bad legal advice is a circumstance to be taken into account, where there was a consent order, there is public good in having finality in litigation and the order would not be interfered with save in the most exceptional case of the cruellest injustice.

Where the parties reach a separation agreement and subsequently apply for financial remedies, the court will consider the *Edgar* principles. If the agreement was fairly reached, then the court will hold it to be one of the most important factors which are highly persuasive, but not binding. In *A v B (Financial Relief: Agreements)* [2005] 2 FLR 730, Black J held that an agreement of this kind should be taken into account under the heading of conduct, as one of the considerations to which the judge must give weight in applying the statutory criteria. See also *S v S (Ancillary Relief)* [2009] 1 FLR 254 where Eleanor King J held that a post-separation agreement reached after round-table meetings, which was then encapsulated in a draft order, was of such magnetic importance that it must necessarily dominate the discretionary process. It was appropriate for the case to proceed on the notice to show cause why the draft order should be not perfected.

4.4.8.3   The millionaire's defence

This 'defence' is essentially a defence against disclosure in cases involving very substantial assets, where the respondent says that he will meet any order the court might make (*Thyssen-Bornemisza v Thyssen-Bornemisza (No 2)* [1985] FLR 1069). If the court considers that any difference between the, say, £400 million that the husband admits to having and the, say, £1,000 million that the wife says he has will not make any significant difference to the award it is likely to make, then it can agree to dispense with lengthy and costly disclosure. There has been some debate as to whether the 'defence' survives post-*White*.

In *J v V (Disclosure: Offshore Corporations)* [2004] 1 FLR 1042, Coleridge J said that there may still be a role for such concessions in some circumstances, such as a marriage involving independently obtained wealth that was of short or medium duration, or where the parties wanted to avoid acrimonious proceedings and expected there to be no order as to costs.

However, in *McFarlane v McFarlane* and *Parlour v Parlour* [2004] EWCA Civ 872, where the wealthy husbands had not bothered with proper financial disclosure, Thorpe LJ stated *obiter*, 'We were told by the Bar that a practice has grown up for substantial earners to decline any statement of their needs on the grounds that they can afford any order that the court is likely to make. These appeals must put an end to that practice.' That sounds like the final word. But in that case the court was annoyed by the husbands' cavalier attitude to disclosure. In addition, the husbands were certainly not saying to the court, 'make any order you like and I'll pay it'. Probably they were not able to make that offer—wealthy though they were, they did not possess the sums involved in *Thyssen*.

Perhaps there is scope for the defence to survive—but only as the *billionaire's* defence!

4.4.8.4   Foreign cultural factors

If the foreign or cultural background of the parties imports significant features relating to marriage or divorce, then the court can take these into account. The court can consider how the matter would be dealt with in the foreign jurisdiction and treat this as a relevant factor, giving it whatever weight seems appropriate to achieve a fair outcome (*Otobo v Otobo* [2003] 1 FLR 192). In *A v T (Ancillary relief: Cultural Factors)* [2004] 1 FLR 977, an Iranian couple had married under shariah law in Iran but the matrimonial home was in England. The marriage broke down after only seven weeks and the wife returned to Iran. The Iranian court ordered the husband to pay the marriage portion—a sum of £60,000—but took no further action. The wife applied for divorce in England. It was held that the husband should pay the wife a lump sum of £35,000 if he gave her a talaq divorce within a specified time, otherwise he must pay the full marriage portion of £60,000, as this was the sum she would have received from the Iranian court in the circumstances.

4.4.9   Deciding on the appropriate basis

After consideration of all the factors and circumstances, an appropriate overall basis must be settled upon for each case. There are no shortcuts; every case turns on its own facts. However, it is possible to make some general observations. They are not comprehensive, and they can overlap, or even conflict in a case, but as a very simple general guide:

(a) If there are young children, their needs will be central to the overall package. Depending on the assets available and the other parent's housing needs, this may require that the former matrimonial home be transferred to or settled on the parent with whom the children live.

(b) If there are no children, the primary objective will be to achieve a clean break, if this is possible with the assets available. A clean break cannot be achieved if the court is not satisfied on the evidence that an applicant spouse can become self-sufficient.

(c) If any factor clearly dominates the case, such as the shortness of the marriage or very bad conduct (rare), this may determine the overall basis for provision.

(d) Even where there are no children, one of the primary concerns of the court will be to ensure that the parties are adequately housed.

(e) As regards level of provision, the balance of needs against ability to provide will be the basic approach. Pensions should be considered as part of this balance.

(f) In any event, whatever broad starting point is appropriate, all the factors can go into the balance in deciding the overall package.

There will not always be a single appropriate basis for a case. There may be some middle ground, for example, between a clean break and continuing provision. If there are, the options should be fully discussed with the client.

4.4.10   The home and the overall package

Once the relevant factors have been assessed and a suitable overall basis for provision has been identified, the details of the overall package must be considered, balancing capital provision, income provision, provision for children, housing needs, pension needs, etc. *The interrelation of all the elements of a package must be considered.* For example, if a spouse gets a capital asset, such as a house, will he or she have sufficient income to pay for it and maintain it? Alternatively, if a spouse has to borrow money to pay a lump sum, the effect of the repayments on his or her own income and the income available to pay maintenance must be considered.

In many cases, where the couple own their own home, that will be central to the package, as it will be the main asset they own. In considering what should happen to the home, it is important to check whether the house is in a sole name or joint names, what its value is, what mortgage attaches to it, and who has made mortgage or other payments in respect of the house.

To outline the main possibilities for the home:

(a) The house may simply be sold, especially if there is to be a clean break. Consideration should be given to the share of the proceeds each spouse will get (noting that it is generally much better to do this in terms of proportionate shares, expressed as a percentage of whatever equity is eventually realised, rather than set figures, in case the expected value is not achieved). Sale may not be an easy option (if the market is poor) or a fair one if a spouse is old or ill, or may have trouble finding alternative accommodation. The costs of sale need to be taken into account—this usually includes solicitors' and estate agents' fees.

(b) The home may be left in or transferred outright into the name of one spouse only. Again this may form the basis for a clean break, and it should help to avoid continuing problems about paying for repairs, and possible future tax liability. However, if the home is the sole capital asset of the parties, it may simply be unfair for one spouse to get the full value, depriving the other spouse of all his or her capital. In such a case, some sort of settlement or charge may be fairer.

(c) The home may be transferred to the ownership of one spouse, subject to a charge in favour of the other, especially if it is needed as a home for the children. This may be an advantage for the custodial spouse, but ties up the interest of the other spouse. Again, it is usually better to express the value of the charge as a percentage of the net equity realised on eventual sale. It is very important to be very clear and unambiguous about when, and in what circumstances, the charge will be realisable (often referred to as 'triggers').

(d) The home may be settled under a trust for sale, although this happens less often these days, the charge back being more commonly used. There are potential difficulties and uncertainty with a settlement, the effect of which leaves both parties in ownership of the former matrimonial home and, therefore, in a continuing financial relationship and both of them dependent on its future sale. Great care must be given to deciding the terms of the settlement, especially what interest each is to have in the house, and when it will be sold. Again, proportionate shares are better than cash figures. Two widely known examples of such trusts follow:

    (i) *Mesher v Mesher* [1980] 1 All ER 126. Home settled to be sold when the children were 18 or left full-time education. The wife to pay the rates and the spouses to pay half the mortgage each (note that this particular feature is very unusual these days—the resident spouse will usually be expected to pay). Each spouse to have a half share in the proceeds of sale.

    (ii) *Martin v Martin* [1978] Fam 12. No children, husband had alternative accommodation. Home settled, not to be sold while the wife was unmarried and lived in it. Each spouse to get half of the proceeds on sale.

(e) If the home is not owned but is rented, then, unless both spouses are to move out, consider what names are on the lease, and whether there may be a possibility, if appropriate, of transferring the lease into another name.

4.4.11   Being realistic

Every aspect of the proposed overall package must be checked to ensure that it works. It must be realistic as regards resources available for payments, realistic as to needs and realistic in terms of what each spouse has left to live on. Check that it is adequate for the payee and affordable by the payer.

Just as you find out full details of the resources each has before the application is made, you should look at the precise position that both parties will be left in, if the suggested provision is ordered. You should do the arithmetic and make it clear to your client what he or she will have in income and capital terms, so that future plans can be made. You should do the same exercise for the other side because you will need to be able to persuade them that your proposals are a practical solution, or, failing settlement, persuade the court of this.

Look ahead as far as possible. It is important to bear in mind what changes in your client's position are reasonably foreseeable, and to make sure that the provision made does provide for the future as far as is reasonably possible. For example, if a house is settled, consider what position the spouses might be left in when it is sold, looking at what their ages and resources are likely to be at that point.

4.4.12 Taxation and benefits

The potential relevance of state benefits must be taken into account and explained to your client. It has been made clear by the courts that it is also part of the barrister's duty in every case to calculate tax implications and explain them to the client.

The principles for the taxation of maintenance are outlined in **Chapter 12**. The income tax effects for the payer and the recipient of maintenance should be calculated and explained to them.

The possibilities of a charge to capital gains tax should never be ignored on divorce, especially if the couple are relatively wealthy (for an example, see *M v M* [1988] 1 FLR 389). The possibility of future liability to capital gains tax where a house is settled is also important, as the spouse who is not living in the home will have no exemption from tax when the house is sold.

4.5 Maintenance pending suit

Marital breakdown can cause immediate financial strains. Maintenance pending suit is simply an interim application for short-term maintenance intended to 'tide' a party over, where necessary, until a final determination of the application(s) for financial provision can be made and put into effect. Such orders, which take the form of requiring one spouse to make periodical payments to the other, are therefore very much a temporary measure.

4.5.1 Law

Once a petition has been filed, maintenance pending suit may be ordered to be paid by one spouse to the other. Of necessity, it will not be possible to have full information available at this stage of the case, so the court will only seek to determine what figure is reasonable for immediate needs and what the respondent's short-term ability to pay is, rather than seeking to make complex calculations or to apply all the factors outlined above. However, it is still important to present the figures you do have and the arguments for what is reasonable as clearly as possible.

The MCA 1973, s 22 states as follows:

On a petition for divorce, nullity of marriage or judicial separation, the court may make an order for maintenance pending suit, that is to say, an order requiring either party to the marriage to make to the other such periodical payments for his or her maintenance and for such term, being a term beginning not earlier than the date of the presentation of the petition and ending with the date of the determination of the suit, as the court thinks reasonable.

4.5.2 Procedure

The procedure for obtaining maintenance pending suit (and other interim orders) is now the same as for any other financial order. An application can be made at any stage in the proceedings: FPR 2010, r 9.7. If the application is made before Form E (which provides details of financial resources and needs) has been filed, the written evidence in support must explain why the order is necessary and give up-to-date information about the party's financial circumstances: r 9.7(3). Applications for maintenance pending suit are commonly listed to be heard at the first appointment (see **5.3.8**).

4.5.3 Practice

When preparing for the hearing, you should bear in mind that at this stage the court will focus on what the applicant really needs to cover reasonable outgoings, together with what the respondent can reasonably afford to pay. To present information on this clearly and concisely, it is best to draw up a schedule which summarises the income of each party from all sources and the reasonable outgoings of each. If relevant, also include other liabilities and assets that may have a bearing on the appropriate order. Ensure that all figures are given on the same basis, ie, monthly or weekly, net or gross (see **5.3**).

If you act for the applicant, your first objective will be to show the shortfall between your client's income and reasonable outgoings; your second is to show how the respondent can reasonably afford to cover this gap. If you act for the respondent, your main aims will be to show that the applicant could earn more, and/or is extravagant, and/or that in any event your client cannot afford to pay the order sought. To convince the judge of your case and your credibility, it is very important to use accurate and full figures.

At the interim stage, the DJ will be concerned to meet immediate needs and not to try to prejudge in any detail what will be ordered when financial provision is finally decided. Therefore, awards tend to be on the low side. It is not possible to obtain interim lump sum orders under s 22—a lacuna which has been much criticised, especially in light of the increasing number of orders that contain an element to cater for legal costs, which would be much more sensibly dealt with by a lump sum.

It is permissible for the court to include in any award an element of legal costs; see *A v A* (*Maintenance Pending Suit: Provision for Legal Fees*) [2001] 1 FLR 377 and *G v G* (*Maintenance Pending Suit: Payment of Costs*) [2003] *Family Law* 393. As sources of funding for financial remedies applications diminish and parties become responsible for more costs, this method of factoring in litigation costs is gaining in importance (as are any other ideas for funding, including bank loans).

Uncertainty was caused by the (apparently inadvertent) introduction of an exceptional circumstance test by Thorpe LJ in *Moses–Taiga v Taiga* [2006] 1 FLR 1074. This was cleared up by the Court of Appeal in *Currey v Currey* [2007] 1 FLR 946, which is now the leading authority. The initial overarching enquiry is into whether the applicant for a costs allowance can demonstrate that she cannot reasonably procure legal advice and representation by any other means. For a case on the process, see *Re G* (*Maintenance Pending Suit*) [2007] 1 FLR 1674, and for an article outlining the problems caused by continuous cuts in legal aid and remuneration, see 'Maintenance Pending Suit and the Costs Allowance' [2007] *Family Law*, March. The position is not likely to improve, given the imminent implementation of further cuts in legal aid.

4.6 The Proceeds of Crime Act 2002 (POCA 2002)

The POCA 2002 came into force on 24 February 2003 and caused lawyers in all areas of practice to reconsider carefully how they go about advising and representing their clients. It seemed to impose a duty on all lawyers in their dealings with clients, to make a report to the National Criminal Intelligence Service (NCIS) (now the Serious Organised Crime Agency (SOCA)) any time they had a suspicion that criminal property might be involved. Criminal property is widely defined and includes any money on which tax might not have been paid, where it should have been. In financial remedies, where there is such emphasis on a thorough investigation of the finances of the parties, it is not uncommon to come across an element of a party's property that might not have been disclosed to HM Revenue & Customs. Often the amounts involved are very small, but POCA 2002 covers every sum, no matter how trivial. Having been compelled to make a disclosure to NCIS, the lawyer then also had to cease acting for the client until getting consent to do so from NCIS and, further, was not allowed to tell the client about the disclosure. It is a criminal offence under POCA 2002 to be involved in an arrangement concerning property and not disclose it to NCIS, with a maximum penalty of five years' imprisonment. Tipping the client off about the disclosure is a further criminal offence.

Happily, the Court of Appeal decision in *Bowman v Fels* (see below) reined back the ambit of POCA 2002. However, the Act in its amended form still exists and there are many activities which lawyers may perform in the course of their profession that may be caught by it. It is important to know the legislation, know the history of its implementation and know the guidance from the Bar Council and other bodies. The most recent guidance from the Bar Council in relation to both POCA 2002 and the Money Laundering Regulations 2007 (MLR 2007) (which came into force on 15 December 2007) was given in January 2008. Most of all it is important to understand that it is the barrister's individual responsibility to be familiar and up-to-date with all the developments and guidance relating to POCA 2002.

The relevant sections of POCA 2002 are summarised here. Essentially, s 328 creates the offence of 'being involved in an arrangement with criminal property' and the ordinary conduct of litigation can be caught under this definition (when, in conducting litigation, the lawyer comes to know about property that he suspects may be tainted).

For wider consideration of POCA 2002, see City Law School's *Professional Ethics Manual*, **Chapter 8**.

4.6.1   The legislation

Section 340 defines 'money laundering', 'criminal conduct' and 'criminal property'. The definitions are wide and include any property that may not have been declared for taxation purposes.

Sections 327–329 create offences of, respectively, dealing with criminal property, being involved in an arrangement concerning criminal property and possessing criminal property. It is a defence under ss 327–329 to make an authorised disclosure to the authorities, usually SOCA.

Section 330 creates an offence of failing to disclose where the person who should make the disclosure is in the regulated sector. Barristers are considered to be within the regulated sector (under MLR 2007).

Section 333, which created an offence of 'tipping off', has been amended (now s 33 A–D) and now only applies within the regulated sector. After a disclosure has been made to the authorities, it is an offence to make any disclosure (eg, to your client) that may prejudice any investigation. There is also an offence under s 342 of prejudicing an investigation *before* any disclosure has been made (eg, destroying relevant evidence). Various defences are available, including legal professional privilege.

Section 338 deals with the making of an authorised disclosure, which provides a defence to s 328.

4.6.2   Relevance to practice

This legislation had a strong effect on the practice of several areas of law, financial remedies being one of them. The whole financial remedies regime relies on an ethos of full and frank disclosure. With such disclosure putting clients at risk of prosecution, lawyers in a position where they have to disclose hitherto confidential information to the police, and proceedings at risk of having to be halted every time this happens to await consent to continue from SOCA, it is not hard to imagine how obstructive this could be to the administration of justice. In effect, in situations governed by POCA 2002, the concept of legal professional privilege had been done away with.

The matter was radically changed by the Court of Appeal in *Bowman v Fels* [2005] EWCA Civ 226, which effectively overruled *P v P (Ancillary Relief; Proceeds of Crime)* [2003] EWHC Fam 2260. The former was a relatively minor civil case concerning interests in a house, where disclosure had been made to NCIS over some work done on the property. The Bar Council, Law Society and NCIS intervened in order that the POCA issues could be fully argued in front of a senior constitution of the court. After dealing with the inconvenient fact that the parties in the substantive matter had settled their dispute at the door of court and the consequent problem of jurisdiction to continue the hearing, Brooke LJ went on to give an exhaustive examination of the issues. His conclusion was that the ordinary conduct of litigation by lawyers was not covered by POCA 2002, s 328. This includes any step taken by lawyers in litigation from the issue of proceedings and the securing of injunctive relief or a freezing order up to its final disposal by judgment. He stated that, 'Parliament cannot have intended that . . . steps taken by lawyers in order to determine or secure legal rights and remedies for their clients should involve them in "becoming concerned in an arrangement which . . . facilitates the acquisition, retention, use or control of criminal property", even if they suspected that the outcome of such proceedings might have such an effect.' He went on to say that s 328 was not intended to override legal professional privilege nor does it affect the terms on which lawyers are to have access to documents disclosed in the litigation process.

Nevertheless, it is important to stress that there are professional activities that may be covered by POCA 2002 and by the MLR 2007. The Regulations and POCA 2002, s 330 apply to activities in the 'regulated sector' and some situations remain where s 328 could still apply to lawyers.

Lawyers acting in the course of business who are deemed to be 'relevant persons' will be subject to additional requirements under the MLR 2007 and are also at risk of criminal liability. Members of the Chancery Bar are those who are most likely to fall within the ambit of the MLR 2007, if they are involved in non-contentious advisory work, particularly in relation to business, taxation or property transactions and the setting up of trusts and companies, see MLR 2007, regs 3(1) and 3(9). You are advised to refer to the Bar Council Guidance on the MLR 2007, issued in January 2008.

The additional requirements under the MLR 2007 include such matters as having procedures for the proper identification of clients, for record keeping, for internal reporting and for the training of staff (see regs 5–9 and 19–21).

The risk of criminal liability is under POCA 2002, s 330, which is an offence (by someone in the regulated sector) of failing to disclose. If such a person suspects, or has reasonable grounds to suspect, on the basis of information that comes to them in the conduct of business in the regulated sector, that another person is engaged in money laundering, then they must make a disclosure to SOCA. Failure to do so is an offence. However, it is a defence if the person is a professional legal advisor and the information came to him in privileged circumstances (s 330(6)(b)). Section 330(10) clarifies situations of legal professional privilege but s 330(11) provides that the defence of privilege will not apply where the information is communicated with the intention of furthering a criminal purpose. The standard is objective and not subjective. It is important, therefore, for any piece of work that you do, to consider whether you have an obligation to disclose under s 330 and, if so, whether the defence under s 330(6) applies.

Note that there are other criminal offences that can be committed under POCA 2002, notably the amended offences of tipping off (s 333A–D) (see **4.6.1**).

So, while most activities are not covered by s 328 and most activities covered by the MLR 2007 are protected by privilege, there are areas that are subject to the force of some or all of the legislation. In his decision Brooke LJ dealt with the situation when parties agreed to the issues between them by settlement rather than in the direct conduct of litigation. His view was that such consensual resolution in a litigious context must also be covered by privilege and exempt from s 328, as, 'The consensual resolution of issues is an integral part of the conduct of ordinary civil litigation.' What is less clear is whether consensual resolution before issue of proceedings is covered. It seems most likely that it is and that the phrase 'consensual resolution in a litigious context' would also cover such situations. To summarise:

- If the settlement is made in contemplation of legal proceedings, then it is normally covered by the ordinary definition of legal professional privilege and there is no obvious reason why POCA 2002 should displace it.

- If parties settle matters during exchanges that take place under the guidance or spirit of a pre-action protocol, then they are doing exactly what the CPR and FPR 2010 intend and encourage them to do—to borrow his Lordship's words: such resolution is also an integral part of the conduct of ordinary civil litigation.

It is then hard to conclude that these situations should be treated any differently in relation to POCA 2002. What his Lordship does make clear is that where litigation is known or suspected to be no more than a pretext for the acquisition, retention, use or control of criminal property, then there would be no protection and s 328 would apply.

It must be stressed again that it is essential that the individual takes responsibility for keeping abreast of the law and the guidance from professional bodies and Bar associations and for assessing whether any work carried out is affected by some or all of the legislation.

Guidance can be found on the Bar Council website at www.barcouncil.org.uk. At the time of writing look under the guidance link, at the alphabetical list, go to 'P' for POCA 2002 and 'M' for Money Laundering Regulations to find the two documents which are both headed 'Guidance for the Bar'.

Financial provision—financial remedies: preparation and process

5.1 Preliminary points

Financial provision following divorce used to be known as 'ancillary relief'. Such applications have for some time been subject to an overriding objective, strong case management by the court and a procedural pre-action protocol, borrowed from and very similar to those central tenets of mainstream civil procedure. The Family Procedure Rules 2010 (FPR 2010) have now extended these features to all aspects of family practice, and now include an overarching protocol relating to mediation information (see **1.7**). The new rules have also re-branded ancillary relief as 'financial remedies', although the former expression may still be used from time to time, not least in the case law. So be prepared for both descriptions.

5.1.1 The overriding objective (FPR 2010, Part 1)

This is a familiar concept to civil practitioners. In the family law context, it has been adapted so as to enable the court to deal with cases justly, 'having regard to any welfare issues involved'. As with the Civil Procedure Rules (CPR), this includes, so far as practicable, dealing with cases fairly, expeditiously, proportionately (both in terms of court time and resources) and in ways which are appropriate to their nature, importance and complexity. It includes ensuring the parties are on an equal footing, and saving expense. One important way in which the overriding objective is achieved is by requiring active case management by the court, to include early identification of the issues and encouraging settlement (see r 1.4). This, in fact, is something judges in financial remedies cases have been doing for the last decade (see also **1.7** and **4.1.2**).

5.1.2 Mediation Pre-application Protocol (FPR 2010, PD 3A)

An application for financial remedies is a 'relevant family proceeding' and so comes within the pre-application protocol for mediation information and assessment (see **11.17** and **11.18**). Therefore, before making an application, a person (save in named exceptional cases, including those involving bankruptcy, recent domestic violence, and where the parties are already in agreement) should contact a family mediator to arrange attendance at an information meeting about family mediation and/or other forms of dispute resolution, as alternatives to court action (para 2). When an application for a financial order is made, evidence of compliance with the protocol must be included with the application. This might be evidence of attendance at an information session or an explanation of why this has not happened (see Form FM1). It is worth noting that it is not compulsory to attend mediation; the point is that it has been given due consideration, although a party's approach to alternative dispute resolution (ADR) is relevant conduct from the point of view of later court orders, especially regarding costs (see **5.6**). This mediation protocol is a brand new procedural requirement, and it will take time to establish what emphasis the courts give to it.

5.1.3 Litigation pre-action protocol

The other relevant protocol for financial remedies cases is now found in FPR 2010, PD 9A and more or less replicates that which was already in existence under the old rules. It is essentially of concern to solicitors, but its purpose should be noted by all practitioners. Like its CPR equivalents, the objective of this protocol is to achieve a fair and consensual settlement without recourse to litigation where this is possible. Therefore, if the parties can and will make full and frank disclosure, sensibly instruct experts jointly and negotiate in a meaningful way without having to involve the court, then they should do so. The current wording emphasises keeping the tone of pre-action conduct conciliatory, the importance of proportionality and limiting costs, as well as the primacy of the overriding objective.

However, in practice not all (some would say not many) disputed financial remedies cases will be suited to attempts to resolve the matter pre-action and the protocol explicitly caters for this. Indeed para 4 of the guidance notes states that 'making an application to the court should not be regarded as a hostile step or a last resort, rather as a way of starting the court timetable'. So where, for example, disclosure is at issue or the parties are at odds (as they often are), it may be more appropriate, both in terms of saving time and costs, to proceed directly to the court managed process.

The Financial Dispute Resolution hearing (FDR) is the central feature of the ensuing process and is the point at which parties are expected to be prepared to make every possible effort to settle their own affairs without the need for a full contest.

Note that by virtue of the Civil Partnership Act 2004 (CPA 2004), same-sex couples who have registered their union will have the same sort of access to financial remedies upon the dissolution of their partnership as married couples do upon divorce. Thus references here to 'spouse' and 'divorce', etc should be read to encompass civil partnerships.

5.2 Getting started: information about your client's position

If you are instructed in a case, getting detailed information about the (lay) client's financial position is very important. This will involve careful investigation, clarity of thought, and realism as to what information may be available—and from what source. It is often not sufficient simply to ask the client general questions—many will not realise what is relevant. Legal advisors must be aware of all the details that may be required. The most successful financial provision application will be that which is based on the soundest preparation.

The first source of information for the barrister will usually be the brief, which is likely to include some form of statement of the client's means. The amount of detail available initially will vary considerably, depending on the stage at which the counsel is instructed and the amount of preparatory work which the solicitor has done. It is, however, unlikely that the statement provided in the brief will be complete, as the client may not have supplied full details to the solicitor, who may well leave it to counsel to suggest what further information is needed.

Whatever information is supplied in the initial brief must, in any event, be carefully analysed. What is there must be sorted out, and any gaps or implications that need to be clarified must be identified. Check that pre-action protocols have been complied with. A list of further information that will be required from the solicitor, from the client and from any other sources should be drawn up.

Depending on the complexity of the case, the next stage may be either a telephone call to the solicitor seeking further information, the arranging of a conference with the client or the writing of an opinion on the case. In any event the following general points will apply.

Get your standpoint clear: is your client seeking financial remedies or trying to resist such an application? What are the client's objectives, and which of these is most important? Do not automatically assume that your client will wish to get as much, or pay as little, as possible. Many divorcing parents are prepared to make reasonable provision, especially for children. Is one specific asset of particular importance to the client? Does your client want to stay in the matrimonial home or move? In considering objectives, be aware of the effects of emotion. One party may want an asset as a matter of status or spite rather than objective need. While legal advisors should seek to fulfil the client's objectives, it may sometimes be necessary to talk to him or her about what is reasonable.

This is just the beginning of a process of gathering and assimilating a large amount of financial and other factual detail. An important aspect of your job is to marshal this information as it comes to you, and not to be overwhelmed by it. You need to understand clearly the context in which it is required and received—and learn how to keep it readily accessible and up-to-date. Various techniques are used to achieve this, to which you will be introduced in the following paragraphs.

Start, first of all, by getting a clear view, with actual or possible values, of your client's finances. As a basic checklist, consider the following.

Income

Employment (including wages, commission, etc)	£
Value of fringe benefits	£
Any other work or business	£
State benefits	£
Pension income	£
Unearned income (eg, dividends, interest)	£
Income regularly provided from another source (eg, from a cohabitee)	£
From any other source	£
	Total £

Outgoings

Mortgage repayments or rent	£
Other costs of the home (eg, repairs, furnishings)	£
Services (eg, electricity, gas, water, telephone)	£
Council tax	£
Food	£
Travel costs	£
Clothes	£
Regular hire-purchase and credit sale payments	£
Costs and expenses of work or business	£
Holidays, entertainment	£
Other regular obligations (eg, supporting a third party)	£
Any other expenses (eg, insurance or other premiums)	£
	Total £

Ensure that all income and expenditure figures relate to the same period (for example, to the same calendar or financial year), and that all figures are annual, monthly or weekly. You need to be able to compare like with like.

Capital assets

Value of home (or share of home)	£
Savings	£
Shares	£
Other investments	£
Household goods, furniture, etc	£
Car	£
Other capital assets (eg, jewellery)	£
	Total £

Debts (liabilities not covered by expenditure)

Balance due on credit cards	£
Bank loans	£
	Total £

Make sure that a client gives current rather than historical values. In considering the matrimonial home, be clear who owns it and what mortgage may be attached to it, and perhaps whether a non-owner spouse may already have an equitable claim to a share in it. If either or both spouses have interests in a business, assessing its value may present particular problems, especially if it is a small business. Other issues, such as the transferability of the shares in an unquoted company, or the value of goodwill due to the involvement of the spouse may need to be considered.

To get a clear picture you need to look at the position as regards both income and capital, so that you can see clearly if the client can afford his or her current lifestyle, or has any money to spare. A quick look at the information required by Form E itself (see **5.3.2**) is the best guide to relevant financial information, although what is relevant will vary from case to case.

Do not just ask for figures, but advise getting written verification and evidence where possible. Not only may this be required as proof, but some clients do make mistakes or overlook points in the replies they give. Think about payslips, bank statements, mortgage statements, receipts, bills, accounts, credit card statements, etc. Be realistic about what records the client may or may not have, but anticipate the documents which will have to be disclosed (see, eg, last page of Form E). In some cases, copies may be available where originals have been lost. But be realistic about the amount of paperwork collected, bearing costs in mind. Focus on what is relevant.

Do not just get figures for each item, but also consider the practical aspects. Could an asset be sold easily or not? Are there any important points regarding the history of the asset? Could an asset be used as security for a loan or not? Does an asset have particular sentimental value to one spouse?

In taking this wide and realistic view, a knowledge of accounts, company law, partnership law, insolvency, revenue law, etc will be valuable where appropriate.

When pursuing a claim, once an application to the court has been made, the procedural timetable is essentially divided into three stages: (a) application to first appointment (FA); (b) FA to FDR hearing; (c) FDR to final hearing.

5.3 Stage one: application to FA

5.3.1 Making the application

This is the initial stage, which is dominated by the mutual exchange of relevant information and getting a 'handle' on the case. A petitioner should ask for the whole range of financial remedies in the divorce petition, to keep all options open. The application is then 'activated' by filing Form A, which should include mortgage details of any relevant property (PD 9A, para 1.3). Respondents to the petition should seek relief in their answer, if there is one. Otherwise, they should initiate an application using Form A.

When Form A is filed the court will list an FA to take place between 12 and 16 weeks from the date of filing. Notice of the FA (in Form C) is served by the court on the respondent, along with a copy of the application (applicants can effect service themselves, but it is usually more convenient to let the court do this). Whether any other person needs to be served with relevant documents will depend on the nature of the application (see r 9.13) or on any allegations made against them (eg, of improper behaviour). Once the date of the FA has been fixed, it can be changed only with the permission of the court (r 9.12(3)).

Consider the following case study, *Cutforth v Cutforth*.

Mr and Mrs Cutforth were married in 2002 when they were in their mid to late twenties. They have two children, now aged 6 and 8. Before the marriage, Mrs C, who has a degree in modern languages and speaks Russian and German, had a well-paid job as an interpreter, working largely at international business conferences. She met Mr C during this time. She gave up work when their children were born. She now works part-time in a local toyshop. The matrimonial home has four bedrooms and three reception rooms. Its value is somewhere between £425,000 and £500,000. The couple separated following an allegation and finding of domestic violence resulting in a court order that Mr C vacate the property. He lives in modest rented accommodation and pays all the outgoings on the former matrimonial home. Even so, Mrs C finds it difficult maintaining her standard of living. She does not wish to move and wants a new car. The elder child will go to boarding school soon. Mr C is employed as a computer engineer and set up his own company in 2005, the value of which is unclear. He can make ends meet, but feels Mrs C was unsupportive of him and his company venture. He is unhappy at the role of Justin Redmond, Mrs C's boyfriend. This affair of his wife's, he says, hastened the breakup of the marriage and caused the row leading to the occupation order. Before the new rules Mr Redmond might have been joined by Mr C as a 'Party Cited', but this is now discouraged, save where such person has a particular interest in the outcome: PD 7A.

5.3.2 Preparing for the FA

Before the FA, the following should happen (r 9.14):

(a) A simultaneous exchange of financial information. The vehicle for this is Form E, which each party must complete, file and serve not less than 35 days before the FA. This is a lengthy, standard-form document, which since 2000 has replaced the narrative affidavit of the past, which often shed more heat than light on a case. Its purpose is to eliminate emotion from the exercise, as well as the lottery involved in finding the lawyers with the best (or better) drafting skills. The overriding objective seeks to ensure that the parties are kept, so far as possible, on an equal footing—and standard forms are one way of achieving this. In any case, Form E contains several boxes inviting comment on standard of living, conduct, contributions (of both a financial and non-financial kind) and the like, so all is not lost for drafters. Form E has recently been updated to request information about pre or postnuptial agreements which a party seeks to rely on (see **4.4.8.2**) and additional pension information.

Form E must have attached to it certain documents required by the form itself and any other documents necessary 'to explain or clarify any of the information' contained on the form itself: r 9.14(2)(b). Specifically, this includes relevant pension information. Exchange between the parties is intended to occur 'simultaneously', which is sometimes easier said than done (a court order may be necessary if one party finds the other is not making adequate progress towards this). It is important to appreciate that once the application for financial remedies has been made, Form E is the principal vechicle for seeking or giving disclosure leading up to the FA: r 9.14(4). The idea is that the detailed information required by Form E is all that will be required by both the courts and the parties. Unusually in this day and age of written evidence verified by statements of truth, Form E is verified by affidavit: r 9.14(2)(a).

(b) No later than 14 days before the FA, each party must file and serve on the other(s) the following documents:

(i)   a concise statement of issues (see **5.3.4**);

(ii) a chronology (see **5.3.3**);

(iii) either a questionnaire, indicating what further disclosure is needed and why, or a statement confirming that no further information is required (see **5.3.6**);

(iv) a notice in Form G stating whether that party will be in a position to use some or all of the FA as an FDR hearing (see **5.4.4**).

(c) In addition, PD 9A, para 4.1 requires that the parties should, if possible and with a view to narrowing the issues between them, exchange and file with the court:

(i) a summary of what is agreed between them;

(ii) an agreed schedule of assets (see **5.3.7**);

(iii) details of any directions they seek, including, where appropriate, the name of any expert they wish to be appointed.

(d) No later than 14 days before the FA, the applicant must file and serve on the respondent confirmation that relevant notice provisions (as required by r 9.13) have been complied with (eg, notice to mortgagors): 9.14(6).

(e) A party with pension rights, within seven days of receiving notification of the date of the FA, must request relevant valuation information (of rights and benefits) from their pension provider (if the information is not already known) and supply that information to any other party and the court (eg, on Form E): r 9.30.

(f) Each side must come to the FA with an estimate of costs (on Form H) up to that point (as they must do at every appointment or hearing): r 9.27(1).

5.3.3 Chronologies

A chronology is an obvious and effective way of getting to grips with a case. It helps you to assimilate the detail and present the history in a meaningful and accessible way. As a matter of common sense, it is one of the first things you will do with a set of papers.

Judges like chronologies too because they help them to keep the background of a case at their fingertips—this is why parties are required to file one before the FA. Note that in this context there may be scope for inserting a bit of 'colour', for these purposes. The chronology is likely to be the judge's initial exposure to the parties, and it may be useful to introduce information to give the court a rounded view of the case.

For example, Mr Cutforth may want to try to 'neutralise' the effect of the occupation order made against him in the following way.

Cutforth v Cutforth—Chronology (Respondent husband)	
DATE	EVENT
14.11.71	Respondent born (40)
7.2.78	Petitioner born (34)
12.12.2000	Parties meet
3.6.01	Purchase of matrimonial home (MH) for £275,000 (4 bedrooms in Mankshott, Oxfordshire)
18.8.02	Parties marry
4.2.04	Damian born (8)
5.6.05	Respondent invests £10,000 in own software business, Jactrad Ltd
30.8.05	Gemma born (6)
Spring 2010	Petitioner starts affair with Justin Redmond
Winter 10/11	Petitioner promises to end affair

25.5.11	Respondent leaves MH after row about Petitioner's extramarital relationship and court order
4.6.11	Respondent moves into one-bedroom flat
12.7.11	Petitioner issues divorce petition
18.9.11	Decree nisi
18.12.11	Petitioner files Form A

Whether and to what extent you want to put such information into the chronology is a matter of judgment—and good sense. You would not want to antagonise the other side if he or she is negotiating constructively, or appear to be giving an inaccurate picture to the court. But sometimes it feels right to try to present a 'balanced' picture here, unless the information already appears elsewhere (eg, the petition or Form E).

5.3.4 Statement of issues

This is an important document. It should set out clearly and succinctly what the areas of dispute are. The aim is to help to identify and narrow the real (not petty) issues, which is the purpose of the FA. In the *Cutforth* case, for example, the dispute over the matrimonial home and the wife's earning capacity might be described as set out below.

ISSUE	WIFE'S CASE	HUSBAND'S CASE
Housing	The wife should remain in the family home. She needs four bedrooms and the children need continuity. She cannot buy other suitable accommodation near the children's school for less than the value of the family home.	The family home should be sold. A three-bedroom house, of the type illustrated in the particulars annexed to the husband's Form E, could be purchased by the wife with some of the proceeds; thus releasing about £50,000 for his housing needs.
The wife's earning capacity	The wife is only able to work part-time and locally until the children are much older. Her language skills are no longer of commercial use; she has been out of the market too long.	The wife has skills she can exploit in the labour market. She can work part-time as a translator from home.

Note that one tends, for the sake of clarity, to refer to the parties as 'husband' and 'wife' (or by name), rather than simply the 'petitioner' and 'respondent', except when drafting formal documents. It is not always the case that the wife is the petitioner, or that the petitioner and the person seeking financial remedies are the same!

5.3.5 Getting information about the other side

Your client's claim for financial provision, or resistance to such a claim, can only be fully considered in the overall context of the income and capital available to both sides. Ideally, you need to know as much about the assets of the other side as you do about your own client's. Realistically, it may not always be easy to get such information if the other side is being obstructive.

Initially, you will ask your own client what he or she knows about his or her ex-spouse's assets. Even if your client has little detailed knowledge, he or she may have a general idea what the other party earns and owns, or at least be able to suggest points to be pursued. This source of information may be inaccurate, may have an emotional rather than an objective basis, and may well include conjecture and hearsay. But it may at least suggest some starting points; and, eventually, a useful basis of comparison.

The next source of information is of course the financial statement provided by the other side. As already suggested, you should go through this with your client, checking it for inaccuracies and omissions. Where the information is vague or incomplete, appropriate steps should be taken, either by way of asking for Form E to be completed properly or seeking additional information by way of questionnaire (see **5.3.6**). Only ask for information you really need from the other side; questionnaires are not the place for scoring tactical points.

5.3.6 Questionnaires

As with the mainstream civil courts, one of the aims of the FPR has been to put an end to cases getting bogged down in endless, expensive and often overwhelming requests for disclosure. This has been achieved in two ways. First, several of the sorts of documents routinely requested for inspection by parties in the past are now required to accompany the Form E financial statements. These are set out in the Schedule of Documents at the end of the form and include:

(a) Any recent valuations of the matrimonial home.

(b) The last 12 months' bank or building society statements for all accounts listed.

(c) Surrender value quotations of all life insurance policies.

(d) The last two years' accounts of any business in which a party has an interest.

(e) The last three payslips, and most recent P60.

(f) The last two years' accounts for any self-employment, or any relevant partnership.

(g) A valuation of pension (or protection compensation) rights if these are available.

A curious omission continues to be credit card statements, so this will remain a typical request in the questionnaire, as will the disclosure of any of the above documents which were not annexed to Form E when it was served and filed.

Second, only documents listed in the checklist may be attached to a party's Form E and requests for further disclosure will not be granted if it would not further the overriding objective. Questionnaires should therefore be *well considered and thorough* and ask for what is needed, but every request *must be related to an issue in the case and, crucially, be proportionate*. This is especially important when seeking orders against third parties. The intention is that the district judge (DJ) deals with *all* disclosure issues based on requests made at the FA, so it is important to get the formal request right. Only with the court's permission will a party be able to require further disclosure after the FA (r 9.16(1)).

Like any other form of drafting, it is necessary to be precise to be effective. Keep the requests as tightly worded as possible. Don't ask: 'Does the Respondent have a credit card?' Be specific.

By way of example, some of Mrs Cutforth's requests might be drafted as set out below.

> ### *Cutforth v Cutforth*—Petitioner's Questionnaire and Request for Documents
>
> 1. The Respondent states in his Form E that Jactrad Ltd 'has few assets and negligible income' but he failed to annex the last two years' accounts as required. Please provide a copy of these accounts, plus any documentary evidence relating to the ownership of shares in and value of the company. Please provide any draft accounts in respect of the period since the last prepared accounts.
>
> 2. The Respondent refers in his Form E to monthly payments of £450 on the matrimonial home, which appears to exceed the amount due under the mortgage. Please explain, by reference to a recent mortgage statement, the basis for this figure.
>
> 3. The Respondent says he cannot afford the Petitioner's stated needs, but does not make clear on what he spends his income. Please provide a schedule of all credit, charge and store cards held by him during the last 12 months, whether in his sole name, joint names or upon which he has signing rights, together with copy statements for the said period.

In his questionnaire, Mr Cutforth might ask as set out below.

> ### *Cutforth v Cutforth*—Respondent's Questionnaire and Request for Documents
>
> 1. What is the Petitioner's case as to her earning capacity? In particular:
>   (a) Does the Applicant contend that, in order to exploit her language skills, she needs to take some form of refresher course or further education? If so, please give details of the course or courses, including cost and duration.
>
>   (b) Is it disputed that, as a translator working from home, the Petitioner could earn approximately £20,000 gross?
>
> 2. Does the Petitioner have any and, if so, what intention to marry or cohabit with Justin Redmond? Without prejudice to the generality of this question, please state with appropriate narrative the precise nature of the Petitioner's relationship with Justin Redmond, giving full details of any direct or indirect financial support the Petitioner has received from him since the beginning of their relationship or expects to receive in future.

Questionnaire requests will tend to focus on controversial matters. There should be an obvious link to the issues in dispute. **You must be clear about the purpose of each question and know what you want to achieve, and why, so you can justify the request to the court.** Nuisance questions, or those which are unnecessarily antagonistic, will be frowned upon, can be counter-productive and are unlikely to be permitted by the court at the FA.

The court does have powers to make more draconian orders regarding disclosure, where that is deemed necessary and proportionate. These include search orders and freezing orders, the setting aside of transactions intended to defeat or reduce a proper claim for financial provision (Matrimonial Causes Act 1973 (MCA 1973), s 37; see **4.2.5**) or even imprisonment (*Lightfoot v Lightfoot* [1989] 1 FLR 414). None of these, of course, will be granted lightly.

If a party fails to provide full, complete and honest information as required by the rules and/or when an order is made, various possibilities may follow:

(a) A party who fails to make proper disclosure may be ordered to pay the costs occasioned by that failure (*P v P* (*Financial Relief: Non-disclosure*) [1994] 2 FLR 381). This would be the typical sanction. See also **5.6**.

(b) A party who fails to produce court ordered documents may be punished for contempt, although imprisonment would be very much a last resort (see, eg, *Bluffield v Curtis* [1988] 1 FLR 170).

(c) There have been cases where parties who were very obstructive in providing information were penalised in the substantive order made because the conduct was so extreme that the court felt it was inequitable to ignore (see *M v M (Ancillary Relief: Conduct: Disclosure)* [2006] 2 FLR 1253 and **4.3.3.10**). Again, this will happen only very rarely.

5.3.7 Use of financial schedules

It is vital to put the financial information you receive into an accessible form. One look at the size and layout of Form E will tell you that however useful for neutrally conveying a large amount of information, it is not convenient for ease of assimilation or reference. This is where the financial schedules come in. They are a crucial part of both the preparation and presentation of a case. They encapsulate the relevant figures in a useful form, and help you, the client and the court focus on the implications of the orders sought. Schedules provide crucial information 'at a glance'. Ensure that they are up-to-date before use in court and that your opponent and the judge have copies.

There is no prescribed format for preparing a schedule—in practice, you will be able to see what other practitioners do and form a view as to what is most effective—but in general the schedule should try to do the following:

(a) Summarise the current situation as to income, outgoings and the capital position (assets and liabilities) of both parties insofar as it is relevant to the application under consideration (eg, if you are applying for maintenance pending suit, you do not need a full summary of the capital position, though it might be relevant to bring in capital that is available to meet immediate needs).

(b) Summarise the proposed position as to income, expenditure and capital that both parties will be in if the order sought is made (which needs to show how this will put your client into a satisfactory position if you are applying for the order, and how this will put your client into an untenable position if you are resisting an application for an unrealistic order). The idea is to demonstrate that the order sought will 'work' for *both* parties—or not, depending on whether you are seeking or resisting the order!

(c) Be adaptable—it is best to have a format that can be used flexibly, so that, for example, it is easy to work out what the effect would be if an order of £10 per week less than that sought were made, etc.

Styles vary, but the following sort of format might be used to support the case of Mrs Cutforth.

Schedule of Income and Assets

Wife: age 34
Husband: age 40

Damian: age 8 (resides with wife)
Gemma: age 6 (resides with wife)

Wife: Income and Outgoings

Current position
Monthly income

Employment	£	500.00	(net)
Payments from respondent (for children)	£	433.00	
Child benefit	£	146.03	
Building Society interest	£	1.30	

Total £ 1,080.33

Monthly outgoings

Listed on separate sheet (does not include housing costs)	£	1,040.00
Balance		
This shows a small surplus of	£	40.33

Proposed position
Monthly income

Employment	£	500.00	(net)
Child benefit	£	146.03	
Building society interest	£	1.30	
Increased payment by respondent	£	450.00	for wife
	£	433.00	for children

Total £ 1,530.33

Monthly outgoings

(As before, plus outgoings on matrimonial home as detailed by the respondent)	£	1,470.00
Balance		
This shows a small surplus of	£	60.33

Husband: Income and Outgoings
Current position

Monthly income	Total	£	2,000.00 (net)
Monthly outgoings	Total	£	1,520.00 (including expenditure on MH)

Surplus per month		£	480.00

Proposed position
Income

Monthly income	Total	£	2,000 (net)

Outgoings
    Estimated monthly expenditure
    (Wife to assume outgoings on MH;
    includes estimated housing costs and
    relevant outgoings on H's Form E)   £   1,350.00
    Proposed payments to petitioner   £   450.00
               (Total £ 1,800.00)

    Surplus per month   £   200.00

Whether one wants to include a 'proposed position' section (and on the same sheet) used to depend on the circumstances and the use being made of the Schedule, which in any event should go on to list *capital* assets and liabilities (joint as well as individual). The new PD 9A requires the parties, where possible, to prepare an 'agreed' schedule of 'assets'. Although this, logically, should also include agreed liabilities, it might also militate towards two separate documents for the two different purposes (existing versus proposed position). In either case, pension details would be apt to be listed under a separate heading.

5.3.8   The FA

Counsel is often instructed to attend the FA. Both parties must do so, unless they are excused by the court. The appointment should not be adjourned or vacated unless there is a good reason (non-service or late service of the other side's Form E could constitute a good reason for an adjournment).

By the time of the appointment, the court will have received, and the judge seen, the documents referred to above, ie, the Form Es, questionnaires and disclosure requests, statement of issues, confirmation of notification to relevant persons, etc. Where a party is seeking a pension-sharing or attachment order, that party should also have notified the fund administrators of this (r 9.31–33), so they can ask to be heard on the matter if necessary. The documents encouraged by PD 9A, para 4.1 to be filed and exchanged for use at the FA (which in addition to agreed financial schedules (see **5.3.7**) should include a summary of what is agreed between the parties and any directions sought, including the name of any experts they want appointed) should help focus attention onto the real issues in the case. The estimate of both sides' costs should concentrate minds on the (negative) implications of a protracted dispute.

An application may be made at the FA for interim maintenance, but if so, you should notify the court beforehand to request a longer hearing (and for interim orders generally, see r 9.7).

The district judge conducts the first appointment and determines the extent to which any questionnaire filed should be answered and what documents or further information should be produced, making such directions as are necessary (which, if appropriate, can include an order that a non-party, for example a cohabitee or business partner, attend and produce specified documents at what has become known as an 'inspection hearing'). The judge will also give directions, where necessary, as to the valuation of assets, obtaining and exchanging expert evidence and any other evidence to be adduced (or further documents to be provided) by each party. He or she may also want to know whether, and to what extent, mediation has been considered by the parties. If not already produced, this would also be the occasion for ordering chronologies and/or schedules to be filed by each party. Remember that it is helpful, when answering questionnaires, to reproduce the original request.

The court may be reluctant to order extensive expert evidence at this stage. In any event, such evidence should be provided by a single joint expert where possible. For guidance on instructing experts, see *Best Practice Guide for Instructing a Single Joint Expert* [2003] 1 FLR 573, issued by the President of the Family Division's Ancillary Relief Advisory Group, PD 25A of FPR 2010 and the useful summary in Bird and King's *Ancillary Relief and Financial Orders Handbook* at 16.26. See also *Martin-Dye v Martin-Dye* [2006] 2 FLR 901.

Rule 9.15(1) states that 'the first appointment must be conducted with the objective of defining the issues and saving costs', so protracted and indiscriminate disclosure is actively discouraged. A party is only 'entitled' to further disclosure if it has been ordered at the FA or with leave of the court (r 9.16(1)). Remember that the judge has extensive case management powers (FPR 2010, Part 4), but will be thinking in terms of the overriding objective, and in particular the need to identify the real issues and keep costs down. For these reasons, you will not necessarily obtain all that you request unless you have prepared cogent reasons for disclosure. Voluntary disclosure happens in practice and advanced disclosure is now part of the pre-action protocol.

Procedure varies slightly from court to court. Applicants usually open, giving reasons for the directions they seek, and the other side responds in kind. Remember that requests will need to be justified by reference to the overriding objective.

If it appears that agreement between the parties may be possible at this stage, the first appointment can be 'converted' into an FDR (see **5.4.4**), in which case any discussion about further disclosure or evidence would await the success or failure of the attempt to settle. In the overwhelming majority of cases, however, the judge will fix an FDR, although a further directions/inspection hearing might be ordered in exceptional circumstances (eg, where a party has failed to file a Form E). If an FDR, which is effectively court-monitored conciliation, seems a waste of time, a date for a final hearing can be fixed at this stage, with any further pertinent directions (including level of court), as can a date for the hearing of an application for an interim order (r 9.15(2)). As part of its case management remit, the court can also order that the case be adjourned for out-of-court mediation or private negotiation or, in exceptional cases, generally: r 3.3.

On rare occasions there may be a good reason for departing from normal procedure to let the court adjudicate on a single issue which will effectively determine the outcome of the case. This might happen, for example, where there has been a prenuptial agreement dictating the parties' financial position post-divorce: *Crossley v Crossley* [2008] 1 FLR 1467.

The FA is heard in private. The new rules on media access to the family courts specifically exempt hearings, like the FDR (see **5.4.4**), which amount to judicially assisted negotiation; but not it seems the FA, unless it is treated as an FDR (or a party's Art 8 rights of privacy prevail). This distinction could well affect one or other party's approach to the FA, for better or worse.

5.4 Stage two: FA to FDR

5.4.1 Analysis of evidence

Whenever, and however, disclosure of financial evidence is made, it is imperative to analyse the information carefully and cross-check it with assertions made by the disclosing party.

When you look at payslips, for example, check that they support the figures presented in Form E. Compare them with the P60.

When going through bank statements, it is important to look out for regular payments which suggest a source of income which has not been divulged. Alternatively, a statement might reveal a bank account, pension, savings account or life assurance policy which has not been disclosed. Check transfers to and from other bank accounts and regular direct debits or standing orders. You will need to look at such statements over time, but by way of example, see the sample below.

UK BANK	**Statement of Account** **Sheet No. 6 44**	**IM 8X 11**
Account Number: 0432366	**Sortcode: 30–20–10**	**Branch Identifier Code:** **GB5UK78995**
MRS S CUTFORTH	**Telephone: 01473 111 222** **Facsimile: 01473 111 333** **Date issued: 1 September 2011**	
Type of Account: Premier		When overdrawn marked OD

Date	Payment type/Particulars		Payments out		Receipts		Balance	
2011	Opening Balance						1,553	51
1 AUG	ATM CASH STMARYSSTREET							
	DATEOFWITHDRAWAL	01 AUG	100	00			1,453	51
7 AUG	CHQ	000073	152	37			1,301	14
	CHQ	000075	500	00[1]			801	14
	ATM CASH STMARYSSTREET							
	DATEOFWITHDRAWAL	05 AUG	100	00			701	14
	ATM CASH STMARYSSTREET							
	DATEOFWITHDRAWAL	06 AUG	20	00			681	14
8 AUG	ATM CASH SOLIHULL							
	DATEOFWITHDRAWAL	08 AUG	60	00			621	14
11 AUG	CR 92600476 CHB				146	03	767	17
	CHQ	000076	400	00			367	17
14 AUG	CHQ	000077	10	94			356	23
15 AUG	ATM CASH MARKSTREET							
	DATEOFWITHDRAWAL	15 AUG	20	00			336	23
	SCOTTISH WIDOWS D/D[2]		44	10			292	13
21 AUG	CR TRANSFER[3]				200	00	492	13
22 AUG	CHQ	000074	15	35			476	78
25 AUG	CHQ	000078	120	50			356	28
	VIS TRAVELFACILITIES[4]		300	00			56	28
	ATM POUNDSTREET							
	DATEOFWITHDRAWAL	23 AUG	60	00			3	72 OD
26 AUG	CAREBEARTOYS CREDIT				500	00	496	28
	S/O VISDEB BP PETROL		25	43			470	85
28 AUG	CHQ	000079	17	63			453	22
	VISDEB SW GAS & ELEC		210	00			243	22
	D/D HOME PHONE/MEDIA		56	27			186	95
29 AUG	CR NETINTEREST					18	187	13
29 AUG	CR CHQ	10048			433	00[5]	620	13

The items and balance shown should be verified. Any interest rates shown are the rates in force only on the date shown. Details of all other rates and calculations of any interest charged are available on request to your branch.

Notes:

1   Investigate large and/or regular withdrawals. Do they correspond to claimed expenditure?

2   Check direct debits/standing orders. Do they tally with Form E? Identify their purpose.

3   Transfers indicate another source of funds.

4   Look for the purpose of significant payments out.

5   Investigate large and/or regular deposits. Cross-refer to Form E.

Reading and cross-checking the bank statements and credit card statements can give clues as to the standard of living of that party—eg, look out for frequent holidays and restaurant bills when a party is pleading poverty.

When you look at business accounts, look at the balance sheet carefully. Watch out for benefits a party receives through the business, eg, entertainment, motor expenses and director's loan accounts and drawings. Also, look at the tax returns and see if they are consistent with the accounts (and do not confuse personal and business tax liability).

5.4.2 Conferences

At an appropriate point, there should be a conference with the client. A conference may take place at a very early stage, perhaps even before the divorce proceedings are commenced if, for example, there is a need to discuss what the client hopes to achieve, or the facts of the case are complex, or there are substantial assets involved. In any case, conferences may be needed at the various procedural staging posts, eg, before Form E is filed (if counsel is asked to draft this); before the FA; before any FDR appointments; and, if no agreement is reached, before the final hearing. Earlier conferences will focus on aspirations and evidence; later ones on priorities, reality, tactics and possibilities of settlement.

It goes without saying, therefore, that good conference skills are important in this context. Getting full information from the client will take great care, and perhaps some diplomacy! You will also need to give clear and practical advice. Special skill will be needed to deal with the emotional reactions of clients, and the effect that such feelings may have on their perspectives. Reality can be a bitter pill to swallow.

5.4.3 Writing opinions

General points

Counsel may be asked to provide an opinion at any stage, but the main possibilities are (a) that an opinion may be sought at an early stage when there is little detail of the financial position but the solicitor and client want general advice, and/or (b) that an opinion or a further opinion may be sought at a later stage when more detailed figures are available. Counsel may be asked to deal with overall entitlement or with particular issues.

The following general checklist for the contents of an opinion dealing with financial provision will of course need to be fully adapted for each individual case. The opinion should:

(a) Show clear appreciation of the standpoint and objectives of the client, and of any particular concerns that the client has.

(b) Identify clearly the factors in the case which favour the client.

(c) Identify clearly the factors in the case which weaken the client's case or favour the other side.

(d) Advise clearly on the likely basis or alternative possible bases for provision.

(e) Deal clearly and comprehensively with the resources and assets that are available.

(f) Use the available facts and figures to practical effect. Be specific.

(g) Advise clearly on further information or figures that should be sought.

(h) Ensure that a summary of clear, practical advice is provided.

(i) Recognise the need to limit costs as far as possible.

In essence, it is vital to be clear, practical and thorough. Do not generalise about statutory provisions and the options available, or deal superficially with figures.

Example opinion

CUTFORTH v CUTFORTH
OPINION

1. I am asked to advise the Petitioner, Sandra Cutforth, with regard to her application for financial remedies on divorce. She has made the usual global application in the Petition. In particular she seeks ownership of the former matrimonial home, a lump sum payment sufficient to enable her to purchase a car and pay off her current credit card bill as well as sufficient income to maintain, for herself and her children, the standard of living enjoyed during the marriage. She has also applied for interim maintenance. The Respondent, Mr Cutforth, is seeking sale of the matrimonial home and a clean break.

Background

2. The parties married in 2002, a year after moving into the matrimonial home together. Mrs Cutforth is now 34 years old; Mr Cutforth is 40. They have two children: Damian (age 8) and Gemma (age 6). The parties separated in May 2011, Mr Cutforth having been ordered to vacate the matrimonial home. The children remain there with their mother. Decree nisi has been granted.

3. After some rather acrimonious pre-action discussion, Form A was issued by Mrs Cutforth on 18 December 2011. Both parties have filed Form E statements. The first appointment (FA) is listed for 22 March 2012, where the further information required from Mr Cutforth mentioned below should, if not forthcoming before that time, be sought.

Summary advice

4. In summary, my opinion is that Mr Cutforth cannot be expected to finance fully Mrs Cutforth's remaining in the matrimonial home. Although the court will not, in my view, impose a clean break in this case, Mrs Cutforth may have to choose between, on the one hand, more financial independence in exchange for the larger share of the matrimonial home and, on the other, sharing the latter more equally in exchange for a higher level of maintenance.

5. This is, of necessity, a provisional view because there is still important information which needs to be gathered, especially as regards the value of Mr Cutforth's business. Until I have the information set out below, I cannot advise more conclusively.

Needs of children

6. In exercising their powers, the court will treat the welfare of the children as the first consideration. There seems to be no dispute about the children living with their mother or having reasonable contact with their father. Mr Cutforth currently pays £100 per week to his wife—she says it is for the two children, but he describes it as 'maintenance for petitioner'. These, of course, are two entirely different things. Assuming the money is intended as child support (and assuming his income figures are accurate), it seems acceptable (possibly generous) by the standards of the

current child support regime. If Mr Cutforth continues to pay for the children at this rate, I certainly would not advise an application to the Child Support Agency (CSA) at this point, but his payments will obviously be taken into account when considering spousal maintenance.

7. There is also no mention of who will be responsible for any school fees (it seems one of the children will soon attend boarding school). This can be catered for in a court order, but it is not clear what the parties intend. If Mr Cutforth is to pay for this, it would add a significant amount to his outgoings.

8. The children are likely to remain with Mrs Cutforth for the foreseeable future and they will need a suitable home for the period of their continued dependency. Mrs Cutforth would like to remain in the former matrimonial home, which is a four-bedroom semi-detached property. The advantages for the children of her doing so are clear, ie, continuity and a sense of security. However, there is some question as to whether the property may be bigger than they need (as Mr Cutforth claims) and whether suitable alternative housing in the same neighbourhood is affordable (Mrs Cutforth says it is not). I suggest that Mrs Cutforth collect particulars of (and see) some three- and four-bedroom properties in the area to help to determine this point.

9. The parties also take very different views of the value of the former matrimonial home: Mrs Cutforth estimates it to be about £425,000, whereas Mr Cutforth puts it at £500,000. Clearly, this discrepancy needs to be resolved, so it is vital to get an agreed, up-to-date assessment. As a matter of priority, could those instructing please invite the respondent's solicitors to agree a valuer to carry out a valuation as soon as possible? It may be worth getting a view on how the house's value has fared and will fare if sold in the current economic climate.

10. Mr Cutforth discloses an outstanding mortgage on the matrimonial home of £50,000. He also says in his Form E that he pays £450 per month 'on the property'—a figure apparently exceeding the probable mortgage (even repayments at, say, 7 per cent would be closer to £370). Mrs Cutforth says Mr Cutforth also pays all the outgoings on the property, so the likelihood is that his figure of £450 per month includes other expenditure, but this needs clarifying. The figure seems rather high for the mortgage alone, especially in view of reduced interest rates. What sort of mortgage do the parties have? Some variable rate mortgages have become very inexpensive, but of course they have a limited lifespan. Accurate information as to the costs of Mrs Cutforth remaining in the house is critical to any application for a transfer of the property into her name. This includes the cost of any mortgage she would have to pay (current lenders are not so apt to pass on the benefits of the low interest rates to new mortgagees). It is unlikely in my view that the court would make an outright transfer to her if she were unable to afford to live there without significant maintenance from Mr Cutforth.

Mrs Cutforth's needs, resources, etc

11. At present, Mrs Cutforth apparently has a monthly income (including Mr Cutforth's current payments to her) of £1,080 to meet current monthly expenses of about £1,040. Although Mr Cutforth pays all of the outgoings on the house, Mrs Cutforth says she still struggles to maintain the standard of living the family enjoyed during the marriage, and has found herself falling into debt. In effect she would like the money Mr Cutforth now pays towards the matrimonial home, paid to her by way of maintenance, to ensure she can stay in the house. She also says she needs a car and looks to Mr Cutforth to provide this.

Contentious Issues in Dispute: Earning Capacity and role of Mr Redmond

12. However, there remain two particularly contentious issues. One is the question of Mrs Cutforth's earning capacity, cited by Mr Cutforth under Part 4 of his Form E. At present, she is working part-time in a small local toy shop but, as she herself says, the pay is inadequate to meet her needs. Mrs Cutforth has a good degree in languages and prior to her marriage had a well-paid job with good career prospects. Not surprisingly, Mr Cutforth is therefore claiming that she is

not exploiting her full earning potential, and this is likely to be an important issue in the case. Could instructing solicitors get from Mrs Cutforth further information on this point. What are her qualifications? What jobs might be open to her as an interpreter? Has she made enquiries about this herself? If so, what did she find out? Could she work as a translator or teacher from home? How much do such jobs pay? Could she take a course to update her skills or increase her job prospects? The other side is bound to ask about these matters in their questionnaire at the FA.

13. The court, however, will only expect Mrs Cutforth to act reasonably. It may, for example, be the case that, while the children are young, she has to work locally and could not take on more lucrative work as an interpreter because this would involve long hours and/or a substantial amount of travel. Clearly, if Mrs Cutforth can only earn what she earns now, this will support her claim for maintenance for herself. But it could detract from her claim for a transfer of property order. On the other hand, if she could earn more, it might be more realistic to argue that she should get the house outright as she will then be in a better position to meet the outgoings on it. What are Mrs Cutforth's views on this? At the moment, it would seem that to cover the existing mortgage as well as the other outgoings on the house would cost at least £450 per month, the figure given by Mr Cutforth.

14. There is also the added complication of Mr Redmond. Mr Cutforth claims that Mrs Cutforth's relationship with Mr Redmond should be taken into account in determining her claim for maintenance. It seems that while Mrs Cutforth has formed a relationship with Mr Redmond (which has endured for some time), it does not have the hallmarks of permanent cohabitation. Mrs Cutforth says that he stays the night from time to time and pays for occasional meals and family entertainment, but makes no direct contribution to the running of the household. She is non-committal about the future of the relationship. On this basis, it would not seem particularly relevant to the outcome of Mrs Cutforth's application. If, on the other hand, the overnight stays were to become a regular event, this would be some evidence of cohabitation, the implications of which on the appropriate level of spousal maintenance would be a circumstance the court should take into account in making any order. Mrs Cutforth should confirm the facts and intentions surrounding her relationship with Mr Redmond—this could be raised in a questionnaire. It should reassure Mr Cutforth to know that any agreement between him and Mrs Cutforth could be upset were the situation to have been shown to be otherwise than stated. Instructing solicitors will no doubt bear in mind and advise Mrs Cutforth of the effects of remarriage or cohabitation should this be relevant.

Mr Cutforth's needs, resources, etc

15. Mr Cutforth says he has a monthly income of about £2,000 (net) to meet current expenses of about £1,520. Were he to pay for Damian's schooling, this would obviously increase his outgoings considerably. Buying a property for himself to live in would also increase his expenditure, although for these purposes he seems to have some room for manoeuvre.

16. It would seem that, in addition to other fringe benefits from his employment, Mr Cutforth has earned various bonuses over the years. It seems likely that these might continue and details should be sought. As to the loan opportunities available to Mr Cutforth referred to by Mrs Cutforth, there is some doubt as to whether Mr Cutforth could qualify because he may leave this employment in the next couple of years.

17. I have very little detail on Mr Cutforth's housing needs. At present, he lives in modest rented accommodation, but the court will want if possible to leave him with sufficient resources to buy suitable accommodation. This would require him to have enough capital for a deposit and sufficient income for mortgage repayments. He will need a property suitable for having the children for overnight stays (ie, at least two bedrooms). Costs of such properties need to be

investigated. If he could borrow money on favourable terms from his employer, then this would be relevant to his purchasing ability, as would his being relieved of mortgage payments on the former matrimonial home. Details of the loan scheme should be requested at the FA.

Capital assets

18. As to capital resources, although the former matrimonial home is registered in Mr Cutforth's sole name, Mrs Cutforth undoubtedly has an equitable interest in it. She apparently put £10,000 towards adding a conservatory (although Mr Cutforth describes this contribution somewhat less generously), but in any event may be taken to be up to 50 per cent entitled if, as seems likely, her contributions to the family over the years assisted Mr Cutforth in making the mortgage repayments. It was apparently agreed, after all, that she gave up a promising career to look after the children. Until I have the information on the value of the property, however, it is impossible to put an accurate value on the parties' existing share in what appears to be the major matrimonial asset.

19. In addition, Mrs Cutforth has £10,000 in savings and £15,000 worth of furniture which she inherited from her parents. As to the value of Jactrad Ltd, there is a dispute between the parties. According to Mr Cutforth, this is a company of few assets but this needs to be clarified. Mr Cutforth's Form E indicates that the accounts of the business will follow. If they do not, they should be sought at the FA. If the company turns out to be of value, then clearly this will improve Mrs Cutforth's prospects as regards her claims. There is, perhaps, a curious lack of disclosure by Mr Cutforth of any other capital assets—does this accord with Mrs Cutforth's memory?

Other factors

20. Although the marriage was not especially long, the court will undoubtedly recognise that Mrs Cutforth has made, and will continue to make, substantial contributions to the family in assuming the primary care of the children. There is also a clear disparity in income and earning capacity between the parties—Mrs Cutforth has been economically handicapped by her withdrawal from the labour market over 10 years ago to have and care for her children. Mr Cutforth suggests that his wife was less than energetic in helping to build up Jactrad Ltd, which he says was intended as a family enterprise. These allegations are far too vague to amount to conduct that would be relevant to Mrs Cutforth's application for financial provision, but it would be useful to have her reaction to them. The standard of living enjoyed during the marriage seems to have been a comfortable one—divorce usually requires both sides to make adjustments in this regard and the court will be alert to the need to ensure the financial burdens are shared as equally as possible. Given the parties' ages and the length of marriage, I doubt that the court would ascribe much value to loss of pension rights in this case, but a degree of offsetting may well take place.

Conclusion

21. It is early days yet and the outcome of this case depends very much on what we find out about the value of the family's capital assets, Mrs Cutforth's true earning potential and the costs of alternative housing. Up-to-date tax advice might also be useful. What I can say at this point is that the court would be very slow to deprive Mr Cutforth of all of his interest in the matrimonial home, unless he is able to raise or has access to other capital for housing purposes. Nor would it, on the other hand, grant a clean break where an applicant's ability to be self-sufficient has been, and continues to be, handicapped by the responsibilities of parenthood. The issue is whether Mrs Cutforth can adjust without undue hardship to the end of financial dependence, not whether she ought to do so: *C v C (Financial Relief: Short Marriage)* [1997] 2 FLR 26, CA. It may seem unlikely that she would not use her specialist skills if she could.

22. Even were Mrs Cutforth to double her income from employment, there would still be a sizeable disparity between the parties' incomes, so it seems likely that a maintenance order would be

made, possibly for a term if the court finds that Mrs Cutforth merely needs time to adjust to the change. She is still quite young and apparently well qualified. In return, Mr Cutforth would keep an interest in the home, either as proceeds of sale or a chargeback. The actual division would depend on the further information sought. In effect, there is likely to be something of a trade-off between provision of income and transfer of property.

23. Even were the court to decide that Mrs Cutforth could become financially independent, I take the view that they would in that case transfer the matrimonial home to her with a nominal maintenance order which could be varied in certain events, eg, Mr Cutforth's business trading at a certain level. This would give her something of a safety net, but feel like (and have some of the psychological benefits of) a clean break for Mr Cutforth. If owning the home outright is a greater priority than remaining in it for the time being, this is perhaps an outcome worth investigating.

24. Whether and to what extent the lump sum payment will form part of the package will again depend on the figures. On the face of it, Mrs Cutforth's need to have a car and pay her credit card bill is reasonable, as both partly relate to the care of the children. Indeed, if having a car would facilitate her realising her earning potential, this would give a boost to her claim. However, unless there is a source of capital from which Mr Cutforth could make such a payment, the court may decide that Mrs Cutforth should look to her own capital to meet some, if not all, of these needs.

Next steps

25. Once the information I have identified is to hand, a clearer picture of the realistic possibilities will emerge. To recap, this includes:
    (i)   an agreed valuation of the matrimonial home (para 9);
    (ii) prices of three and four-bedroom properties in the area (para 8);
    (iii) more precise information on the nature and value of Jactrad Ltd, including the loan scheme and Mr Cutforth's rehousing costs (paras 17–19);
    (iv) more precise information on Mr Cutforth's resources and expenditure (para 17ff);
    (v)   who will pay Damian's boarding-school fees? (para 7);
    (vi) details of Mrs Cutforth's qualifications and employment prospects (para 12);
    (vii) Mrs Cutforth's priorities in term of outcome (paras 22–23).

    In the meantime, if Mrs Cutforth is falling into debt, a claim for interim maintenance can be dealt with at the FA. Those instructing should inform the court of the need for some extra time for this purpose. Interim maintenance is intended to tide an applicant over temporarily to assist with immediate needs, but without prejudging the outcome of the case as a whole. Given how much Mr Cutforth now contributes to the upkeep of the matrimonial home, in my view the court would expect that Mrs Cutforth also tighten her belt somewhat, and would only ask Mr Cutforth to pay more if he really can afford to do so. If she is to pursue such an application, Mrs Cutforth will need to show the court what steps she has taken to economise.

26. As soon as it is feasible, attempts should again be made to narrow the issues and agree an outcome with the other side. Neither party is publicly funded and, as always, it is important that costs should not be built up unnecessarily. To the extent that agreement has not been reached, the FA should help serve this purpose. The usual documents should be filed and served on the other side before the hearing (including costs estimate) as, ideally, should agreed financial schedules and details of any directions to be requested (including names of relevant experts).

301 Gray's Inn Place Chambers   *Sue D. Nym*
10 February 2012

5.4.4   The FDR hearing

The FDR is the focal point of any case; its aim is to achieve settlement through 'discussion and negotiation' (r 9.17(1)). The idea is that the parties be given the chance to put their fundamental positions, not only to each other, but also to the district judge, who will make such observations and comments as may be thought to 'facilitate settlement' of the case: PD 9A, para 6.1. To this end, not later than seven days beforehand, applicants must file at court details of all offers, and proposals received, with responses (r 9.17(3)), as well as up-to-date costs estimates.

It is important to arrive early and, again, unless the court orders otherwise, both parties must attend. Legal representatives are expected to have a full working knowledge of the case so that the opportunity for settlement is not wasted—it is not uncommon for negotiations to take place, on and off, all day long.

Hearings are privileged and heard in private. FDRs are specifically exempted from the new rules on media access to private hearings, since they are 'conducted for the purpose of judicially assisted conciliation or negotiation'. And although all offers and responses are required to be filed with the court beforehand, this does not make them admissible in evidence if they would not otherwise be so (r 9.17(2)). It is important that the parties approach the occasion 'openly and without reserve': PD 9A, para 6.2.

At the appointment, you should use your 'best endeavours' to reach an agreement, as indeed should all concerned. Be prepared to open the case to the judge. It goes without saying that it is essential to have a good working knowledge of all the facts and figures. You must be able to make brief submissions in support of the orders you seek. Counsel usually each prepare a 'Note', similar to a skeleton argument, which is handed in to the court on arrival. The FDR allows each side to put their positions to the district judge, who will guide the case towards a settlement, if that is possible. In particular, the judge should point out to either party any argument or expectation which he or she considers unrealistic. If you reach an agreement, you should be ready to draw up a consent order for the judge to make at the hearing or submit after the hearing for his or her consideration (see **5.9**). If you are close to agreement, but need more time, the judge can give you more time, fix another date for a further FDR, or the FDR can be adjourned for out-of-court mediation. If there is no agreement, the proceedings are usually listed for a final hearing. You should then collect all documents containing offers, proposals and responses. The appointment is without prejudice and none of these documents should stay on the court file.

In *W v W (Ancillary Relief: Practice)* [2000] Fam Law 473, it was suggested that if, at the FDR, it is clear that the case is 'going to fight', the FDR judge may order 'narrative affidavits' to be filed if this would help 'illuminate' the conduct and contributions of each party. This sounds like a retrograde step, but it generally only happens in 'big-money' cases, where allegations of lack of disclosure and good faith abound. The whole idea behind the rules is that by the time one gets to the FDR, all the relevant information is already to hand and attempts to widen the debate at that point are contrary to the overriding objective. But there are always exceptions.

One answer to the problem of disputes over disclosure of complex and sizeable family fortunes is to deal with that matter early on as a preliminary issue. In *OS v DS (Oral Disclosure: Preliminary Hearing)* [2005] 1 FLR 675, Coleridge J did just that. He ordered a three-day preliminary disclosure hearing at the end of which he made findings of fact, which saved time and costs further down the line. This was a somewhat novel approach at the time, and would only rarely be necessary, but both the overriding objective and the widening of the court's case management powers under the FPR 2010 support practical solutions of this kind. It is a route regularly taken in commercial cases.

In *Rose v Rose* [2002] 1 FLR 978, the Court of Appeal considered a number of aspects of the FDR. It was said that the judge might offer an early, but *considered* neutral view of the case, along with an objective risk assessment should the case go to a contested final hearing. This could well concentrate the minds of the parties on what is, and what is not, important, and so conduce to settlement. Having said that, there will still be cases where the issues cannot be properly determined without a full hearing.

It is important to note that the judge who hears the FDR is not permitted to have any further dealings with the case, except to make trial directions, hold further FDR appointments or grant consent orders: r 9.17(2). It is unclear whether a judge who granted a consent order can hear the application to vary it: *Myerson v Myerson* [2008] EWCA Civ 1376.

The FDR appointment is a crucial feature of the process and it is important to explain to your client just what it is all about and what may or may not happen. You too need to be clear about the dos and don'ts as you and your clients approach the FDR, including being very clear about what your 'bottom line' is so that you do not lose sight of it in the heat of negotiation. It is also imperative to reduce any agreement into writing, ideally as a proper consent order or at the very least set out in sufficient detail to qualify as an 'unperfected order' (which can later be perfected by the court): see *Rose v Rose* (above), where the husband sought to resile from an agreement which had not been properly drawn up at the end of the FDR due to lack of time. The Court of Appeal treated it as an 'unperfected order' and the husband was held to it.

5.4.5 Negotiations and offers to settle

The importance of trying to negotiate agreed terms for financial provision cannot be overstated. One way or another, the costs of any case will come out of the family coffers. Leaving aside the impetus and requirements of the FPR 2010, which encourage mediation from the outset, an agreed settlement offers many advantages for the parties:

(a) Terms can be fine-tuned to meet the needs of a particular case.

(b) An agreement can include terms which a judge might not have power to order.

(c) An agreement gives the client more control over the outcome than going to court (subject to the wide powers of the court).

(d) Spouses are more likely to abide by an order they have agreed to.

(e) An agreed solution can save costs.

Unless the parties are very well informed, a first move to try to negotiate an agreement is most likely to be formally made when sufficiently detailed information is available (eg, after Form Es have been filed), although you should be prepared to consider a settlement at any stage. To negotiate sensibly, it is crucial to have a thorough knowledge of the facts and figures of the case since once the settlement is agreed, an appeal or an application for further provision may be impossible. In preparing for a negotiation, you must have a *clear view* of what the client wants, and the parameters of the *most* and the *least* that the client might reasonably get and/or be prepared to accept.

Until recently, the so-called '*Calderbank* offer' was very much part of the financial remedies negotiation landscape. This worked like Part 36 offers in mainstream civil cases, and conduced to settlement by means of putting pressure on the other side so far as costs were concerned. However, it became increasingly apparent that there was potential, if not actual conflict between the open offer(s) which the court knows about and the

Calderbank offer, which it does not (until the question of costs is determined). This posed problems, the solution to which has been found in the decision to depart, in financial remedies cases, from the notion that 'costs follow the event'. This has effectively killed off the *Calderbank* letter (see further **5.6**).

Because the negotiated settlement will usually end all the client's claims, it cannot be stressed too strongly that the terms must be clear and comprehensive—and clearly explained to and sanctioned by the client.

5.5 Stage three: FDR to final hearing

For cases which do not settle, the matter will have to go to a final hearing.

5.5.1 Preparation

Certain matters must be given particular attention when preparing for the final hearing:

(a) *Bundles*. A bundle of documents relevant to both parties' cases should be prepared for the hearing *by the applicant*, properly indexed and paginated. For a complete guide to what goes into the bundle, see: *Practice Direction (Family Proceedings: Court Bundles) (Universal Practice to be Applied in All Courts Other Than the Family Proceedings Court)* [2006] 2 FLR 199. What follows is an outline summary only.

The trial bundles must now be divided into separate sections, namely:
(i)   preliminary and other case management documents;

(ii) applications and orders;

(iii) statements and affidavits;

(iv) experts and other reports;

(v)   care plan (where relevant); and

(vi) other documents.

Bearing in mind that each case is different, the sorts of documents which might typically be relevant and so be included in the bundle would be:
- payslips;
- relevant P60 forms;
- business accounts (if either party is self-employed or a director of a small company);
- bank and building society statements (going back over an informative but not excessive period);
- investment details;
- pension details;
- insurance policy details;
- credit card statements (going back over an informative but not excessive period);
- property valuations; and
- mortgage redemption figure.

At the beginning of the bundle should be:

(i)   a short (one-page if possible) up-to-date summary of the background to the case;

(ii) statement of issues;

(iii) position summary of each party (including orders/directions sought);

(iv) a chronology (if a final hearing or the summary of background is insufficient);

(v)   skeleton arguments as appropriate (for more information on these see City Law School's **Drafting Manual**, published annually by Oxford University Press); and

(vi) list of essential reading.

It is the applicant's responsibility to prepare and keep track of the bundle, which should if possible be agreed with the respondent. The bundle, which should include a time estimate for the hearing, must be lodged before the relevant hearing and in accordance with the rules. A paginated index to the bundle must be given to all parties not less than four working days before the hearing, regardless of whether the bundle has been agreed or not. Bundles are now lodged and relodged as a case progresses.

(b) The *issues in dispute*. Continue to review the evidence carefully so that you do not waste time on matters which are agreed, but are able to deal effectively with areas in dispute. Decide in advance how relevant facts will be proved. Consider what evidence may be needed to support relevant allegations, eg, regarding costs of alternative accommodation (estate agents), availability of (re)mortgage (lender), availability of council housing (local authority). Plan any cross-examination so that it will be focused and efficient. You must also have a clear and accurate view of the range of possible outcomes. Applicants must file and serve, at least 14 days before the hearing, a concise statement setting out the nature and amount of any orders they propose to invite the court to make. Respondents must respond within seven days thereafter: r 9.28. Both are open offers and no privilege attaches to them. *Calderbank* offers have effectively been consigned to history (although they are not banned as such), but financial remedies cases often settle at the door of the court and so, right up to the very last minute, you must be able to recognise and make acceptable offers of compromise.

(c) *Tax considerations*. It is important to calculate in advance (so far as this is possible) the likely tax implications for all parties of any order sought. In some courts, judges require such calculations to be agreed between the parties.

(d) *Benefit considerations*. Similarly, if any party is in receipt of any state benefits, it is important to consider in advance the effect that any order may have on entitlement or the amount of such benefit.

(e) *Child support*. If there are children in respect of whom a statutory child support assessment will, may or could be made, an estimate of the level of the amount of such payment ought to be made and included in the bundle.

(f) *Schedules*. Agreed financial schedules (see **5.3.7**) should have been available to the court throughout. Ensure that they are up-to-date and accurate.

(g) *Chattels*. Do not overlook this aspect of the case. Ideally, this should be dealt with before the final hearing, with a clear schedule included in the bundle setting out who is getting what. But this is not always possible—couples who get this far are often willing to fight over the strangest things. In such cases, a Scott Schedule should be drawn up setting out who claims what, and why. See generally *K v K* (*Financial Relief: Management of Difficult Cases*) [2005] 2 FLR 1137.

(h) *Costs statements.* Each party should prepare a statement of costs, including an estimate of costs to date, an estimate of the anticipated costs of the hearing and any anticipated consequential costs such as costs of sale, purchase or remortgage of any property (see *Practice Direction* (*Family Division: Costs*) [1988] 2 All ER 63 and FPR 2010, r 9.27(2)). This is now to be filed and served in Form H1, which is a far more detailed document than Form H (which has been used on all previous occasions up to this point). Its purpose is to enable the court to take account of the parties' costs liabilities when deciding the outcome of the case. This is particularly important in publicly funded cases, where the effect of the statutory charge must be borne in mind at all times (see **5.7**). It is an expensive exercise in itself to complete form H1 and there may be occasions when the court can be persuaded that using Form H would be more proportionate.

5.5.2   The hearing

The hearing usually takes place before a district judge (except in complex cases when it may be heard by a more senior judge). Even if the parties have agreed terms for provision, these should be referred to the judge for the court's approval, with sufficient information as to the resources of the parties. The hearing is in private, but (like the FA) there is now scope, it seems, for media access, and publication of what was heard or seen (subject to longstanding restrictions relating to the welfare of children, etc).

It is usual for the parties to attend the hearing to give oral evidence, as the other side will wish to cross-examine them. Others may also be asked to attend to give evidence; for example, expert valuers, if a valuation is not agreed. The essential informatiom about the parties' means will be contained in Form E, but the judge has a discretion over the evidence received.

Some judges set their own procedural agendas (eg, by inviting discussion on a provisional view he or she has taken on the papers), but many require proceedings to run as follows.

Counsel for the applicant (whether this is the petitioner or respondent to the divorce proceedings) will, as a general rule, go first. Where there are cross-applications, the convention is that the first in time opens, but if logic or convenience suggests otherwise, a different order may be adopted by agreement and with the court's permission. The party opening has the advantage of the first and last word.

5.5.2.1   The applicant's opening

Ensure that the judge has all relevant documents, including the chronology, any schedules and, as appropriate, your skeleton argument.

In the opening, you should:

- introduce yourself and the other advocates, indicating who is appearing on behalf of whom;

- outline briefly the nature of the application, referring to any relevant dates and application forms;

- give a brief outline of the background to the case (ie, names and ages of parties, date of marriage, names and dates of birth of children, etc), referring to any chronology which has been filed. This puts the application into context, but should not be overlong. In particular, remember that marital conduct (or misconduct!) is usually not relevant to applications for financial provision and so should not be emphasised. Any attempt to make capital out of the behaviour of the other party (unless it is relevant) is likely to backfire;

- set out the parties' financial position, using the schedules. Refer as necessary to any relevant documents in the agreed bundle (eg, revaluation of the matrimonial home);

- summarise the evidence you intend to call, making reference to the more important paragraphs in the written evidence, reports, etc. Check, as you go along, that the judge has all of the documents to which reference will be made;

- indicate whether agreement has been reached on any issue and make clear what the outstanding issues in dispute are;

- tell the judge what order your client is seeking and why, indicating briefly the factors under the MCA 1973, s 25, on which you rely. For example, a case might be such that you would argue: 'the children reside with the applicant wife. They need to be housed and she is resisting sale of the former matrimonial home because the husband is already adequately housed. And while his share in the equity will be tied up by way of a charge, this is justified because of the contributions the wife made, and will continue to make, to the welfare of the family and her reduced earning capacity.' If appropriate, outline any points of law, making brief references to any skeleton argument and/or authorities to be cited; and

- lastly, give a costs estimate of each of the parties.

Pace yourself so that the judge can easily follow you and ensure that he or she has had or is given the opportunity to read the statements, reports, etc. Even if the judge has read the file before you open your case, you should still summarise the main issues and deal with the matters above. However, do so *briefly*—be as concise and to the point as possible. In particular, be receptive to any hints the judge gives you that he or she has understood the point being made (and would like you to move on to the next one).

At the end of the opening (and once the judge has read the file) indicate that, unless the court wishes to hear further on any preliminary matter, you propose to proceed to the evidence.

5.5.2.2 The applicant's evidence

As a general proposition, Form E and other disclosed documents will contain all the relevant information. It will not normally be necessary (or desirable) to read or repeat this wholesale to the court. Keep the oral evidence succinct and to the point.

The evidence of the applicant will usually be tendered first but other witnesses may be taken first, for convenience sake.

Where the witness has made a statement and is then called upon to give oral evidence, this must be given on oath or affirmation. As in mainstream civil cases, get the witness to state his or her name and address and confirm that the contents of the relevant statement are correct. Examination-in-chief is now limited to:

- updating the witness's evidence, if there has been a change in circumstances;

- allowing the witness to expand on issues in dispute—for example, why the applicant can only work part-time when the other party says he or she can work full-time; or why the alternative properties suggested by the respondent are not suitable (a good tip, in this context, is to advise the client to go and look at the properties which have been put forward by the other side); and

- allowing the applicant to say what order is being sought from the court and how that order would meet his or her needs.

Cross-examination will then follow. Keep it polite and purposeful. Discursive or discourteous cross-examination is counter-productive and should be avoided. Common areas of cross-examination of a party include: questions on bank statements; questions on lifestyle and expenditure; questions on rehousing; questions on cohabitees and their contributions to the household. Big-money cases tend to invite detailed scrutiny by way of cross-examination. In any event, there should always be a link between questions asked/put and the points you hope to make in your closing.

Any re-examination should be kept very brief. Remember only to use re-examination to clarify matters arising out of the cross-examination.

After cross-examination and (if appropriate) re-examination of the applicant, each succeeding witness will be called and dealt with in the same way. In the unlikely event that a witness is called to give oral evidence without first having made a statement, then all of that witness's evidence will have to be brought out in examination-in-chief and tested in cross-examination in accordance with general principles.

After all of the evidence for the applicant has been called, indicate to the court that the applicant's case is closed.

5.5.2.3   The respondent's case

As with any conventional civil case, the respondent is not entitled, as of right, to an opening speech. Otherwise, the respondent's case should be presented in the same way as the applicant's case.

5.5.2.4   Closing speeches

It is usual for the applicant who opened the hearing to make the final speech, preceded by the other party. However, the court has a wide discretion as to the order of speeches and the judge may determine, or the parties (with the court's permission) may agree, a different order.

Your closing speech should, in short, attempt to *persuade* the court to make the order your client seeks. This is done by reference to your 'theory of the case' (which should have informed your questioning of witnesses), backed up by the relevant facts as disclosed by the evidence, and in particular those factors under the MCA 1973, s 25 which support your case. Be practical and realistic. Demonstrate, by use of the relevant figures, how the order would work *in practice* (from both the applicant's and respondent's perspectives). It is rarely relevant what happened in some other case, but any pertinent law should be cited. Use common sense and keep your closing speech focused.

Counsel should not, of course, go over ground that was covered in an opening speech. Do not be tempted to regurgitate all of the evidence the judge has just heard—simply highlight the important points. Be persuasive not long-winded. If you have omitted, or not had the opportunity to give, an up-to-date costs estimate, do so in your closing speech.

5.5.2.5   Costs

Once judgment has been given, there may follow argument on costs. If there is a reason to depart from the general rule, which in such cases now is that the court shall make no order as to costs (ie, leaving parties to pay their own costs), then these should be put forward (see **5.6**). Remember to ask for a detailed assessment of costs and also, if necessary, for a declaration pursuant to the Community Legal Service (Financial)

Regulations 2000, reg 52, which allows postponement of the legal aid charge against a property, if applicable (see **5.7**). Barristers will also need to ask for a certificate for counsel.

5.5.2.6 Court order

Having made his or her decision, it is possible that the judge will ask the parties to draw up the terms of the order to be referred back to the judge for approval. If appropriate, the court may refer the order for financial provision to conveyancing counsel if it involves complexities in securing payments or in a property adjustment order (MCA 1973, s 30). This is very rare.

5.6 Costs

Keeping track of and controlling costs is a very important aspect of financial remedies litigation. Parties are kept informed about the costs of the litigation as the case progresses, while the overriding objective and active case management means that costs are kept proportionate. After all, whoever pays the costs, this will effectively reduce the total amount of available family resources.

Until 2006, costs in ancillary relief cases followed the philosophy of mainstream civil cases, ie, the 'loser' paid the costs of the 'winner'. It was a context in which the *Calderbank* offer thrived (see **5.4.5**). However, over time, it became increasingly clear that there were more differences than similarities between family feuds over money following divorce and, say, your average negligence action. Several criticisms were levelled at the *Calderbank*-friendly costs regime. First, in many cases it is difficult to say who has 'won' and who has 'lost'. Secondly, marital breakdown and its financial consequences should be regarded as a misfortune befalling the family rather than the fault of either party. Thirdly, such costs orders, which might be for a significant sum, often had a destabilising effect on the substantive order. As a result, the *Calderbank* system had come to be used more and more as a tactical tool, rather than a genuine offer of settlement. Finally, the whole issue of costs gave rise to an increasing amount of expensive and time-consuming satellite litigation, which was often conducted with some venom. In such circumstances, the issues between the parties were not being disposed of at final hearing, as was the intention. Although the system had its proponents, most practitioners felt the time had come for a change.

This came first in the form of the Family Proceedings (Amendment) Rules 2006 (SI 2006/352), as explained in the accompanying *President's Direction (Ancillary Relief: Costs)* [2006] 1 FLR 865, which have now been replicated more or less unchanged in the 2010 rules. As a result, for all claims for financial remedies commenced on or after 3 April 2006, the general rule is that 'the court will not make an order requiring one party to pay the costs of the other party': r 28.3(5). In other words the fundamental presumption is that each side should be responsible for his or her own costs (which is the position in Children Act cases). The (unstated) idea is that the costs which have been expended by each party (which are obvious to the court from the running total set out on Forms H and H1) should be treated as part of the financial needs of each, to be accounted/paid for when dividing up the family assets. This approach has been generally upheld as sound: see, eg, *Currey v Currey* [2007] 1 FLR 946.

Notwithstanding the general principle, the rules go on to say that a costs order can be made at any stage of the case where a party's *litigation* (not matrimonial) conduct (whether before or during the proceedings) justifies it: r 28.3(6). A checklist has been set out in r 28.3(7) of the matters to which the court is to have regard, namely:

- any failure by a party to comply with the rules, or any relevant order or Practice Direction;
- any *open* offer to settle made by a party (my emphasis);
- whether or not it was reasonable for a party to raise, pursue or contest a particular allegation or issue;
- the manner in which a party has pursued or responded to the application or a particular allegation or issue;
- any other aspect of a party's conduct in relation to the proceedings which the court finds relevant;
- the financial effect on the parties of any costs order.

Note the explicit reference to *open* offers; the court is no longer able (after the FDR anyway) to look at *Calderbank* letters (ie, without-prejudice offers) in determining liability for costs. But it will look at litigation behaviour and this includes how a party responds to offers of settlement (whether in the form of a counter-offer or not), as Heather Mills found (quite literally) to her cost: *McCartney v Mills McCartney* [2008] 1 FLR 1508. The President's Direction makes clear that where a party is seeking an order for costs against the other, this should be made clear in open correspondence or in skeleton arguments before the date of the hearing. In addition, that party must serve a written notice of the costs concerned in Form N260. If the judge does decide to make an order for costs, all of the options open to the mainstream courts are available (modified as necessary) in family proceedings (see, eg, CPR 44.3(6), which lays down various permutations which can be adopted and adapted to the circumstances of the case). For detailed guidance on the costs rules, see David Burrows, *The New Ancillary Relief Costs Regime* (Jordans, 2006) and Bird and King, Chapter 17.

Remember that when negotiating a consent order, the payment of costs should form part of the agreement (see **5.9**).

Note, too, the possibility that a legal or other representative may be liable for wasted costs as a result of improper, unreasonable or negligent acts or omissions. See, eg, *C v C* (*Wasted Costs Order*) [1994] 2 FLR 34 and *B v B* (*Wasted Costs: Abuse of Process*) [2001] 1 FLR 843.

5.7 Public funding

The future of public funding for financial remedies cases is very much in doubt. The government has proposed removing entirely from the scope of legal aid all advice and representation in financial remedy cases, except those where issues of related domestic violence, forced marriage, international child abduction and the like are involved. The stated hope is that individuals will settle such disputes without recourse to the courts (mediation services are still being funded to an extent); the objective is to slash the burgeoning legal aid budget (see **1.8**). To a large extent, therefore, what follows will either in due course be rendered irrelevant, or applicable only in very limited circumstances.

If a party is publicly funded, this raises certain matters requiring close attention. Although being legally aided can be considered advantageous, there are pitfalls, the largest of which is the statutory charge, which must always be borne in mind, and explained to the client (see *Singer v Sharegin* [1984] FLR 114). The statutory charge arises whenever the Legal Services Commission (LSC) has to pay out more to finance the funded party's litigation than it gets back by way of that person's own contribution to his legal costs and any costs paid by the other side: Access to Justice Act 1999, s 10(7). It plugs the gap by giving the LSC a first charge on any property 'recovered or preserved' in the proceedings. The charge can attach to any property that is in issue in the proceedings, not just property which changes hands (*Hanlon v Law Society* [1981] AC 124). It can arise even if the claim for provision is settled (*Curling v Law Society* [1985] 1 WLR 470).

Given that the usual costs order now is that each side pays its own costs, the statutory charge can be problematic.

It is important to note that the charge arises whenever a *capital* lump sum is recovered, as the charge can then be realised immediately, even if the lump sum is awarded in lieu of continuing maintenance (*Stewart v Law Society* [1987] 1 FLR 223). The same could happen if the money was awarded for the purchase of a house (*Simpson v Law Society* [1987] AC 861), but it is provided that if a lump sum is specifically ordered for this purpose, the charge (registered against the property) can be postponed until that house is sold. If a house is sold, costs can be enforced from the proceeds of sale (*Chaggar v Chaggar* [1996] 1 FLR 450).

In many cases, the major asset is the matrimonial home, which may need to be preserved as a home for a spouse and for children. In appreciation of this, where the matrimonial home or an interest in it is transferred on divorce, the statutory charge can again be postponed until the home is sold. It is also possible for the charge to be transferred from one house to another if the spouse moves. This is clearly beneficial in one sense but, where a charge is postponed, interest will accrue on the charge. Consideration must always be given to paying off the charge if, and as soon as, possible.

There are various ways of keeping the potential effects of the legal aid charge to a minimum:

(a) All reasonable efforts (by the parties and the courts) should be made to keep costs down as the case progresses.

(b) Efforts should be made to reach a reasonable settlement rather than pursue the matter to trial and build up costs. The most obvious way to avoid the impact of the charge is to settle the case through mediation, not litigation. This is the line of argument the government is pursuing with its proposals (see **Chapter 11**).

(c) If your client is publicly funded and the other side is not, try to get agreement that the latter pay the costs (this can be part of the 'deal') or, where appropriate (see **5.6**), seek an order that they do so from the court.

(d) Orders for periodical payments to a spouse will not be caught by the charge, nor will any provision ordered for children. Courts may have regard to the implications of the type, as well as the amount of any order it makes.

(e) Try to keep the property that is in issue in a case to the minimum. If, eg, both sides agree that the applicant owns half the matrimonial home, it may be arguable that only the other half will be 'up for grabs'. This is a complex area and much will depend on the facts of the case.

(f) If there will inevitably be a charge, try to ensure that it attaches to a family home and can therefore be postponed, though note that this option is not so attractive now that interest is payable on the charge.

Clearly, the effects of any charge must be taken into account in agreeing provision. The approach taken by the courts has not been entirely consistent. It has been said that a judge should take the effects of a charge into account when ordering provision (*Simmons v Simmons* [1984] Fam 17). However, it has more recently been suggested that a judge should not do so (*Collins v Collins* [1987] 1 FLR 226).

It is less clear the extent to which the principles and provisions relating to possible costs orders against funded parties and against the Community Legal Service Fund itself still apply to family law cases.

In 2009, Roger Bird devoted several pages to legal aid in ancillary relief cases; in 2011 he gives just four lines to the subject on the basis that there seemed 'little point' repeating information soon to be consigned to history. Having said that, there has been considerable opposition (from those on the front line) to the government's proposals, and the precise fate of public funding in family cases may not be known for certain for some time. In any event, funding will remain for a narrow band of cases. So, as the saying goes, watch this space!

5.8 Tactics

As in mainstream civil cases, tactics in the negative sense (eg, delaying tactics) have been largely eliminated by the procedural rules. But there are still lots of positive judgments to be made, from how things are worded, to offers put and concessions made in negotiations.

Be aware of other factors that may be tied in with a financial remedies application. For example, one spouse may be prepared to consent to a divorce under the MCA 1973, s 1(2)(d) (that is, two years' separation and consent) if the other is prepared to make some financial concession. Another illustration might be a dispute over the residence of children where the spouse who gets custody is likely to have a better claim, in financial remedies proceedings, to stay in the matrimonial home.

An understanding of the relationship between the spouses can also help you in doing the best for the client. Emotional strain can cloud the judgment of some divorcing couples, but others will be able to behave reasonably to each other, and will wish to achieve a fair solution. Few couples want to see their children suffer unnecessarily. The relationship between the parties may be critical to getting information and in reaching a solution.

As so many cases result in agreed orders, effective negotiation skills are clearly important. Even if a consensual outcome is likely, there are still decisions to be made as to which side should make the first offer, what precisely they should offer, and when.

5.9 Orders and consent orders

5.9.1 Orders

Although the court will, officially, be the one to make or sanction the order for financial provision, it is vital to know how to draft these effectively and efficiently. Whether drawing up agreed terms or responding to suggestions from the other side (or indeed a request from the court to do the drafting!), you are likely to be actively involved in this aspect of the case. Financial remedies orders need to be drafted with care and foresight—the devil is often in the detail. This is particularly critical when drafting consent orders.

The importance of reaching a consensual order has been mentioned and is strongly underlined in the procedure for seeking financial remedies. The overriding objective provides that active case management should help the parties to settle the whole or part of the case and encourages the parties to use mediation where appropriate. As regards the FDR appointment, details of all offers and responses should be filed, and the parties are enjoined to use their 'best endeavours' to reach agreement on all matters in issue, with the express possibility of a consent order being made at the end of the hearing. In fact, the impetus to settle permeates the rules from beginning to end and the costs rules are designed to the stop parties gambling on the outcome.

5.9.2 Powers to make consent orders

The judge hearing an application for financial provision on divorce has an inherent power to make an order in terms suggested by the parties, but can refuse if he or she thinks the terms are clearly inappropriate. The court should not interfere lightly, but equally it is not a mere 'rubber stamp': *Pounds v Pounds* [1994] 1 FLR 775. It follows that the court must have sufficient information before it in order to make an assessment as to whether the proposed order is within the reasonable bounds of the court's discretion. The information which the applicant must file, and the form this should take, is set out in r 9.26 and PD 5A.

The rules make it possible for a consent order to be made at a first hearing in a straightforward case, and do all they can to encourage a consent order by the end of the FDR appointment through the clarification of issues and offers.

Note that a consent order can only be made after a decree nisi (*Pounds v Pounds*, above), and that orders relating to capital can only become effective after decree absolute. This may need to be taken into account if drafting at an early stage.

5.9.3 The role of the consent order

Although negotiations for financial relief are common, a settlement must never be seen as an easy way out. The settlement should be based on full information just as much as a contested court order would be.

It is vital that the lawyer and the client keep at the front of their minds that, save in exceptional circumstances, the consent order will form a final settlement of all claims. An application for variation may not be possible (see **5.11.3**). In *H v B* [1987] 1 WLR 113 it was held that once a spouse has agreed to a consent order, he or she cannot seek further provision. There is a duty to make full disclosure in carrying out negotiations for a consent order, or the order may be set aside (*Livesey v Jenkins* [1985] AC 424).

The terms of a consent order must be clearly explained to the client. Although an agreement may have advantages, there should be no undue pressure on a client to accept terms, particularly bearing in mind that the spouse may be very emotional at the time of a divorce (*Tommey v Tommey* [1983] Fam 15). As always, you must act within the client's instructions in negotiating. In the exceptional case of *Dutfield v Gilbert H Stephens & Sons* [1988] *Family Law* 473, a wife sought a quick divorce settlement but later sued her solicitors for not thoroughly investigating her husband's assets. The wife failed in her claim as her solicitors had acted within her instructions. Note, however, that it is no defence to a claim for negligence against a lawyer that a court has approved a consent order (*B v Miller & Co* [1996] 2 FLR 23).

5.9.4 Drafting an order

The draft order must be clear, comprehensive and accurate (*Dinch v Dinch* [1987] 1 WLR 252). Judges have frequently criticised poor drafting in this area, as in the case of *Dinch* itself, in which Lord Oliver of Aylmerton said:

> The appeal is yet another example of the unhappy results flowing from the failure to which I ventured to draw attention in *Sandford v Sandford* [1986] 1 FLR 412 to take sufficient care in the drafting of consent orders in matrimonial proceedings to define with precision exactly what the parties were intending to do in relation to the disposal of the petitioner's claims for ancillary relief so as to avoid any future misunderstanding as to whether those claims, or any of them, were or were not to be kept alive. The hardship and injustice that such failure inevitably causes, particularly in cases where one or both parties are legally aided and the only substantial asset consists of the family home, are so glaring in the instant case that I feel impelled once again to stress in the most emphatic terms that it is in all cases the imperative professional duty of those invested with the task of advising the parties to these unfortunate disputes to consider with due care the impact which any terms that they agree on behalf of the clients have and are intended to have upon any outstanding application for ancillary relief and to ensure that such appropriate provision is inserted in any consent order made as will leave no room for any future doubt or misunderstanding or saddle the parties with the wasteful burden of wholly unnecessary costs. It is, of course, also the duty of any court called upon to make such a consent order to consider for itself, before the order is drawn up and entered, the jurisdiction which it is being called upon to exercise and to make clear what claims for ancillary relief are being finally disposed of. I would, however, like to emphasise that the primary duty in this regard must lie upon those concerned with the negotiation and drafting of the terms of the order and that any failure to fulfil such duty occurring hereafter cannot be excused simply by reference to some inadvertent lack of vigilance on the part of the court or its officers in passing the order in a form which the parties have approved.

The vital importance of absolute accuracy in drafting is illustrated by *Richardson v Richardson* [1994] 1 FLR 286. It was recorded in the consent order that maintenance for a wife should continue at the rate of £8000 for three years. Shortly before the end of the three-year period (which the husband thought was about to bring to an end his liability to pay maintenance) the wife applied to increase the amount payable and to extend the period of the order. It was held that this could be done as nothing in the wording of the consent order prevented this. Precise wording may be vital for many purposes, eg, possible tax relief (*Billingham v John* [1998] *Family Law* 175). See also *B v B (Consent Order: Variation)* [1995] 1 FLR 9, *L v L (Lump Sum: Interest)* [1994] 2 FLR 324 and *Richardson v Richardson (No 2)* [1997] *Family Law* 14.

Once terms are agreed, the draft order may be prepared by lawyers for both sides acting together, or may be prepared by the lawyer for one side and then sent to the other for amendment and approval. Rule 9.26 deals with the procedure for seeking consent orders.

The draft should follow the formal structure of a court order, illustrated in the examples below (see **5.9.7**). Each item agreed should be set out in a separate paragraph. It is important to note that, in addition to including orders which the court is empowered to make, the order can record matters agreed between the parties as well as undertakings. It is important to be aware of which of the agreed terms can and should be orders and which should not. Judges will pull you up if you attempt to make them order something outside their jurisdiction.

The possible problems of failing to draft in sufficient detail were illustrated in *Rooker v Rooker* [1988] 1 FLR 219, where there was a consent order that the home be sold, but the husband failed to sell for two years. It was held that the wife could get no compensation for this delay. It would have been far better if the original order had been drafted more specifically to protect her.

Adequate flexibility is also important. In *Masefield v Alexander* [1995] 1 FLR 100 it was only on appeal that a husband escaped difficulties brought about by a strict time limit in the order, and in *N v N (Valuation: Charge-Back Order)* [1996] 1 FLR 361 the husband found that he could not avoid problems arising from a specific valuation clause.

Being thorough is also important. Everything that is agreed by the parties should be covered in the order. Although it might be argued that an agreed aspect could be enforced even if it is not included, any omission may lead to real difficulties (see *Edgar v Edgar* [1980] 3 All ER 887 and *Brown v Brown* [1980] 1 FLR 322).

5.9.5 Body of the order

The court can make orders it is empowered to make (eg, MCA 1973, ss 23 and 24—see **4.2**). These will be contained in the body of the document. Certain aspects relating to implementation may go beyond what the court is empowered to order, and merely record what the parties have agreed.

As a basic checklist for what might be ordered (and the matters to consider):

(a) Maintenance for a spouse. How much? At what intervals (weekly, monthly)? When should payments start? Should payments be for a set period? Should payment be by a particular method, eg standing order? Should any provision for review be built in? Even if there is no substantial order for maintenance, should a nominal order be included? On potential problems here, see *Richardson v Richardson* (above) and *Flavell v Flavell* [1997] *Family Law* 211.

(b) Maintenance for children. Is an order necessary, or is this dealt with by the statutory authority? How much? How often? When should it start? Should it be paid to the child or the custodial parent? How should payment be made? Any overlap with future statutory payments?

(c) Lump sum. If a lump sum is to be paid, how much? When? Linked to any other part of the order? Payable by instalments? Any penalty if it is not paid on time? Interest penalty?

(d) Sale of the home. If the home is to be sold, do you need a time limit linked with a penalty for delay? How should the proceeds be divided? Who should conduct the sale? What about price? What if it doesn't sell?

(e) Settlement of the home. Be very clear about the terms of settlement. When should the home be sold? Should there be any options for time of sale? How should the proceeds be divided? Who should occupy the home? Are other orders or undertakings needed to deal with the mortgage or other obligations?

(f) Transfer of property. Precisely what is to be transferred? When? Any penalty for failure to comply? Does it need to be linked to, eg, a lump sum payment?

(g) Pensions. This is a complex area. If either a pension-sharing or pension attachment order is included, relevant information must be annexed (in form P1 or P2). For further guidance consult specialist texts.

(h) Dismissing claims. Should the court be asked to dismiss any further possible claims by a spouse? It is especially important to consider this where there is to be a clean break. For example, the possibility of claims for maintenance in the future, and the possibility of claims for provision from the estate of the spouse on death may be dismissed.

(i) Costs. If, and to the extent that, one party is to pay the other's costs, this must be recorded. If a party is publicly funded, additional provisions (eg, relating to the statutory charge) may be necessary.

(j) Liberty to apply. This can be given to allow the parties to return to court if there are any difficulties in enforcing the order, but not to deal with substantive issues.

If orders are required in respect of the care of the children, the practice is that they should be separately recorded on the appropriate form. Care is needed if a decision on any application is adjourned (*D v D* (*Lump Sum Order: Adjournment of Application*) [2001] *Family Law* 254).

5.9.6   Preamble and undertakings

The lead-in to the substantive order is sometimes referred to as the preamble. If appropriate, this records the basis of the order or any relevant historical detail (eg, the fact that the matrimonial home has already been sold). In particular, it also includes any relevant undertakings.

Undertakings are not an essential element of a consent order. In a relatively straightforward case, they may not be required. However, the undertaking is another extremely useful and flexible way of adding extra details to an order. The point is that the court can only actually order those things which it has the *power* to order by statute, which includes the main items outlined in **5.9.5**. If the parties wish to agree to further details, such as one party allowing something to be done, or one party making specific payments to third parties, this cannot be directly ordered by the court, but may be recorded as part of the agreement (eg, who shall have conduct of the sale of the matrimonial home) or be the subject of an undertaking. For example, in *Milne v Milne* [1981] 2 FLR 286 it was held that a party could not be ordered to take out a mortgage or an insurance policy, but these matters could be the subject of undertakings.

It is important to appreciate the apparently subtle differences between the various aspects of a consent order. For example, an undertaking, although not an order *of* the court, is a promise *to* the court to do something, and breach would amount to contempt (just as breach of an order would be). A failure of one party to do what he promised or agreed with the other is a matter of breach of contract.

5.9.7   Sample consent orders

The following samples are intended to cover some of the most common types of financial provision, and to illustrate possible variations in drafting style. All the samples are loosely based on the *Cutforth* case study used in this chapter, but they make use of a range of scenarios so that it is possible to illustrate a variety of possible orders. Note that if child maintenance is being left entirely to a CSA assessment, it does not need to be referred to at all in the order.

For further examples, see the Precedents section (G) of *Duckworth's Matrimonial Property and Finance*. See also examples in Bird and King.

5.9.7.1   Consent order providing for a clean break based on a transfer of property order, and ordering child maintenance by consent. Neither party in receipt of public funding:

This is a fairly simple and straightforward order, appropriate where property is to be divided and there will be a complete clean break, save as regards children, for whom provision is agreed in the form of maintenance and school fees.

IN THE OXFORD COUNTY COURT   Matter No D

BETWEEN

MRS SANDRA ANNE CUTFORTH   Petitioner

and

MR JAMES ANDREW CUTFORTH   Respondent

CONSENT ORDER

BEFORE District Judge   on the   day of   20
UPON hearing Counsel for both parties and upon reading Form E and other evidence of each party;
AND UPON the Petitioner undertaking to make application for decree absolute in this matter forthwith;
AND UPON the Petitioner undertaking

(a) to pay from the date of the transfer to her sole name of the property at 13 Jasmine Road, Oxford, Oxfordshire (registered at HM Land Registry title no) ('the property') all instalments in respect of the mortgage in favour of the Bland Building Society (Roll No 123456) ('the mortgage') secured upon the property as they fall due;

(b) to use her best endeavours to secure the release of the Respondent from his covenants and liabilities in respect of the mortgage, and in any event to indemnify him against any claims and liabilities in respect thereof;

AND UPON the Respondent undertaking to pay or cause to be paid all payments due under the mortgage and collateral endowment premiums relating to the property up to the date of transfer of his legal and beneficial interest in the property to the Petitioner;
AND UPON it being deemed that the Petitioner and the Respondent have made all forms of application for financial remedies under sections 21A, 23, 24 and 25 of the Matrimonial Causes Act 1973;
BY CONSENT IT IS ORDERED THAT:

(1) The Respondent within 28 days of the date of the order shall transfer all his legal and beneficial interest in the property to the Petitioner, subject to the existing mortgage in favour of the Bland Building Society but otherwise free of encumbrance.

(2) Simultaneously with the transfer referred to in paragraph (1), the Petitioner shall execute a charge upon the property in favour of the Respondent as to 25 per cent of the net equity therein (as defined in paragraph 3 below). The said charge shall be realisable upon the earliest of the following events:

— the remarriage of the Petitioner

— the Petitioner cohabiting with another man for a continuous period of six months or more

— the death of the Petitioner

— the youngest surviving child of the family attaining the age of 18, or finishing full-time education if later, save that in any event the charge shall become realisable upon that child attaining the age of 21 years.

Upon the occurrence of the earliest of these events, the property shall be placed upon the market for sale and sold at the best price reasonably obtainable, save that the Petitioner shall have the option of buying out the Respondent's charge for a sum calculated in accordance with paragraph (3) below.

(3) The term 'net equity' as referred to above is defined as the selling price of the property less the mortgage thereon at the time of the realisation of the charge, and less reasonable legal and estate agent costs of sale. In the event that the Petitioner shall exercise her right to buy out the charge, the net equity will be calculated with reference to value of the property at that time rather than the selling price. In the event of any dispute as to the value or selling price of the property, the valuation of a jointly agreed and paid surveyor (being a member of the Royal Institute of Chartered Surveyors) shall be final.

(4) The Respondent shall pay periodical payments to the Petitioner for the benefit of the children of the family, Damian John Cutforth and Gemma Jane Cutforth, at the rate of £50 per week in respect of each child, the first payments to be made on 4 June 2012 and the payments to last until each child respectively attains the age of 17 years or ceases full-time education (whichever is the later) or until further order.

(5) Upon the transfer and charge referred to in paragraphs (1) and (2) above, the claims of both parties for periodical payments, secured periodical payments, lump sum or sums, property adjustment orders and pension-sharing orders (all such claims being deemed to have been made) shall stand dismissed, and it is directed that neither party shall be entitled to make any further application in relation to the marriage for an order under s 23(1)(a) or (b) of the Matrimonial Causes Act 1973 or the Married Women's Property Act 1882 as amended.

(6) Further, upon the transfer and payment referred to in paragraphs (1) and (2) above, the court considering it just to do so, neither party shall on the death of the other be entitled to apply for an order under s 2 of the Inheritance (Provision for Family and Dependants) Act 1975.

(7) There be liberty to apply as regards the timing and implementation of the terms of this order.

(8) No order as to costs.

Note the following:

(a) There is an undertaking to apply for the decree to be made absolute as the property orders can only come into effect after decree absolute.

(b) It is important to describe the property fully, including the Land Registry title number at one point in the order. Note the link between the transfer of the property to the Petitioner and her taking over the mortgage payments.

(c) Undertakings as regards the mortgage can be useful where the property has been in joint names and will be put into one name. The building society that has granted a mortgage cannot be directly ordered to change any responsibilities under the mortgage so that must be achieved here through undertakings. An undertaking may not be necessary if there is no doubt that the party getting sole ownership will pay the mortgage (which it will be in his or her interests to do). Note the use of the expression 'best endeavours'. This is used where the consent or cooperation of a third party is necessary to achieve the desired result.

(d) If one party is to get sole ownership of the home, it will often be fair for the other party to get some of the capital value. This may be achieved by an immediate lump sum payment if possible, or by a deferred charge back (as here) if there is no free capital to pay an immediate lump sum.

(e) When dealing with shares in or charges on capital, it is important to be clear about how figures will be calculated, eg, by defining net equity.

(f) Child support is now often a matter for the statutory authority so that no order may be required although parents are to be encouraged to agree maintenance (see **Chapter 7**).

(g) A clean break is achieved by the court ordering that no further applications can be made. Here there can be no other applications by either spouse. However, it is possible to order a clean break as regards only one spouse, leaving open the possibility for the other to make applications.

(h) 'Liberty to apply' only relates to the detailed enforcement of the order and cannot be used to go back to court on a substantive issue.

(i) You should be explicit that there is to be no order as to costs, if that is what is agreed.

5.9.7.2 Consent order providing for a clean break based on the sale of the matrimonial home, a lump sum payment by instalments, and additional child maintenance to cover school fees. Neither party is publicly funded

This is again a fairly simple and straightforward order, appropriate where the home has to be sold and the proceeds divided as the basis for a clean break. Note that here the clean break is delayed by maintenance payments for the wife for a limited period (appropriate where she is likely to be able to support herself after retraining or when the children are old enough for her to work). Here it is assumed that a CSA assessment will provide for child maintenance, although there is an order to cover school fees.

IN THE OXFORD COUNTY COURT   Matter No D

BETWEEN

MRS SANDRA ANNE CUTFORTH   Petitioner

and

MR JAMES ANDREW CUTFORTH   Respondent

CONSENT ORDER

BEFORE District Judge   on the   day of   20
UPON hearing Counsel for both parties and upon reading the sworn Form E and other evidence of each party filed herein;
AND UPON the parties agreeing that the contents of the former matrimonial home are the absolute property of the Petitioner;
AND UPON the parties further agreeing that the Respondent shall pay the amounts ordered in paragraph (4) below directly to the Bursar of the said school, and that receipt by that payee shall be a sufficient discharge;
AND UPON it being deemed that the Petitioner and the Respondent have made all forms of application for financial remedies under sections 21A, 23, 24 and 25 of the Matrimonial Causes Act 1973;
BY CONSENT IT IS ORDERED THAT:

(1) The property at 13 Jasmine Road, Oxford, Oxfordshire (registered at HM Land Registry title no) ('the property') shall be placed on the market for sale forthwith, and upon sale the net proceeds of sale shall be divided between the Petitioner and the Respondent as to two-thirds

to the Petitioner and one-third to the Respondent. The term net proceeds of sale shall mean the gross sale price less the amount outstanding in respect of the mortgage in favour of the Bland Building Society and the legal costs and estate agent charges in respect of sale. The Petitioner's solicitors shall have conduct of the sale.

(2) The Respondent shall pay to the Petitioner a lump sum of £30,000 payable as follows:
— £5000 within 28 days of the date of this order
— £5000 within three months of the date of this order
— £20,000 within six months of the date of this order.

(3) The Respondent shall pay or cause to be paid to the Petitioner periodical payments at the rate of £400 per calendar month, payable in advance, for a period of three years commencing on 2 April 2012 (and it is directed that the Petitioner shall not be entitled to apply for any extension of the period of three years).

(4) As from the date of this order, the Respondent shall pay or cause to be paid to the Petitioner for the benefit of Gemma Jane Cutforth, until such time as she shall cease full-time secondary education or until further order, periodical payments of an amount equal to the fees payable at the Royal Girls' School, Oxford (including reasonable extras), such sums being payable on the first day of each school term.

(5) Upon the sale and payment referred to in paragraphs (1) and (2) above, the Petitioner's and Respondent's claims for lump sum, property adjustment orders and pension-sharing orders (all such claims being deemed to have been made) shall stand dismissed, and neither party shall be entitled to make any further application in relation to the marriage for orders of a capital nature pursuant to the Matrimonial Causes Act 1973 or the Married Women's Property Act 1882 as amended.

(6) Further, upon the same events referred to in paragraph (5) above, the Respondent's claims against the Petitioner for periodical payments or secured periodical payments shall stand dismissed and it is directed that he shall not be entitled to make any further application in relation to the marriage for an order under section 23(1)(a) or (b) of the Matrimonial Causes Act 1973.

(7) The Respondent shall not be entitled on the death of the Petitioner to apply for an order under section 2 of the Inheritance (Provision for Family and Dependants) Act 1975, the Court considering it just to so order.

(8) There be liberty to apply as regards the timing and implementation of the terms of this order.

(9) The Respondent shall pay the Petitioner's costs on the standard basis, to be assessed if not agreed, including the costs of negotiations, up to a maximum of £7500.

Note the following:

(a) There does not need to be an undertaking to apply for decree absolute if that decree has already been granted, as is assumed for this draft.

(b) An agreement about personal property may usefully be recorded in the undertakings section for the avoidance of doubt.

(c) A payment of school fees involves third parties who are not involved in the divorce, and this must be carefully dealt with in deciding on appropriate orders/undertakings.

(d) If a property is to be sold, the court can make detailed orders as regards the carrying out of the sale. The sample order here is very short and simple.

(e) The court can make detailed orders about the payment of lump sums, including instalments, interest, etc (compare the lump sum order in the next example). An order needs to reflect the reality of what can reasonably be raised and when payments can be made.

(f) Ideally, if a home is to be sold, all capital provision would be dealt with in the division of the proceeds of sale without a separate lump sum. This is not done here purely to provide a wide range of sample orders.

(g) Maintenance payments for the former wife are here limited to three years. Such a limitation would depend entirely on the practicalities of the individual situation. Note that, as a result, the clean break orders in paras 5 and 6 leave open applications for maintenance by the wife for the time being.

(h) Here the agreement is that the husband will pay the wife's costs (within certain limits, which detail is recorded).

5.9.7.3 Consent order providing for a continuing financial relationship between the parties, with periodical payments and a settlement of the house. Petitioner is publicly funded

If there will be ongoing provision, the order may need to be more complex than that for a clean break as the ongoing terms will need to be clear and there will be more possible eventualities to be provided for. The following is a fairly simple example.

IN THE OXFORD COUNTY COURT   Matter No D

BETWEEN

MRS SANDRA ANNE CUTFORTH   Petitioner

and

MR JAMES ANDREW CUTFORTH   Respondent

CONSENT ORDER

BEFORE District Judge   on the   day of   20

UPON hearing Counsel for both parties and upon reading Form E and other evidence of each party;

AND UPON the Petitioner undertaking to make application for decree absolute in this matter forthwith;

AND UPON the Petitioner undertaking to pay or cause to be paid as from the date of this order all monies which shall become payable in respect of the former matrimonial home at 13 Jasmine Road, Oxford, Oxfordshire (registered at HM Land Registry title no) ('the property') and the building insurance premium, the water rates and the council tax on the property;

AND UPON the parties agreeing that all property and possessions shall remain the property of the party in whose possession they currently lie except as otherwise provided in the order below;

BY CONSENT IT IS ORDERED THAT:

(1) The Respondent shall pay or cause to be paid to the Petitioner from 4 June 2012 periodical payments for herself during their joint lives or until the Petitioner shall remarry or until further order at the rate of £800 per month, payable monthly in advance.

(2) The Respondent shall forthwith transfer the property into the joint names of himself and the Petitioner, to be held by the Petitioner and the Respondent upon trust for themselves as

beneficial tenants in common in equal shares, on condition that the property shall not be sold until the earliest of the following events:

— the death of the Petitioner

— the remarriage or cohabitation for a period in excess of six months of the Petitioner

— the children of the family both attain the age of 18 years or cease full-time education (whichever is the later).

(3) The Respondent within 28 days of the date of this order shall pay or cause to be paid to the Petitioner a lump sum of £10,000, the sum to carry interest at the rate of 10 per cent per annum if not paid by the due date.

(4) The Petitioner shall forthwith transfer to the Respondent all legal and beneficial interest in the Peugeot 306, car registration number CB09 LRT.

(5) It is hereby certified for the purposes of the Community Legal Service (Financial) Regulations 2000, regulation 52 that the property at 13 Jasmine Road, Oxford, Oxfordshire has been preserved/recovered by the Petitioner for use as a home by herself and her dependants.

(6) There shall be no order as to costs save public funding detailed assessment of the Petitioner's cost.

Note the following:

(a) If a home is to be settled rather than sold or transferred to the ownership of one spouse, the details of who pays all the household bills will need to be agreed. The court cannot make orders as regards specific liabilities, but this can be covered by undertakings.

(b) A settlement of a house may be quite complicated and the sample order here is a relatively simple one. It is vital to reflect accurately whether the house is or is not already jointly owned, and to include any appropriate details of the settlement of the house.

(c) It is possible for the court to order the transfer of ownership of any specific asset if required.

(d) The final paragraphs may be relevant where the applicant is publicly funded.

5.10 Enforcement of orders

5.10.1 Ensuring compliance

Methods of enforcement in financial remedies cases largely mimic, or incorporate, the rules in mainstream civil cases. It is typically a solicitor's area of expertise, and is not without its complexities. What follows here is a brief overview.

The first and most important point is that many possible enforcement problems can and should be avoided. In a financial remedies case, potential difficulties can be foreseen, because of the assets involved, the attitude of one or both spouses, or the circumstances of the case. Going back to the court for enforcement will itself cost money and cause stress, so any need to return to court should be avoided if at all possible. Some suggestions for avoiding or alleviating enforcement problems are:

(a) If the spouses can agree the details of provision they are more likely to abide by them, so a negotiated settlement should be reached where possible.

(b) The precise effects of an order should be explained to the client to avoid any misunderstanding.

(c) The details of every order must be carefully drafted to avoid ambiguities and omissions that may cause problems.

(d) Some provision for enforcement may be included in an order, for example, by providing a penalty if something is not done by a set date, or only dismissing a spouse's claims once the other spouse has fulfilled a term (but avoid doing this if it would simply make the order more complex, or be irritating rather than productive).

(e) If there are any alternatives in making provision, consider whether one may be easier to enforce than another.

As an obvious practical point, once an order is made, the solicitor should if appropriate check with the client that the steps ordered are being taken, and should take action quickly if there is any difficulty. Delay in enforcement may itself cause problems, if, for example, the capital value of property alters, or arrears of maintenance accumulate to such an extent that they have to be remitted.

Enforcement is primarily a matter of returning to court once there has been some default on an existing obligation, but because of the delays and difficulties this can cause, the powers of the High Court and of the county court when making a maintenance order have been extended by the Maintenance Enforcement Act 1991 (MEA 1991), s 1. These courts may now order that payments be made by standing order or some similar method, and may order the payer to open a bank account for this purpose. It is now also possible to make an attachment of earnings order when making the maintenance order rather than waiting for a default in payment.

5.10.2 Modes of enforcement

An appropriate mode of enforcement must be chosen, depending on the type of order breached, and the form of the breach. Procedural points relating to enforcement must be kept in mind. For example, even though an order is not made in the Family Proceedings Court (ie, magistrates' court), it can be enforced there if it is first registered there (Maintenance Orders Act 1958 and FPR 2010, r 32.15).

The starting point for most financial remedy orders is r 33.3(1), which requires that an application for an order to enforce an order for the payment of money must be made in a notice of application accompanied by a statement, verified by a statement of truth, setting out relevant details about the amount due and so forth. Applicants who know which particular method of execution they seek can indicate this; those who do not may apply for such order 'as the court may consider appropriate' (using Form D50K; r 33.3(2)). In the latter case, the court will require the respondent to attend, to provide relevant financial information and be warned of the possible methods of enforcement which may be ordered (r 33.3(3)). Some of these are set out below.

5.10.2.1 Attachment of earnings

An order can be sought to get maintenance paid directly from an individual's salary to the recipient under the Attachment of Earnings Act 1971. This Act has been amended by the MEA 1991, primarily to allow attachment orders to be made at the same time as the maintenance order is made. This can be useful, but only if the payer is in steady employment. It can also be used to deduct payments from a pension or recover an unpaid lump sum over time. The rules are essentially the same as for mainstream civil cases, although application should be to the relevant family court.

5.10.2.2   General civil remedies

Many other forms of enforcement for civil claims are appropriate in a family case, and indeed the FPR 2010 cross-refer to the CPR for much of the procedure. These include charging orders, execution against goods, third-party debt orders, and judgment summons (see Sime, *A Practical Approach to Civil Procedure* for more detail and *Gandolfo v Gandolfo* [1981] QB 359). The appropriateness of such proceedings must be properly considered (see, eg, *Clark v Clark* [1989] 1 FLR 174, where lawyers were criticised for seeking sequestration where the resulting funds did not cover costs, let alone the sum due).

5.10.2.3   Imprisonment

This is a last resort, which will not generally be available or used for a simple failure to pay. However, it may be a possibility where a spouse has flouted court orders and is therefore in contempt of court, as in *Lightfoot v Lightfoot* [1989] 1 FLR 414.

5.10.2.4   The international element and reciprocal enforcement procedures

If an ex-spouse lives or moves abroad, it may be possible to register and enforce an order in the country in question. Similarly, orders made abroad can sometimes be enforced here. This is a complex area, and you will need to refer to relevant reciprocal enforcement orders and conventions.

5.11   Returning to court: appeal and variation

5.11.1   Context

A party may be able to appeal against an order or, if appropriate, seek a variation or further provision. However, there are limits and difficulties in returning to court which must not be overlooked in considering the original order.

The different possibilities for returning to court should be clearly distinguished and the correct option chosen for the case at hand:

(a) Returning to the court which made the order. This may be done without commencing new proceedings, but generally only to assist in implementing the terms of the order made, not to make any radical alteration or addition. To allow the parties to return to the court if necessary, 'liberty to apply' should be added to an order.

(b) Appeals/setting aside. On normal principles, an appeal will lie to challenge an order made if there is cause. Permission to appeal is now required in most cases. Attempts to set aside a consent order, which is effectively an agreement between the parties, pose special problems (see **5.11.2**).

(c) Variation. If there is a later change of circumstances, a party may be able to apply to court to vary the original order (see **5.11.3**).

(d) Additional orders. A further order may be sought in some circumstances. For example, the powers of the court on divorce under the MCA 1973, ss 23 and 24 may be exercised on divorce or at any time thereafter. Note, however, that a court will be slow to add to an existing order without good reason, especially if the existing order was made by consent and was intended to end all claims.

It may be possible to vary or add to an order without actually returning to court. This may be done either if the terms of the original order allow for variation without return to court, or if the parties agree to a variation by consent.

Problems arise particularly in the case of a consent order, where the court will be very slow to interfere where the parties have expressly agreed provision; and in the case of a clean break, where the court will be reluctant to undermine the order by making further provision.

5.11.2 Appeals and setting aside

Where an order is made by a district judge (or a costs judge) following a contested hearing, either party may appeal, if dissatisfied with the outcome, to a judge in chambers. As part of a process of harmonising the CPR with the FPR, the new rules now require that permission to appeal is required in such cases, except where the liberty of the person is at stake (eg, committal or secure accommodation order): r 30.3(1),(2). This is a change from the previous practice. Permission is still not required for an appeal from the magistrates' court.

Permission is also required for appeals from circuit or High Court judges. Permission can be sought from either the lower court (at the hearing where the order was made) or the appeal court in an application notice: r 30.3(3). Practitioners now need to be alert to the need to seek permission from the district judge whose order they challenge, bearing in mind that it is always good practice to raise matters of concern before the order is made. If he or she refuses permission, an application may be made to the circuit or High Court judge. Such applications are normally considered without a hearing, although if permission is refused a request may be made that the decision be reconsidered at a hearing: r 30.14(5). Not surprisingly, permission should only be given if there is a real prospect of success or some other compelling reason why the appeal should be heard. Any permission to appeal can be subject to conditions or limitations (eg, as to the issues): r 30.10.

In deciding whether to allow an appeal, the following principles still apply (see r 30.12):

(a) the decision of the lower court should only be interfered with if it was clearly wrong or unjust because of a procedural irregularity;

(b) the appeal is limited to a review of the lower court's decision unless the appeal court considers that in all the circumstances it would be in the interests of justice to hold a rehearing (or some other enactment or Practice Direction provides otherwise);

(c) the appeal court will not hear oral or other evidence before the lower court unless it considers that in the circumstances it would be in the interests of justice to do so (see *Kaur v Matharu* [2010] EWCA Civ 930).

So, for example, in *Lyons v Lyons* [2010] EWCA Civ 177, the appeal was allowed where the trial judge had made an obvious error, but the court of appeal commented that the mistake ought to have been picked up at the time.

In the case of a consent order, the possibilities for setting aside are very limited. A party who has agreed terms with the other side (and thus, in effect, to the order being made) will rarely be allowed simply to change his or her mind, or the finality of consent orders would be in doubt. The court will be looking not at the merits of the order as such, but rather the basis on which agreement was made. For example:

(a) *Barber v Barber* [1987] *Family Law* 125. As a wife knew of her husband's pension rights when she agreed to provision, she could not later seek to set aside the agreement to get further provision in respect of those pension rights.

(b) *Cook v Cook* [1988] 1 FLR 521. As it was agreed that the wife should get the home in any event, the fact that she was cohabiting with another man did not undermine this agreement. Equally, if a wife agrees to leave on cohabitation, that is enforceable (*Omeilan v Omeilan* [1996] 2 FLR 306).

(c) *Cornick v Cornick* [1995] 2 FLR 490, *Harris v Manahan* [1997] 1 FLR 205. A dramatic change in the value of property, if at all foreseeable, cannot be a basis for setting aside. However, an appeal will be allowed if one party has knowingly misled the other (*Middleton v Middleton* [1998] 2 FLR 821).

Thus, only where the order has been undermined by a procedural irregularity or by serious misconduct, such as fraud, material non-disclosure or mistake, will it be set aside. For example:

(a) *Munks v Munks* [1985] FLR 576. Consent order set aside because the fact that it was made before decree nisi was a procedural irregularity.

(b) *Redmond v Redmond* [1986] 2 FLR 173. A wife's application to set aside was allowed when she agreed to provision on the basis that her husband would not apply for redundancy, which he later did.

(c) *Vicary v Vicary* [1992] 2 FLR 271, CA. A consent order was made on the basis that the husband's assets, including his shares in a private company, were £430,000. He did not disclose the fact that negotiations were taking place for the sale of the company, which included the sale of his shares for £2.8 million. The order was set aside (but compare this with the case discussed in the next paragraph).

(d) *I v I* (*Ancillary Relief: Disclosure*) [2008] EWCA 1167 (Fam). A consent order had been made after an FDR at which the husband failed to disclose that he was negotiating a new employment contract. The wife applied to set aside the order on grounds of material non-disclosure. It was held that, even had the situation been disclosed, it would have made very little difference to the final order and so the appeal was dismissed.

Unforeseeable supervening events and mutual mistake can also be a basis for setting aside. See generally the interesting range of cases set out in Bird and King.

5.11.3   Variation

Some time after a financial remedies case, one of the parties may wish to vary the provision agreed and/or ordered for many reasons. There may be a notable change in the financial fortunes of one person, such as a significant inheritance of capital or a redundancy. Alternatively, one of the parties may change his or her views as to how or where he or she wishes to live, for example, taking early retirement. The details of variation of orders are beyond the scope of this Manual, but it is important to be aware broadly of when variation may or may not be possible in negotiating and drawing up the original order.

The court has little power to make more than one lump sum or property transfer order, and it cannot vary a transfer or settlement of property. It is therefore best to work on the basis that variation of such capital orders will be unlikely, if not impossible, and that the widest view of potential events should be taken when drawing up the original order.

However, variation may be possible in a case where there is *ongoing* provision for maintenance. Not only may the amount and term of maintenance be ordered, but a lump sum may be ordered to replace maintenance (thereby potentially achieving a clean break some time after the divorce). The powers for variation are contained in the MCA 1973, s 31 (as amended). It should be noted that these powers can be used even where an order has been made by consent, and that an order can relate to pension provision (*Burrow v Burrow* [1999] 1 FLR 508).

In deciding whether a variation should be ordered, the court will consider any material change of circumstances respecting either party since the order was made. This will often primarily consist of reviewing changes in financial resources and/or needs, and therefore such should be fully investigated just as they would be before an initial application. The court will also take into account any change in other factors that are relevant to provision. The court might consider, for example, whether one of the spouses is now cohabiting and therefore has extra resources or liabilities.

If there has been a material change then the court will reassess financial provision to decide what is now appropriate, taking into account all the factors it would take into account on an original application. Having said that, the court will try not to deviate from the *spirit* of the original order: see, eg, *VB v JP* [2008] 1 FLR 742.

As with an appeal, it may be difficult for a party to seek a variation of an order to which he or she has consented. It is possible to apply (*Jessel v Jessel* [1979] 1 WLR 1148) but the court will be slow to order the variation without good reason. In *T v T* [1988] 1 FLR 480 there was a consent order for provision for a wife to last until she married or her ex-husband retired. When the latter did retire, it was held that she could not have these terms varied to provide extra provision. If claims for financial provision have been dismissed, it will not be possible to seek a variation to get provision (*De Lasala v De Lasala* [1980] AC 546). On a variation linked to a clean break, see *Jones v Jones* [2000] *Family Law* 607.

Variation of a consent order may be possible if the welfare of a child is at stake (*N v N (Consent order: Variation)* [1993] 2 FLR 868). In addition, some limited relief may be available in exceptional circumstances. In *Thwaite v Thwaite* [1982] Fam 1 it was held that, although the consent order could not be varied, the court would refuse to enforce it in favour of a party who had not complied with its terms.

5.11.4 Professional negligence

If other routes fail, the lay client may feel driven to blame the lawyers for an unsatisfactory divorce settlement. This is clearly an unhappy situation for all concerned, and one to be avoided wherever possible! Bear in mind that a legal advisor/representative should always ensure that a client is fully advised of the terms and implications of any settlement, including any possible drawbacks, and that the client is aware of the options and takes informed personal decisions.

The issue of the public interest in maintaining advocates' immunity from suit in the conduct of litigation was considered by the House of Lords in a series of consolidated cases, reported as *Hall and Co v Simons* [2002] 1 AC 615, [2000] 2 FLR 545. The House of Lords held that there was no longer any justification for continuing this immunity. In summary, it is clear from these cases that advice given before a hearing will not necessarily be immune from legal action. This makes it more important than ever that clear and accurate advice is given as regards what financial relief may be awarded on divorce, and what might be offered or accepted by way of settlement.

6

Financial provision within marriage

This chapter outlines briefly the power of the courts to deal with financial matters when no divorce is sought. Although there are circumstances in which it may be necessary or desirable to seek, vary or enforce orders for financial provision even though divorce proceedings are neither pending nor contemplated, these provisions are infrequently used. Nevertheless spouses may separate experimentally, or temporarily, or there may be personal or practical reasons why they wish to separate without divorcing, and it is in this area that most of those provisions continue to have some application. Financial problems can arise very quickly if there are housing and food bills to be met and previous financial arrangements have broken down. More practical detail on how to prepare and present a case is provided in **Chapter 5**. Financial provision for children is dealt with in more detail in **Chapter 7**.

6.1 The High Court and county courts

The High Court and the county courts have the following powers to make orders relating to financial provision and property rights within marriage. Applications must be supported by appropriate evidence. The provisions of Part 9 of the Family Procedure Rules 2010 (FPR 2010), Applications for a Financial Remedy, will apply as regards process and information to be made available.

6.1.1 Financial provision in case of neglect to maintain

Either party to a marriage can seek a maintenance order that the other should provide maintenance on the basis of:

- failure to provide reasonable maintenance for the applicant; or
- failure to provide or make a proper contribution towards reasonable maintenance for any child of the family.

The relevant statutory provision is the Matrimonial Causes Act 1973 (MCA 1973), s 27. The orders that can be made and the factors that are relevant to the level of provision made are similar to those on divorce. In fact, s 27 directs the court to have regard to the factors mentioned in s 25(2) (see **4.3**).

Applications for failure to maintain are uncommon and, where they are made, are more likely to use the fuller provisions under the Domestic Proceedings and Magistrates' Court Act 1978 (DPMCA 1978) (see **6.2**).

6.1.2 Maintenance agreements

It is possible for spouses to make enforceable agreements for the payment of maintenance by contract or deed without going to court. There are powers relating to the validity and variation of maintenance agreements in MCA 1973, ss 34–36, although these are not widely used.

6.1.3 Ownership of property

Orders as to the ownership of property can be made under the Married Women's Property Act 1882, s 17. Note that this section does not provide any discretion, but simply a power to declare existing rights. One spouse may have an interest in property owned by the other under an implied, constructive or resulting trust, due to contributions made to the purchase price, etc.

6.2 Family proceedings courts

Although they have no jurisdiction in respect of divorce, family proceedings courts have powers to order financial provision for spouses and children. The powers of the magistrates and the factors that they can take into account in making orders are closely aligned to the powers of the higher courts, but their jurisdiction is much more limited. The powers of the court are set out in the DPMCA 1978. Orders made under this Act are often referred to, inaccurately, as 'separation orders'.

The possible advantages of going to a family proceedings court are that it may be cheaper, and possibly also quicker, as the procedure is relatively straightforward. There are limits on the orders that can be made and the purpose behind the Act is really one of maintenance rather than significant consideration of capital.

6.2.1 Powers to award maintenance and lump sums

The powers of the family proceedings courts (see DPMCA 1978, ss 1 and 2) are broadly similar to those of the High Court and the county courts already outlined, but the powers are wider in that, in addition to being able to make an order where there is a failure to provide reasonable maintenance for a spouse or child, an order can be made where the respondent has deserted the applicant, or has behaved in such a way that the applicant cannot reasonably be expected to live with the respondent. An order may provide for periodical payments or a lump sum, but cannot include secured periodical payments, or a lump sum in excess of £1,000 (a limit that can be raised by the Lord Chancellor). The factors relevant to making an order are similar to those on divorce.

The duration of any order should be specified and is essentially at the discretion of the court. An order cannot be backdated before the making of the application for provision, although the order can cover liabilities and expenses already reasonably incurred. It is quite common for periodical payments to be payable for a set period of years, or 'until further order'. The courts can make interim orders (s 19) and can vary or revoke orders (s 20).

Payments to or for the benefit of a child will not normally be made under the DPMCA 1978 since the enactment of the Children Act 1989, Sch 1 (CA 1989) and Child Support Act 1991, s 8(3) (see **Chapter 7**). In fact DPMCA, s 8 mandates that the court shall not dismiss or make a final order under the Act until it has decided whether to exercise any of its powers under the CA 1989 with respect to the child. Where such orders are made they will normally stop when the child reaches school-leaving age, and should in any event cease when a child is 18 unless the child is still undergoing education or training or there are other special circumstances justifying ongoing provision (DPMCA 1978, ss 4 and 5).

6.2.2 Agreed provision

Magistrates have powers under the DPMCA 1978, ss 6 and 7 to make an order where provision has been agreed. An order can be made where the court is satisfied that there is an agreement that provision be made and it would not be contrary to the interests of justice to make an order in those terms (s 6). Alternatively, an order can be made where the parties have been living apart for at least three months and maintenance has in fact been paid, to ensure that such maintenance continues and becomes enforceable (s 7). Orders under these sections can include maintenance for a spouse or child. An order by agreement under s 6 can also include a lump sum.

6.2.3 Procedure

The proceedings for an order under the DPMCA 1978, ss 2 or 6 are commenced by written application. Following this, a summons will be issued to the spouse from whom provision is sought. Affidavits do not have to be filed, but it is necessary for a statement of means to be completed, for which there is a standard form. The documents are lodged with the court for service on the respondent.

The applicant will make his or her claim and the other side will reply. Evidence will be partly oral, with skills in examination-in-chief and cross-examination required in getting out the facts of the case. There is advance disclosure of argument and evidence, including a schedule of figures relating to the current and proposed financial position of the client. As you might expect, the practical arithmetic of the situation is at the heart of the case.

Financial provision for children

7.1 Introduction

7.1.1 Overview and sources

These materials seek to provide no more than an introduction to the principles in this area and a general guide to child support calculations. A final section deals with applications for financial provision for children under Sch 1 of the Children Act 1989 (CA 1989).

This is a complex area as there have been a number of changes to the child support system since its introduction in 1991 with the enactment of the Child Support Act 1991 (CSA 1991). The principal changes implemented by the Child Support, Pensions and Social Security Act 2000 (the 2000 Act) were outlined in the previous edition of this Manual. The Child Maintenance and Other Payments Act 2008 (the 2008 Act') introduced further amendments to the CSA 1991. At the time of writing, applications for child support are still calculated under both the 1991 and 2000 regimes. However, a new calculation system is planned to be introduced from 2012, which means that there will be three systems running concurrently, until claimants under the 1991 and 2000 regimes are phased over to the third scheme. It is anticipated that this will begin in 2012.

Assistance can be obtained on this confusing area of law from the practitioner texts. There is a short overview in Bird and King at paras 11.5 to 11.8 and a comprehensive section in Duckworth at Part B, Section 2, from para 19. See also *Child Maintenance: The New Law*, by Roger Bird and David Burrows (Jordan Publishing, 2009). The annual publication *At a Glance* (FLBA) includes sections on all three regimes, including useful calculation tables for each. Child Poverty Action Group also annually publishes *The Child Support Handbook,* which comprehensively details all the legislation and common practice on the child support system. The website for the Child Support Agency ('CSA') can be found at www.csa.gov.uk.

7.1.2 The changing ethos

The theory behind the CSA 1991 (which came into force on 5 April 1993) was that parents should take proper financial responsibility for their children. Child support payments should be set at a realistic and reasonably uniform level by the use of a standard formula for calculation. The CSA was set up to gather relevant information, make assessments using the set formula and assist in the enforcement of payments due. There would be little, or no, need for the courts to be involved and using the CSA was to be virtually compulsory.

Despite the introduction of a new set of rules advented by the 2000 Act (see **7.1.5**), the child support regime continued to be the subject of considerable criticism. In December 2006, following publication of a report by Sir David Henshaw, the government published its White Paper 'A New System of Child Maintenance', the consultation period for which ended on 13 March 2007. This resulted in the enactment of the 2008 Act, which introduced a shift in direction, with the removal of the obligation on parents in receipt of income replacement benefits to apply to the CSA. All parents are encouraged to reach a voluntary arrangement. An advisory body for parents was established, Child Maintenance Options, which assists parents to make agreements and provides advice on how to make calculations applying the rules introduced under the 2000 regime. The 2008 Act also established a new umbrella public body, the Child Maintenance and Enforcement Commission (the Commission), through which the CSA now operates.

In January 2011 the government published a Green Paper 'Strengthening Families, promoting parental responsibility; the future of child maintenance'. The proposals placed even greater emphasis on parents making voluntary, family-based arrangements before resorting to the statutory maintenance system; proposed a 'gateway' to the statutory system through which all parents could be advised and encouraged to agree; and proposed to charge parents for using the system, if they could not agree. The proposal to make a charge emanates from the report by Sir David Henshaw and provisions to enact this are already contained in the 2008 Act. On 12 July 2011 the coalition government published its Response to the consultation process. It reported that there was overwhelming agreement with the principle that support for child maintenance should be more joined up with other types of support for separating and separated families. Paragraph 9 of the executive summary contains this critical commentary on the current financing of the child support system:

Whilst the Child Support Agency has improved over the years, it remains a flawed and expensive system costing £460 million each year to run. Weaknesses in the IT systems mean around 100,000 cases have to be managed off the system, each costing around double what it costs to manage an on-system case, and significant arrears have built up over the past 18 years. Furthermore it costs more than 40 pence to collect every £1 of maintenance from parents.

The proposed range of charges appears to be £100 for making an application, but if the applicant is on benefits this will be £50 maximum, and £20–£25 for seeking a calculation only. The estimated actual costs are put at £220 per application. There are as yet no draft regulations to implement the government's proposals and the Response is couched in very general terms; it appears that the proposals for the gateway, for charging and for a new child maintenance system will be implemented, largely by bringing into force further sections of the 2008 Act. The expectation that parents should reach agreement sits happily with the proposals in the Interim Family Justice Report (see **1.9**).

7.1.3 The Child Support Agency and the courts

The establishment of the CSA took control and responsibility for child maintenance out of the hands of the court system. In essence, where the CSA has power to make a maintenance calculation, the court may not make an order for child maintenance (CSA 1991, s 8(3)).

'Maintenance' generally means the making of orders for periodical payments. However, there are residual areas of jurisdiction for the court and the inter-relationship between the powers of the court and the CSA is not simple (see **7.3**). Where the court does have the power to order maintenance for children, one of three statutes will apply:

- the MCA 1973—financial provision on divorce;
- the DPMCA 1978—married parents; or
- the CA 1989—unmarried parents or the child itself.

7.1.4   Inflexibility—the CSA 1991; the old rules

The CSA 1991 in its original form was unfair in a number of ways. The formula for calculating child maintenance was both too complicated and too inflexible. This led to much dissatisfaction from both parents, with the effect that many calculations were disputed and arrears built up. Legislation was introduced to try to address this, but eventually a new calculation formula was introduced by the 2000 Act.

7.1.5   The 2000 Act; the new rules

The most important amendment resulted in a complete change to the way child support is calculated (see Sch 3). The 2000 regime is known as the new rules and applies to all cases with an effective date on or after 3 March 2003. At the time of writing, these new rules apply to the majority of parents using the CSA. The proposed changes yet to be enacted under the 2008 Act are considered at **7.4** below.

7.1.6   Terminology

This is about the only thing that has not changed over time. The 'absent' parent is the non-resident parent (NRP); the child maintenance assessment is the 'calculation'. The claimant, almost always the parent with care (PWC), has always been, and still is, described as 'she' in all three statutes. This chapter adopts the same approach for the sake of simplicity, though of course a PWC could be either mother or father. It should also be noted that in spite of the establishment of the Commission, the CSA remains the body responsible for calculating and distributing child maintenance.

7.2   The CSA

7.2.1   Jurisdiction of the CSA

Essentially, the CSA has jurisdiction where there is a PWC, an NRP and a 'qualifying' child within the United Kingdom. It should be noted that a qualifying child must be the natural or adoptive child of the parent (CSA 1991, s 3(1)).

7.2.2   The CSA and parents receiving benefit

A claimant in receipt of income replacement benefit is in no different position from any other PWC. Since April 2010 all child maintenance payments, whether paid through the CSA or through private agreement, have been disregarded in full for all means tested benefits.

7.2.3   Procedure for child support application

A PWC who chooses to make an application for child support may do so either orally or in writing, using a prescribed form.

7.2.4 The formula for calculating what is payable under the new rules

The starting point under the new rules is the net income of the paying parent (NRP) and the number of children in each household. The income of the parent in receipt is ignored for the purposes of the calculation. The CSA 1991, Sch 1 lays down four rates:

- the basic rate;
- the reduced rate;
- the flat rate; and
- the nil rate.

7.2.4.1 The basic rate

One qualifying child	15 per cent of net weekly income
Two qualifying children	20 per cent of net weekly income
Three or more qualifying children	25 per cent of net weekly income

Where the NRP has 'relevant other children' the amount payable is reduced. Relevant other children are children living with the NRP, either his own or his partner's: CSA 1991, Sch 1, para 10C(2). The reduction for the number of relevant children is the same percentage as the number of qualifying children.

7.2.4.2 The reduced rate

A reduced rate is payable where the NRP's net income is between £100 and £200 per week. For example, the reduced rate for one child will range from a minimum of £5 to a maximum of £27.50 per week.

7.2.4.3 The flat rate

A flat rate of £5 is payable where:

- the NRP has a net income of less than £100 per week;
- he or his partner are on income support or income-based jobseeker's allowance; or
- he is in receipt of a state pension, incapacity benefit, invalid care allowance or certain other benefits set out in the Child Support (Maintenance Calculations and Special Cases) Regulations 2000, reg 4.

If either of the first two points applies and the NRP looks after a qualifying child for at least 52 nights a year, he is eligible for the nil rate.

7.2.4.4 The nil rate

Nothing is payable where the NRP is:
- a student;
- a pensioner;
- a geriatric patient;
- a prisoner;
- a child;
- a person whose net weekly income is less than £5;
- a person in receipt of an allowance in respect of work-based training for young people.
- a 16/17-year-old (or their partner) in receipt of income support/jobseeker's allowance.

7.2.5 Apportionment

Where an NRP has qualifying children living with different parents, a simple apportionment system is applied (CSA 1991, Sch 1, para 6.1). For example, an NRP earns £400 per week and has three qualifying children aged 2, 5 and 14. The two younger children live with A and the eldest lives with B. The NRP's maintenance liability would be £100 (25 per cent of £400). A would receive two-thirds of this sum (£66.66) and B would receive one-third (£33.33). The ages of the children are immaterial.

7.2.6 Shared care

For NRPs who have qualifying children staying with them overnight, a reduction is made to their calculation (CSA 1991, Sch 1, paras 7–9). A sliding scale of reduction in payment applies depending on the number of nights the child stays with the NRP. The scale starts at one-seventh of the amount payable where the NRP has a qualifying child stay between 52 nights a year rising, to one-half at 175 nights each year. If a child stays with the NRP for more than half the year, the NRP can apply to claim child benefit and thus become the PWC. See *At a Glance* for the full table.

7.2.7 Cap

Under the new rules, net weekly income over £2,000 is ignored for the purpose of child support. The court retains the power to top up under the CSA 1991, s 8(6).

7.2.8 Variations

The system has always endeavoured to make allowance for situations where the strict application of the rules would lead to unfairness to either parent. Variation rules were introduced under the new rules to address this. The system of variations is the means by which an element of discretion can be exercised to take account of a large range of factors, from the costs of contact to a lifestyle of the NRP inconsistent with his declared income; see CSA 1991, ss 28A–28G. A variation may only be made if it would be 'just and equitable'. In coming to this decision, the CSA is to have regard to the welfare of all children affected and other factors laid out in the CSA 1991, Sch 4B and the Child Support (Variations) Modification of Statutory Provisions Regulations 2000. The Regulations also set out factors that must not be taken into account.

7.2.9 Interim/default maintenance decisions

Where the CSA is required to make a maintenance calculation and does not have sufficient material to enable it to do so, it may impose a 'default' maintenance decision. This requires the NRP to pay a fixed rate, currently £30 for one qualifying child, £40 for two qualifying children and £50 where there are three or more qualifying children.

7.2.10 Appeals

Where a parent is aggrieved by a decision of the Secretary of State, the first step is an application for 'revision'. If this fails and where the right of appeal exists, the parent may apply to the First Tier Tribunal. The next stage, if the right of appeal exists, is to the Upper Tribunal. There may be an appeal from the Upper Tribunal, but only on a point of law, to the Court of Appeal. Judicial review of the Secretary of State's decision may be possible in some cases. A number of cases have made it clear that the CSA, as an independent agency, is outside the court system and there can be no appeal to a court on the substance of the agency's decision (*Farley v SSW&P* [2006] 1WLR HL; *Secretary of State for Social Security v Shotton* [1996] 2 FLR 241).

7.3 The powers of the court

7.3.1 Where the court retains exclusive jurisdiction

The court retains the power to order financial provision for children where the CSA has no jurisdiction:

(a) Where the parents are still living in the same house.

(b) Where one of the parents is not habitually resident in the UK. However, CSA 1991, s 44(2A) provides that a Reciprocal Enforcement Maintenance Order (REMO) could be sought. A list of the countries which have signed up to the REMO agreement can be found on the CSA website.

(c) If the child is not a qualifying child but is, for example, a stepchild.

(d) If the child is aged 17–19 but not in full-time education.

(e) If the order is for a lump sum or property adjustment rather than maintenance (see **7.5** below). Note, however, that in *Phillips v Pearce* [1996] 2 FLR 230, Johnson J made it clear that the court must not award a lump sum as a form of capitalised maintenance when the matter is within the jurisdiction of the CSA.

7.3.2 Where the court has jurisdiction in addition to the Commission

The court has power to make orders under Sch 1 CA 1989 under the MCA 1973 in three cases where a CSA calculation has been made:

(a) If the maximum amount payable under the CSA formula is reached ('topping up'): s 8(6) CSA 1991. Currently, this is reached where the NRP earns more than £2,000 net per week.

(b) For educational expenses—used for the payment of school fees, for example: CSA 1991, s 8(7).

(c) In respect of a disabled or blind child: CSA 1991, s 8(8).

For a most helpful article on how to maximise the chances of applying for a top up order, see Sharon Mahmood and Catherine Hallam's article 'Schedule 1 and the CSA: Getting into the Top Up Zone' [2011] *Fam Law* 266 (March 2011). The article considers how to marshal arguments in relation to assets in excess of £65,000, income not previously taken into account and a lifestyle inconsistent with the declared income of the NRP.

7.3.3 Contracting out of the CSA

The court retains the power to make a maintenance order in the terms of a written agreement reached between the parents for child support: s 8(5). This could be an order by consent, but need not be, provided the terms of the written agreement are embodied 'in all material respects' in the order. The court will have power to vary such an order on the making of an application to do so: s 8(3A)(a). Another option, if parents wish to give the court jurisdiction but cannot agree as to amount, is to agree a nominal order at the outset and then allow the court to vary the level as it thinks fit. However, once 12 months have elapsed from the making of an order under s 8(5), either parent may apply to the Commission for a maintenance calculation and the order will cease to have effect on the assessment being made. In order to give the s 8(5) order the best chances of remaining effective, therefore, the court will consider the likely amount of any CSA maintenance calculation, see *E v C* [1996] 1 FLR 472.

The court also retains jurisdiction in relation to an order for child maintenance made before 3 March 2003.

7.4 The 2008 Act and the future of child support

As set out above, the Commission was established by this statute, but the CSA continues to make the calculations and recover child support. The 2008 Act provides a third regime (the 2008 regime) with a new set of formulae for making the maintenance calculation. Much of the 2008 Act, including the 2008 regime, has not yet been brought into force. Transfer of old and new rules cases to the new third regime is expected to begin in 2012 and be completed by 2015.

Key features of the 2008 regime include:

- use of gross rather than net income for assessment basis;
- a change to the percentage rates to be used for calculation. For gross incomes of £200 or more per week up to £800 pw basic rates will be 12 per cent, 16 per cent or 19 per cent for one, two or three children respectively. In excess of £800 the percentages are 9 per cent, 12 per cent and 15 per cent respectively. Gross weekly income in excess of £3,000 will be disregarded;
- a reduced rate for gross incomes between £100 and £200 per week;
- a flat rate of £7 per week for gross income under £100 per week;
- nil rate on similar terms as the new rules (ie, the 2000 regime: see **7.2.4.4**)
- awards fixed for yearly terms with restriction on applications for variation; and
- more effective enforcement procedures including curfews and passport confiscation.

Despite significant criticisms of the operation and effectiveness of the whole child support system, there does appear to be some evidence that changes already brought into effect by the 2008 Act have had some beneficial effects, in particular in relation to enforcement. The Commission appears to be having some success in recovering arrears owed, by using its powers under CSA 1991, s 32L, introduced by s 24 of the 2008 Act. These powers enable an application to be made to court to restrain or set aside a disposal of assests made for the intention of avoiding the payment of child support: see the Newsline section for [2010] Fam Law. Further information on the Commission's own claims to the improvements effected are summarised at page 5 of the 2010/2011 issue of *At a Glance*. For example, it is suggested that the amount of maintenance collected or arranged through the statutory scheme has increased by 39 per cent to £1.132 billion and that the number of NRPs who pay maintenance has increased from 63 per cent to 71 per cent in the last four years.

The strong focus on parental agreement for child support in the Response to the Green Paper, the suggestion that some decisions may await the final report of the Family Justice Review and the lack of draft regulations may all serve to put a question mark over the anticipated timetable for the introduction of the 2008 regime, and the transfer to it of cases under the old and new rules.

7.5 Applications under the CA 1989, Sch 1

Where a PWC seeks provision for a child or children from the other parent to whom he or she is not married, the appropriate statutory provision is the CA 1989, s 15 and Sch 1. A person over the age of 18 whose parents are living separately may also in certain circumstances make an application for an order on his or her own behalf (CA 1989, Sch 1, para 2(a) and (b)).

Orders under the CA 1989, Sch 1 continue in force until the child's seventeenth birthday unless the court thinks it right to specify a date not beyond the child's eighteenth birthday. Orders may be extended beyond the eighteenth birthday if the child is a student or there are special circumstances. These special circumstances are not set out in the statute but might include, for example, disablement.

The language of the Schedule echoes that of the MCA 1973, s 23 and the orders that can be made are as follows:

- periodical payments;
- secured periodical payments;
- lump sum orders;
- settlements;
- transfer of property orders;
- interim periodical payment orders; and
- orders altering a maintenance agreement.

Such orders may be sought in the county court or the Family Proceedings Court (FPC), although the FPC is restricted to making orders for periodical payments, interim periodical payments and lump sum orders to the level of £1,000.

Orders under the CA 1989, Sch 1 may direct payment to the child itself or to the applicant 'for the benefit of the child'. Thus, it is possible for the court to order the transfer of a tenancy into the sole name of a parent for the benefit of a child (see *K v K (Minors: Property Transfer)* [1992] 2 FLR 22).

The court's jurisdiction to make orders for periodical payments under Sch 1 is set out at **7.3** above. Where, as in many cases, however, the court has no jurisdiction to make periodical payments for the benefit of the child as a result of the CSA 1991, s 8(3), lump sum orders may still be awarded. This is the main use of Sch 1 in practice for the children of unmarried parents, where the PWC (usually the mother) is unable to apply for provision in her own right. For the interplay of Sch 1 applications and prenuptial agreements, see *K v K (Ancillary Relief: Pre-nuptial Agreement)* [2003] 1 FLR 120. For an article on the development of Sch 1 proceedings since 2003, see 'Schedule 1 to the Children Act 1989: Consider the Mother's Future' [2007] *Family Law*, March.

7.5.1 Definitions

In contrast to the CSA 1991, under CA 1989, Sch 1 a 'parent' includes any party to a marriage in relation to whom the child concerned is a child of the family. Unmarried fathers are included whether or not they have parental responsibility for the child concerned. However, for the purposes of the CA 1989, Sch 1, an unmarried cohabitee who is not the father or mother of the child is not a parent however long he or she has lived with the child. If the parties marry, the parent will become a step-parent and thus a 'parent' for the purpose of Sch 1.

7.5.2 Procedure

The procedure for making an application under the CA 1989, Sch 1 is now the same as under the MCA 1973; Part 9 of the FPR 2010 applies. An application under the CA 1989 may be free-standing or may be attached to an application for any other order under the Act. It is also possible for the court to make a Sch 1 order of its own motion whenever it makes or discharges a residence order (CA 1989, Sch 1, para 1(6)). This is, however, somewhat unusual.

7.5.3 Statutory criteria

Once again, the language of the CA 1989, Sch 1 echoes that of the MCA 1973. The relevant paragraph is set out below:

4 Matters to which court is to have regard in making orders for financial relief

(1) In deciding whether to exercise its powers under paragraph 1 or 2, and if so in what manner, the court shall have regard to all the circumstances including—

(a) the income, earning capacity, property and other financial resources which each person mentioned in sub-paragraph (4) has or is likely to have in the foreseeable future;

(b) the financial needs, obligations and responsibilities which each person mentioned in sub-paragraph (4) has or is likely to have in the foreseeable future;

(c) the financial needs of the child;

(d) the income, earning capacity (if any), property and other financial resources of the child;

(e) any physical or mental disability of the child;

(f) the manner in which the child was being or was expected to be educated or trained.

(2) In deciding whether to exercise its powers under paragraph 1 against a person who is not the mother or father of the child, and if so in what manner, the court shall in addition have regard to—

(a) whether that person has assumed responsibility for the maintenance of the child and, if so, the extent to which and basis on which he assumed that responsibility and the length of the period during which he met that responsibility;

(b) whether he did so knowing that the child was not his child;

(c) the liability of any other person to maintain the child.

(3) Where the court makes an order under paragraph 1 against a person who is not the father of the child, it shall record in the order that the order is made on the basis that the person against whom the order is made is not the child's father.

(4) The persons mentioned in sub-paragraph (1) are—

(a) in relation to a decision whether to exercise its powers under paragraph 1, any parent of the child;

(b) in relation to a decision whether to exercise its powers under paragraph 2, the mother and father of the child;

(c) the applicant for the order;

(d) any other person in whose favour the court proposes to make the order.

The child's welfare, while relevant, is not required to be the court's paramount concern as the court is not determining a question with respect to the 'upbringing' of the child

(CA 1989, s 1). Nor does the 'no order' principle (CA 1989 s 1(5)) apply in such an application (*K v H (Child Maintenance*) [1993] 2 FLR 61).

It is in the bigger-money cases, where the 'top up' criteria is readily met, that the court has been able to exercise the fullest range of powers. The leading case is still *Re P (Child: Financial Provision)* [2003] 2 FLR 865, where the Court of Appeal gave guidance on the exercise of the discretion, emphasising that the child's welfare would in most cases be a constant influence on the discretionary outcome. It established that, where resources permit, the parent with care will require suitable accommodation during the child's minority and carer's allowance as part of the periodical payments order. There is a useful summary of the principles to be distilled from this case at para 99A of Duckworth. Depending on the financial circumstances of the parents, there is certainly scope to argue that these principles apply in other cases.

7.6 Further reading

For detailed consideration on guidance and practice in relation to Sch 1 applications, see *Applications made under Schedule 1 to the Children Act 1989* by a team of contributors from 1 Garden Court, Family Law Chambers (Jordans, 2010).

Children—private law

8.1 Introduction

The law relating to children in both private law and public law situations (see **Chapters 9 and 10**) can mainly be found in the Children Act 1989 (CA 1989), as amended by the Adoption and Children Act 2002 (ACA 2002) and the Children and Adoption Act 2006 (CAA 2006). Part 12 of the Family Procedure Rules 2010 (FPR 2010) contains the main rules concerned with applications in relation to children.

These rules should be read subject to the procedural guidance introduced from July 2005 in the Private Law Programme, which was subsequently revised and can now be found in Practice Direction (PD) 12B of the FPR 2010. The aim is to speed up proceedings, achieve greater resolution by consent and give courts greater case management responsibility: see **8.6.1**. Forms must be used in all applications to issue proceedings—PD 5A lists the forms to be used in family proceedings after 6 April 2011. Under the FPR 2010, the court has a duty to consider whether alternative dispute resolution (ADR) is appropriate (Part 3). The pre-action protocol for mediation applies to private law children proceedings (except those relating to enforcement of an order or emergency proceedings (see **Chapter 11**).

Much of the philosophy underpinning the legislation is of non-intervention—a belief that, in the main, parents know best what is good for their children and will act in their children's best interests. It also provides for a unified structure of both law and jurisdiction, with concurrent jurisdiction and cases capable of being transferred from one court to another.

The Handbook of Best Practice in Children Act Cases (HMSO, June 1997) contains detailed guidance from the Children Act Advisory Committee.

The Human Rights Act 1998 (HRA 1998) also has an impact in child cases as it incorporates the European Convention on Human Rights directly into UK law. There are a number of areas where the HRA 1998 is relevant in child cases, in particular Art 6, which provides the right to a fair trial, and Art 8, which provides the right to respect for family life. The HRA 1998 imposes obligations on the state, both negative and positive, and applies to public authorities. The individual is, therefore, able either to bring proceedings directly against public authorities under the HRA 1998 or to rely on Convention rights in any legal proceedings. The most obvious areas in which the HRA 1998 applies in child cases relate to unmarried fathers, same-sex couples, care plans, the enforcement of contact orders (COs), abduction and the disclosure of information (see *TP and KM v United Kingdom*, Application No 28945/95 [2001] 2 FLR 549). Where a local authority fails to act to protect children from abuse, then Art 3 (inhuman and degrading treatment) can be used (see *Z and Others v United Kingdom*, Application No 29392/95 [2001] 2

FLR 612, where pecuniary damages were awarded for this breach under Art 13). A breach of Art 8 has been found where, following the granting of a care order, the local authority abandoned the care plan without informing the mother (*Re C* (*Breach of Human Rights; Damages*) [2007] 1 FLR 1957).

8.1.1 'Old terminology'

Old terminology used prior to the CA 1989 such as 'custody' may still be used (particularly by litigants-in-person). It is important to have some familiarity with the former law if you practise in this area.

On divorce or separation, a parent could apply for an order for 'custody' of a child, which if awarded would give the person with custody the right to take most major decisions 'with regard' to the child. Custody was normally awarded to one parent alone and might therefore be strongly contested, though a joint order could be made if it was thought there would be cooperation.

A separate order for 'care and control' could be made for the day-to-day care of the child as distinct from the power to take decisions about the child. There might therefore be an order for joint custody of a child with care and control to one parent.

An order could also be made for 'access', which was roughly equivalent to the current CO.

8.2 Parental responsibility (PR)

This concept makes clear that being a parent creates responsibilities rather than rights, and hence that these responsibilities exist whatever the state of the parents' relationship with each other. It emphasises the view that each will retain a (shared) continuing responsibility for the children. Where more than one person has PR for a child, each of them is given power to act alone (CA 1989, s 2(7)) unless each person with PR is by law required to give his or her consent, for example, to adoption. PR can be shared by a range of people and with a local authority where the child is in care, and an order can be made even though the child was neither born nor is resident in the UK.

8.2.1 What does PR mean?

The concept of PR replaced that of custody while incorporating into it much of the common law meaning of custody. The CA 1989, s 3(1) states that PR encompasses 'all the rights, duties, powers, responsibilities and authority which by law a parent of a child has in relation to the child and his property'. At common law the meaning of custody has never been absolutely clear with most writers relying on the definition of it by Sachs LJ in *Hewer v Bryant* [1970] 1 QB 357, at p 373:

'custody' … embraces … a 'bundle of powers' … These include power to control education, the choice of religion, and the administration of the infant's property. They include entitlement to veto the issue of a passport and to withhold consent to marriage. They include, also, both the personal power physically to control the infant until the years of discretion and the right … to apply to the courts to exercise the powers of the Crown as *parens patriae*.

In practice PR impacts on such matters as deciding the child's name, religion, consenting to medical treatment, using corporal punishment and giving consent to marriage. The 'bundle of powers' has often been described as a dwindling one because the more mature the child is, the more difficult it is for a parent to justify exercising total power over him or her. A particular example of this can be seen in the discussion surrounding the power to control the medical treatment of a child (see *Gillick v West Norfolk & Wisbech Area Health Authority* [1986] AC 112).

The main addition is to make clear that there are responsibilities which automatically follow parenthood. The Children (Scotland) Act 1995 defines PR and includes matters such as safeguarding and promoting the child's health, development and welfare, giving direction and guidance, the maintenance of personal relations and direct personal contact, and the right to live with the child (see s 1(1)).

8.2.2 Who has PR?

(a) **Mother**: always has **PR**—CA 1989, s 2 (ACA 2002).

(b) **Father**: if married to the mother at the time of the child's birth, he will automatically acquire **PR**—CA 1989, s 2(1).

Previously, fathers not married to the mother at the time of the child's birth did not have **PR** unless the following positive steps were taken:

(i)   Entering into a PR agreement with the mother

An agreement must comply with the Parental Responsibility Regulations 1991 (SI 1991/1478), reg 2 (as amended by SI 1994/3157). Agreements must be signed, there must be proof of identity of the parents and the child; the agreement must then be registered in the Principal Registry of the Family Division. It should be noted that an agreement can be terminated by order of the court either on application by a person with PR or, with leave, by a child with sufficient understanding (CA 1989, s 4(3) and (4), see *Re A* [1994] 2 FCR 709, CA).

(ii)   Court order

If the mother does not consent to the father obtaining PR, it is open to the father to apply to court.

The European Convention on Human Rights has been used by unmarried fathers to determine their rights. In *X, Y and Z v UK* [1995] 2 FLR 892 and *Keegan v Ireland* (1994) 18 EHRR 342 the court was asked to consider the meaning of family life (Art 8) in relation to unmarried fathers and concluded that a number of factors would be relevant as to whether Art 8 was engaged, including whether the couple had lived together, the length of the relationship and whether they had demonstrated their commitment to each other by having children.

The court considers the child's welfare as the paramount consideration (*Re G (A Minor) (Parental Responsibility Order)* [1994] 1 FLR 504), and the making of the order must be better for the child than making no order at all. Factors that will be taken into account include the degree of commitment shown to the child, the degree of attachment that exists and the reasons for applying (see *Re H (No 3)* [1991] Fam 151).

(iii)   Obtaining a residence order (RO)

Section 12(1) of the CA 1989 directs the court to make a PR order under s 4 if the father obtains an RO and does not have PR.

(iv)   Marrying the child's mother

(v)   Being appointed a guardian

(Appointment in this manner can relate to another person other than the father too.)

(vi) Adopting the child

The unmarried father never automatically acquired PR.

Section 4 of the CA 1989 was amended by ACA 2002, s 111 in December 2003, which altered the unsatisfactory position in relation to unmarried fathers and PR.

The position now is that an unmarried father can obtain PR from 1 December 2003 when his name is included on the child's birth certificate (CA 1989, s 4(1)(a)).

In relation to a birth registration which does not mention the father's name the birth can be reregistered—see Births and Deaths Registration Act 1953, s 10A.

If reregistering the birth is not an option, the unmarried father can attempt to obtain PR by any of the routes detailed in (i)–(vi).

(c) Step-parent

They will be able to use the procedure open to a father by applying for a court order or entering into an agreement with the mother to share responsibility (ACA, s 112 amending CA 1989, s 4).

If an RO is made in favour of a step-parent then he will have PR for the duration of the RO. There are a number of restrictions to the exercise of a step-parent's PR—see CA 1989, s 12(2)–(4).

There are other parties who may apply for an RO (see **8.3.4**)—if they are successful in such an application they will acquire PR, subject to the same restrictions as a step-parent.

(d) Local authority

The local authority obtain PR when an interim care order, a full care order or an emergency protection order is made (see **9.8.3.1**).

(e) Adoption

When a child is placed for adoption, PR vests in the adoption agency and the prospective adopters (ACA 2002, s 25(2) and (3)). When the child is placed for adoption, the adoption agency may restrict the PR of any parent or guardian (ACA 2002, s 25(4)). When the adoption order is made, the PR of all others save for the adopter or the adopters is extinguished (**ACA** 2002, s 46(2)).

8.2.3 Transferring PR

A person who has PR may not transfer responsibility to another. However, he or she can arrange for the responsibility to be met by some other person acting on his or her behalf (including someone who has PR for that child) while remaining responsible for the failure by that delegate to act (CA 1989, s 2(9)–(11)).

8.3 Section 8 orders

8.3.1 Types of s 8 order

Section 8 of the CA 1989 empowers the court to make, vary or discharge the following orders.

8.3.1.1   Contact order (CO)

This is an order which imposes on the person with whom the child lives a legal obligation to allow the child to have direct contact with the person named in the CO. This may include, for example, a visit, stays, including overnight, long or short visits and holidays, telephone calls and contact at contact centres. Contact can, however, be restricted to indirect contact, for example, letters, birthday or Christmas cards, as in *Re P (Contact: Indirect Contact)* [1999] 2 FLR 893 where a father who had just served a long prison sentence was limited to sending cards to the child.

Supervised contact is used where a child has suffered or is at risk of suffering harm during contact where a third party provides one-to-one supervision to ensure that nothing untoward occurs. It is only justified if the person presents a risk to the child. A local authority cannot be directed to supervise contact and finding funding for supervised contact can prove problematic. Supported contact where contact takes place in a confined area alongside other children having contact with people monitoring the contact is less intrusive and is preferred by the courts to supervision.

Orders can be made for 'no contact' and this will mean that contact is prohibited. COs are directed against the person with whom the child is living, and so, when the court is seeking to prevent that person allowing contact with someone unsuitable, a no contact order will be appropriate. However, it may be more effective to seek an order prohibiting contact when this is directed to the person who is not to have contact, as it can then be enforced against that person.

When making a CO, the court may also make a contact activity direction in connection with the CO (CA 1989, s 11A). Such a direction will require an individual who is party to the proceedings to take part in an activity that promotes contact with the child concerned. The direction should specify the activity and the person providing the activity. This is a useful tool when there is a particularly hostile relationship between the resident and non-resident parents.

There is a presumption of contact between parents and their children (see **8.4**). The same presumption does not apply as between children and their step-parents or grandparents. A CO made in favour of a parent no longer living with his or her spouse and children will cease to have effect if the parents resume cohabitation for a continuous period exceeding six months (CA 1989, s 11(6)). Orders can be made without notice or by consent, on written evidence or after an oral hearing, and in favour of any person, including grandparents and siblings.

A CO may contain directions about how it is to be carried out or may impose certain conditions to be complied with by any person to whom the conditions are expressed to apply: for example, that the child should not be exposed to a particular religious group, that contact be supervised by another person, that contact must be at a particular location, etc. Further conditions may be imposed concerning the duration of the order or concerning the duration of express provisions of the order. The court may also make any incidental, supplemental or consequential directions as it sees fit (CA 1989, s 11(7)) or it may order that a particular activity is undertaken alongside a CO (CA 1989, s 11A as amended by CAA 2006, s 1).

Where matters have to be investigated, eg, allegations of violence and/or inquiry by the Children and Family Court Advisory and Support Service (Cafcass—see **8.4.1**), the outcome of which may effect whether a CO should be made or the type of contact that should be ordered, an interim CO may be appropriate pending a final hearing. This is always a short-term position. In cases where allegations of domestic violence are made regard must be had to the case of *Re L (Contact; Domestic Violence)* [2000] 2 FLR 334. In particular it is important to have regard to the impact of domestic violence on children and how this in turn may require the imposition of safeguards or conditions around contact. Where allegations of violence are made a fact-finding hearing should be listed at the earliest possible date to deal with this issue. The best practice in such cases was detailed in *Re A (Contact; Risk of Violence)* [2005] EWHC 851. This was supplemented by a PD issued by the President of the Family Division (*Practice Direction Residence and Contact Orders: Domestic Violence* [2008] 2 FLR 103) which stated that where domestic violence was raised as an issue, the court must identify at the earliest opportunity the factual and welfare issues involved. This PD was reissued on 14 January 2009 to confirm that a fact-finding hearing is part of the process of trying a case and not a separate exercise; where a case is then adjourned, it remains part-heard—see PD 12J of the FPR 2010 (also reported at [2009] 2 FLR 1400). The PD also emphasises that it is a matter of discretion for the judge as to whether or not to have a fact-finding hearing. This was underlined by the Court of Appeal in *Re C (Domestic Violence: Fact Finding)* [2010] 1 FLR 1728. In May 2010 the President of the Family Division issued further guidance, *President's Guidance in relation to Split Hearings* [2010] 2 FLR 1897, which stresses that fact-finding hearings should only be ordered if the court takes the view that the case *cannot* be decided without one—see **10.6.3**.

The courts decide issues relating to contact by having regard to the child's welfare as the paramount determinant and may decide to deny contact, for example, where there has been violence towards the mother, although the presumption in favour of contact between children and their parents will generally prevail (see **8.4**).

8.3.1.2   Residence order (RO)

This form of order specifies with whom the child is to live and nothing more, each parent with PR retaining the right to act independently. Orders can be made without notice in exceptional circumstances but an 'on notice' hearing will be listed shortly thereafter to allow both parties to make representations on the issue.

If an RO is made in favour of a father who is not married to the mother of the child and does not have PR, then the residence order must also give PR to that father (CA 1989, s 12(1)). If a residence order is made in favour of a person without PR, then that person will be given that responsibility (excluding the power to consent to adoption or free for adoption or appoint a guardian) for the duration of the order (CA 1989, s 12(2) and (3)). An RO gives no power to any person to change the child's surname, or to arrange for the child's removal from the jurisdiction for more than one month without the consent of all persons with PR or the leave of the court (although the court can include in the order general or specific leave to remove the child from the jurisdiction) (CA 1989, s 13). In *Re K (Minor) (Residence Order)* [1999] 1 FLR 583, on an application by the mother for leave to remove the child from the jurisdiction the court found the mother to be untrustworthy (having refused to allow the father to visit his child at an earlier stage). There was therefore concern that the father would not be allowed to see his child and so it was appropriate to refuse the application and also to deny the mother's claim for residence although she was granted contact.

In *Payne v Payne* [2001] 2 WLR 1827, CA, the court held that, in relocation cases, the rights of all the parties have to be balanced under Art 8 of the European Convention on Human Rights and any interference has to be both justified and proportionate. However, the Convention did not affect the requirement to balance the factors influencing the operation of the paramountcy of the welfare principle. In such a case, the courts have to balance the reasonable proposals and motivation of the parent wishing to relocate, the effects on the child of seriously interfering with the life of a resident parent and the denial of contact to the absent parent. The principles stated in *Payne v Payne* have been reaffirmed in another Court of Appeal decision, *Re W (Children) (Relocation: Permission)* [2011] EWCA Civ 345. But see also the Court of Appeal decision in *Re K (Children)* [2011] EWCA Civ 793 where the Court of Appeal held that the principles stated in *Payne v Payne* were only guidance to be applied or distinguished depending on the circumstances—the judge should still apply the statutory checklist in s 1(3) to exercise his discretion and all the facts of the case should be considered. The key distinguishing circumstance in *Re K* was that the parents were looking after their children under shared care arrangements; the approach in *Payne* did not apply. However, the considerations relevant to an application for temporary removal are different. The more temporary the removal from the jurisdiction, the less regard should be paid to the principles laid out in *Payne v Payne*. See *Re A (Temporary Removal from Jurisdiction)* [2004] EWCA Civ 1587, where the CA held that weight had to be attached to the value to mother and child of a two-year move to South Africa for future career and development.

Interim ROs which last for a limited period are possible but should be strictly limited in time to avoid delay. As stated above, applications can be made without notice, although only exceptionally (*Re G* [1993] 1 FLR 910), for example, where a child has been snatched or is in some other immediate danger. In order to challenge an order made without notice, it is necessary to apply for discharge or variation on notice although usually a return hearing will also be listed soon after the 'without' notice hearing.

An RO may be granted in favour of two or more persons who do not live together (known as a 'shared residence order'). In this instance, the order may specify the periods in which the child is to reside at the different homes. The long held view was that shared residence orders were 'exceptional'. The Court of Appeal in *A v A (Minors) (Shared Residence Orders)* [1994] 1 FLR 669 moved away from this by indicating that they were still 'unusual' but must incur a positive benefit to the child. Dame Butler-Sloss in *D v D (Shared Residence Order)* [2001] 1 FLR 495 endorsed a more relaxed approach to making such orders if the best interests of the child dictated the necessity. In *Re C (A Child) (Shared Residence Order)* [2006] EWCA Civ 235, the Court of Appeal made it clear that such orders are no longer to be considered exceptional and are in fact appropriate if they reflect the reality of the child's circumstances. It is not necessary for the time to be divided equally between both parents in order for there to be a shared residence order. This more relaxed approach in relation to shared residence orders was further endorsed by the President of the Family Division in *Re A (A Child: Joint Residence/Parental Responsibility)* [2008] EWCA Civ 867 where the Court of Appeal stated that any lingering idea that a shared residence order was apt only where the children alternated between the two homes evenly was erroneous. If the home offered by each parent was of equal status and importance to a child, an order for shared residence could be valuable. A useful summary of the authorities on shared residence was provided by Wilson LJ in *Re W (Shared Residence Order)* [2009] 2 FLR 436.

A shared residence order may be made in favour of a step-parent or the partner of a parent who is not biologically related to the child, after the parties have separated, for example in *Re G (Children) (Residence; Same-sex Partner)* [2006] UKHL 43. The shared residence order may be made to include a parent's current partner in the order (as well as mother and father) to safeguard the situation should one parent die (see *T v T (Shared Residence)* [2010] EWCA Civ 1366).

8.3.1.3 Prohibited steps order (PSO)

This form of order prevents a parent with PR or a third party from taking any step which is specified in the order without the prior consent of the court, for example, taking the child out of the jurisdiction or changing the child's surname. A number of cases have considered the vexed question of changing children's surnames. In *Re PC (Change of*

Surname) [1997] 2 FLR 730 it was held that where both parents have PR, either may change the child's surname provided the other consents, although such consent need not be in writing. In *Dawson v Wearmouth* [1997] 2 FLR 629 the court held that an unmarried father could apply to have the child's surname changed to his own but the court had discretion to decide whether to grant the application which was of major significance to the welfare of the child. Here, the mother's surname (that of her former husband and other children) was ordered to be retained by the child. This issue was revisited in *Re W, Re A, Re B* (*Change of Name*) [1999] 2 FLR 930 where the court provided a list of factors the court will consider when hearing such an application.

Where an RO or care order is in place (CA 1989, ss 13(1) and 33(7)), the child's surname cannot be changed without the written consent of every person having PR, or the leave of the court. See *Practice Direction* (*Child: Change of Surname*) [1995] 1 FLR 458. Leave will only be granted in exceptional circumstances (*Re B* (*Change of Surname*) [1996] 1 FLR 791). See also *Re C* (*Minors*) (*Change of Surname*) The Times, 8 December 1997 and *Re C* (*A Minor*) (*Change of Surname*) The Times, 2 February 1998. Where there is no RO, an application can be made under CA 1989, s 8 either for a PSO to prevent the surname being changed or for a specific issue order to allow the surname to be changed.

Applications made without notice are possible in accordance with r 12.16 of the FPR 2010, although permission is required in the magistrates' court. Where a s 8 order is made without notice, the applicant must serve a copy of the order and the application on each respondent within 48 hours (r 12.16(4)–(5)). See *Nottingham CC v P* [1994] Fam 18. Here, the local authority sought an *ex parte* order to oust the father from the family home where there was evidence of the possible sexual abuse of a daughter. The court found that the appropriate procedure here would have been through the public law provisions of the CA 1989. Otherwise, the effect of the application, if granted, would have been a 'no contact order' when the authority had no power to apply for a CO (see CA 1989, s 9(2)). In *Re H* [1995] 1 FLR 638 a PSO was made to prevent contact between the children and the mother's former cohabitant because of the possible risk to the children. To have made a 'no contact order' would effectively have put the mother under an obligation to prevent contact; the PSO was therefore the more sensible course.

8.3.1.4 Specific issue order (SIO)

This form of order directs the way in which a disagreement about a specific issue which has arisen or may arise in respect of any aspect of PR should be resolved. For example, where those with PR do not agree on the form of education or religious upbringing which the child should have, the matter can be referred to the court for it to make an SIO. Applications made without notice are possible, with permission required in magistrates' courts. In *Camden LBC v R* [1993] 2 FLR 757, an application for the court to authorise the use of blood products on a child whose parents were Jehovah's Witnesses was successful. It was considered an appropriate use of the court's powers under the CA 1989, s 8, in preference to wardship, since there was no wider issue concerning the future welfare of the child. A contested issue relating to emergency medical treatment in *Re O* [1993] 2 FLR 149 was thought better dealt with under the wardship jurisdiction, although an application to allow a sterilisation operation to be carried out on a mentally retarded girl could be authorised (see *Re HG* [1993] 1 FLR 587). More recently in *Re S* (*Specific Issue Order: Religion: Circumcision*) [2004] EWHC 1282 (Fam) the court rejected the application from a Muslim mother who sought permission for both children to become practising members of the Islamic faith and for the 8-year-old boy to be circumcised. The Hindu father sought to promote the children's cultural heritage and the children's right to choose, when old enough, their religious preference.

The court may not make a PSO or SIO if the result envisaged could be obtained by making an RO or CO (CA 1989, s 9(5)). The court may not make a PSO or SIO which in effect places a child in the care or under the supervision of a local authority, or which requires the child to be accommodated by or on behalf of the local authority, or confers power on a local authority to determine any issue on parental responsibility which has arisen or may arise.

A s 8 order may contain directions about how it is to be carried out, impose conditions on parents or other persons and specify when it is to come into effect and how long it is to last for, and any other provisions which the court thinks fit (CA 1989, s 11(7)) (see *Re M*, The Times, 10 November 1993). In *Re E (Residence: Imposition of Conditions)* [1997] 2 FLR 638 a mother successfully appealed against the imposition of a condition requiring her to live at a specific address, the court taking the view that the issue of location of residence should have been determined through cross-applications for residence and not through the imposition of conditions aimed at interfering with the ordinary rights of the resident parent. The imposition of conditions on an RO restricting the primary carer's right to choose his or her place of residence should be seen as exceptional (see *Re B (A Child) (Prohibited Steps Order)* [2008] 1 FLR 613) even when there is a shared residence order in place (see *Re T (A Child)* [2009] EWCA Civ 20, [2009] 1 FLR 1157).

A s 8 order will be discharged by a care order (CA 1989, s 91(2)). Orders under s 8 will end after the child has reached the age of 16 unless the court is satisfied that the circumstances of the case are exceptional (CA 1989, s 9(6)). It is also possible for orders to specify a time period during which it shall apply.

8.3.2 Situations in which the court can make a s 8 order

Under CA 1989, s 10, a s 8 order with respect to a child can be made in any family proceedings in which an issue arises with respect to the welfare of the child. The application must either be made by a person entitled to apply for such an order, or where the court has granted leave, or if, in any event, the court considers that such an order should be made.

Equally, orders can be made in other proceedings on the application of a person entitled to make such an application or where the applicant has obtained the leave of the court. The application for leave is governed by the principles in the CA 1989, s 10(9).

8.3.3 What are family proceedings?

For the purpose of CA 1989, family proceedings are defined by s 8(3) and (4) of the Act. These subsections are subject to regular update as legislation evolves. Currently the definitions include: proceedings under CA 1989, Parts I (general principles), II (orders in respect of children in family proceedings) and IV (local authority support for children); proceedings under MCA 1973 (financial remedies etc); Civil Partnership Act 2004, Sch 5 and Sch 6; ACA 2002; Domestic Proceedings and Magistrates' Court Act 1978 (DPMCA 1978) (limited financial provision in the magistrates' court); Matrimonial and Family Proceedings Act 1984, Part III (financial relief after overseas divorce); Family Law Act 1996 (FLA 1996) (injunctions in domestic violence and associated issues); and the Crime and Disorder Act 1998, ss 11 and 12 (child safety orders).

8.3.4 Who can apply for a s 8 order?

Certain people can apply as of right; others require the leave of the court. Those entitled to apply for s 8 orders vary according to the nature of the order sought. For example, where a child is in the care of a local authority, the only order which the court has power to make is a residence order (CA 1989, s 9(1)). Once a child has reached the age of 16, the court has no power to make any s 8 order (except for discharge or variation) unless the circumstances are exceptional (CA 1989, s 9(6)).

Those who can apply as of right without leave are:

> Parents or guardians and persons who have an RO in respect of the child can apply for any s 8 order (CA 1989, s 10(4)). This includes the unmarried father but not former parents whose child has been adopted. Parents can apply for leave on behalf of their child where the child is too young to do so on his or her own behalf, where this would enable the child to receive public funding for representation.

> The following persons are entitled to apply for an RO or CO without the leave of the court:

> (i)   Any party to a marriage where the child is a 'child of the family' of that marriage. 'Child of the family' includes both the natural children of the parties to the marriage and step-children treated as a child of the family, excluding foster children.

> (ii) Any civil partner in a civil partnership in relation to whom the child is a child of the family.

> (iii) Any person with whom the child has been living for a period of at least three years (subject to CA 1989, s 10(10)).

> (iv) Other persons who have the consent of the person in whose favour an RO has been made, or the consent of the local authority which has the child in its care, or the consent of each person with PR can apply for an RO or CO (CA 1989, s 10(5)). Local authorities *cannot* apply for or have such orders made in their favour.

Rules of court may provide for additional persons to be entitled to make such an application; FPR 2010, r 16.14 covers a child's litigation friend.

All other parties require the permission of the court to make an application for a s 8 order.

An application is made by application notice (FPR 2010, Part 18) and a decision may be made by the court on the papers only. Where an application for permission to begin proceedings is refused, the court must, at the request of the applicant, re-list the application and fix a date for a hearing (see FPR 2010, r 18.9(2), although this does not apply to the magistrates' court—r 18.9(3)). Natural parents of an adopted child must seek leave (*Re S* The Times, 8 March 1993), as must a child (see *Re C* [1994] 1 FLR 26; *Re SC* [1994] 1 FLR 96).

Foster parents who have had the child *living with them* within the previous six months cannot apply for leave unless they have the consent of the local authority, they are related to the child or the child has lived with them for the past three years (CA 1989, s 9(3) and (4)).

8.3.5   When will the court grant leave to apply for a s 8 order?

Factors which the court is required to take particularly into account in deciding whether or not leave should be given (in relation to a person other than the child concerned) can be found in CA 1989, s 10(9). Factors include: the nature of the application, the applicant's connection with the child, the risk of harmful disruption to the child's life and, if the child is being cared for by the local authority, any plans which the authority has for the child's future and the wishes of the child's parents (see *Re A* [1992] Fam 182).

However, s 10(9) does not provide an exclusive list of the factors to be taken into account and the CA 1989, s 1(3) checklist does not apply to leave applications nor does CA 1989, s 1(1) (see *Re S (Contact: Application by Sibling)* [1998] 2 FLR 897). It has also been held that the court can have regard as to whether or not the substantive application has a chance of success (but not whether it would be bound to succeed) (see *G v Kirklees MBC* [1993] 1 FLR 805 and *C v Salford CC* [1994] 2 FLR 926). *Re J (Leave to issue Application for Residence Order)* [2003] 1 FLR 114 emphasised that the European Convention on Human Rights, Arts 6 and 8 apply to leave applications made by grandparents. *Re A* concerned an application by a former local authority foster mother for leave to apply for an RO over her former foster child. It was held that courts are required to take into account the local authority's plans for the child (see CA 1989, s 10(9)(d)(i)), which must be based on the duty to safeguard and promote the child's welfare. They should not determine the application for leave on the basis that the welfare of the child is the paramount consideration.

There is also concern that cases will involve too many parties and so where, for example, the interests of grandparents coincide absolutely with those of the parents, there is no good reason to grant them leave to be separately represented (see *Re M (Sexual Abuse: Evidence)* [1993] 1 FLR 822). However, a court may tend to look favourably on an application for leave from grandparents particularly in care proceedings. In *Re J (Leave to Issue Application for Residence Order)* [2003] 1 FLR 114, the Court of Appeal gave further guidance on the correct approach to such applications under s 10(9).

Where a child is in the care of a local authority the courts will be circumspect about granting leave when, in effect, the purpose of the application is to act purely as a review of the local authority's decisions in respect of the child (see *Re M (PSO: Application of Leave)* [1993] 1 FLR 275).

If the application for leave is made by the child who is the subject of proceedings, then the court can only grant leave if satisfied that the child has sufficient understanding to make the proposed application (CA 1989, s 10(8)). The s 10(9) guidelines do not apply to applications made by children; there has, however, been a conflict of opinion as to whether or not the welfare principle should be paramount (see *Re C* [1994] 1 FLR 26 and *Re SC* [1994] 1 FLR 96 at **8.3.4**. The latter case followed the thinking of the Court of Appeal in *Re A and W (Minors)* [1992] 1 WLR 422 that an application for leave does not involve a decision about the future upbringing of the child and therefore the child's welfare need not be the paramount consideration. This approach was adopted by the Court of Appeal in *M v Warwickshire County Council* [2008] 1 FLR 1093. The current criterion which is taken into account is therefore the likelihood of the success of the application, so as to avoid situations where the child is embarking on proceedings which are doomed to failure.

8.3.6 Section 91(14)

The court has the power to require a person who otherwise would be entitled to apply for an order without the need to obtain leave, to obtain leave for a particular application, s 91(14). See *Re R* [1998] 1 FLR 149 for an example and *C v W* [1998] 1 FCR 618 where it was said that the power was not just for hopeless or fruitless applications, but also where a parent pursues litigation unreasonably and in a manner damaging to the interests of the child.

Guidelines on when, and to what degree, such power should be exercised were laid down by the Court of Appeal in *Re P* [1999] 2 FLR 573. *Re C (A Child)* [2009] EWCA Civ 674 provides a checklist of the steps the court should undertake when faced with a s 91(14) application. The obvious conflict with the right of access to justice led the court to stress that the power should be used as the exception rather than the rule and that the section should be read in conjunction with the welfare principle outlined at **8.4**.

The power has been exercised where there have been repeated applications which have become or are becoming oppressive; and, pre-emptively, where the conduct has not yet reached that level or where there is no criticism of the applicant's conduct, but nonetheless the interests of the child require it. For example, in *Re M* (*Section 91(14) Order*) [1999] 2 FLR 553 the children were already confused, unhappy and unsettled and urgently needed to settle down and make their permanent home away from the mother, so contact needed to be put on a new footing and their mother had to come to terms with the arrangement. The court order was intended to be a long-term arrangement and a premature application by the mother would disrupt, upset and confuse the children more. However, s 91(14) orders should not be made in cases where there was substantial contact and the parents find communicating with each other difficult—see *Re W* (*Children*) (*Restriction on Applications*) [2006] All ER (D) 229. Nor should s 91(14) orders be made summarily and without the judge hearing proper submissions on the matter: see *Re A (A Child) (Contact: Section 91(14))* [2010] 2 FLR 151.

An absolute prohibition on applications falls outside s 91(14) and any such order would have to be made under the inherent jurisdiction of the court.

8.3.7   Duration of PR and s 8 orders

Agreements and guardian appointments last until the child reaches the age of 18. Section 8 orders end when the child is 16, unless the CA 1989, s 9(6) applies (ie, the circumstances are exceptional). If s 9(6) applies, the order will end when the child is 18 (CA 1989, s 91(11)).

8.3.8   Enforcement of s 8 orders

The enforcement procedure adopted depends on the type of order and its breach.

Where a person disobeys the terms of an RO, eg, refuses to return the child to the holder of an RO, there are two options available:

1. FLA 1986, s 34 empowers the court to make an order authorising an officer of the court or a police officer to take charge of a child and deliver to another.

2. An order can be sought without notice under the inherent jurisdiction of the court for the tipstaff (an enforcement officer of the Supreme Court) to find and recover a child.

Where there has been failure to comply with a CO or certain terms of an RO or injunctive relief this may amount to contempt of court, which is punishable with a fine or imprisonment. In the Family Proceedings Court (FPC) the court may impose a fine or sentence a person to up to two months in prison of its own motion for breach of a court order under s 63(3) of the Magistrates' Court Act 1980. In the county court a penal notice may be attached to an order and a subsequent breach may result in a committal to prison. Alternatively, it may be advisable to consider a PSO.

An order is not capable of enforcement unless the order is clear and precise, eg, an order providing for 'reasonable contact' would not be enforceable but an order stating that 'the child will be made available for contact every Wednesday between 6 pm and 7 pm with handover to be at the mother's home' is clearly defined and thus enforceable by attaching a penal notice.

A county court judge has jurisdiction to proceed of his or her motion with a committal order where the other party has not requested such action. Such procedure should only be used in exceptional cases and as a last resort where all other remedies have been exhausted (*Re M (A Minor) (Contact Order: Committal)* The Times 31 December 1998).

Generally, committal orders for breach of a CO or RO are thought to be orders of the last resort but imprisonment is used in exceptional cases. In *A v N (Committal: Refusal of Contact)* [1997] 1 FLR 533 a mother who had shown implacable hostility towards contact between the father and the child was committed to prison for flagrant breach of a court order. The court held that the child's welfare was a material consideration but not the paramount consideration and so, even though the child would be affected by the imprisonment of the mother, there was ultimately a limit as to what the court would endure by way of breach of its orders. The Children Act Sub-Committee of the Lord Chancellor's Advisory Board on Family considered, in a report called '*Making Contact Work*', ways in which to address the problems of implacably hostile parents, fines or imprisonment being, in their view, 'crude weapons'. See *Re D (Intractable Contact Dispute: Publicity)* [2004] EWHC 727 for Munby J's recommendations on how to resolve the problems. In *V v V (Contact: Implacable Hostility)* [2004] EWHC 1215 (Fam) the court made an RO in favour of the father when the mother had consistently failed to make the children available for contact. The court found the children had suffered emotional harm by the mother and this would continue if the children were deprived of the relationship with their father. However, in *Re L-W (Children) (Contact Order: Committal)* [2011] 1 FLR 1095 the court held that when considering whether to enforce a CO, it was not incumbent on the custodial parent to ensure that the child went on a contact visit with the other parent if the child does not wish to do so.

With effect from 1 November 2008, CA 1989, s 11 was amended by the CAA 2006 and provides for a more robust mechanism for the enforcement of COs. Under the new provisions, the court can order that a particular activity is undertaken during the period of contact (see **8.3.1.1**) and require Cafcass to monitor a person's compliance with the activity. The court can also direct Cafcass to monitor whether a person is complying with a CO and report to the court. New enforcement powers where a CO is breached include requiring the person in breach to undertake unpaid work. Financial compensation may also be ordered for losses sustained through non-compliance with a CO. All COs made or varied after 8 December 2008 must have a warning on them, setting out the consequences of not complying with an order.

For detailed consideration of the procedure on applications to commit, see **Chapter 13**.

8.4 The welfare principle and the welfare checklist

The CA 1989, s 1 states that the court should have regard to the child's welfare as the paramount consideration when determining any question relating to the child's upbringing or the administration of the child's property. The principle can also apply therefore to wardship proceedings, non-convention (that is, non-European and Hague Convention cases) child abduction cases and the exercise of the inherent jurisdiction in general. However, it does not apply in those cases described above, where the child's upbringing is not directly in issue, for example, where the application is for leave to make an application under s 8, or in restricting publications that might be harmful to a child. In proceedings brought under the ACA 2002 concerning placement orders and adoption orders the welfare of the child is, as in CA 1989 cases, the paramount consideration.

In *Re H* [1994] 2 AC 212, the court held that the welfare of the child who is the subject of proceedings should have paramountcy in the proceedings even if the parent of the child is also under 16. The welfare principle is made subject to the general non-interventionist principle that the court shall not make the order or any order *unless it considers that doing so would be better for the child than making no order at all* (CA 1989, s 1(5)). This means that the court must be assured that there is actually some benefit to the child in making the order sought.

CA 1989 provides a list of circumstances to which the court is directed to have particular regard when considering whether or not to make a s 8 order, or when deciding whether or not to make, vary or discharge a care or supervision order. These are set out in CA 1989, s 1(3) and are widely known as the welfare checklist. The circumstances include:

(a) The ascertained wishes of the child (subject to the age of the child), ie, what the child has said he or she wants to happen, if he or she is considered old enough or mature enough to reach such a decision. However, in *Re J* [1992] Fam Law 229, the court said that the fact the wishes and feelings of the child were first on the s 1 welfare checklist gave them no priority over other items which included any harm the child was suffering or at risk of suffering. The case concerned a 16-year-old anorexic girl who was in local authority care and who was refusing medical treatment.

(b) The child's physical, emotional and educational needs, ie, who can best provide for all the needs of the child. Issues such as with whom the child has a bonded relationship, the impact which an order is likely to have on the child's sense of security and the importance of maintaining the status quo are of importance here, as is knowing both parents (see *Re F (Paternity Jurisdiction)* [2008] 1 FLR 225 where the Court of Appeal confirmed that the court can, where appropriate, order a mother to inform her children of the identity of their natural father).

(c) The likely effect of any change in the circumstances (eg, if another adult is to be introduced into the child's life because one parent is to remarry or cohabit with someone new, a move to new accommodation or to a new school, etc). See *Re H* The Times, 7 September 1992.

(d) The age, sex, ethnicity, background and any other characteristics of the child which the court thinks relevant. In *Re B* [1998] 1 FLR 520, the court stated that there had been a major shift in expert opinion on the weight to be given to the ethnic background of children in residence cases, and so confirmed that two Nigerian boys could remain with their white foster mother who had cared for them since birth, which was in accordance with the boys' vehemently expressed wishes. When it comes to the care of a child of either sex, there is not a presumption existing in favour of one or other parent. The courts are keen not to endorse a gender bias when dealing with s 8 cases. You may be aware of pressure groups such as Fathers for Justice, which campaign for a change to the law as they feel that an anti-father bias exists. This is an ongoing debate—but the starting point for the courts is to make no assumptions and to consider how to deal with each case based on its own circumstances. Other issues which may be relevant here relate to bringing up a child in circumstances that could be said to be slightly unusual and hence which might potentially affect the child's welfare, for example, where a parent belongs to a religious cult group or is a Scientologist, or, where grandparents are seeking a s 8 order, their age may be a relevant consideration.

(e) Any harm which has been suffered or of which there is a risk (eg, where a child has been neglected or physically or sexually abused or it is feared that there is a risk of such abuse).

(f) The ability of the parents or other relevant people to meet the child's needs (eg, where the adult carer suffers from some disability which affects the care which he or she can offer, this will be a relevant consideration). Sexual preference such as being a lesbian will not be seen as making a mother unfit to have the future care of her child (see *C v C* [1991] 1 FLR 223).

(g) The range of powers available to the court in the proceedings (ie, whether it is right for the court to exercise its powers in a particular way).

In *Re P* [1999] 2 FLR 573, the House of Lords held that the Roman Catholic foster parents of a Down syndrome child born to orthodox Jewish parents could have an RO made in their favour with reasonable contact to the child's natural parents. The House of Lords confirmed that the benefit to the child of continuing to be brought up by the foster parents, to whom she had become greatly attached, outweighed the benefit to her in being brought up as an orthodox Jew, as she did not have the capacity to understand fully or appreciate her Jewish heritage. In effect, this case has added consideration of religious background to the checklist of matters to be taken into account when assessing the welfare principle.

A failure by the court in reaching a decision to run through the checklist may make it easier for a dissatisfied party to appeal against the decision, made on the grounds that the judge below was 'plainly wrong' (see *M v M* [1987] 2 FLR 146).

The general principle in disputed contact cases has been that the child has a basic right to know both its parents, but there are an increasing number of cases in which there have been cogent reasons why the child should be denied that opportunity. All decisions, however, must be made in accordance with the welfare checklist. In *Re D* [1993] 2 FLR 1, the cogent reason for denying access was the 'implacable hostility' to contact of both the mother and her parents with whom she and the child lived. In *Re D* (*Contact: Reasons for Refusal*) [1997] 2 FLR 314, the Court of Appeal held that implacable hostility could occur in cases where there were good reasons for that hostility as well as in cases where there were no good reasons for that hostility. In that case, there were good reasons because of the violence of the father to the mother. In *Re L* (*A Child*) (*Contact: Domestic Violence*) [2001] 2 WLR 339, it was held that, while there is no presumption against contact simply because of domestic violence, it was one factor among many which might offset the assumption in favour of contact when carrying out the balancing exercise under the welfare principle. Further, in interim contact applications, where allegations of domestic violence have yet to be adjudicated upon, the court should give particular consideration to the likelihood of harm, whether physical or emotional, if contact is granted or denied, and try to ensure that any risk to the child is minimised and the safety of the child and residential parent protected, during, before and after contact. The court further suggested that, under the European Convention on Human Rights, Art 8(2), the interests of the child must prevail where there is a serious conflict between the interests of the child and a parent. In all cases, the power to order no contact or no direct contact should be exercised sparingly.

The FLA 1996, s 11 also makes provision for the making of orders under the CA 1989 over children of the family (either those under 16 or those over that age but in respect of whom the court directs that the section should apply) where there are proceedings for divorce or separation. The concept of the welfare of the child being paramount applies, but in application of that concept the court is required to have particular regard to:

(a) The wishes of the child, having regard to its age.

(b) The conduct of the parties in relation to the upbringing of the child.

(c) The general principle that in the absence of evidence to the contrary, welfare will be best served by:
   (i) regular contact with those who have PR and with members of the family;
   (ii) maintenance of as good a relationship as possible with the parents.

(d) Any risk attributable to:
   (i) where, and the persons with whom, the child will reside;
   (ii) any other arrangements for the care and upbringing of the child.

However, FLA 1996, s 11 is not yet in force and it is not known when it will be.

8.4.1 Welfare reports

In order to help the court make an informed decision about the welfare of the child, the CA 1989, s 7 empowers the court to seek expert evidence in the form of a written or oral welfare report (or ask the local authority to arrange for such a report to be made). In the past, such a report would have been compiled by a court welfare officer. In April 2001 the three branches of the welfare services (the Official Solicitors' Department, guardians *ad litem* and court welfare officers) were merged into one body known as Cafcass. Unless prepared by a local authority officer, the new title for those compiling court welfare reports is a Cafcass officer.

The court can ask that such reports concentrate on certain specified matters or ask for a general report. The court can override legal professional privilege in proceedings and order disclosure of reports adverse to a party's interests if it is relevant to a determination (*Re R* [1993] 4 All ER 702).

Cafcass has the power to interview a child to ascertain wishes and feelings, contact the school, read social services' files and observe contact.

8.5 Rules of evidence

You should note, in particular, that the rules relating to the admissibility of hearsay evidence can be ignored by the court if it considers that any statement or evidence is relevant to any issue before the court (see Children (Admissibility of Hearsay Evidence) Order 1993, SI 1993/621). Civil courts may thus admit hearsay evidence, such as evidence of interviews conducted by psychiatrists and social workers in which children disclose physical or sexual abuse (CA 1989, s 96(3)–(5)). In civil proceedings before a juvenile court, a statement made by a child (or by a person connected with, or having control of the child) that he or she has been assaulted, neglected or ill-treated, or a statement in any report made by a children's guardian or by a local authority, is admissible in connection with any proceedings relating to the upbringing, maintenance or welfare of the child, regardless of whether or not it is also hearsay. In *Re G* [1993] 2 FLR 293, it was suggested that the fundamental rules of evidence should only be relaxed in the most exceptional circumstances amounting to a serious threat to the welfare of the children. The Act also allows civil courts to accept unsworn evidence from young children if the court deems the child capable of understanding the duty to speak the truth and is of sufficient understanding (CA 1989, s 96(2)(a) and (b)).

The CA 1989, s 98 removes the privilege against answering questions which might elicit incriminating replies in any proceedings relating to care, supervision or emergency protection. The witness is, however, protected against the criminal consequences of making a damaging admission but not in proceedings relating to COs or ROs or proceedings for perjury. The CA 1989, s 98 gives protection against statements being admissible in evidence in criminal proceedings except for the offence of perjury but it does not protect against their use in a police enquiry into the offence (see *Re EC* (*Disclosure of Material*) [1996] 2 FLR 725).

Each party must file written statements containing the major thrust of the oral evidence to be called at trial and copies of any documents which are to be relied upon, including experts' reports. See also *Re D* The Times, 11 March 1998, as to abiding by Home Office Guidance on interviewing children on video.

Copies must be served on all parties to the proceedings (or their legal representatives) including the children's guardian or Cafcass officer appointed by the court but is otherwise confidential (except that copies may be supplied to the Legal Services Commission). The timetable for compliance will be fixed at the directions hearing and the court has the general power to control the evidence to be adduced (see FPR 2010, r 22.1 and **10.6.4**). Evidence which is not served in accordance with the direction of the court may not be adduced at trial without the leave of the court (FPR 2010, r 12.19).

A witness summons can be issued against a child but only if it would not be oppressive. In *Re N* The Times, 25 March 1996, it was held that where allegations of sexual abuse are made and expert evidence is admitted as hearsay evidence in relation to a videoed interview with the child, it is for the judge alone to decide the weight to be given to the child's evidence. Here, the interview had been very pressured with leading questions being put to the child and so the father's application for contact was ordered to be reheard. See also *Re W (Children) (Family Proceedings: Evidence)* [2010] UKSC 12; [2010] 1 FLR 1485 and the discussion at **10.6.3**.

In *Re CH* [1998] 1 FLR 402, the Court of Appeal said that it was undesirable to allow significant discussion about the future care of a child to be held in the judge's private room; rather, any such discussions should be held in private in the court room so that those discussions can be recorded and a transcript made. However, see also *Re Z (Children)* [2009] 2 FLR 877 where the Court of Appeal held that the days for private consultations between the judge and counsel were over. The Court of Appeal held that such discussions could not properly survive the HRA 1998.

For procedure, see **9.7**.

8.6 Avoidance of delay

One of the major criticisms of the operation of this area of the law has been the inordinate time that it has taken for cases finally to be resolved by order of the court. Delay in reaching a final decision in these important matters can be extremely damaging to the children concerned, particularly since a child's sense of time is very different from that of an adult. Children can feel extremely insecure while waiting for a case to be resolved. In some cases, courts have been forced to give judicial authority to the *de facto* situation rather than risk the psychological damage which could result from moving the child.

8.6.1 The Private Law Programme

On 21 July 2005 Dame Butler-Sloss, then-President of the Family Division, introduced a new framework to the court process when dealing with private law cases. This has been subsequently revised and is now contained at PD 12B of the FPR 2010. The child's welfare remains the paramount concern and the court must have due regard to the over-riding objective which will enable the court to deal with a case justly, having regard to the welfare principles involved (see **1.7**).

The Revised Private Law Programme operates in the following manner:

(a) Where practicable a First Hearing Dispute Resolution Appointment (FHDRA) must take place within four weeks (and in any event no later than six weeks) of a private law application made. Before the FHDRA, Cafcass shall identify any safety issues relating to the application in order to outline these (if any exist) to the court.

(b) The parties and Cafcass officer are to attend the FHDRA. A mediator may also attend where available. The Cafcass officer will speak separately to each party before the hearing, and the court, in collaboration with the Cafcass officer, will attempt to assist the parties to resolve the issues between them. Any remaining issues will be identified and directions will be given for the further resolution of such issues, including considering whether any interim order should be made, whether a Cafcass report should be ordered, whether there should be a fact-finding hearing and timetabling for evidence.

(c) If an agreement is reached between the parties, no order can be made without the scrunity of the court. Any order should be clear as to the issues which the parties are agreed on and what remains unresolved. Consideration at the county court should also be given to transferring the case to the relevant FPC.

8.6.2   Conduct of proceedings

The CA 1989, s 11 attempts to deal with the problem of delay by requiring the court to draw up a timetable and give directions to enable it to deal with the matter without delay. Part 12 of the FPR 2010 governs the conduct of proceedings. These include providing for directions appointments in all courts, including the magistrates' courts. Attendance at the hearing is obligatory unless the court directs otherwise. Proceedings are conducted by the clerk in the magistrates' court and by the district judge in the county court. Hearings may deal with the timetabling of the case, the appointment of a children's guardian or solicitor for the child, the submission of evidence, the preparation of welfare reports, the transfer and consolidation of proceedings, the service of documents and the attendance of the child at hearings. Directions can also be given about the order of speeches and evidence. Directions can be given of the court's own motion subject to the parties having been given notice and having the opportunity to make representations. Directions hearings tend to be oral hearings and parties can be required to attend. In the magistrates' court, directions hearings are held by the clerk whose powers are very restricted.

Section 11(3) gives the court power to make what is, in effect, an interim s 8 order.

8.7   Special Guardianship Orders

8.7.1   How are Special Guardianship Orders made?

Special Guardianship Orders (SGOs) can be made under CA 1989, s 14A and were introduced by way of an amendment in the ACA 2002. An SGO appoints a person to be the child's special guardian. A special guardian has PR for a child which he can exercise to the exclusion of other holders of PR. The aim of the SGO is to provide a child who is placed with a non-parent with some permanence but it is not an adoption. They are considered to be particularly suitable to placements with family members who are not parents which may, for example, result from care proceedings. In *Re S (Adoption Order or Special Guardianship Order)* [2007] 1 FLR 819, the Court of Appeal gave detailed guidance as to the making of SGOs resulting from a child's placement with a family member. An SGO does not entitle the holder to change a child's surname or to remove the child from the UK for more than three months without the permission of either the court or other holders of PR.

8.7.2 Who may apply for an SGO?

The following persons may apply for an SGO:

- a guardian;
- a person with an RO;
- a person with whom the child has lived for three years;
- if there is an RO in place, any person who has the consent of the person with the RO;
- if the child is in local authority care, any person who has the consent of the local authority; or
- a local authority foster carer with whom the child has lived for at least one year.

8.7.3 SGOs, local authorities and notice period

No person can make an application for an SGO unless it gives at least three months' notice to the local authority. If the child is being cared for by the local authority, it must give notice to that authority. Alternatively notice is to be given to the authority in whose area the child is ordinarily resident.

8.7.4 SGOs, local authorities and procedures

A local authority on receipt of notice must carry out an assessment and complete an SGO report. A list of the factors to be considered and reported on are to be found in the Special Guardianship Regulations 2005. The Regulations allow the local authority to provide financial and other support to special guardians. In addition, a court making an SGO has an obligation to consider the arrangements for contact between the child and its parents. Section 8 COs can run alongside SGOs.

8.8 Wardship and the inherent jurisdiction

The CA 1989 has curtailed the powers of the High Court in relation to use of its inherent jurisdiction and wardship. Section 100 provides that the wardship court (be it the High Court or some other court exercising the wardship jurisdiction) does not have the power to put children into the care or under the supervision of the local authority. Equally, local authorities are no longer entitled to use the wardship jurisdiction without the prior leave of the court, and leave will only be granted if the court is satisfied that the result which the local authority wishes to achieve could not be achieved through the making of any other order and there is reasonable cause to believe that, if the inherent jurisdiction is not used, the child is likely to suffer significant harm. See *Re J* (1992) 142 NLJ 1123, where the local authority sought leave for a court order for medical treatment of a girl suffering from anorexia nervosa. The court also has power to order that such a child can be detained in hospital until treatment is complete (*Re C* [1997] 2 FLR 180 and *Devon CC v S* [1994] 1 FLR 355). Courts have recommended that applications for AIDS tests on children should be made under the wardship jurisdiction.

The CA 1989, s 100 means that, in effect, the wardship jurisdiction is being used only by those who have no other means of seeking the court's help to protect a child, for example, for some non-therapeutic surgical interventions, to protect the child from the publication of information which might be harmful to that child or where there is a threat of removal from the jurisdiction of the court.

The procedure is by originating summons with an affidavit in support, and is immediate once issued so that no step can be taken without prior court permission (see also FPR 2010, PD 12D for more details on the court's powers). The procedure is particularly useful for threatened child abduction.

In *Kelly v BBC* [2001] 2 WLR 253, it was held that the publication of information about a ward was not of itself a contempt of court. The media did not need the permission of the court to interview a ward or to publish the results of such an interview where the interview did not raise any questions about the ward's upbringing and there was a clear public interest in broadcasting the interview, which, if suppressed, would involve a derogation from the right to freedom of expression, guaranteed by Art 10 of the European Convention on Human Rights.

Likewise, the inherent jurisdiction is invoked by originating summons supported by affidavit; local authorities need the leave of the court. The power in wardship to protect children is probably greater (see *R v Central Television plc* [1994] Fam 192).

The courts will not interfere through either jurisdiction with the exercise of powers clearly vested in other bodies, eg, local authorities, the immigration authorities, or to interfere with the normal criminal process, or to order a medical practitioner to treat a child in any manner contrary to his or her clinical judgment.

Local authorities can use the jurisdictions to help to resolve issues which they have no power to deal with under their statutory powers and must seek leave to apply for the jurisdiction on the basis that they do not have the powers they seek. Section 8 will often provide the powers they need under SIOs or PSOs.

The court can only exercise its jurisdiction where there is evidence that, without it, the child would suffer significant harm—for example, the prevention or sanction of an abortion, medical treatment for an anorexic, sterilisation operations, the continuation of medical treatment and cases where there is no other way to prevent, for example, a paedophile having contact with children (see *Devon CC v S* [1994] 1 FLR 355).

8.9 International custody problems

If it is feared that an attempt may be made to remove a child improperly from the jurisdiction, the child may be made a ward of court or an injunction may be sought preventing the removal of the child.

It is possible for a parent who is worried about a possible improper removal of a child to give notice to the passport office to stop a passport being issued for the child without consent. The Home Office will try to assist in preventing the illegal removal of a child from the jurisdiction if they are informed.

Because of the problems of international child abduction, the Hague Convention on the Civil Aspects of International Child Abduction of 1980 and the European Convention on Recognition and Enforcement of Decisions Concerning Custody of Children and on the Restoration of Custody of Children of 1980 provide procedures for tracing a child and returning him, put into effect through the Child Abduction and Custody Act 1985. The aim of the Hague Convention is to protect rights of custody and access and to provide for the expeditious return of any child under the age of 16 who has wrongfully been removed or retained in another Contracting State. Under the 1985 Act, it is an offence to attempt to take a child from the UK without requisite consents. The Family Law Reform Act 1987 allows for orders made in one part of the UK to be directly enforceable in another part. If the child has been taken to a non-Convention country, there is little hope, although the UK can enter into bilateral agreements with non-Convention countries (see *Protocol (Child Abduction Cases between the UK and Pakistan)* [2003] Fam Law 199).

Where children are brought from a state which is not a signatory to either the European or Hague Conventions, then the court is free to determine the case on its merits under the wardship jurisdiction, although the court will commonly have regard to the factors specified in the Hague Convention in reaching its decision. If the child is brought from a Convention country, then the provisions of the Convention are applied instead of those of wardship, but the wardship will apply if the Convention application fails.

The Hague Convention makes exceptional provision for the court to consider the welfare of children where the needs of the child require the court to take action other than the summary return to the country of habitual residence under Art 13 (see *Re M (Abduction: Psychological Harm)* [1997] 2 FLR 690). The Supreme Court in *Re E* [2011] UKSC 27 has recently held that the summary return procedure laid out by the Hague Convention retains at its heart the best interests of the child and is compatible with Art 8 of the European Convention. The case also provides important guidance as to the approach to be taken to Art 13(b). Where the foreign jurisdiction concerned does not take account of the child's welfare in its determinations as to the arrangements for the child's future, the court is justified in refusing return to the court of habitual residence (see *Re JA (Child Abduction: Non-Convention Country)* [1998] 1 FLR 231).

Children's views can be taken into account provided they are sufficiently mature and their views can therefore overturn the presumption of return (see *Re B (Abduction: Children's Objections)* [1998] 1 FLR 667). For these purposes, separate representation is possible (see *Re S* [1997] 1 FLR 486).

For the situation in respect of unmarried fathers, see *Practice Note (Child Abduction and Custody Act 1985): Hague Convention: Applications for Return Orders by Unmarried Fathers* [1998] 1 FLR 491.

It is possible for the court in exercising its inherent jurisdiction to order that a father who had previously abducted one of his children should be required to keep his passport with his solicitors from where it was not to be released without either the order of the court or the consent of the mother (*Re A-K (Minors) (Foreign Passport: Jurisdiction)* [1997] 2 FLR 563).

An interesting development can be seen in *Re T (Staying in Contact in Non-Convention Country)* [1999] 1 FLR 262 where the court required undertakings to be given to apply for 'mirror orders' in Egypt to ensure the child's return from the father's home in Egypt. Egypt is not a party to the Hague Convention. The court emphasised the importance for children to be aware of their cultural identity.

In *Re E* [2000] Fam 62, the court underpinned the importance of the cultural background (unless there are exceptional circumstances, such as persecution or ethnic, sex or other discrimination) in assessing the welfare of the child. The Court of Appeal noted that it would be unrealistic to expect that child welfare would be equally understood and applied throughout the Member States to the Hague Convention.

The Convention on Jurisdiction and Recognition and Enforcement in Certain Family Matters of 1998 regulates concurrent matrimonial proceedings in courts of different Member States involving the same parties and allows for recognition and enforcement throughout the EU. In *Osman v Elasha* [2000] 2 WLR 1037, CA, it was held that, when making an order for the immediate return of a child to his or her habitual residence in a non-Convention country, the court should consider the welfare of the child as the paramount consideration. In that case, the welfare principle had to be considered in the light of Sudanese custom and culture, which applied Islamic law and which was familiar and acceptable to a practising Muslim family.

In *Re M* [1997] 1 FCR 109, a child, who was habitually resident in Scotland but physically present in England, could be subject to the jurisdiction of the English court for the purposes of the court to implement a care plan.

When making applications under the Hague Convention advocates should also consider the impact of the Brussels II (*bis*) Regulation which came into force in March 2005 and which governs the recognition of orders dealing with custody, access and PR.

8.10 Separate representation of children

8.10.1 When this might occur

As a general rule, children are not directly involved in or represented in private law applications for contact, residence, SGOs, etc. However, under r 16.2 of the FPR 2010 the court may make a child a party to the proceedings if the court considers it in the best interests of the child to do so. If a child is made a party to the proceedings, a guardian will usually be appointed to them (under r 16.4). A child may be made a party to the proceedings if the proceedings are particularly complex, if they involve an international element or if the child's views cannot accurately be ascertained by a Cafcass reporter. Further guidance is to be found in PD 16A of the FPR 2010. In *Mabon v Mabon* [2005] All ER DL, the Court of Appeal made it clear that a court should allow older children to directly instruct solicitors rather than have a guardian appointed to them who would instruct the solicitor because it was wrong to exclude articulate adolescents from the decision making process. In proceedings under the Hague Convention, the court in *Re C (Children) (Abduction: Separate Representation of Children)* [2008] EWHC 517 (Fam) has stated that the proper test for the court in considering the question of party status was whether the separate representation of the child would add enough to the court's understanding of the issues that arose to justify the intrusion, expense and the delay that might result.

8.11 Surrogacy

The term 'surrogacy' basically covers those situations where a woman agrees to have a baby for another couple, whether or not for payment. The law on this area is far from clear, but prima facie PR for the child will vest in the natural mother, not in the couple who hope to bring up the baby. Although the father can be given PR by agreement or by order of the court (see **8.2.2**), there is a substantial problem over whether any contract to hand the baby over should be enforceable. It seems doubtful that any contract to pay money for a child would be enforceable if the money were not paid voluntarily.

The welfare of the child would be paramount in any case coming to court. In the 'Baby Cotton' case—*Re C* (*A Minor*) (*Wardship: Surrogacy*) [1985] FLR 846—it was held that the 'parents' should take the child as the mother was quite happy to hand it over. Also, it seems that the 'parents' can adopt the child (*Adoption Application: Surrogacy* AA 212/86, The Times, 12 March 1987). Under the Human Fertilisation and Embryology Act 1990, s 30, the court can make a parental order on an application of a married couple in respect of a child who is born to a surrogate mother and the gametes used are those of one or other of the couple. However, if the natural mother wished to keep the child, it seems unlikely that she would be prevented from doing so unless she was unsuitable.

It is an offence under the Surrogacy Arrangements Act 1985 to be involved in negotiating or making a surrogacy arrangement on a commercial basis, or to advertise to make such arrangements.

Children—public law: procedure and law

9.1 Introduction

This chapter will start with an overview of how child protection decisions are made at local authority level prior to proceedings being issued. It will then consider the legal responses available when the parents or carers of children are considered to be unable to care for them properly. You will already be familiar with some of the key concepts from your reading of **Chapter 8**. For example, the concept of parental responsibility (PR), the paramountcy of the child's welfare and the no order principle are relevant in public law proceedings too.

The practice of care law is complex, intellectually demanding and emotionally fraught, regardless of which party you appear for. Unlike adoption proceedings, you can become involved in care proceedings at a quite early stage of your practice—for example, you might be asked to represent the parents at an emergency protection order (EPO) hearing as a matter of urgency. Whatever your initial level of involvement, you will need an understanding of the whole process. This chapter will explain the key aspects of the legal framework underpinning this area of practice. The next chapter aims to address the practice of care proceedings work. It will introduce you to the more common practical, evidential and procedural issues in public law, some of which can confront you very early on in the process, and to consider some of the common patterns of argument and outcome at final hearings for care and supervision orders.

Be aware that this chapter and the next are designed to give you an 'entry point' for your understanding of this area of law. They are not designed to replace the need for wider reading and regular use of key practitioner texts, but they will give you an overview of the issues for you to use to direct your further research using such texts. Probably the key practitioner work in this area is Hershman and McFarlane, *Children Law and Practice*—it is an indispensable source of reference for all practitioners, regardless of experience. Any references to Hershman and McFarlane ('Hershman') in this chapter and the next are to the edition as it stood at August 2011. If you cannot find the precise reference, it has probably changed during updating, and should not be hard to find nearby. You should be aware of the Munro Review and the government's response in July 2011; the detailed proposals for implementing the recommendations for reform of the child protection system are expected at the end of 2011.

9.2 Child protection decision making

9.2.1 Introduction and sources of information

The local authority's duty to investigate a child's circumstances is dealt with at **9.9.1**. Investigations pursuant to the Children Act 1989 (CA 1989), s 47 relate to discovering whether a child is suffering or likely to suffer significant harm—the threshold criteria for a full care or supervision order (see **9.4.4**). The government's publication *Working Together to Safeguard Children* contains vital guidance for all agencies involved in child protection. It was revised in 2010 following the publication of Lord Laming's progress report in March 2009, *The Protection of Children in England: A Progress Report*, which was commissioned following the *Baby P* case. It seeks to address 23 of Lord Laming's 58 recommendations. You can download it from the Department of Education website: www.education.gov.uk/publications/standard/publicationdetail/page1/DCSF-0030502010.

The current guidance defines the various forms of abuse and neglect of a child as follows (paras 1.33–1.36):

Physical abuse

Physical abuse may involve hitting, shaking, throwing, poisoning, burning or scalding, drowning, suffocating, or otherwise causing physical harm to a child. Physical harm may also be caused when a parent or carer feigns the symptoms of, or deliberately causes, ill health to a child whom they are looking after. This situation is commonly described using terms such as factitious illness by proxy, or Munchausen's syndrome by proxy.

Emotional abuse

Emotional abuse is the persistent emotional ill-treatment of a child such as to cause severe and persistent adverse effects on the child's emotional development. It may involve conveying to children that they are worthless or unloved, inadequate or valued only insofar as they meet the needs of another person. It may include not giving the child opportunities to express their views, deliberately silencing them or 'making fun' of what they say or how they communicate. It may feature age or developmentally inappropriate expectations being imposed on children. These may include interactions that are beyond the child's developmental capability, as well as overprotection and limitation of exploration and learning, or preventing the child participating in normal social interaction. It may involve seeing or hearing the ill-treatment of another. It may involve serious bullying (including cyberbullying), causing children frequently to feel frightened or in danger, or the exploitation or corruption of children. Some level of emotional abuse is involved in all types of ill-treatment of a child, though it can also occur alone.

Sexual abuse

Sexual abuse involves forcing or enticing a child or young person to take part in sexual activities, whether or not the child is aware of what is happening. The activities may involve physical contact, including penetrative (eg, rape or buggery) or non-penetrative acts. They may include non-contact activities, such as involving children in looking at, or in the production of, pornographic material or watching sexual activities, or encouraging children to behave in sexually inappropriate ways. Sexual abuse is not solely perpetrated by adult males. Women can commit acts of sexual abuse, as can other children.

Neglect

> Neglect is the persistent failure to meet a child's basic physical and/or psychological needs, likely to result in the serious impairment of the child's health or development. Neglect may occur during pregnancy as a result of maternal substance abuse. Once a child is born, neglect may involve a parent or carer failing to provide adequate food, shelter and clothing, failing to protect a child from physical harm or danger, or the failure to ensure access to appropriate medical care or treatment. It may also include neglect of, or unresponsiveness to, a child's basic emotional needs.

The guidance in *Working Together* is very informative for those involved in care proceedings. Its 'sister' document, *The Framework for the Assessment of Children in Need and their Families*, provides guidance for assessing children in need and/or thought to be at risk of significant harm and is considered in more detail at **10.3.1** and the sections that follow it. A summary can be found at Appendix 2 of *Working Together*. The *Framework* document has become a very lengthy document and you may find the practitioner guide and/or the web based version on the Department of Education website to be helpful tools. However, you may also find it helpful to read the whole document—Chapters 1 to 8 give statutory guidance; Chapters 9 to 12, non-statutory practice guidance. It is worth noting the following:

- The Executive Summary gives a useful overview, explains some of the changes since the 2006 version (but it is not guidance itself).

- The introduction at Chapter 1 stresses the importance of an integrated approach between the various professionals and agencies involved and the shared responsibility of these agencies. It also deals with the context of the revisions and the government's response to the Laming progress report. It sets out the key definitions used.

- Chapter 2 is worth 'skim-reading' in order to gain a sense of which agencies have a role to play in child protection and the statutory framework within which they operate. Any of these agencies can be a source of evidence on which local authority decision making regarding your client is made. In particular, there is reference to the role of the police (paras 2.123–2.132); the Children and Family Court Advisory and Support Service (Cafcass) (paras 2.172–2.175); schools and other educational institutions; and the health services.

- Chapter 5, 'Managing individual cases', is a valuable description of the decision making process which can (in certain cases) lead to the institution of proceedings. This is probably the most useful chapter for a practitioner in this area; for example, the principles underpinning work to safeguard children are set out at para 5.4 (p 134 and following). The process is summarised below at **9.2.2**.

- Chapter 9 is also very useful as it outlines the *impact* of abuse and neglect upon a child; sources of stress for children and their families (eg, drug abuse by a parent, mental health problems, social exclusion, domestic violence); and key lessons to be learned by child protection agencies from research done into the operation of child protection processes.

9.2.2 The decision making framework in child protection

The following is a summary of Chapter 5 of *Working Together*, which should assist you to put the information generated by the local authority and disclosed in care proceedings in context. You may well find the flow charts produced at the end of that chapter (from p 187) very helpful. (See also the pre-proceedings flow chart referred to at **9.7.4**) If a child is found to be in immediate need of protection *at any stage* of the process, the local authority can apply for an EPO (see **9.8.3**)—there is no requirement that the whole process is undertaken *before* action to protect a child is taken if the matter is urgent.

9.2.2.1   Referral

A parent, a professional (eg, the police) or another person (such as a concerned neighbour or family member) may bring to the attention of the local authority concerns regarding a child. Alternatively the concern could arise within the social services department itself, as new information is gained on a child already known to the service. The local authority will then review the referral and decide on a course of action within 24 hours—usually after checking records and discussing the matter with other agencies involved (eg, police or health visitor). Generally, referral and action on referral should be undertaken with permission from parents unless this would place the child at risk. The result of a referral will be either no further action, or the carrying out of an initial assessment. Whatever the outcome, the referrer should be told.

9.2.2.2   Initial assessment

The local authority is expected to complete an initial assessment within a maximum of 10 working days of the referral. However, the guidance states that the initial assessment can be undertaken very quickly where a s 47 inquiry is called for. This latter focuses on establishing whether the child is in need, and further whether there is reasonable cause to suspect that the child is suffering, or likely to suffer, significant harm.

The process of initial assessment will include seeing and speaking to the child and family members; analysing information from a range of sources (including historical information on the family); and obtaining information from relevant professionals (eg, the child's general practitioner or the health visitor). The family should be informed of decisions taken as a result of the initial assessment (unless this would jeopardise the child protection process, for example, police investigations). See the diagram depicting the assessment framework (at Figure 1 on p 146 of *Working Together*) and the questions that should be addressed (at para 5.40). See also *Birmingham City Council v AG and A* [2010] 2 FLR 580 for a case where it was held that there had been an inadequate initial assessment and the local authority should have considered a s 47 enquiry.

9.2.2.3   Next steps where actual or likely significant harm is not suspected

In these circumstances, the local authority will obviously not be considering legal proceedings or the need for a child protection plan. However, if the initial assessment demonstrates that the child is 'in need' (see CA 1989, s 17), a core assessment (see **10.3.1**) may be carried out in order to decide how those needs should be met, including what services the local authority can offer in this regard.

9.2.2.4   Next steps where actual or likely significant harm is suspected

These are the circumstances in which the local authority is obliged to make inquiries under CA 1989, s 47. They will require a 'core assessment' under the *Framework* (see **10.3.1**). The results of that assessment *must* form part of the local authority's evidence if it commences proceedings for a care or supervision order. At this stage in the investigation, its role is to confirm whether further intervention will be required to protect the child, and if so, what that intervention should be—this could be legal proceedings, or some lesser step.

Emergency proceedings may be required to protect the child at any stage where it becomes apparent that the child is at immediate risk of serious harm, but normally it is expected that there will be a 'strategy discussion' between social services, the police and other agencies involved before action is taken: see Flow Chart 3 in Chapter 5 of *Working Together* (pp 189–190). Where action is required immediately, this discussion should occur as soon as possible afterwards. Where the immediate removal of a child is needed, the guidance indicates that the local authority should rely on an application for an EPO and not police protection powers (see **9.8.2** and **9.8.3**).

9.2.2.5 Strategy discussion

The purpose of the strategy discussion is to enable the social services department and other relevant agencies (eg, education department, health services) to share information, make decisions about initiating or continuing a s 47 investigation, what inquiries will be made and by whom, whether there is a need for action to immediately safeguard the child, and what information about the strategy discussion will be provided to the family. Decisions will be made about providing any relevant medical treatment, how to handle inquiries in the light of any criminal investigation, and whether other children affected are in need or at risk.

9.2.2.6 Decisions following s 47 inquiries

The outcome of the s 47 inquiries should be discussed with relevant professionals involved in the inquiries, and recorded. The parents should be provided with a copy of that record before any initial child protection conference. There are three possible outcomes according to the guidance in *Working Together*:

(a) First, the concerns may not be substantiated but the child is nevertheless in need. An agreement should be reached with the family and other professionals for ensuring the child's safety and this should be recorded. For example, it may be that the concerns about significant harm remain, but there is insufficient evidence to bring proceedings—in which case, the local authority's response may well be to monitor the child's well-being through, for example, the health visitor.

(b) Secondly, the concerns are borne out by the investigation, but the child is not considered to be at *continuing* risk of significant harm. The local authority has a choice as to whether or not to hold a child protection conference. If it does not, the social worker leads the completion of the core assessment and, as with the first option, an agreement is reached with the family and other professionals for ensuring the child's safety. That agreement is recorded. Where no conference is called, the guidance states that the agencies most involved with the family, social services and the child and family themselves should develop and implement a plan to ensure the child's future well-being. This plan should be clearly developed according to the findings of the assessment, with clear indications of who is responsible for its implementation and what will happen if it is not properly implemented: 5.78–5.80 of *Working Together*.

(c) The third possible outcome is that the inquiries and assessment show that the concerns are substantiated and the child is judged to be at continuing risk of significant harm. In these circumstances, a child protection conference should be convened in order to enable the family, and professionals involved with the family, to assess available information and plan for the protection of the child.

9.2.2.7   Initial child protection conference

If called, this should occur within 15 working days of the strategy discussion. The purpose is (para 5.82 of *Working Together*):

- to bring together and analyse in an inter-agency setting the information that has been obtained about the child's developmental needs and the parents' or carers' capacity to respond to these needs to ensure the child's safety and promote the child's health and development, within the context of their wider family and environment;
- to make judgments about the likelihood of the child suffering significant harm in future; and
- to decide what future action is needed to safeguard the child and promote his or her welfare, how that action will be taken forward, and with what intended outcomes.

The guidance in *Working Together* (at para 5.84) is very specific about who should be invited to the conference: 'Those attending conferences should be there because they have a significant contribution to make, arising from professional expertise, knowledge of the child or family or both.' Between the knowledge and expertise of those invited, and the written reports, there should be sufficient information to enable the conference to make well-informed judgments about action to safeguard the child and what is realistic and workable in terms of taking that action. Guidance is also provided about the information which should be provided in advance to the parents.

The decisions to be made by the conference include a decision on whether the child is at continuing risk of significant harm; what an outline child protection plan for the child should contain; and under what category of abuse the child protection plan should be recorded (see **9.2.1** for the categories of abuse, and **9.2.2.10** for recording the Child Protection Plan). A core group must be established at the conference.

There is detailed guidance on what decisions need to be made about the child protection plan at paras 5.101–5.102 and 5.105 of *Working Together*. These include appointing a lead statutory body and a lead social worker for the child, deciding on the membership of the core group of professionals (including any foster carers) and family members who will develop and implement the plan, establishing the timescales for production of the plan and review meetings, contingency planning and what further assessments if any are required. A date must also be decided upon for a review conference. In particular, the requirements for decisions at the conference on the child protection plan are set out at para 5.106 and include identifying risks of significant harm to the child, establishing short-term and longer-term objectives linked to reducing the risk of harm to the child.

Records of the conference (which are confidential and should not be passed to third parties without the consent of the conference chair or the lead social worker) should be sent to all persons invited to attend it, including family members. These minutes are usually disclosable in any ensuing proceedings; they are listed in the pre-proceedings checklist as part of the list of documents which should generally be disclosed before the 'First Appointment' (see the table at para 10.2, PD 12A of the FPR 2010).

9.2.2.8   Child protection plan, and action following the initial child protection conference

The lead social worker is responsible for making sure that the outline child protection plan is developed into a more detailed inter-agency plan, and for acting as the lead professional for the inter-agency work with the child and family. He or she should coordinate the contribution of family members and other agencies, plan the actions which need to be taken to put the child protection plan into effect and review progress against the planned outcomes set out in the plan.

The core group is responsible for developing the child protection plan as a detailed working tool and implementing it within the outline plan agreed at the initial child protection conference (para 5.116). The first meeting should occur within 10 days of the initial child protection conference, and decisions and action agreed at core group meetings should be recorded.

The child protection plan aims to safeguard the child from further harm, promote their health and development, and (if consistent with the protection of the child) support the family in promoting the child's welfare. A key part of this is the carrying out of the core assessment which is the responsibility of the lead social worker and should be completed within 35 working days. Core group members commission other specialist assessments as necessary.

The importance of the child's family understanding, agreeing to and being prepared to work with the plan are emphasised in para 5.127. A written agreement as regards implementation of the plan is recommended by the guidance as good practice—this would reflect the causes of concern leading to the decision that the child needs a child protection plan, what has to change, and what is expected from the parents in order to safeguard the child. From a practical point of view, it is often the case when proceedings are commenced that the family has failed to cooperate with such a plan, and this failure is a large part of the reason for the local authority applying for a care order.

9.2.2.9   The review conference

The progress of the child protection plan will be considered at a review conference. The first of these must occur within three months of the initial child protection conference, and thereafter at intervals of a maximum of six months for the whole of the period of time during which the child's name remains listed as being the subject of a child protection plan (see **9.2.2.10**). This aims to prevent 'drift' in the child's case—it ensures that the child's circumstances and protection plan are regularly reviewed. This may involve changes in the plan, including a need for legal proceedings, or removal of the child's name from the child protection plan record if circumstances are sufficiently improved that he or she is no longer at continuing risk of significant harm. The core group is responsible for providing reports to the review conference on each occasion (see paras 5.137–5.140 of *Working Together*).

9.2.2.10   Recording the Child Protection Plan

A formal record that a child is the subject of a child protection plan should be recorded by each local authority on its Integrated Children's System. This replaces the child protection register previously in operation, but has a similar effect. It forms a vital tool for all agencies in child protection, since this aspect of the child's records will be available to all legitimate inquirers. Children should be recorded under one or more categories of physical, emotional or sexual abuse or neglect, as decided at the conference. The fact that the categories are consistent across all local authorities means that the information the record provides can be understood in the same way throughout the country. There are strict rules regarding the record—it is confidential, to be shown only to legitimate inquirers, and must be accessible at all hours. The contact given to inquirers who request it is the name of the child's lead social worker.

9.3 The statutory framework

9.3.1 Threshold for intervention

Public law children work involves state intervention in the lives of families. Generally speaking, it is thought that parents are best placed to make decisions about what is best for their children, so state interference should only happen as a last resort. It is therefore not surprising that in applications for all types of order, the child's circumstances must be shown to be very serious indeed before the court even has *power* to act. This is commonly referred to as 'the threshold criteria' because the threshold must, as a matter of fact, be crossed before the court has any *jurisdiction* to make the order in question. This is a very important safeguard for the family—local authorities and courts cannot intervene in their lives on a spurious or insufficient basis.

Establishing the threshold criteria, however, is only the first step. For most of the orders in public law children matters, the proof of the threshold criteria just gives the court the power to act. It still has to consider whether such an order should be made, taking into account the paramountcy of the child's welfare and the 'no order' principle. Therefore, for most applications in this area, there are two key questions:

- Has the threshold been crossed? If not, no orders can be made.

- If so, what order, if any, should be made? This is commonly referred to as the 'disposal' or 'welfare' stage, since the welfare of the child is paramount in any decision taken.

In addition, the human rights of the people involved must be respected. Any intervention in their family life must be no greater than is proportionate to the risks posed to the children.

The next sections will consider the main orders and procedures that are available in this area. It will begin with the most serious order, the care order, and will then consider in turn other order possibilities in descending order of seriousness. The more a court order interferes in the life of a family, the more serious it is. For each order or procedure, consideration will be given to the *effect* of the order; the *duration* of the order; its *interaction with other orders*; and the *tests to be applied* on the making of the order.

9.4 Care orders

Apart from adoption, a care order represents the most fundamental intervention in the life of a family, and will only be made where the court is satisfied that no lesser measure will protect the child or children in question.

9.4.1 Effect of a care order

By CA 1989, s 31(1), a care order is an order:

placing the child with respect to whom the application is made in the care of a designated local authority.

A care order can only be made in favour of a local authority. It places a duty on the local authority to safeguard and promote the child's welfare, which will include providing for his maintenance and accommodation. It gives the local authority PR. This does not always mean that the child is placed away from his parents—in appropriate cases, the 'care plan' (see **10.7**) can provide that the child is placed with his parents or a member of the maternal or paternal family who is willing and able to care for him. In many cases, however, the plan might be for permanent placement away from the family, eg, adoption or fostering. The plan (now called a s 31A Plan) must be approved by the court before it can make a care order. Independent reviewing officers monitor how local authorities implement the care plan. The independent reviewing officer will chair each review of the care plan in an effort to provide some safeguards to parents and children. The parents must be involved in the decision making process (*Re G Care: Challenge to Local Authority Decision*) [2003] 2 FLR 42). Note that the court does not continue to intervene in the day-to-day life of the child; once a full care order is made, this ends any control by it over the local authority's implementation of its care plan. However, there is now a requirement for the authority to review the care plan and revise it as necessary, together with a route for returning it to the court through the intervention of a Cafcass officer where appropriate: CA 1989, s 26(2)(e).

9.4.2 Duration

The order can remain in force until a child reaches 18 years. However, it can be ended earlier in a number of ways, such as discharge by the court; discharge by way of a residence or a Special Guardianship Order (SGO) being made; or substitution by a supervision order (see **9.5**). It will also end upon the making of a placement order or on adoption.

9.4.3 Interaction with other orders

A care order is incompatible with all s 8 orders (see **Chapter 8** and note that contact with a child in care is governed by CA 1989, s 34, not s 8); a supervision order; an interim care or supervision order. See also Hershman at C 904. For a useful summary of orders that can be made upon the application for (and instead of) a care order, see Hershman at C 983. Many of these are incompatible with a care order but you need to know what orders are available as an *alternative* if the court decides not to make a care order.

9.4.4 Grounds for a care order

The court must apply the following steps and principles:

- First, are the statutory threshold criteria satisfied? If not, there is no jurisdiction to make a care or supervision order. This is often referred to as the 'threshold' stage of the decision.

- If so, should an order be made at all?

- If so, what sort of order should be made? These latter two questions relate to the 'disposal' (welfare) stage of proceedings, where the court is deciding what approach best promotes the child's welfare.

- The paramountcy principle, the welfare checklist at CA 1989, s 1(3), and the no order principle do not apply to the question of whether the threshold criteria are satisfied—that is a question of factual proof alone. However, they do apply to the question of whether an order should be made, and if so, the type of order.

- In deciding on whether an order is appropriate, and what sort of order should be made, the court will additionally scrutinise the local authority's care plan (see **10.7**) and proposals for contact with the child (see **9.10**).

The threshold criteria for a care order are set out at CA 1989, s 31(2):

(2) A court may only make a care order or supervision order if it is satisfied—

(a) that the child concerned is suffering, or is likely to suffer, significant harm; and

(b) that the harm, or likelihood of harm, is attributable to—

    (i)   the care given to the child, or likely to be given to him if the order were not made, not being what it would be reasonable to expect a parent to give to him; or

    (ii) the child's being beyond parental control.

Clearly, there are two elements to the threshold test—first, establishing the existence, or likelihood, of significant harm to the child; and secondly, establishing that that harm is *caused by* one of the two circumstances in (b). Both elements must be shown. For example, a child could be suffering significant harm because of a serious disability, but that disability could have occurred without any fault on the part of the parents and their care of him could be totally appropriate, and so the threshold test would not be made out. By contrast, a child might be suffering the consequences of neglect, and the evidence shows that this is due to insufficient care by his parents—clearly, he is suffering significant harm, which is due to inadequate care by his parents, and the threshold is made out.

Note that the test for the adequacy of care given to the child in question is an *objective* one and refers to the care which it would be reasonable for a parent to give. This means that there need not necessarily be blameworthiness on the part of the parent; parents may be trying their best to care properly for the child and simply be unable to do so. The threshold would still be met. Equally, parents are not required to provide ideal care (which in any event is a subjective notion), but only that which it is reasonable to expect. Where the child's needs are unusual, complex or demanding, it may be that expert evidence is required as to what care such a child would be given by reasonable parents.

9.4.5 Key definitions in the threshold criteria

The threshold criteria in CA 1989, s 31(2) raise a number of issues, including what is meant by 'harm', or what makes harm 'significant'. The concepts discussed below occur and apply throughout this area of law so it is useful to begin with them. Remember that some of these will apply to the tests for other applications, not just those for care orders.

9.4.5.1 'the child concerned'

This relates to the child who is the subject of the application. It may be that the court is considering applications in relation to several children at one hearing (generally because they are siblings), but decisions as to threshold and order must be made on each child individually. A child is someone under the age of 18 years old, although an application cannot be made in respect of a child who has reached 17 years (16 if married). Further, it is not possible to make an order, or indeed for an application to be made, in relation to a child who is not yet born.

9.4.5.2 'is suffering'

The time at which the child is suffering the harm is an important point. *Re M (A Minor) (Care Order: Threshold Conditions)* [1994] 2 AC 424, [1994] 2 FLR 577 (HL) provides the key principle: the *relevant date* for deciding whether the child 'is suffering' significant harm is *either*:

- the date of the hearing for a care or supervision order; or
- the date on which the local authority first initiated the procedure for protection of the child, *provided that* the protection has then been continuously in place up to the date of the hearing.

This has an important practical consequence. Generally speaking, care proceedings can take many months to come to a final hearing. During that time, the carers of the child might have made substantial progress in their parenting skills, or in addressing the area of risk. If so, the situation at the time of the final hearing could be much improved to the point where it is questionable whether the child 'is' at that time suffering harm. Alternatively, the child's situation could be much improved *because of* protective arrangements made by the local authority (eg, removing the child to foster care). It would then be hard to say that the child 'is suffering' harm at *the time of the final hearing*. This principle enunciated in *Re M* enables the court to look back to the time of the initial intervention when assessing the 'is suffering' part of the test, provided that the provision of protective arrangements has not been withdrawn at any time. From a tactical point of view, this makes it unlikely, for example, that a local authority would agree to the discharge of an interim care order, unless they had no intention of proceeding to the final hearing in any event.

9.4.5.3 'is likely to suffer'

This part of the test enables the court to intervene in situations where the child has not as yet suffered harm, but there is a likelihood of harm. A classic example might be where there are several children in the household and it can be shown that one or more are suffering or have suffered significant harm due to their parents' care, and yet the other or others are as yet unharmed. The fact of harm to one child, if proved, *may* provide *evidence* of the likelihood of harm to others in that household (see **9.4.6**). Another example (which shows that the risk can arise *in utero*) would be where a baby had been born withdrawing from heroin taken by the mother during pregnancy and removed from her care shortly after birth.

As to the time at which 'likelihood of harm' should be demonstrated, see **9.4.5.2** above—the principle is the same.

9.4.5.4 'harm'

This is defined at CA 1989, s 31(9) as:

> *ill-treatment or the impairment of health or development including, for example, impairment suffered from seeing or hearing the ill-treatment of another.*

Hershman and McFarlane make the point that 'ill-treatment' and 'impairment of health or development' are alternatives—so the ill-treatment does not need to have caused some impairment, and impairment does not have to have arisen due to ill-treatment (it could, for example, be due to neglect).

It is also interesting to note that in the definition specific recognition is given to the fact that witnessing ill-treatment of another constitutes harm. This is important where, for example, a child has witnessed domestic violence. The child may not have personally been attacked but the attack on another (his mother, say) could be sufficient to cause emotional harm.

The Act provides further definition of the terms within s 31(9):

> *'development' means physical, intellectual, emotional, social or behavioural development; 'health' means physical or mental health; and*
> *'ill-treatment' includes sexual abuse and forms of ill-treatment which are not physical.*

Clearly, the definitions are cast widely in order to maximise the chances of protecting children from a wide range of abuses. For example, obvious physical maltreatment, such as physical abuse or sexual abuse, is clearly included, but so are neglect and emotional abuse by reference to treatment which impairs health and development, and the definition extends to impairment of mental health, and to ill-treatment which is not necessarily physical. It is of course possible, and quite common, that a child has suffered more than one form of abuse.

An obvious question arises as to how to judge whether health and development are 'impaired'. The CA 1989 again provides a clear definition. By s 31(10):

where the question of whether harm suffered by a child is significant turns on the child's health or development, his health or development shall be compared with that which could reasonably be expected of a similar child.

This introduces a need to compare 'like with like'—the child subject to the application is compared to a hypothetical 'similar child'. For example, a child with Down syndrome is inevitably going to be delayed in his development, and it would be misleading for his development to be compared with that of a child without the disability. Therefore, the effect of s 31(10) means that his development would be compared with that of a similar child suffering from Down syndrome. From a practical point of view, this will inevitably require expert evidence regarding what level of development could be expected from a similar Down syndrome child and how the child in question compares. Generally speaking, expert evidence is often required regarding whether a child has suffered 'harm' where the issue is developmental (as opposed to ill-treatment, which is likely to be more obvious). The 'like for like' comparison that s 31(10) envisages might also mean that other factors are relevant, such as race or culture.

9.4.5.5 'significant harm'

This is a very difficult term to define—as Hershman and McFarlane point out, it is a qualitative term. What matters is that the *harm* is significant—the focus is not so much on the seriousness of the acts that caused it. It could vary according to the child, so for example a nervous and sensitive child could be harmed to a greater extent than a more robust child by the same type of emotional abuse. Alternatively, there may be racial or cultural factors which put a different complexion on the harm. The definition referred to by the courts is: 'considerable, noteworthy or important …' (see *Humberside County Council v B* [1993] 1 FLR 257). For further recent discussion on this, see *Re MA (Care Threshold)* [2010] 1FLR 431, where the members of the Court of Appeal disagreed and where Ward LJ defined significant as 'enough to justify the intervention of the state and disturb the autonomy of the parents to bring the child up themselves in the way they choose'.

9.4.6 Applying the risk of harm test

The obvious question is to what extent does the applicant have to show that suffering is 'likely'—what does it mean in this context? The key authority is now *Re B (Care Proceedings: Standard of Proof)* [2008] 2 FLR 141, where the House of Lords emphasised there are no special rules in family cases and that there is only one civil standard of proof. It follows that the standard of proof in finding the facts necessary to establish the threshold under s 31(2) or the welfare considerations in s 1 of the CA 1989 is the simple balance of probabilities. The court emphasised that neither the seriousness of the allegation nor the seriousness of the consequences should make any difference. This was reaffirmed by the Supreme Court (as the judicial wing of House of Lords has been rebranded) in *Re S-B* [2009] UKSC 17, [2010] 1 FLR 1161.

Difficulties arise where it is not clear who is responsible for causing the harm. In these cases, past facts must be established on the balance of probabilities and this includes the identity of the perpetrator of any harm (para 34 *Re S-B*). Having said that, it is not an essential ingredient of the threshold criteria to name the perpetrator, but the pool of possible perpetrators should be identified. The likelihood of *future* harm cannot be established on the balance of probabilities—it is enough if there is a real possibility of future harm. But the finding of fact on which a prediction of future harm is based must be made on the balance of probabilities: *Re S-B*. The Supreme Court held that where the issue is whether there is a risk of harm if a child remains with one of a pool of possible perpetrators (the mother, say), it is not enough to say that there is such a risk based *only* on the possibility that the mother was the perpetrator. It follows, therefore, that *Re S-B* has overruled *Re CB and JB (Care Proceedings: Guidelines)* [1998] 2 FLR 211.

9.4.7   The decision to make a care order

As stated earlier, the court has no jurisdiction to make a care order until satisfied on the balance of probabilities that the threshold criteria with respect to the child in question are made out. This is a question of factual proof. Once the court has decided that this is so, it then moves to the decision regarding whether to make an order, and if so, what type of order. This stage of the decision making at a final hearing is often referred to as 'disposal'.

9.4.7.1   Applicable principles

The no order principle applies to this stage of the court's decision making. The court must ask itself, in accordance with CA 1989, s 31(9), whether making an order in respect of the child would be better for the child than making no order. Normally, local authorities do not wish to spend precious social services resources upon court proceedings, and therefore the type of cases that come before the courts tend to involve very serious problems with the parenting of these children. It is, therefore, frequently the case that the threshold criteria are satisfied and the problems are such that intervention of some sort is required. In care proceedings, therefore, a proper application of the no order principle probably demands that the order or orders made reflect the *least intervention consistent with proper protection of the child's welfare*: see *Re O (Care or Supervision Order)* [1996] 2 FLR 755. Therefore, a care order might not be appropriate where a supervision order would sufficiently safeguard the child's welfare; or where there was insufficient evidence before the court for a final decision to be made and therefore an adjournment under an interim care order was appropriate for further assessment (see **10.8.3.2**).

Such an approach would be consistent with European law. Clearly, the European Convention on Human Rights, Art 8 would apply, protecting the right to a family life both for parents and child; equally, Art 6 rights to a fair trial may have an impact on proceedings. Proportionality is a key issue in care law as it is in European law and this is further underlined by the fact that it is enshrined in the overriding objective (FPR 2010, r 1). See further, Hershman at C 965–C 966, *Re C and B (Care Order: Future Harm)* [2001] 1 FLR 611; and *Re B (Care: Interference with Family Life)* [2003] 2 FLR 813.

The welfare principle and welfare checklist are the central part of the court's decision making on disposal. Key checklist factors which are likely to influence the decision will be the child's educational, emotional and physical needs; the parents' capabilities of meeting the child's needs; and the risk of future harm to the child.

The s 1(2) principle that delay is inimical to the welfare of a child is also relevant and courts strive to minimise the delay in establishing the child's long-term future. However, you will find that in public law proceedings this does not mean that a final placement must be found at all speed regardless of the cost. In particular, the court will take into account the notion that 'planned and purposeful delay' can be in the best interests of a child (see **10.8.3**).

9.4.7.2 Effect of a care order

Under a full care order, the local authority acquires PR: s 33(3). Anyone who previously had PR does not lose it, but in order to safeguard or promote the child's interests, the local authority has the power to determine how others may exercise their PR: s 33(3) and (4). This is reinforced by s 2(8) of the CA 1989, which provides that a person with PR is not entitled to act in a way that would be incompatible with any order made under the CA 1989. In effect, parents do not lose their PR, but the local authority has the first say in how they are able to exercise it.

9.4.8 Discharge of a care order

9.4.8.1 Substitution of a supervision order for the care order

The court can substitute a supervision order for a care order upon the application of a person with PR, the local authority or the child (see CA 1989, s 39). It cannot do so of its own motion. The abiding principle is the paramountcy principle, and the court will apply the CA 1989, s 1(3) welfare checklist. There is no need to prove that the statutory threshold criteria are still made out (s 39(5)). CA 1989, s 91(15) restricts repeat applications to substitute—where an application has been made before, another cannot be made before six months from the disposal of the original application unless the applicant first obtains permission of the court.

9.4.8.2 Discharge of the care order

Section 39 of the CA 1989 also governs discharge of care orders. The same applicants (see **9.4.8.1**) can apply for the discharge of a care order, and again, by CA 1989, s 39(5) there is no need for the threshold criteria to be shown to still be made out. Again, the welfare principle and checklist apply, as do the same restrictions on repeat applications.

From a tactical point of view, it is difficult for the parents to succeed in applications to substitute or discharge. The child's situation may have substantially improved as a result of the care plan—eg, he or she may be happy and well settled with a long-term foster family. Even if the parents can show that they have made significant improvements in the matters that led to the initial proceedings (eg, a mother who has successfully overcome problems with depression and drug dependency), they will still need to show that it is in the child's best interests to disrupt their current placement for an untested new placement with themselves. This can be a tough comparison. It is even harder where the parents have not sufficiently addressed the original problems with their parenting. Of course, the task will be easier if the improvement in the parents' position is sufficient to safeguard the child's welfare, and the child's placement under the care plan is perhaps not working well enough.

9.5 Supervision orders

A supervision order is a less draconian measure than a care order. One crucial difference is that under a supervision order *the local authority does not acquire PR*. The parents or carers of the child are therefore responsible for meeting the child's needs and the local authority has a much more limited say on how they do this (although they may not act inconsistently with the supervision order, s 2(8). Additionally, there is greater potential for court control of how the supervision is exercised by the local authority, in that the local authority will have to return to court for a care order if the situation deteriorates. This contrasts with the care order, where the local authority can simply change the care plan (eg, from rehabilitation with the parents to foster parent care) without further recourse to court.

9.5.1   Effect of a supervision order

A supervision order places a child under the supervision of a designated local authority (CA 1989, s 31(1)) and imposes duties (CA 1989, s 35) on the appointed supervisor to:

- advise, assist and befriend the supervised child;
- take such steps as are reasonably necessary to give effect to the order;
- where the order is not wholly complied with, or the supervisor considers that the order may no longer be necessary, consider whether or not to apply to court for variation or discharge of the order.

A supervision order without requirements simply requires the supervisor to advise, assist and befriend. It does not appear to give the supervisor the power to give directions to the child, although if the order is not working, the supervisor could apply to court to attach requirements to the order, or even for a care order to be substituted.

9.5.2   Requirements

The court can attach requirements to a supervision order. The available requirements are:

- for the supervised child to comply with directions of the supervisor on certain matters (contained in CA 1989, Sch 3) such as living in a specified place, participating in specified activities, allowing the supervisor to visit him;
- a requirement for the person with whom the child lives to comply with directions of the supervisor. Such an order requires their consent;
- that the supervised child submit to medical or psychiatric examination;
- that the supervised child undergoes specified treatment for his mental health (provided that certain conditions are satisfied).

For further detail, see Hershman C 1517–1532.

9.5.3   Duration

A supervision order will automatically end one year after it was made (it can be made for a period of less than a year). A supervisor can apply for it to be extended, and it can be extended for a period of up to three years from the original order. It will also automatically end if a care order is made (the two orders are incompatible) or on the child's eighteenth birthday.

9.5.4   Interaction with other orders

A supervision order is incompatible with a care order. However, on an application for a care order, the court can make a supervision order, and vice versa. They are therefore alternative outcomes. A supervision order is compatible with any s 8 order.

9.5.5 Grounds for a supervision order

The threshold test in CA 1989, s 31(2) applies to supervision orders in exactly the same manner as it applies to care orders (see **9.4.4**). So, too, does the no order principle, and in particular the idea that the order made should be the least interventionist order possible which is consistent with protecting the child's welfare, which, of course, remains the paramount consideration (see **9.4.7.1**).

The factors influencing the court in deciding between making a care order or a supervision order will be considered at **10.8.3.3**.

9.6 Interim orders

9.6.1 Introduction

An interim care order (ICO) or an interim supervision order under s 38 of the CA 1989 can be made at the time that an application for a care order or supervision order is adjourned. Interim orders may also be made in any other proceedings at any time that the court makes a direction that the local authority investigate under s 37 of the CA 1989 (see **9.9**). An interim supervision order has the same effect as a full supervision order, save that it may last for a lesser period and the court has power to make directions. The significance of ICOs should not be underestimated and this section will focus on them. Whilst the ethos of the CA 1989 suggests that they should not be a routine step in care proceedings, the realities are often different: where the evidence shows that there are real child protection concerns, it would be unusual for an ICO not to be granted (see **10.2**). Further, even with the tightest possible case management (see **9.7.2**), it is inevitable that such orders will last for many months, whilst necessary assessments are carried out and evidence is gathered.

9.6.2 Effect and duration

The effect of an ICO is to grant the local authority PR for the duration of the order. As with full care orders, the PR of the parents is not extinguished, but they cannot exercise their rights inconsistently with that of the local authority. For example, they cannot remove a child from a foster care placement chosen by the local authority. The first ICO can last for eight weeks and may be renewed at four weekly intervals after that until the final hearing in the case.

9.6.3 Grounds for the interim order

The same two-stage process applies to the making of interim orders: has the threshold been proved and, if so, what order, if any, should be made? The threshold, however, is lower than for a full care order, since under s 38(2) the court has only to be satisfied that there are *reasonable grounds for believing that* the threshold criteria in CA 1989, s 31(2) are made out. If it is so satisfied, the court must then consider the welfare checklist and the no order principle. Like any interim order, the court is seeking to strike a balance pending the final hearing and must limit itself to dealing with issues that cannot wait till trial: *Re F (Care Proceedings: ICO)* [2010] 2 FLR 1455. The Court of Appeal has repeatedly emphasised that the making of an ICO is an impartial step to preserve the status quo and does not give the local authority a tactical advantage: *Re G (Minors) (Interim Care Order)* [1993] 2 FLR 839 (see further **10.2**).

This is a developing area of law. There have been a number of recent Court of Appeal authorities on the test to be applied on an application for an ICO when the plan is to remove the child from the parents' care. The test is whether the risk to the child's safety demands immediate separation: *Re H (a child) (Interim Care Order)* [2002] EWCA 1932, *Re L-A (Care: Chronic Neglect)* [2010] 1 FLR 80 and *Re GR (Care Order)* [2011] 1 FLR 669, where it was also held that safety was not confined to physical safety but included emotional and psychological welfare. Where the child has already been removed from the parents' care (perhaps by an EPO (see **9.8.3**) or at an uncontested ICO application), the court should ask itself whether the continued separation of the child from the care of its parents is proportionate to the risk of harm to which it would be exposed if it were allowed to return to its parents' care: *Re B (Care Proceedings: Interim Care Order)* [2010] 1 FLR 1211.

9.7 Procedure—the Public Law Outline

9.7.1 Introduction

A new protocol, the Public Law Outline (PLO), was introduced in April 2008 in an attempt to combat the continuing delay in care proceedings. At the same time, the Department for Children, Schools and Families (DCSF) revised their statutory guidance for local authorities (The Children Act 1989 Guidance and Regulations). In April 2010 a revised form of the PLO was introduced and it has been incorporated in full into the FPR 2010 at PD 12A.

9.7.2 The stages of proceedings

There are four stages, the first three of which must be completed within a specified time frame from the issue of proceedings:

- Stage 1: pre-issue to the end of the First Appointment (FA), which must be by day 6;
- Stage 2: to the Case Management Conference (CMC), no later than 45 days from issue, with the Advocates' Meeting no later than two days before the CMC;
- Stage 3: to the Issue Resolutions Hearing (IRH), to be held between 16 and 25 weeks after issue, again with the Advocates' Meeting between two and seven days before the IRH;
- Stage 4: to the final hearing.

9.7.3 Key elements of the PLO

- The most significant change introduced by the PLO was the expectation that significant work will be done by local authorities (including involving families) *before* proceedings are instigated. This does not apply where action needs to be taken in urgent circumstances to protect a child. The expectation is that the core assessment (in accordance with the *Framework for the Assessment of Children in Need and Their Families*) will have been carried out before a s 31 application is made. This should include a careful consideration of the possibility of placing the child with relatives or friends.

- There is a detailed pre-proceedings checklist to encourage improved preparation of materials to support the application. This checklist includes, for example, a schedule of proposed findings and a care plan.

- A letter before proceedings should be written to the parent(s) to alert them to the local authority's concerns and give them the opportunity to obtain legal representation.

- The overriding objective is repeated at para 2 of PD 12A. The court must apply it when exercising any of its case management powers or interpreting any provision of the PLO. The parties also have a duty to further the overriding objective and the expectation is that all parties will cooperate in case management, seek to avoid delay and attempt agreement out of court, if possible.

- The emphasis on cooperation is significant. The parties and their representatives are expected to cooperate wherever reasonably practicable to help towards securing the welfare of the child as the paramount consideration (para 20.1, PD 12A).

- Analysis from a Cafcass officer is to be available for the CMC, providing objective quality control to the local authority's position.

- The court *must*, early on, set a Timetable for the Child, which must be considered at every stage of the proceedings and kept under review. It must take into account the significant steps in the child's life.

- Greater judicial continuity should follow from the allocation of each case to a maximum of two judges, who are responsible for every CMC stage and one of whom should, where possible, conduct the final hearing.

- The court will actively case manage each case, using the range of powers in FPR 2010, r 1.4, and also maintain various case management documents, including a Case Management Record for each case.

- The Advocates are required to meet to narrow the issues for consideration by the court, and to draft proposed Case Management Orders. There is a suggested draft Case Management Order at para 26(12) of PD 12A.

9.7.4 Guidance

Volume 1 of the Children Act 1989 Guidance and Regulations, which was first published in 1991, was revised by the DCSF and should be read in conjunction with the PLO. It can be accessed via the Children and Young Person section of the Department of Education website, under the 'Strategy and Working Practice' tab. Two useful flow charts from the guidance are reproduced in Hershman and McFarlane: the guidance on the decision making process pre-proceedings (at para 1040) and the stages of proceedings (at para 1031A).

9.7.5 Developments

At the same time as the PLO was introduced, the court fees for bringing care proceedings rose from £150 to £4825, of which £2,225 must be paid on issuing the application. The number of care proceedings being issued swung wildly after this, with a dramatic reduction in the immediate aftermath of the fee rise, but with an equally dramatic increase in the autumn of 2008, in the wake of the intensive press publicity surrounding the *Baby P* case. *Family Law Week* (www.familylawweek.co.uk) reported in its July 2011 bulletin that the figures for May and June suggest further record numbers of care proceedings are being issued.

The interim report of the Family Justice Review (March 2011) contains various proposals in relation to public law proceedings. The most significant are that the court should move away from its close scrutiny of the care plan and focus on whether the threshold criteria have been made out, and that the reliance on expert evidence should be reduced. On the time frame, it also proposes that cases be completed within six months of the application (see **1.9**). This Manual does not have the capacity to discuss the merits or possible effects of these proposals. One can say with certainty, however, that significant procedural change must follow if the proposals are implemented.

The Family Justice Review also places increased emphasis on judicial continuity and proactive case management. As a result of this aspect of the Review, in April 2011 the President of the Family Division issued further Guidance to the courts (*President's Guidance Bulletin Number 3, Listing and Hearing Care Cases*). This seeks to promote even greater discussion between the various layers of the family judiciary and lawyers involved in cases to promote and improve both judicial and representative continuity and reduce delays. As the bulletin put it: 'the legal advisers and judges must fit their availability around the case, not the other way around' (para 16).

9.8 Emergency protection

9.8.1 Introduction

This section will consider the protection of children in an emergency. While care proceedings for some children will commence in quite a measured way, with an application for a care order accompanied by one for an ICO (see **9.6** and **10.2**), others begin with an emergency. For example, the child might be brought to hospital with injuries highly indicative of physical abuse, and social services and hospital staff are concerned that the parents could discharge the child from hospital and disappear; or the child might come to social services' attention through the police, where the police have been called to an incident and discovered a child they consider to be at risk. There are two principal ways in which children can be protected in such a situation: police protection (which does not require a court order); and an EPO (which does).

9.8.2 Police protection

This is governed by s 46 of the CA 1989. By s 46(1):

Where a constable has reasonable cause to believe that a child would otherwise be likely to suffer significant harm, he may—

(a) remove the child to suitable accommodation and keep him there; or

(b) take such steps as are reasonable to ensure that the child's removal from any hospital, or other place, in which he is then being accommodated is prevented.

Clearly, this covers two alternative situations—either the child needs to be *removed* from a situation of risk (s 46(1)(a)) or the child needs to be *kept* in a safe place where removal might put the child at risk (s 46(1)(b)—the specific example used is a hospital).

Neither the police officer taking the child into protection, nor the 'designated' officer who then inquires into the case acquires PR for the child. The child can be kept in police protection for up to 72 hours and no order is required. Thereafter, an EPO will have to be applied for (and the 'designated officer' is one of the persons entitled to apply for such an order on behalf of the local authority).

In terms of how parental rights are affected, although PR is not transferred to the police, a child cannot be removed from police protection unless either the designated officer decides such protection is no longer necessary (according to the test in s 46(1)), or the time limit (72 hours) has expired and no other order—such as an EPO—has been made with regard to the child.

The officer taking the child into police protection has a number of duties. These include informing the local authority and anyone with PR as to what has occurred and ensuring that the case is inquired into by the 'designated officer'. The 'designated officer' also has duties, principally doing 'all that is reasonable in the circumstances of the case to safeguard or promote the child's welfare' (CA 1989, s 46(9)(b)). This will also include consideration of appropriate contact, if considered in the child's best interests, with certain people such as those with PR. Where a child has been transferred to accommodation provided by the local authority (as is almost always the case) the obligations regarding contact transfer to the local authority.

Practically speaking, the police officer taking the child into police protection is obliged to inform the local authority. The local authority then has a duty to investigate to establish what action, if any, it should take (CA 1989, s 47(1)). Generally speaking, if the local authority considers that action should be taken, it will itself apply for an EPO rather than requesting the designated officer to do so on its behalf. If the local authority applies, the time limits for the EPO will not include time in police protection, in contrast to an application by the designated officer.

Police protection is therefore very much a 'first aid' provision where a child is at immediate risk. If local authority investigation does reveal cause for concern, matters progress to proceedings taken by the local authority very rapidly. This would often be by application for an EPO.

9.8.3 EPOs

9.8.3.1 Effect

While in force, by CA 1989, s 44(4), an EPO has three effects. It:

(a) gives the applicant PR for the child (s 44(4)(c)). This does not replace the PR of anyone else who has it;

(b) authorises removal of the child to accommodation provided by the applicant; or alternatively, the prevention of the child's removal from a hospital or other place in which he was being accommodated immediately prior to the order (s 44(4)(b)); and

(c) operates as a direction to any person who is in a position to do so to comply with any request to produce the child to the applicant (s 44(4)(a)).

Therefore, the order gives the applicant the power to remove the child to, or keep the child in, a safe place; it operates injunctively to demand the handover of a child to the applicant; and the applicant acquires PR. The exercise of that PR is, however, somewhat restricted by s 44(5), whereby it can only be exercised to safeguard and promote the child's welfare, with regard to the duration of the order—in other words, measures must reflect that this order is very much temporary—actions and decisions regarding the child with a long-term effect would not be appropriate. During the order, the PR of others who have PR appears to be 'suspended'. For further information on what the applicant can and cannot do during an order, see Hershman C 537–570. In particular, action under the EPO must be proportionate (see *P, C and S v UK* [2002] 2 FLR 631); removing—or failing to return—a child where the risk has been removed, for example where a known abuser has been excluded from the home, would be disproportionate if it went beyond what was required to safeguard or promote the child's welfare. If practicable, the local authority should work in partnership with a parent: *A v East Sussex County Council and Chief Constable of Sussex Police* [2010] 2 FLR 1596.

There is also a requirement to allow 'reasonable contact' with a category of persons including the child's parents. Where there are difficulties, such as an inability between the parties to agree 'reasonable' contact, or where the court agrees that a specific person should have no contact at all, this can be dealt with on the hearing by way of directions from the court.

Further directions can be added to the order by the court if it is felt appropriate. These include directions entitling the applicant to enter and search specified premises for the child or for another child; to require any other person to disclose information on the whereabouts of the child; warrants to authorise a constable to assist the applicant, and for a doctor, nurse or health visitor to accompany the constable; directions authorising medical or psychiatric examination of the child; directions with regard to contact with named persons; and exclusion requirements (see **10.6.2**). For further details regarding these important powers, see Hershman C 494–534.

9.8.3.2   Duration

An EPO can be made only to last for eight days at the first hearing (s 45(1)), although there are special provisions where a public holiday falls on the eighth day. If the applicant is a designated officer applying on behalf of the local authority (see above, **9.8.2**), the eight days include any period the child has been in police protection—this is not the case if the local authority applies for itself. Lastly, the order can be extended once, by seven days (CA 1989, s 45(5)). Normally speaking, an applicant local authority would be expected to have made a decision on whether to apply for a care or supervision order within that time, so reasons will be required by the court as to why the applicant is not ready to proceed.

9.8.3.3   Who can apply?

As seen previously, both the local authority and a designated officer can apply on behalf of the local authority. Additionally, an 'authorised person', normally an officer of the NSPCC, can apply. Lastly, 'any other person'—although if the application is to remove the child (rather than to keep the child in his current accommodation), such a person must prove that he has suitable accommodation available. In reality, these applications are almost always made by the local authority.

9.8.3.4   Grounds for the order

An order can be made without notice, and in emergency situations this is often the case. There are detailed rules covering the procedure, the giving of notice and time limits— you should familiarise yourself with these using a text such as Hershman (C 351–430).

The court must be satisfied of three matters before an order is made:

(a) that one of the grounds in CA 1989, s 44(1) is made out;

(b) that the child's welfare requires that the order be made (the paramountcy principle); and

(c) that making the order would be better for the child than making no order (the 'no order' principle).

The principal ground in s 44(1), and the ground which is available to all types of applicant is that the court must be satisfied that:

there is reasonable cause to believe that the child is likely to suffer significant harm if—
   (i)   he is not removed to accommodation provided for or on behalf of the applicant; or
   (ii)   he does not remain in the place in which he is then being accommodated.

This is the most common ground relied upon. Additionally, s 44(1)(b) and (c) provide alternative grounds for local authorities and 'authorised person' applicants only—these relate to where inquiries are being made and there is reasonable cause to suspect that a child is suffering or is likely to suffer significant harm. If access to the child for the purpose of such inquiries is being unreasonably refused, these 'frustrated access' grounds can be relied upon in an application for an EPO.

Returning to the first, and most commonly used ground, the test is evidently less stringent than that for a full care order. The applicant only has to prove, as a question of fact, *reasonable cause to believe* that the child is likely to suffer significant harm, although this must be proved objectively ('reasonable')—it is not simply a question of the applicant's personal belief. This lower standard is clearly appropriate to an emergency procedure. There are two other significant differences with the threshold for care and supervision orders. First, here, the facts must relate to *likelihood* of harm—in other words, a future state of affairs. Obviously, the fact that a child can be shown to have suffered, or be suffering significant harm at present will be evidence that this will continue into the future. Secondly, this ground requires the applicant to show that (depending on the facts of the case) removal from, or retention of the child in, his current accommodation will prevent the harm. For further definitions, see **9.4** above. See *X Council—B (Emergency Protection Orders)* [2005] 1 FLR 341 for 14 key considerations proposed by Munby J.

9.8.3.5   Discharge of order and appeal

Given that the order is quite limited in time, the rules surrounding opposition to the order, application for its discharge and appeal against any decision regarding the EPO application are quite restrictive.

A party may apply to discharge an EPO only if he was not present when it was initially made. Therefore, one can oppose the initial making of the order, or one may apply to discharge it—but not both (s 45(8) and (11)). An application to discharge an EPO can be made immediately upon the making of the order, but the court cannot hear it before 72 hours have elapsed from the time of the order. Such applications are always on notice (contrast the making of an EPO, which can be without notice). Again, there are detailed rules on procedure which you will need to be familiar with. Application can also be made to vary directions made on the making of the EPO.

There is no right of appeal regarding any decision on the making or discharge of an EPO—including a refusal to make the order. The only method of review would be judicial review if grounds to support it are present.

In reality, while these rules may appear restrictive, the short-term nature of an EPO needs to be borne in mind. In particular, extensions are often not required and, if the child is not returned, the local authority will apply for a care or supervision order, together with an interim care or supervision order within a short space of time. At that point, the parents will have a full opportunity to be heard on the position pending the final hearing (see **9.6** and **10.2**).

9.9 Investigation

This section will consider the local authority's powers of investigation of a child's circumstances. Bear in mind that such investigations may not necessarily lead to proceedings being initiated. The result of an investigation could be that the local authority is satisfied that the child's needs are being adequately met by his carers. Alternatively, it may conclude that the provision of services for the child and his carers may best meet the needs of the family at this time. See further **9.2**.

9.9.1 Local authority duty to investigate

The local authority has a specific duty to investigate in a variety of circumstances. Under CA 1989, s 37, a court hearing family proceedings (such as an application for a s 8 order) may be sufficiently concerned about a child's circumstances that it considers that a supervision or care order may be appropriate, and it can order the local authority to investigate. The local authority should consider whether to apply for such an order, or whether provision of services would be appropriate, or whether other action with regard to the child should be taken. There are also duties to investigate in relation to education supervision orders where a court discharges such an order and directs the local authority to investigate; or where a child is persistently not complying with directions under such an order.

Apart from the above requirements, there is an obligation to investigate pursuant to CA 1989, s 47(1). This duty relates to children within the local authority's area. By s 47(1), where a local authority:

(a) are informed that a child who lives, or is found, in their area—

    (i)   is the subject of an emergency protection order; or

    (ii)   is in police protection; or

    (iii) […]

(b) have reasonable cause to suspect that a child who lives, or is found, in their area is suffering, or is likely to suffer, significant harm, the authority shall make, or cause to be made, such enquiries as they consider necessary to enable them to decide whether they should take any action to safeguard or promote the child's welfare.

The standard *reasonable cause to suspect* is a low threshold—in *Re S (Sexual Abuse Allegations: Local Authority Response)* [2001] 2 FLR 776 it was made clear that this does not require conclusions or facts to be established on the balance of probabilities. The purpose of the investigation is to establish whether action is required to safeguard and promote a child's welfare—in particular, the local authority will be considering whether an application for an order is necessary or whether other powers that it has under CA 1989 should be exercised. The local authority will need to obtain access to the child— and if this is unreasonably refused, then there is a ground for application for an EPO (see **9.8.3.4** above), and the local authority should apply for an EPO, a child assessment order, or a care or supervision order unless satisfied that the child's welfare will be safeguarded without such an order (s 47(6)). By s 47(9) and (11), a variety of organisations are required to assist a local authority with their investigation, including housing authorities, NHS trusts, education authorities and so forth.

9.9.2 Child assessment orders

Under CA 1989, s 43, a court may make a child assessment order if satisfied that:

(a) the applicant has reasonable cause to suspect that the child is suffering, or is likely to suffer, significant harm;

(b) an assessment of the state of the child's health or development, or of the way in which he has been treated, is required to enable the applicant to determine whether or not the child is suffering, or is likely to suffer, significant harm; and

(c) it is unlikely that such an assessment will be made, or be satisfactory, in the absence of an order under this section.

The point of such an order is to facilitate CA 1989, s 47 enquiries into a child's circumstances where the family or carers of the child are not cooperating with the assessment process—most obviously by denying access to the child.

Clearly, the standard *reasonable cause to suspect* is relatively low, as is appropriate to an order designed to address a situation where there is concern but insufficient opportunity to assess the degree of risk, if any, to a child. In terms of seriousness, therefore, it is less interventionist than an EPO. Only a local authority or an 'authorised person' (eg, NSPCC) can apply, unlike the EPO.

If satisfied that these grounds are made out, the court will then consider the no order principle and the paramountcy principle.

The court may treat the application as one for an EPO (s 43(3)), and by s 43(4) must make an EPO rather than a child assessment order if it appears to the court that there are grounds for the EPO and such an order should be made. The court does not have power to make any other kind of order on the application (such as a s 8 order) of its own motion.

The order lasts for seven days only, and there is no provision for it to be extended—at which point the local authority would have to apply for an EPO with directions for assessment or an interim care order in order to continue an incomplete assessment.

The court has considerable control over the assessment process. In particular, the child can only be kept away from home if necessary for the assessment, for such periods as specified in the order only, and only in accordance with directions in the order (s 43(9)). It seems that the child cannot be removed from home without a court direction approving such a measure. Hershman and McFarlane suggest that, given that this type of order is supposed to fall short of the severity of an EPO, then if preventing contact with the child's carers for the duration of an order is necessary, it may be that an EPO is in fact more appropriate. Provision for contact is subject to court direction (s 43(10)).

The order operates as a direction to any person who is able to produce the child to produce him to a person named in the order and to comply with such directions as to assessment as the court specifies in the order (s 43(6)).

A child who has sufficient understanding to make an informed decision may refuse consent to a medical or psychiatric assessment—s 43(8). This would appear to accord with the principles of *Gillick* competence.

While there is no specific guidance on the sort of directions that a court might impose as to the carrying out of the assessment, Hershman and McFarlane suggest a detailed list of matters that need consideration when making such an order. See Hershman C 276–280. In particular, directions may be necessary as to who carries out the examinations, the nature of examinations to be permitted, the number of examinations to be permitted and the people who may or must be present during examination. Further, specific directions will be necessary as to what contact the child should have with persons, such as his parents, during the period of the order.

An order can be varied or discharged on application of specified persons, including the child's parents or carers; and there is a right of appeal with regard to the making or refusal of a child assessment order.

9.10   Contact with a child in care

9.10.1   Powers of the court

Contact with a child in the care of the local authority is governed by CA 1989, s 34. Section 34(1) provides the 'default position' which should pertain whenever there is no specific court order as to contact—the local authority must allow *reasonable contact* with certain people specified by s 34(1), notably the child's parents. Of course, what is 'reasonable' can vary according to the circumstances (eg, once a care order is made, where rehabilitation is planned a higher level of contact is appropriate than where the child is to be placed for adoption). Parents and other relevant persons may be unhappy with the levels of contact granted by the local authority. For this reason there is provision in s 34(3) for persons named in s 34(1) to apply to the court for a contact order (CO) (other persons not named in s 34(1) would need the court's leave to make such an application), and in s 34(2) for the child or the local authority to apply for COs as well. By s 34(4), the court can authorise the local authority to refuse contact between persons named in s 34(1) and the child. This is an order that should only be made where there is exceptional risk to the child (see *A v M and Walsall Metropolitan Borough Council* [1993] 2 FLR 244), and should never be made routinely as a first step to a care plan entailing adoption. Court orders may carry conditions (s 34(7)—an example might be that the contact be supervised by a named person or take place at a specific address) and when making a care order, a court can make an order for contact under s 34 of its own motion if appropriate. There is an important power for the local authority to suspend contact (even contact ordered by the court) for no more than seven days if necessary to safeguard the child's welfare and an urgent decision is required. If a suspension is required for longer, then clearly the local authority would have to apply for a s 34 CO, or even an order authorising refusal of contact. By s 34(11), the court is required to scrutinise and invite parties to comment upon the plans for contact put forward by the local authority before granting a care order. Section 34 applies to interim care orders, since by s 31(11) the definition of 'care order' includes interim care orders.

There is a particularly important provision to remember when making a s 34 contact application—by CA 1989, s 91(17), where an application is made and *refused*, the applicant may not make another application under s 34 for a further six months, unless the court gives leave for such an application. This is to prevent the potentially destabilising effect on the child of frequent, unmeritorious applications. You should note that this applies to all care orders, including interim care orders—and so careful consideration needs to be given to the timing and merits of any application made prior to the final hearing since it may prevent a further application being made at the time of the final hearing.

Just as with a s 8 CO in private proceedings, 'contact' includes all forms of contact, such as staying or visiting contact, supervised contact and indirect contact (telephone calls, letters and so forth).

9.10.2   Applicable principles

The paramountcy principle applies to contact proceedings under s 34. Contact with a child in care raises particular difficulties since what is in the child's best interests will depend to a large degree upon what his likely future is to be. The court has to balance the value of contact to the child against how that contact might affect the child's long-term placement—and in some cases, where there is any doubt, the long-term placement will have to be prioritised, as being the child's greatest need. Where the person seeking contact is not able to take full-time care of the child (such as a parent whose parenting abilities are such that he or she cannot meet the child's needs), the degree of contact that is appropriate will depend on the likely long-term placement of the child and whether and to what degree contact would destabilise that placement. For example, if the care plan is for the child to be placed for adoption, direct contact between parent and child will almost certainly be inappropriate. If rehabilitation is intended, then contact will be essential and will probably be at an increasingly high level. If the child is to be fostered by an experienced foster family long term, some direct contact could be appropriate but at a level that enables the child to integrate properly into his foster family and which is not unduly disruptive to the life of the foster family. In such a situation, the parent who can be supportive of the child's new home is likely to be more successful in gaining direct contact than the parent who seeks to undermine the new home in the child's eyes. It is also important that the parent seeking contact can demonstrate that he or she will be consistent and maintain contact so as not to undermine the child's sense of security and self-worth.

The fact that a care order is made with a care plan for placement away from the family does not necessarily mean that there will not be long-term contact between the child and his family—much depends on the child's placement, as set out above. There are certain advantages that contact with the birth family gives a child and which may be important enough in the individual case to be worth preserving. These were considered in *Re E (A Minor) (Care Order: Contact)* [1994] 1 FLR 146—Simon Brown LJ (at pp 154–155):

In short, even where the s 31 criteria are satisfied, contact may well be of singular importance to the long-term welfare of the child; first in giving the child security of knowing that his parents love him and are interested in his welfare; second, by avoiding any damaging sense of loss to the child in seeing himself abandoned by his parents; thirdly, by enabling the child to commit himself to the substitute family with the seal of approval of the natural parents; and fourthly, by giving the child the necessary sense of family and personal identity. Contact, if maintained, is capable of reinforcing and increasing the chances of success of a permanent placement, whether on a long-term basis or by adoption.

See also *Re B (Minors) (Care: Local Authority's Plans)* [1993] 1 FLR 543.

The issue of contact to a child in care is dealt with comprehensively, both as to substantive law and as to procedure in Hershman and McFarlane, Section C 1131–1370.

Children—public law: preparation and practice

10.1 Introduction

There are about 60,000 children being looked after by local authorities in England at any one time. This includes children subject to a care order (under the Children Act 1989 (CA 1989), s 31) and those who are being looked after under a voluntary agreement with their parents (under CA 1989, s 20). It seems that about 59 per cent of those being looked after are in care.

Statistics released for the year ending 31 March 2010 reveal that there were 375,900 children in need, which is equivalent to a rate of 341.3 per 10000 children. There were 603,700 referrals to children's social services in the year, during which time 395,300 initial assessments and 142,070 core assessments were completed. There were 64,400 looked after children, which represents an increase of 6 per cent since 2009 and 7 per cent since 2006. The main reason that social services first engaged with children who started to be looked after during the year was because of abuse or neglect (52 per cent). 73 per cent of the children looked after to 31 March 2010 were in foster placements. The number of children placed for adoption in this period was 2300. Finally, looking at the number of children who were the subject of a child protection plan (ie, those to be compared with children whose names were on the child protection register), as at 31 March 2010, the figure was 39100. More than 13 per cent of the children who became the subject of a child protection plan in the year had already been the subject of one or more previous plans.

The purpose of including these figures is to give you an idea of the scale of the problem. By way of further example, the number of core assessments has increased by more than two and a half times since the 2003 figures given in the previous edition of this Manual. The figures have been extracted from the summaries of information in each survey, and should of course be understood subject to the guidance and caveats in those survey reports. These statistics have been taken from the Children in Need (CIN) Census. You can find this information on the Department of Education website: www.education.gov. uk. General information on children and social services matters is in the Children and Young People section of the website at 'Safeguarding and social work reform'. Statistical information is found at the data research and statistics section of 'Every Child Matters'.

You may also wish to look at the statistics on 'Outcomes for Children Looked After by Local Authorities' in England in the 12 months to 31 March 2010. These measure outcomes such as educational achievement, health and criminal involvement. Sadly, although perhaps not surprisingly given their difficult upbringings, these children tend to underachieve significantly compared to the general population of children.

This chapter will first consider the investigative process in care proceedings, including the use of interim care and supervision orders to maintain a 'holding position' between local authority and parents to protect the child prior to a final hearing; discussion of local authority evidence, expert evidence and the role of the Children's Guardian in proceedings follows. Some of the main issues which can arise at any stage in the care proceedings will then be summarised. Finally, consideration will be given to arguments and outcomes at a final hearing.

10.2   Interim care orders and interim supervision orders

Children may become the subject of court proceedings in a variety of ways. An application for a care or supervision order may be made after a s 47 (CA 1989) investigation (see **9.9.1**); as a result of a core assessment prepared for that investigation; or following a child being taken into police protection (see **9.8.2**); and/or becoming the subject of an emergency protection order (EPO) (see **9.8.3**). As discussed in **Chapter 9**, the Public Law Outline (PLO) requires the local authority to carry out significant work before proceedings are instigated. While it is possible for a child to remain in his parents' care, or in voluntary accommodation with the local authority whilst care proceedings are ongoing, it would be unusual for the local authority to accept either situation if there is concern that the child could be at risk. Usually, it will feel the need to share parental responsibility (PR) under an interim care order (ICO), so that it can protect the child without further recourse to the court if need be.

10.2.1   The importance of interim care orders

An interim order can be made whenever an application for a care or supervision order is adjourned. They are made under CA 1989, s 38(1) and are intended to be a strictly neutral step to preserve the status quo, giving no advantage to the local authority in terms of the final hearing: see *Re G (Minors) (Interim Care Order)* [1993] 2 FLR 839. The legal framework for interim orders is set out in detail at **9.6**. This section seeks to look at the practical considerations and consequences. While the guidance (*The Children Act 1989 Guidance and Regulations, Volume 1, Court Orders*) suggests that an interim order is never a 'routine' step in proceedings, in reality ICOs are made in a significant number of cases.

The issue is crucial where the plan is to remove the child from its parents' care under the ICO. There are cases where it would be very difficult for parents to contest an ICO; for example, where the child has serious, unexplained injuries and an EPO has already been granted. It might well be difficult to persuade a court that the child's safety does not demand immediate separation from the parents (see **9.6.3**). However, there may also be cases where the nature of the case against the parents is much less strong, where there has been no physical harm and appears to be no real threat of it. Parents and their advisors face difficult decisions. Should they contest the ICO application or should they adopt a pragmatic approach and neither contest nor oppose the ICO? These difficult issues and the competing pressures faced by parents are discussed in an excellent article by Andrew Bainham, 'Interim care orders: Is the bar set too low?' at [2011] Fam Law 374 (April). He suggests that the practice of neither opposing nor consenting to ICOs is prevalent, but questions whether it should be so.

Another relevant consideration is that, unlike the position after a final care order, the court has much more control over the local authority's actions on the grant of and during the life of an ICO. In particular, it can prescribe what assessments the local authority can carry out either by requiring the court's permission for an assessment (see **10.4**) or by directing that the local authority carry out certain assessments under s 38(6) (see **10.6.1**). Further, because the threshold is lower (reasonable grounds to believe), a finding of fact that the threshold criteria are met for an ICO *does not* constitute a finding that the threshold criteria are met for a full order—the local authority will have to prove this to the higher standard in CA 1989, s 31 at a final hearing. The court hearing an application for an ICO should not seek to make findings on whether the threshold is met for a final order. Further, it is possible for parents to concede that the threshold is met for the ICO or interim supervision order and go on to argue 'disposal' (whether an ICO should be made, or another order, or no order) in just the same way as for a full care or supervision order—see **10.8.2** and **10.8.3.2** below.

However, given the amount of time that an ICO might be in force whilst the necessary investigations and assessments are carried out, parents will need to be advised that the status quo is likely to change. Parents have to attempt to balance the risk of unsuccessfully opposing an ICO (with a finding against them that there *are* reasonable grounds to believe that the threshold is made out) against attempting to cooperate with the local authority as much as possible (although not conceding the case against them), but still running the risk of time working against them. Andrew Bainham presents forceful arguments that ICOs are not, in reality, as neutral as the CA 1989 ethos suggests; he also makes some interesting proposals for alternative solutions. In practice, it is important to give careful consideration to the issue of ICOs; for a good example of how to put the arguments against removal when the evidence of future risk is thin, see: *Re M (Interim Care Order: Removal)* [2006] 1 FLR 1043.

10.3   Local authority evidence

10.3.1   The Framework for the Assessment of Children in Need and their Families

This guidance, first produced by the Department of Health in June 2000, is a key document for professionals involved in child protection work. Assessments produced pursuant to this guidance (usually called 'core assessments') are key documents in care proceedings and, therefore, you should familiarise yourself with the *Framework*'s contents. It will provide you with an insight into social service decision making in the individual case, and may well inform the decisions you take about how to challenge (or defend, depending on your client) the local authority's case. The entire document can still be accessed through the Department of Health website, at www.dh.gov.uk/en/ Publicationsandstatistics/Publications/PublicationsPolicyAndGuidance/DH_4008144. However, there is a very useful and pithy summary of the *Framework* at Appendix 2 of *Working Together to Safeguard Children* (see **9.2.1**). To gain a useful insight into the investigations that social services carry out on families for the purpose of assessments, do look at the guidance given for practitioners in the field. The most recent was published in August 2009: '*Early identification, assessment of needs and intervention – The Common Assessment Framework (CAF) for children and young people: A Guide for Practitioners*'. A downloadable pdf or hard copy can be viewed or obtained on the Department of Education website: www.education.gov.uk/publications/standard/publicationDetail/Page1/IW91/0709.

10.3.2   Ascertaining whether a child is 'in need'

The purpose of the guidance is to assist social work practitioners to identify whether a child is 'in need', including whether he is suffering or likely to suffer significant harm, and how his needs might best be met through appropriate provision of services to the child and his family. This is key to fulfilling the local authority's statutory duty under CA 1989, s 17 to safeguard and promote the welfare of children in need within its area. It is intended to provide a *systematic way of analysing, understanding and recording* what happens to a child within his family. It does not have the force of statute but must be complied with unless circumstances are exceptional. One of the crucial principles behind its use is that it is a *framework and not a practice manual*. Social work practitioners are expected to adapt its requirements to the needs of the individual case rather than apply it in a dogmatic and 'tick box' way. It also aims to facilitate effective collaborative work between professionals from different disciplines and agencies so that parents and children do not experience inconsistent treatment by these professionals. A vast array of different agencies may have had dealings with the family—Chapter 2 of *Working Together* will give you an indication of who is likely to be involved (see **9.2.1**). They include education and health professionals, the police (in some cases) and many others. They will frequently be required to assist in and contribute information and/or professional skills to an assessment.

Throughout the *Framework* (as in *Working Together*), there is emphasis on the importance of communication with the family and the child (as far as the child is able to understand), sharing information with the family, and seeking where possible to secure their agreement to plans made as a result of an assessment. The PLO requires the involvement of the parents at an early stage. Key principles informing the mindset of child protection professionals are that it is in a child's best interests to be brought up by his or her family wherever possible and that parents have a right to call upon the local authority for services, including voluntary accommodation (CA 1989, s 20) and help, when needed. To this end, whilst the focus is always clearly on the child, services might address needs of the adults (eg, counselling) if that will have an impact upon the child's welfare. One of the main messages of the guidance is that assessment and provision of services are not mutually exclusive—the family should not have to wait for the completion of an assessment to access services if the need for such help is clear during the assessment. In the individual case, you will be looking to see whether, and to what extent, these principles have informed the way professionals have worked with the family so far. Has proper and timely support been provided to enable this child to be brought up by the family as far as possible? There are many cases in which social work practitioners have worked very hard with the family and explored all possibilities to enable the child to be cared for by them, despite which the family have made insufficient effort, or are simply incapable of providing adequate care. There are others in which intervention by the professionals has been poorly targeted, or issues have been prejudged and not properly assessed. You need to be able to spot the differences.

10.3.3   How does the carrying out of a core assessment under the Framework relate to care proceedings?

A core assessment does not necessarily have to be carried out with legal proceedings in mind. Primarily, they are begun where initial assessment has demonstrated that the child may be a child in need, and they are aimed at giving the local authority the necessary information to develop a 'child in need plan' for that child and identify necessary services for that child and his parents. However, legal proceedings may become an issue at any time in the assessment process if the professional(s) carrying out the assessment suspects that the child is suffering or is likely to suffer significant harm. At this point, the assessment would not end, but the local authority would have to consider its s 47 obligations to inquire and decide whether action is necessary to protect the child. This might affect the focus and pace of the assessment at that point. The result could be proceedings for a care order—beginning with an application for an ICO. If the situation is truly urgent, then an EPO could be sought.

The PLO requires disclosure by the local authority of all the relevant assessments when proceedings are instituted. The Timetable for the Child and the Case Management Conference (CMC) should ensure that the court has control over all further necessary work by the local authority and other professionals. In contested care proceedings, the professional who undertook the core assessment will often have to 'speak to the report' (give evidence) orally and be cross-examined on it.

10.3.4   What is being assessed?

From the point of view of legal proceedings, the assessment may provide evidence to support the local authority's case as follows:

- proof that the threshold criteria are met; and/or
- evidence demonstrating what the child's welfare requires; and/or
- evidence justifying and supporting the care plan or part of the plan.

More widely, whether the core assessment relates to legal proceedings, or whether it simply seeks to identify whether the child is in need and what support the local authority can provide to promote his welfare, there are three key elements being assessed (known within the *Framework* as 'domains'):

- the child's developmental needs;
- the capacity of the parents to respond appropriately to those needs;
- family and environmental factors and their impact upon the parents' capabilities and the child.

The various aspects of these three domains are set out in Boxes 1 to 3 respectively of Appendix 2 to *Working Together* (the summary of the *Framework*). Assessors are strongly advised to *observe* the interactions between parents and child as well as discussing these with the parents. Further, assessment will take in the impact of the parents' relationship with each other on their abilities to respond to the child's needs. This may involve considering a distinction between an abusing parent and a potentially protective parent. In particular, it is sometimes the case that one parent could parent better alone than if the parents are together.

Section 6 of the Guide for Practitioners (see **10.3.1**) sets out a step-by-step guide to carrying out the *Framework*, includes the pre-assessment checklist and details of how to complete the relevant forms themselves and can be found at pages 43 to 56.

10.3.5   Decision making and judgments

This section of the main *Framework* document will be of particular interest to the lawyer, dealing as it does with the conclusions drawn from the core assessment process and subsequent planning. It should now be read in conjunction with Chapter 5 of the updated and amended *Working Together* (see **9.2.2**) and bearing in mind the overriding objective in the PLO (see **9.7.3**). The process of analysis should lead to the following results:

- identifying the child's needs and the parents' ability to respond appropriately to those needs;
- identifying whether, and if so, what intervention is necessary to secure the well-being of the child;
- a realistic plan of action, including what services should be provided to the family, and a timetable and process for review.

The crucial judgments to be made are outlined at 4.15:

- determining what has been happening and whether this is a child in need or a child suffering significant harm;
- understanding the child and family context sufficiently to be able to secure the child's well-being or safety;
- assessing the likelihood of change;
- and later, on review, reviewing whether such change is being achieved.

The latter two judgments are often the crucial points for the lawyer in care proceedings—likelihood of change is a fundamental issue when considering the 'disposal' (welfare) stage of the final hearing. The decisions of and plans by the local authority will be apparent from its care plan, disclosed at the outset of proceedings.

The remainder of Chapter 4 is very important in terms of local authority planning for the child, and you should read it. In particular, at 4.21, the guidance states that the content and timing of the plan for the child is informed by three key aspects of the child's health and development:

- ensuring the child's safety;
- remembering that a child cannot wait indefinitely;
- maintaining a child's learning.

Again, the particular issue for the lawyer is likely to be the second of these points. The court and advocates must always bear in mind the Timetable for the Child which is of prime importance in the PLO. Where parents have not improved their parenting sufficiently for return of a child at a final care hearing, the argument on their behalf will usually relate to allowing more time for assessment of their abilities, or a new type of work or assessment; the court will need to be persuaded that any delay is constructive. The concern is the child's timescales—children cannot wait for a permanent placement for ever and to expect them to do so could cause them harm in itself. The younger the child the more urgent the need for permanency and secure attachments with a carer become. Sections 4.22 and 4.25 raise the importance of secure attachments between parents and child in deciding the future of the child, and the issues of permanent placement elsewhere.

Sections 4.26, 4.28 and 4.30 are of particular interest for the lawyer since they identify criteria indicative of poor, or good, prospects for reuniting a child with his family. In making judgments about the long-term placement of the child, the professionals involved are likely to have relied upon a combination of such factors. At 4.26, the following criteria are identified as suggesting a poor outcome for reuniting the child with abusive parents:

- the abusing parent completely or significantly denies any responsibility for the child's developmental state or abuse;
- the child is rejected or blamed outright;
- the child's needs are not recognised by its parents, who put their own needs first;
- parents have frequently failed to show concern, or acknowledge, longstanding difficulties such as alcoholism or psychiatric problems; and
- during therapeutic interventions, the relationships within the family and with professionals are at breaking point.

One imagines that many of these issues must have been seen in the *Baby P* case, but were not followed up.

Key themes in the care case will therefore be whether the parents *minimise* the problems rather than being realistic about them; whether they *accept responsibility* for the problems in their parenting or deny that they exist (in particular, do they blame the child or do they have some insight into their own responsibility); whether the parents put the child's needs first and above their own (eg, does the mother in an abusive relationship continue that relationship 'because she can't help it' or seek to end it in order to protect the children; or a parent with an addiction to narcotics makes insufficient effort to give up, putting their need for their addiction before their children's needs to be properly parented); whether the parents *deny* that they have their own problems (such as alcoholism) or acknowledge them and attempt to resolve them; and whether the parents are *able to work with professionals, or resist attempts to improve their parenting.*

Therefore, when looking at the evidence in a case where the local authority's care plan is for permanent placement away from the family, the lawyer needs to identify and evaluate evidence demonstrating these factors, and evidence which suggests the contrary. For example, in a case where the mother is alleged to have failed to cooperate with the professionals, is there evidence that she has in fact attended appointments made for her? Is there reason for non-compliance, for example that she was suffering from post-natal depression which was undiagnosed at the time? See further, **10.3.7** below.

10.3.6   The initial social work statement

This is a document which will only be prepared for care proceedings (unlike the core assessment, which has a number of roles in child protection work). Under the PLO, the initial social work statement must be filed on the issue of the application. The PLO strictly defines its contents: FPR 2010, PD 12A, para 25(23).

A social work chronology will also be filed in the prescribed format.

PD 12A strictly limits the contents of the initial statement to the matters set out in para 25(23)(a)–(g). It will not contain the whole of the history of social services' involvement with the family but only 'the precipitating incident(s) and background circumstances relevant to the grounds and reasons for making the application'. The evidence is to be focused on the findings sought by the local authority, their initial proposals under their care plan, any referral and assessment processes that have already occurred and their initial proposals for further assessment of the parties during the proceedings. It is normally made by the lead social worker, who is likely to be the author of the core assessment. Further statements may well be filed in accordance with the court's case management directions at stages during the proceedings. These later statements will update the court on events occurring since the initial statement and progress of assessments and work with the family, if any, which are ongoing.

10.3.7 Challenging the local authority evidence

It will immediately be noted that the local authority evidence has a distinct advantage over that of the parents. The evidence that the parents will give about past events may well be confused and incomplete. It may be that their recollection is affected by the problems they face, for example drug abuse or depression or simply chaotic lives. They certainly will not have recorded salient details as they occur! By contrast, social services will have routinely recorded their interaction with the family throughout their involvement, as will other agencies (eg, the health visitor) coming into contact with the family. It can also be difficult to challenge the local authority version of events because—at least in theory—it relies upon observation by professionals who have no personal interest in the outcome, in stark contrast to the parents. That is not to say that the credibility of local authority witnesses cannot on occasion be undermined; for example, there may be evidence to show that a key social work practitioner allowed personal feelings of dislike towards a parent to affect her professional judgment, or prejudged the outcome (eg, failing to investigate an important allegation made by the mother which later proves to be true; or failing to consider a realistic alternative to some quite draconian step without good reason).

Of course, you must always take your client's instructions on the history of the matter, and look at each case on its facts. There may be good evidence to contradict historical allegations of fact, or those made may be susceptible to being undermined. But in many cases, the focus of the lawyer will be less on challenging the past and more on trying to demonstrate change in the parents' attitudes and abilities. The factors referred to in 4.26 of the *Framework* (see **10.3.5** above) will provide a starting point in many cases for what you have to attack—both historically and in relation to the events during the lifetime of the proceedings. Parents, unfortunately, frequently react to social services' intervention by denying all the problems, minimising their own responsibility, and refusing to cooperate—or at least cooperate in any meaningful way—with those professionals trying to work with them. These attitudes will be something the lawyer will need to explore with the clients in conference, and advise them about as early as possible in the case—a continuation of this behaviour is likely to prove disastrous for their prospects of success. Where parents cannot see that there is any cause for concern regarding their parenting, their motivation for change will be low—and demonstrating potential for change will often be the key argument. The lawyer will be looking at all times for the following, for purposes of cross-examination (whether at a contested ICO hearing or a final hearing) and argument:

- Evidence of cooperation with professionals from the parents. For example, an open attitude to social services' visits (rather than refusing to open the door, or being away from home when a visit is prearranged) and engagement with social work practitioners (attending planning meetings, being prepared to discuss assessments and so forth). More importantly, evidence of engagement with assessment and therapeutic work—eg, regular attendance at parenting work sessions and a clear attempt to put what is learned into practice. The lawyer will attempt to 'accentuate the positive' by putting to the social work practitioner the instances of positive engagement by the parents. The more it can be shown that the parents are cooperating, and are likely to continue to cooperate with professionals in the interests of the child, the better the chance of a successful outcome.

- Demonstrations of insight into the problems by the parents. Are there examples of real attempts to understand the problems by the parents? Do they accept any responsibility for the problems, and what instances demonstrate this? What work has been done with them, or is planned, to assist them to gain insight into these issues? Insight is important because an understanding and acceptance of the problems are good indications that change will be possible.

- Are there good reasons for a failure to cooperate, or to engage properly with work designed to improve their skills? It may be that attention can be turned on the way in which the social work practitioners handled the situation—for example, contrary to the principles of the *Framework*, there may have been little effort to consult parents about key decisions and include them in decision making (eg, were there genuine efforts to invite them to planning meetings and share information with them?). It may be that parents have a good relationship with one practitioner and not with another—was this taken into account in decisions about who would deal with the family? More fundamentally, there might be good reason for the parents' inability to engage with work—they may have low learning ability, and the intervention, however well meaning, did not take this into account; or one might have been suffering depression in a way which reduced their motivation, and this was untreated at the time they are alleged to have failed to cooperate.

- Have the right assessments been undertaken, or the right work targeted? Some interventions, however well intentioned, may be ineffective compared to others—a classic example would be where learning difficulties were not taken into account.

- What efforts have been made to support compliance by the parents? For example, if a resource is not available locally, was assistance given to enable the parents to travel? What resources could have been supplied by the local authority but were not? Again, while the social services department cannot make decisions about housing and provision of accommodation, they can, under CA 1989, s–27, ask the housing authority for assistance—have enquiries been made?

- Consider the key principles outlined in the *Framework*. Does social services' intervention demonstrate a commitment to those principles or not? For example, given the key principle that *where possible* children should be brought up in their families, on deciding that the child could not be permanently placed with the parents, did the social worker make a genuine effort to consider placement within the wider family (eg, grandparents) if that was an option on the facts of the case?

- To a degree, social work practitioners have some similarities to expert witnesses (see **10.4** below). Their evidence may be susceptible to being undermined in terms of important assumptions they have made about the facts, or key information relied upon by them which has come from other sources being incorrect, in particular where a fact is subsequently shown to be false.

10.4 Expert evidence

Care proceedings do not simply focus on past events—unlike many forms of litigation, there is a strong focus on the likely future. The court is trying to predict the future in order to decide what the child's welfare will demand. If a care order is not made, will the child suffer significant harm? Will the parents be able to meet the child's needs in the long term? Will the therapy or work needed to enable the parents to meet the child's needs be successful—and how quickly? Would the child's needs be better met by adoption or fostering? These are a few of the questions that the court may be seeking to answer in a typical care case.

The local authority evidence discussed at **10.3** will in part seek to answer these questions. Additionally, expert evidence may be sought to help the court predict the future in this way. It may also play a role in determining past events, for example, whether a child has suffered non-accidental injuries, sexual abuse or emotional damage as a result of the care given to him. Many care cases will therefore involve some element of expert evidence and it is usually of great importance. For this reason, your cross-examination of an unfavourable expert can be vital. In the modern context, this can become even more difficult because it will frequently be expected that parties will jointly instruct one expert and therefore you do not have the benefit of an expert instructed by your party who can assist you to identify appropriate cross-examination of other experts in the case.

This section will look at the legal requirements for expert evidence, the role of the expert in proceedings, and throughout the discussion, practice requirements for the instruction of experts. There will also be some brief consideration of the methods of undermining unfavourable expert testimony.

10.4.1 The rules

The rules on expert evidence in family proceedings are now contained in FPR 2010, Part 25 and PD 25A. Part 25 of the FPR 2010 closely follows Part 35 of the Civil Procedure Rules (CPR). The guidance in the Practice Direction (PD) (which also covers assessors) incorporates and supersedes the previous Experts' Practice Direction which came into force at the same time as the PLO in April 2008. Part 25 and PD 25A together provide a comprehensive guide to expert evidence in family cases.

10.4.2 Leave for the instruction of experts

In proceedings to which FPR 2010, Part 12 apply (which includes all private and public law children cases), the leave of the court must be obtained for a child to be medically, psychiatrically or otherwise examined: r 12.20. Further, as a result of rr 12.73 and 14.14 (and in particular for the purposes of the law of contempt), disclosure of the case papers to the expert should only happen once the court has authorised the instruction of an expert. A failure to obtain leave for these purposes means that the evidence thereby obtained may not be adduced without leave of the court.

Clearly these rules are important—they ensure that the court has control over any assessment of the child. This protects the child from unwarranted intervention which may not be in his best interests and helps to protect the privacy of the family. As indicated in para 1.7 of PD 25A, in practice, the need to have the court's permission to disclose information to an expert and/or to have the child examined or assessed means that in proceedings in relation to children the court strictly controls the number, fields of expertise and identity of the experts who may be first instructed and then called.

There is another important rule relating to litigation privilege—in other words, the privilege that attaches to expert evidence and other evidence prepared for pending or anticipated litigation. In CA 1989 proceedings, litigation privilege does not apply. Therefore, if the court gives leave to disclose the relevant case papers to an expert, any resulting report from the expert *must be disclosed* to the court and other parties, even if unfavourable to the party commissioning the report. (Litigation privilege should be contrasted with legal professional privilege—communications between client and lawyer for the purpose of obtaining legal advice—which *does* apply to CA 1989 proceedings to protect the confidentiality of lawyer–client communications, unless it is waived: see the salutary tale of the consequences of inadvertently waiving privilege in *Re D (A Child) (Care proceedings: professional privilege)* [2011] EWCA Civ 684.)

The aim of the guidance on experts and expert evidence is set out at para 1.3 of PD 25A. It is to help the court identify at an early stage whether matters are outside its expertise, to help the court and the parties to identify and narrow the issues in the case, to encourage the early identification of any experts and to formulate the questions for them and to encourage disclosure of full and frank information between the parties, the court and any expert instructed. The guidance does not pretend to be comprehensive to cover every eventuality, but should be complied within the spirit of the overriding objective.

10.4.3 Role of the expert in the proceedings

Any expert witness should be referred to Wall LJ's *A Handbook for Expert Witnesses in Children Act Cases* (2nd edition). As its title suggests, it is aimed specifically at the expert body and has useful summaries of practice and guidance. When an expert is instructed before proceedings are issued, it should be made clear to the expert that he may in due course be reporting to the court, and should consider himself bound by Part 25 of the FPR 2010.

As with any other proceedings, the purpose of expert evidence is to provide evidence and information on areas outside the court's expertise. Experts can give opinion evidence on any matter within their expertise which is relevant to the court's decision. That can include the ultimate issue, although the decision is that of the judge—and the judge makes that decision on the basis of all the evidence in the case, not just that of the expert.

Following *M v R (Child Abuse: Evidence)* [1996] 2 FLR 195, it was established that a suitably qualified expert can give evidence as to the credibility or accuracy of a child or other witness, although it was always for the judge to determine the relevance of such evidence and the weight to be attached to it. This might be important, for example, in a sexual abuse case where the physical evidence is limited or even non-existent and reliance is placed on allegations by the child or another witness.

10.4.4 Instructing the expert

One of the first points to note about the instruction of an expert is that generally it is inappropriate for an expert involved in therapeutic treatment of a child to make a forensic report to the court. There are several good and obvious reasons for this: the therapeutic expert will probably have built up a relationship of trust with the child—and/or with the parents—which might be compromised by the same expert having duties to the court; equally that relationship could make it difficult for the treating expert to fulfil the role of court reporter objectively due to sympathy for the child's plight. It is generally better that an independent expert reports and makes recommendations for the child's future. That is not to say that a treating expert will not be expected to give evidence or be involved in proceedings at all—for example, they may have valuable factual information to give on the child's medical history which they are best placed to provide, and indeed, their information as to the child's history will probably form part of the reporting expert's investigations. For consideration of when the treating clinician may be useful as an expert, see *Oldham Metropolitan Council v GW & PW* [2007] 2 FLR 597.

What sort of expert is appropriate? Different expertise might be required for different stages of the court's decision making process. For establishing the threshold criteria, the type of expert evidence required depends very much on the type of harm the child has suffered and which is feared might occur in the future. For a case of neglect (the most common form of abuse), generally speaking, a child psychiatrist would be appropriate to comment upon the emotional harm occasioned by the neglect. Where there are allegations of non-accidental injury or, less dramatically, physical harm occasioned by neglect, a consultant paediatrician would be appropriate. It may very well be necessary to instruct a consultant radiologist as well should there be bone injuries to be assessed. For suspected sexual abuse, there will be a need for medical evidence regarding the child's physical condition and also a child psychiatrist to consider other evidence regarding the abuse, and the emotional effects of abuse that is shown to have occurred.

It may well be that different types of expertise are required in the same case at the 'disposal' (welfare test) stage. The issues in the case will dictate who is required. For example, in a non-accidental injuries case, there may be a need for expert evidence from a psychiatrist or psychologist regarding the abusing parent's ability to control their anger as well as the attachments between the child and the parents and the prognosis for successful rehabilitation of the child to his parents. This evidence will be essentially 'forward looking' in an attempt to predict the outcomes. It must be always borne in mind that the court will need to be persuaded to give leave and has a duty to consider all aspects of the overriding objective; in this context, proportionality is probably the most important.

Duties are placed on the advocates to identify any proposed experts and draft questions for them (in accordance with the PLO and PD 25A) at the Advocates' Meeting which must take place before the CMC. Detailed consideration will, therefore, need to be given to all these matters as early as possible in the proceedings. The questions must be clear and precise.

An example might be the case of a couple whom social services suspect have neglected their 4-year-old child. The child appears to be suffering from developmental delay—she is not putting on weight or growing at a normal rate; she is still in nappies; she was late to learn to walk and her speech and comprehension seem to the social worker to be delayed. Her parents appear largely indifferent to her presence and are not noted to interact with her in a frequent or meaningful way.

You will probably need to instruct a consultant child psychiatrist to consider the following:

(a) To what extent is this child's development delayed by comparison with other children of her age?

(b) What reasons are there for any delay established—in particular, what indications are there that the delay is due to parental neglect?

(c) Comment on the nature and quality of attachment between the child and her parents.

(d) Comment on the degree of insight and understanding her parents have in relation to their child's emotional and developmental needs.

(e) To what extent are her parents capable of meeting her needs at present?

(f) To what extent are her parents capable of improving their capacity to parent, including consideration of their insight into their parenting skills problems and their motivation to address those problems?

(g) What work and resources are likely to be necessary for such improvement to take place?

(h) Over what timescale is such improvement likely to take place, and at what point, if at all, would rehabilitation be feasible?

Questions (a)–(c) are relevant to establishing the threshold by addressing the question of what developmental harm, if any, the child has suffered, and the causation of that harm. Note the comparison to a child of her age without developmental difficulties—CA 1989, s 31(10), see **9.4.5.4**. Questions (c)–(h) address 'disposal'—the child's welfare—by addressing the issue of the parents' ability to understand and overcome problems in their parenting, together with the issue of what resources will be necessary and what timescale is likely. This will help the judge to decide whether a rehabilitation to the parents is feasible and in the child's best interests. The questions asked are very clearly defined according to the issues in the case.

10.4.5   The duties of the expert and the contents of his report

An expert in family proceedings in relation to children has an overriding duty to the court which takes precedence over any obligation to the person from whom he has received his instructions or by whom he is paid (FPR 2010, r 25.3 and para 3.1 of PD 25A). This now mirrors the position in civil proceedings under Part 35 of the CPR. Para 3.2 of PD 25A sets out details for experts of their duties:

1. to assist the court in accordance with the overriding duty;
2. to provide advice which conforms to the best practice of the expert's profession;
3. to provide an independent opinion;
4. to limit his opinion to material issues and to matters within his area of expertise;
5. to alert those instructing to areas outside his expertise on which his advice has been sought and volunteer an opinion as to whether another expert is required;
6. to take into consideration all material facts including those arising from ethnic, cultural, religious or linguistic contexts, when providing his opinion;
7. to inform those instructing without any delay of any change in opinion and the reasons for such change.

In addition, para 3.3 of PD 25A gives detailed guidance on the content of the report:

The expert's report shall be addressed to the Court and filed in accordance with the Court's timetable and shall:

1. Give details of the expert's qualifications and experience.
2. Contain a statement setting out the substance of all material instructions (whether written or oral) summarising the facts stated and instructions given to the expert which are material to the conclusions and opinions expressed in the report.
3. Identify materials that have not been produced whether as original medical or other professional records or in response to an instruction from a party.
4. Identify all requests to third parties for disclosure and their response.
5. Make clear which facts in the report are within the expert's own knowledge.
6. State who carried out any test, examination or interview which the expert has used for the report and whether or not the test, examination or interview has been carried out under the expert's supervision.

7. Give details of the qualifications of any person who carried out the test, examination or interview.

8. In expressing an opinion:
   (a) take into account all material facts as set out under his duties at 6 above and give details of any literature or other research material upon which the expert has relied in giving an opinion;

   (b) describe his own professional risk assessment process and process of differential diagnosis;

   (c) indicate whether a proposition is a hypothesis (in particular a controversial one) or an opinion deduced in accordance with peer-reviewed and tested technique, research and experience accepted as consensus in the scientific body.

   (d) indicate whether an opinion is provisional or qualified and giving necessary consequential details.

9. Where there is a range of opinion:
   (a) summarise the range;

   (b) highlight and analyse within the range an 'unknown cause', (eg too little information to form a scientific opinion);

   (c) give reasons for any opinion expressed, the court finding it of great assistance if a balance sheet approach is used with factors that support and undermine the opinion.

10. Contain a summary of the expert's conclusions and opinions.

11. Contain a statement that the expert understands his duty to the Court and has complied with that duty.

12. Contain a statement that the expert has no conflict of interest (other than one already disclosed), does not consider that any disclosed interest affects his suitability as an expert in the case and that he will notify the instructing party if there is any change in this.

13. Be verified by a statement of truth in prescribed form.

In this way, the PD seeks to ensure that the basis of the report is made clear—the factual assumptions made, the ambit of the expert's instruction, the methods used must all be stated. This is important since any of these matters can form the basis of cross-examination to test the reliability and significance of the report. Experts no longer have immunity from a claim for professional negligence arising out of their involvement as an expert in court proceedings: *Jones v Kaney* [2011] UKSC 13.

10.4.6   Dealing with expert evidence at a hearing

This section will focus on the cross-examination of experts. Experts do give evidence-in-chief but this tends to be quite limited—rather like a witness statement, their report stands as their evidence-in-chief and so examination-in-chief is restricted to explaining and expanding matters which are not clear from the report and/or obtaining the expert's views on any new matters which have arisen since the time of the report.

It may be that the expert is never called to give evidence and the report is accepted. In addition, if there is more than one expert, an experts' meeting (see FPR 2010, r 25.12 and para 6.2, PD 25A) may have narrowed the actual disagreements between them quite sharply, so that their evidence and your cross-examination can be narrowly focused on those areas.

Cross-examining any expert is a considerable challenge for an advocate. The expert inevitably knows far more about his area of expertise than you do. There are a number of matters that it is useful to bear in mind.

First, there are particular differences between the evidence of an expert and the evidence of most other witnesses.

- Experts tend to speak in 'probabilities' rather than absolutes. For example, when predicting the child's future, a child and adolescent psychologist may state that it is 'unlikely' that the parents can improve their parenting difficulties sufficiently 'within an appropriate timescale' for the child. He cannot say definitely that they will or will not, or what that timescale truly is—nobody can. He is having to express an *opinion* based on facts and analysis of what is known so far.

- Normally, experts draw conclusions and give evidence without first-hand knowledge of many of the facts they rely on. Of course, an expert will have direct experience of some facts—eg, if they have observed a play session between parent and child they can give direct evidence of what they saw as a question of fact. But much of the information on which an expert relies in drawing conclusions is at second hand—provided by others, for example, social work records and the papers disclosed with leave of the court.

With this in mind, David Bedingfield states three questions that an advocate must consider when preparing to cross-examine an expert:

(1) How did the expert conduct his assessment? The advocate must always seek to understand the methods used by the expert in order to reach the opinion that was reached.

(2) What did the expert assess? The advocate must seek to understand the factual matrix used by the expert, and seek to pin down the expert on what factual assumptions were made.

(3) Why is the assessment wrong? Why did the assessment reach that conclusion?

(See David Bedingfield, *Advocacy in Family Proceedings: A Practical Guide*, Jordan's Family Law, 2005.)

As Bedingfield goes on to point out, in order to undermine the expert's evidence, the expert must be shown to have made an error on one of these three fundamental questions. Cross-examination will therefore seek to show a problem with the expert's method(s), and/or an erroneous factual assumption on which the conclusion is based which then renders the conclusion unreliable (or where a fact relied on is the subject of dispute in the proceedings, that the expert would have concluded differently if the fact relied on was incorrect—disproving the fact relied on is then an issue for cross-examination of the witness who provided the challenged fact).

As Bedingfield explains, challenging the expert on an error on the third question will almost always fail unless a successful attack can be made on either or both of the first two questions—unless there is other evidence in the case which contradicts the expert's conclusion—normally a report from an equally well-qualified expert disagreeing with the expert in question.

You should never attempt to prepare or carry out a cross-examination without having a clear idea of what you want to be able to say about this witness's evidence in a closing speech—and experts are no exception. Have a clear idea about what helpful evidence this expert could give for your case; and in what way he or she damages your case. The content of your cross-examination will be driven by the issues in the case, but the following grounds of challenge may be appropriate:

- **Difference between your case and expert's view is a question of degree**. Because experts speak in probabilities (see above), a major aim of cross-examination will often be to establish that the difference between your case and his view is a question of degree—and obviously, the closer the case, the more powerful this point becomes. For example, say you are acting for the local authority. Your case is that even if the parents could improve their parenting and overcome drug dependency with intensive work, they cannot do so soon enough—this child is 2 years old and needs permanent placement very soon. The parents' expert has stated that progress could be made by the parents within three months. In cross-examination you will be seeking to 'extend' that period to introduce doubt—so you will make reasonable suggestions such as that a lapse in the drug rehabilitation programme could easily extend the time the parents need by many months. The expert would probably agree—enabling you to 'chip away' at the parents' suggestion that they can improve in a time suitable for the child.

- **Expert has based conclusions on facts reported by others.** It is therefore possible to 'separate' the facts on which the expert relies from his personal expertise and credibility—you are not attacking his judgment, rather the facts on which he has drawn conclusions—if the facts were different, would his conclusion have been different? Usually the answer will be 'yes'. You will then aim to undermine the important fact(s) when cross-examining the witness who reported them.

- **Alternative version.** You can suggest alternative versions of the facts to an expert to establish how that would change his conclusions. You *must* ensure that those alternative versions are facts for which you have evidence in support (such as the evidence of the parents) and that the facts you suggest accurately reflect the version of events that your other evidence will prove—otherwise a positive answer from the expert proves nothing. As with all these questions, be very careful how you prepare the line of questioning—if it becomes muddled, the effect is lost.

- **Alternative interpretations of facts.** This can be quite a tricky area. Evidently you will never be as 'expert' on the area as the person you are cross-examining, but you will have made an effort to try to understand the area. The same facts relied upon might support other interpretations. For example, petechial marks on a child's neck (these are little rash-like areas of tiny red dots—they are the result of little capillaries bursting) can be highly indicative of abuse—but an alternative cause is a child having a coughing fit while wearing a collar that is too tight; or a badly fitting seatbelt.

- **Reasonable suggestion.** Provided the alternative facts or the alternative interpretation you put is reasonable, an expert who resists such a suggestion too strongly looks less credible.

- **Method.** The methods employed by the expert may have weaknesses—eg, a test may take account of one feature of someone's personality, but take insufficient account of, or be a poor test of, another feature. It might be reliant on the quality of the information 'fed into' the test, which might be erroneous or contain assumptions. Certain factors may have been overlooked or gone untested. This area of cross-examination would be easier if you are fortunate enough to have an expert instructed for your party who can advise you on the adequacy of the other expert's methods.

- **Bias.** It is very rare for an expert to lie, but it is not unknown for them to be biased or in some way have a personal interest. It may be helpful to find out prior to cross-examination whether the expert tends to give evidence for one side (eg, local authority, or parents) rather than the other. Equally, the expert may be strongly identified with a 'pet theory' and therefore feels his personal reputation is as much at stake as the interests of the parties in the proceedings. Occasionally, experts have 'relied upon' facts which have not been observed by either themselves or any other witness—clearly, that would lend doubt to the expert's credibility.

- **Qualifications**. Exceptionally, the expert's qualifications to provide the evidence may be insufficient. This would, however, be most unusual in care proceedings, and there would almost certainly be fault on the part of the lawyer or lawyers instructing him for such an expert to be chosen in the first place.

Further reading and information

- Expert Witness Pack—draft letters of instruction, guidelines for report writing, etc. Published by the Expert Witness Group, and Family Law
- Brophy J. (ed), *Child Psychiatry and Child Protection Litigation* (Gaskell, 2001)

Experts—key authorities

- *Re U (Serious Injury: Standard of Proof); Re B* [2004] 2 FLR 263—guidance on treatment of expert evidence by courts post-*R v Cannings*
- *Oldham Metropolitan Borough Council v GW & PW* [2007] 2 FLR 597
- *R v Henderson; Butler and Oyediran* [2010] EWCA Crim 1269—guidance on conflicting expert evidence in baby shaking cases
- *Jones v Kaney* [2011] UKSC 13, [2011] 2 FLR 312

10.5 Role of the Children's Guardian

10.5.1 Appointment of the Children's Guardian

Apart from the local authority and the parents, there is almost always another party to the proceedings—the Children's Guardian (see CA 1989, s 41(1) and FPR 2010, r 16.3), for there is a presumption favouring appointment of a Children's Guardian in specified proceedings—which include applications for care and supervision orders. This will be a person drawn from the Guardian ad Litem and Reporting Officer Service of the Children and Family Court Advisory and Support Service (Cafcass), and the Children's Guardian is an officer of the court. The appointment of the Guardian in public law proceedings is governed by r 12.6 and his duties are set out in r 16.20 and PD 16A. The Children's Guardian acts for the child in public law proceedings, since a child is, by law, a person under a disability. The Children's Guardian will usually select a solicitor to act as advocate in the proceedings on the instructions of the Children's Guardian—it would not be compatible with the Guardian's obligations as a witness in the proceedings for the Guardian to also act as advocate. For rules governing appointment of a solicitor for the child, and what happens when the child is sufficiently mature to instruct the solicitor for himself, see Hershman and McFarlane at C 2707 and C 2811–20. In relation to the law on Children's Guardians and the responsibilities of the solicitor for the child generally, see section 6 of part C, Hershman and McFarlane.

The local authority has obligations to consult with the Children's Guardian where one is appointed. It would be wrong for the local authority to change a child's circumstances in a major way without first discussing the matter with the Guardian; equally, an application for a care or supervision order should not be withdrawn without such prior discussion.

10.5.2 Responsibilities of the Children's Guardian

By s 41(2)(b), the Children's Guardian is under a duty to safeguard the interests of the child in the manner prescribed by the rules. Upon appointment, he or she must appoint a solicitor for the child (see **10.5.1** above). The requirements imposed by the rules can be summarised as follows:

- give advice to the child as appropriate to his age and understanding;
- instruct the solicitor representing the child on matters relevant to the child's interests;
- notify any person whose joinder to the proceedings would assist in safeguarding the child's interests (in the Guardian's view) of their right to apply to be joined;
- attend all hearings, including directions hearings, unless excused by the court, and provide the court with such other assistance as it may require;
- prepare a written report where ordered to do so, and in any event prepare a written report for the final hearing; and
- accept service of documents on behalf of the child and advise the child on the contents of the documents in as far as appropriate given his age and understanding.

Most importantly, the Children's Guardian is empowered, and indeed obliged, to investigate and advise the court on the basis of that investigation. He or she will give evidence at a final hearing (and if appropriate at earlier hearings, such as a contested ICO), and will be cross-examined by the other parties in the normal way, although the court has the power to limit the issues on which cross-examination may take place. The Guardian's background is almost always as a child protection social work practitioner, and they therefore tend to be regarded as independent social work—ie, child care—experts. Their views carry significant weight with the court. The Guardian must have regard to the principle of the CA 1989 that delay is likely to be prejudicial to the welfare of the child, and to the elements of the welfare checklist (CA 1989, s 1(3)).

10.5.3 Investigation by the Children's Guardian

This is a vital part of the Guardian's role. The Guardian has access to relevant records of the local authority (see CA 1989, s 42), including the right to take copies, and can bring relevant records and documents to the court's attention. The Guardian's access is quite wide ranging (see Hershman and McFarlane at C 2747–49) and will include certain records held by voluntary organisations and registered children's homes.

Further, the Guardian may interview those persons he or she considers relevant, and as directed by the court. Evidently, this will involve seeing the child (on a fairly regular basis), the family, the social work practitioners involved, health visitors and other agencies involved with the family, plus other professionals who have been involved in the child's care (eg, hospital staff, day nurseries, etc).

The Guardian may also obtain other professional assistance where necessary. The Guardian's expertise is in child care—it would therefore be wrong for him or her to attempt to express expertise in other areas, such as paediatrics. In such cases, the Guardian can obtain expert evidence to assist, with the leave of the court.

10.5.4   The Children's Guardian's report

PD 16A, para 6.6 sets out the matters on which the Children's Guardian must advise the court. The Children's Guardian may be asked to assist the court at interim hearings—this might be by way of written evidence or oral report. Examples could be as to the desirability of an assessment of the child being sought by another party, or on the question of a contested application for an ICO. At a final hearing, a written report must be filed in advance of the hearing, and the guardian will give evidence and be cross-examined. The report for a final hearing will summarise the Guardian's investigations and his or her conclusions from those investigations as to the options available to the court and the suitability of the local authority's care plan. A Children's Guardian can make specific recommendations, and a court should not depart from these without giving reasons in the judgment (*Re D* (*Grant of Care Order: Refusal of Freeing Order*) [2001] 1 FLR 862). See further Hershman and McFarlane C 2751. The report is confidential and distribution of the report carefully controlled beyond its provision to the parties in the case.

10.6   Key issues during proceedings prior to a final hearing

This section aims to provide you with a starting point to consider a number of common problems and issues which can confront you prior to (and sometimes even at) a final hearing.

10.6.1   Section 38(6) CA 1989 directions for assessment

As you have seen, there is often a considerable body of assessment available at the early stages of proceedings—eg, an initial assessment and a core assessment by the local authority. Once proceedings have commenced, the court's leave is required for any assessment of the child (see **10.4.1**). It may be that the parties can agree that further assessment is required, and on the specific type of assessment—alternatively, there may be disagreement on these issues. Under CA 1989, s 38(6), the court can direct that further assessment be carried out, whether by the local authority or upon instruction by another party. The section reads as follows:

Where the court makes an interim care order, or an interim supervision order, it may give such directions (if any) as it considers appropriate with regard to the medical or psychiatric examination or other assessment of the child; but if the child is of sufficient understanding to make an informed decision he may refuse to submit to the examination or other assessment.

This is an important section—the local authority may have PR under an ICO, but this is one example of the fact that the court has some control over its exercise—the court can order an assessment in an appropriate case even if the local authority does not want it.

There was once a sharp distinction drawn by the courts between 'assessment' and 'therapy'—the former was permissible, the latter was not. This distinction was problematic—for example, some organisations (eg, The Priory) provide assessment which has elements of therapy. The distinction is still relevant and was considered by the House of Lords in *Re G* (cited below). The court emphasised that the purpose of the subsection was to enable the court to obtain the information it needed and to control the information gathering activities of others. The principal focus of the assessment must be the child and any services which were provided must be ancillary to the aim of obtaining the necessary information.

The key point in a s 38(6) application is whether or not the assessment is *necessary for a court to have sufficient information* before it to make the final decision in the case. 'Assessment' is wider than psychiatric or medical assessment, and can include assessment of the *parents* together with their child (often as a *residential assessment*)—a significant point in many cases where the ability of the parents to care properly is doubted. Such assessments are not limited, however, to residential settings and the court has power to direct an assessment in a family setting under the umbrella of an ICO (see *Re A* cited below). The court will not ignore the resource implications for funding by the local authority—some assessments are simply prohibitively expensive—although the court can direct the assessment is funded in any event. Section 38(6) of the CA 1989 can be used to prohibit an assessment. What is clear, however, is that s 38(6) cannot be used simply to provide therapy for any of the parties. It is essential that you are familiar with the key authorities in this area before you seek to argue such an application.

> ### Key authorities
>
> - *Re G (Interim Care Order: Residential Assessment)* [2006] 1 AC 576, [2006] 1 FLR 601
> - *Re J (Care: Rehabilitation Plan)* [1998] 2 FLR 498
> - *Lambeth London Borough Council v F* [2005] 2 FLR 1171
> - *Re A (Residential Assessment)* [2009] 2 FLR 443
> - *Re W (a child)* [2011] EWCA Civ 661

10.6.2 Exclusion orders in care proceedings

The ability to attach an exclusion requirement to an ICO under CA 1989, s 38A(2) is a relatively recent power, and a welcome addition to the court's armoury. The order is dependent on an ICO being made, and ss 38A(2) and 44(A) set out the conditions: see **2.19.2**.

The exclusion order can include a provision requiring the relevant person to leave a dwelling-house in which he or she is living with the child; prohibiting the relevant person from entering a dwelling-house in which the child lives; and excluding the relevant person from an area in which a dwelling-house in which the child lives is situated (s 38A(3)). The court has power to attach a power of arrest to such an order: s 38A(5). You should familiarise yourself with the other provisions of s 38(A). By s 38(B), the court has power to accept an undertaking from the relevant person instead—a power of arrest may not be attached to an undertaking but it is otherwise enforceable as an order of the court. Note that both the order and the undertaking would cease to have effect if the child is removed from the house in question for more than 24 hours continuously. For procedural requirements, see Hershman and McFarlane C 1468–75.

The significance of these powers is clear. It may be apparent on the evidence that the harm or threat of harm to the child would be eliminated or sufficiently reduced if an abuser in his household were to be removed. For example, the father may have perpetrated appalling violence on the mother of which the child is aware. If the father is excluded, the immediate risk reduces (provided that the mother stays away from him) and this may mean that the child does not have to be removed from his home or main carer. Notice the need for consent to the order from the person remaining to care for the child. Another example would be where one adult in the household is suspected of physical or sexual abuse of the child and another adult is willing to accept the need to protect the child. These powers are important in such circumstances because, where possible, it is likely to be far less disruptive for a child to remain with familiar carers and significant adults in his life, and to stay in his home.

10.6.3 Split hearings

The final determination of the case is often dependent on the nature of the findings of fact made about the abuse suffered by the child. The difficulty is that in the classic final hearing, the court considers whether the proven facts meet the threshold criteria, and then what the decision should be on the child's future (disposal) *at one hearing*. However, the findings of fact relevant to the threshold *inform and determine* the shape of the investigation that occurs during the proceedings, and sometimes it is necessary to prove the relevant facts for the threshold *before* the final hearing in order to decide what assessments and information the court needs to make the decision on disposal at the final hearing. In a typical neglect/emotional harm case, there may be little need to prove facts in order to work out what assessments are required—the key focus will often be on how parents respond to intervention and parenting skills work done during the life of the case. However, in other, perhaps more dramatic, situations, it may be essential to decide what the factual position is *first* in order to work out what assessments if any are then necessary for the court to make a final decision. Take this example:

> The parents are a young married couple. They take their 14-month-old child to the casualty department at the local hospital, explaining that the child had a fall the previous evening and still seems to be uncomfortable. The treating consultant paediatrician is suspicious of their story, which seems to vary in the detail, especially as to when the fall occurred. Radiological examination shows multiple injuries of apparently different ages, some of which are indicative of non-accidental injury.
>
> The local authority's case is that this is non-accidental injury. The parents deny this, saying the injuries must be the results of accidents.

Clearly, this is essential to a finding on the threshold criteria at a final hearing—and also to decisions on disposal. There are three possibilities: the injuries were deliberately inflicted—a very serious form of abuse; the injuries were a result of innocent events which were nevertheless avoidable—indicating a failure to provide proper care by not keeping the child safe; or the injuries were from innocent causes which were simply unlucky and not due to a failure of care.

The difficulties for the court, if findings of fact have to wait to a final hearing, are that the response and required assessment in order to have the right information for a final decision on the child's future would be quite different for each circumstance. For the deliberate abuse, assessment would have to focus upon trying to assess which parent was the abuser and which was not; whether the abusive parent accepts responsibility and has insight into the causes of the loss of control; whether the non-abusive parent is able to protect the child from the abusive parent and put the child's safety before their own needs to trust the other parent and have a relationship with the other parent; and whether the abusive parent can change their behaviour. Clearly the degree of risk is high, and will require specialist assessment. For the 'neglect' circumstances, the assessment will probably focus on work with the parents to improve their ability to recognise risks and protect the child from such risks—in order to provide an important aspect of child care properly. It may be that other aspects of their care—which would be assessed by way of a local authority core assessment—are acceptable. The final scenario—accident which the reasonable parent's care could not have avoided—probably does not even require intervention.

Other examples might be where it is unclear who the perpetrator of the abuse was; or whether the child has suffered sexual abuse.

It is in cases like these, where the facts need to be established in order to determine what information will be necessary for the court to make a final decision on the child's future, that a split hearing is likely to be required. Fact-finding hearings are regularly held as the first part of a contested care case. The findings will then inform the preparation for the disposal hearing, which must be heard by the same judge: *Re B (Care Proceedings: Standard of Proof)* [2008] 2 FLR 141.

There is one special class of case in which split hearings could be appropriate, and which is worth specifically mentioning here. Situations arise in which a child has apparently suffered significant harm, but it is unclear *who the perpetrator is*. For example, a child may have suffered non-accidental injuries, but neither parent admits responsibility. In this case, it is hard to tell who presents the risk to the child, and therefore what the future level of risk is, what future assessments need to be carried out, whether the risk can be ameliorated by intervention (eg, anger management counselling with the abusing parent) and whether the child could be safely placed with one parent if the other parent were no longer part of the household. It makes future planning for the child very difficult indeed. The situation can be complicated still further if the parents seek to blame their babysitter, or child minder, or another family member—any of whom may be responsible because the child has at relevant times been in their care. Not only does this present problems for future work with the family and the assessment of risk for long-term planning—it also causes difficulties in establishing whether the threshold is met, since it has to be shown that the significant harm, or risk of significant harm, is due to the child not receiving the care that a reasonable parent would give.

In regard to the threshold criteria, the leading authority is *Lancashire County Council v B* [2000] AC 147, where the House of Lords held that the threshold can be met by a finding that the child suffered harm in the care of his parents or other carers—there is no need to precisely prove who was responsible for the injuries. See also, however, *Re S-B* [2010] 1 FLR 1161 and the discussion at **9.4.6** on the proof required for the risk of harm.

For purposes of the welfare part of the decision (disposal), it is obviously better if the perpetrator of the harm can be identified for the reasons given above. The judge hearing the preliminary hearing should attempt to give such assistance as is possible for social services and those experts having to carry out assessment as to the facts. For further consideration of this issue, see Baroness Hale in *Re B* (below) at paras 59–61. However, it would appear that the courts began to order split hearings unnecessarily and there were concerns that this was both leading to delay and increasing the difficulties in maintaining judicial continuity. In May 2010 the President of the Family Division issued *Guidance in Relation to Split Hearings*. This applies to both private and public law proceedings and reminds the judiciary that fact-finding hearings should only be ordered if the court takes the view that the case *cannot* be decided without one.

Another crucial aspect to consider is whether (and if so, how) evidence from children the subject matter of alleged abuse should give evidence. The Supreme Court has held that the presumption against a child giving evidence in such circumstances was not consistent with Art 6 of the European Convention on Human Rights: *Re W* (cited below). It has given guidance on how to strike the balance between Art 6 and Art 8 by weighing the advantages that it would bring to determine the truth by calling the child against the damage it might do to the welfare of that child or any other child.

> **Key authorities**
>
> - *Re S (Care Proceedings: Split Hearings)* [1996] 2 FLR 773
> - *Re P (Children) (Care Proceedings: Split Hearing)* [2007] EWCA Civ 1265; [2008] 1 FCR 72
> - *Re B (Care Proceedings: Standard of Proof)* [2008] 2 FLR 141
> - *Re W (Children) (Family Proceedings: Evidence)* [2010] UKSC 12; [2010] 1 FLR 1485

10.6.4 General principles of evidence

Part 22 of the FPR 2010 sets out the evidential rules which apply in family proceedings. The court effectively has complete control over the evidence it receives, having the power both to exclude relevant evidence and to admit evidence which does not strictly comply with the rules. It will determine the issues in respect of which it requires evidence and the form that evidence should take. It may also limit cross-examination: r22.1. Evidence is generally given by witness statement and the rules are the same as in general civil proceedings, namely that the witness statement stands as the evidence in chief of the witness, and the witness must generally be called and be available for cross-examination.

10.6.5 Criminal proceedings and care proceedings

It is often the case that the circumstances that have given rise to child protection concerns for the child have simultaneously become the subject of criminal proceedings, or at least a criminal investigation. This is scarcely surprising—assault, sexual abuse and similar allegations in care proceedings are criminal offences as well as child abuse. However, the fact that there are two sets of proceedings ongoing can cause difficulties. First, the standard of proof in care proceedings, being civil proceedings, is lower than that in criminal proceedings (where the allegation must be proven beyond reasonable doubt). This has two effects—if the factual allegation is proved in the criminal proceedings, then it has been proved to a higher standard than it would need to be in care proceedings. Conversely, the finding of a fact against a respondent in care proceedings, who is also facing criminal charges arising out of the same circumstances, is of little relevance to the criminal proceedings given the higher standard of proof. The main principle is that pending criminal proceedings are not necessarily a reason to adjourn the care proceedings. Obviously, findings of guilt in criminal proceedings on an allegation common to the care and criminal proceedings can be helpful for the local authority in the care proceedings; however, the disadvantage of awaiting the result of the criminal proceedings is likely to be a substantial delay in determining the future of the child.

The most important issue relates to the sharing of information between police, or the Crown Prosecution Service (CPS) conducting an investigation, and the local authority involved in child protection. This section will look at the following aspects: the privilege against self-incrimination in care proceedings; problems of confidentiality and disclosure of documents in care proceedings; and the obtaining of documents from the police for use in child protection and care proceedings. For wider questions of public interest immunity, refer to Chapter 7, section 5 of part C, Hershman and McFarlane. This is a particularly complex area.

10.6.5.1 No privilege against self-incrimination in care proceedings

By CA 1989, s 98:

(1)   In any proceedings in which a court is hearing an application for an order under Part IV or V, no person shall be excused from—

(a) giving evidence on any matter; or

(b) answering any question put to him in the course of his giving evidence on the ground that doing so might incriminate him or his spouse of an offence.

(2)   A statement or admission made in such proceedings shall not be admissible in evidence against the person making it or his spouse in proceedings for an offence other than perjury.

It is therefore clear that there is no privilege against self-incrimination in care proceedings. This is perhaps unsurprising, given the prime importance of protecting the welfare of children. Subsection 2 seems to give some protection against use of statements and admissions made in care proceedings from being used in subsequent criminal proceedings. While 'statement or admission' is given a wide meaning (it includes statements while giving oral evidence and in a written statement of evidence filed in the proceedings, and admissions made to the Children's Guardian and to expert witnesses while preparing assessments), note that the protection is only against such statements being *admissible* in criminal proceedings. It would not prevent, for example, a third party such as the police using in a criminal *investigation* documents properly disclosed to them. The question is, in what circumstances will such documents be disclosed to third parties?

10.6.5.2 Confidentiality and disclosure to third parties

As a general rule information relating to private court proceedings, which include the majority of family cases, is to be kept confidential. This is a part of the point of conducting the proceedings away from the glare of publicity. However, parties clearly need to speak to their legal advisors and lawyers need to speak to expert witnesses, and so forth, so the FPR 2010 set out the circumstances when information can be exchanged. This includes: communications between parties, their legal representatives, with the Children's Guardian, with the Legal Services Commission (to obtain legal aid, etc) and so forth (r 12.73(1)(a)); court sanctioned experts (r 12.74); and other persons (eg, a mediator) intimately connected with the legal process and only for very narrow purposes (see r 12.75). Otherwise, no disclosure of information can be made to third parties without the permission of the court: r 12.73(1)(b). Note that when allowing disclosure, the court can order the withholding of specific confidential information: see *Re R (Securing Editing of Documents)* [2007] below, in relation to documents where key information *must* remain confidential.

The first point to make is that the confidentiality of information in such cases is not absolute, since the court can order disclosure. But the new rules may be more liberal in terms of sharing information since there would now seem to be more persons to whom disclosure can be made without the permission of the court. Under the previous rules, for example, the police always needed the court's permission to obtain documents in care proceedings which revealed possible criminal activity. Now, they may come under the description of 'a professional acting in furtherance of the protection of children' (r 12.73(1)(a)(viii)).

Where permission is required, it seems that the principles in the leading case of *Re EC* (cited below) apply, subject to the comments in *Re C* and *Re H*. These say that the court will seek to balance the welfare of the child, the importance of encouraging frankness in the care proceedings, the public interest in the proper administration of justice and prosecution of serious crime, and fairness to the person when deciding whether to give permission. There will obviously be a difference between cases where there is a factual link between the care proceedings and any criminal proceedings, and those where they are unconnected. But the fact remains that there can be no guarantee of confidentiality in any case.

Hershman and McFarlane also reproduce (at C 2967) Munby J's examination of these factors in *Re X* (*Disclosure of Information*). You should read this section of the judgment (citation below) and also the summary (at C 2968) of cases where disclosure has been allowed for a variety of purposes.

Key authorities—10.6.5.1 to 10.6.5.2

- *Re EC* (*Disclosure of Material*) [1996] 2 FLR 725
- *Re X* (*Disclosure of Information*) [2001] 2 FLR 440
- *Re C* (*Disclosure: Sexual Abuse Findings*) [2002] 2 FLR 375
- *Re R* (*Securing Editing of Documents*) [2007] 2 FLR 759
- *Re H* (*Care Proceedings: Disclosure*) [2009] 2 FLR 1531

10.6.5.3   Obtaining documents from the police for use in care proceedings

Of course, it often happens that matters are 'the other way around'—the local authority in particular may wish to obtain documents from the police for use in care proceedings. The grounds would be that information contained in the documents may well assist the local authority in discharging its statutory duties in relation to a child in the care proceedings. As Hershman and McFarlane point out, there are actually two stages to the issue of disclosure in such circumstances:

(a) disclosure by the police to the local authority; and

(b) further disclosure by the police or local authority to parties to the care proceedings.

(See *Nottinghamshire County Council v H* [1995] 1 FLR 115.) The normal procedure would be a witness summons against the chief constable for the force in question requiring production of the material requested. The test for the court is to balance the public interest in maintaining confidentiality of materials whose disclosure could prejudice an investigation or prosecution against the public interest in ensuring that a local authority has available all material which will assist in proper development of proposals for the future of the child in question. See further, Hershman and McFarlane C 2976–77 for the full procedure and specifically the procedure regarding further disclosure of information obtained by the local authority to other parties in the care proceedings.

Where there are no pending care proceedings, the rules are different—it is again a question of inter-agency sharing of information for effective child protection.

10.7   The care plan

10.7.1   Purpose of the care plan

In every application for a care order, the local authority must produce a 'care plan' for the court's scrutiny: CA 1989, s 31A. Indeed, rigorous scrutiny of the care plan is an essential part of the 'disposal' decision on such applications (see *Re J* cited below), but it will also be scrutinised regularly by the court and when an ICO is sought. The purpose of the document is to provide the essential information about long-term planning for the child—this enables the court to see what the local authority's plans are for that child if the order sought is granted. The proposals should be supported by evidence and proper details of proposed placements should be given.

10.7.2 What should the care plan contain?

The care plan must accord with the Care Planning, Placement and Case Review (England) Regulations 2010 SI 2010/959, which came into force on 1 April 2011. The new Regulations are accompanied by four sets of statutory guidance: *Putting Care Into Practice: Statutory Guidance for Local Authorities On Care Planning, Placement and Case Review For Looked After Children*. The four sets of statutory guidance form the new revised Volume 2 of the CA 1989 statutory guidance which can be found on the Department of Education website. There is specific guidance on the contents of a care plan in Regulation 5 and Schedule 1 of these Regulations, and paragraph 2.44 of the Guidance summarises the matters that the care plan should contain:

- information about the long-term plans for the child, including timescales (permanence planning);
- the arrangements to meet the child's needs in line with the child's developmental domain of the *Framework*;
- in particular, the child's need for contact with any siblings;
- details of any court orders made under s 8 or s 34 of the CA 1989;
- arrangements for promoting and maintaining contact with a parent and anyone else with PR;
- details of the placement plan and why the placement was chosen;
- details of the child's health and personal education plan;
- the wishes and feelings of relevant people about the arrangements for the child and about any proposed changes to the care plan.

The local authority should have a contingency plan, should the care plan not be achievable.

10.7.3 Permanent placement options

The care plan will indicate where the local authority proposes to place the child should the order be granted. The most common alternative possibilities are now considered.

- Rehabilitation with parents/family. This would obviously be the preferred option for the family. The local authority will have taken the view from evidence available from the various assessments and work with the family during the care proceedings that the parents have shown sufficient improvement in the aspects of parenting skill that had caused initial concern, and that the child can now be returned to their care within a suitable period of time. This will usually be pursuant to a careful plan for phased return (eg, increasing contact over a period of time coupled with ongoing work on parenting skills or counselling). Sometimes, this will have begun by the time of the final hearing (in consultation with the Children's Guardian). Under the care order, the local authority will continue to share PR with the parents (see **9.4.1**), so can act quickly to protect the child should things go wrong. If rehabilitation is successful, the parents might apply at some suitable time in future to discharge the care order, for a residence order (RO) in their favour (automatically discharging the care order) or to substitute for a supervision order (see **9.4.8**). Sometimes rehabilitation to the parents is not possible, and placement is planned with another family member who has been assessed as suitable and who is willing to assist. This could be under a care order—an alternative possibility is that that person is granted an RO or a Special Guardianship Order (SGO) and the local authority does not share PR. This could occur if it is clear that such a placement will eliminate the risks.

- Permanent placement with foster parents. In this situation, the foster parents do not acquire PR—this is held by the local authority under the care order. The parents continue to hold PR, but cannot exercise it inconsistently with that of the local authority. The foster family will become the child's main home, providing all care for the child and a permanent substitute family. The parents (and possibly other significant members of the child's natural family) will usually be granted contact with the child as appropriate to the child's welfare (see **9.10**), and proposals for contact will become an important part of the court's decision. Generally, contact will be encouraged although there may be a need to restrict it where it undermines the child's sense of security with the foster family (often because of undermining tactics by the parents). As a very general rule of thumb, foster care tends to be a suitable disposal where the child is too old (or possibly too damaged by his experiences) for adoption—very approximately, children of about 5 years of age and above may be unsuitable for adoption. Because foster care therefore concentrates largely on older children, many of those children have suffered abuse or neglect over some considerable period of their lives, and can present considerable challenges to foster carers.

- Adoption. This is perhaps the most extreme outcome for parents. Upon adoption, the parents lose their PR for the child (as indeed does the local authority, for the care order would also lapse), and the adoptive parents acquire it. It is effectively a 'family transplant'. There is likely to be very little contact allowed to the birth family. Direct contact is almost never allowed, there may or may not be some heavily controlled provision for indirect contact (such as a birthday card for the child once a year), and 'life story' work will at some stage usually be done with the adopted child so that he or she has a sense of their own identity. Birth parents may be permitted to provide photographs and the like for that purpose. This is usually the preferred option where the child is relatively young—the younger the child, the more likely the success of the adoption. There are often issues where the child has older siblings who cannot be adopted—a desire to maintain the children's relationships with each other can in such situations either indicate fostering for all the children, or some agreement for contact with siblings where some of the children are adopted.

- Care homes, special schools. These are obviously the least preferable outcome for any child, since they do not involve a family environment. There are some children for whom rehabilitation is not possible, and who are unsuitable for fostering or adoption. An example may be a child who has been sexually abused and who has become a threat to other children as a result of sexualised behaviour; or a child whose behaviour is so challenging that it cannot be handled within a family environment. Specialist professional care could be the only option. In these cases, contact with the birth family may be feasible, again with due consideration for its effect on the child's welfare.

10.7.4   Care plans and human rights

Clearly, permanent placement away from the natural family has the potential for interference with the Art 8 rights of the child and those of the family for family life with each other. This is all the more so with adoption, involving the permanent destruction of ties between child and family. There are, of course, the competing Art 8 rights of the child to proper care and a stable, loving permanent home. The court must balance these competing rights when making a final decision on whether to grant the care order with the care plan proposed. The principle of proportionality in European human rights law is of particular importance. In *Re C and B* (*Care Order: Future Harm*) [2001] 1 FLR 611, Hale LJ stated:

> The principle has to be that the local authority works to support, and eventually reunite the family, unless the risks are so high that the child's welfare requires alternative family care.

And later:

> Intervention in the family must be proportionate, but the aim should be to reunite the family when the circumstances enable that, and the effort should be devoted towards that end. Cutting off all contact and the relationship between the child and their family is only justified by the overriding necessity of the interests of the child.

There are further human rights issues which arise with respect to care plans, considered in the next section.

10.7.5   The court cannot alter the local authority's care plan

The scheme of the statute, the CA 1989, empowers the court to decide whether to make, or withhold, the care order. However, once the care order is made, the court has no ongoing control over the way in which the local authority implements its care plan (see *Re J* cited below). This presents two problems. First, the court may consider that a care order is necessary to safeguard the child's welfare, but that the local authority's care plan is inappropriate. An example might be that the local authority plans that the child should be adopted, whilst the court considers that a proper attempt should be made to rehabilitate the child to the parents. *The court has no power to order the local authority to change the care plan*—it can only make, or refuse to make, the care order. The court could be faced with an awkward situation—the child will not be safe unless the local authority shares PR with the parents under a care order, but if the care order is made, the child's ties with his parents will end because the local authority will pursue adoption. This—and similar dilemmas—can result in a sort of 'stand-off' situation between the local authority and the court. In such situations the court will encourage negotiation between the parties over the care plan, and it retains the power to make contact orders (COs) under CA 1989, s 34. More importantly, and perhaps more controversially, the court has power to continue to make ICOs in the proceedings to safeguard the child and retain control of the child's position whilst still withholding a full care order (at which point control passes to the local authority), and may do so in an effort to put pressure on the local authority to reconsider the plan. This is a very difficult situation—the court can properly use ICOs to postpone the final decision on a care order if there is a need for further assessment or further clarification of the care plan because this is 'planned and purposeful delay' and so does not offend the principle that delay is damaging to the child's welfare (see **10.8.3.2**). However, in a situation where the necessary information is available to the court and it is simply a question of disagreement over permanent placement of the child the question arises whether the continuing postponement of the decision on the child's future by way of a series of ICOs is appropriate in terms of the no delay principle. At some point, the court has to choose between leaving the child with the parents without the protection of the care order, and making a care order with a care plan of which it does not approve. As was stated in *Re S and D* (*Children: Powers of Court*) [1995] 2 FLR 456, the court may be forced to choose the lesser of the two evils.

The second situation that can arise is that the court approves the care plan proposed by the local authority and makes a care order. The court then plays no further role unless a party makes a further application (eg, to discharge the care order). The local authority may subsequently change the care plan. This can have profound consequences, for example, a change from a permanent foster placement where the parents could have good contact, to adoption where their ties with the child are cut. The local authority must involve the parents if it proposes to make a significant change to the care plan once the care order has been made: *Re S and Re W* (cited below). However, do also refer to **9.4.1**, where the new provisions of CA 1989, s 26 are discussed, whereby independent reviewing officers now monitor how local authorities implement the care plan. The difficulties of challenging a care order where the parents cannot realistically offer adequate alternative care for the child are discussed at **9.4.8.2**. This is also a difficult area for the court, since courts have no power to intervene regarding how local authorities exercise their statutory powers once the care order is made. Once the care proceedings are concluded, the alteration of a care plan in such a way as to breach the parents' human rights can be challenged by way of an application for the court to exercise its powers under ss 7 and 8 of the Human Rights Act 1998 (HRA 1998). A local authority is a 'public authority' and may therefore not act incompatibly with the European Convention on Human Rights (ECHR)—to do so is unlawful under HRA 1998, s 6. The difficulty with breaches of human rights is that although an applicant may establish a breach, this does not necessarily mean that he or she will be given a remedy. However, under HRA 1998, s 8, the court has access to remedies including the power to grant an injunction restraining a breach of human rights. Of course, it should be remembered that alteration of the care plan is not automatically a breach of human rights—it may have been done as an essential response to the requirements of the child's welfare, which could have significantly changed since the production of the original care plan. Whilst proceedings are pending, the challenge should be made in the course of the care proceedings. For an excellent review of the law in this area, see Hershman and McFarlane C 1138–41.

10.7.6   Twin-track planning

Twin-track planning is a very important aspect of an interim care plan where (as in many cases) the alternatives at a final hearing are likely to be rehabilitation of the child with the family (depending on progress made and assessment done during the proceedings), and permanent placement in an adoptive family. The aim is to minimise delay in permanently placing the child should rehabilitation fail, or not be feasible in the first place. The effect is that at the same time as the possibility of rehabilitation is being explored in the care proceedings, the local authority will also have taken the child's case before the adoption panel, and identified suitable adopters. This means that the court has full information on the two possibilities at the final hearing. In addition, should rehabilitation not be chosen, the adoption can proceed much more quickly than if the process had not been started before the final care hearing, and this means that the child can have a permanent placement much sooner. This is certainly desirable from the point of view of the child's emotional development and security. There is also a similar process known as 'concurrent planning', whereby work is done towards rehabilitation whilst at the same time establishing a plan for alternative placement elsewhere. See *Re D and K (Care Plan: Twin-Track Planning)* [1999] 2 FLR 872.

Further reading and key authorities

- Children Act 1989 Guidance and Regulations Volume 2: Care Planning, Placement and Case Review

- *Re J (Minors) (Care: Care Plan)* [1994] 1 FLR 253

- *Re D and K (Care Plan: Twin-Track Planning)* [1999] 2 FLR 872

- *Re C and B (Care Order: Future Harm)* [2001] 1 FLR 611

- *Re S (Minors) (Care Order: Implementation of Care Plan), Re W (Minors) (Care Order: Adequacy of Care Plan)* [2002] 1 FLR 815

- *Re B (Care: Interference with Family Life)* [2003] 2 FLR 813

10.8 The final hearing—arguments and outcomes

This section aims to give you an outline understanding of common issues and arguments at a final hearing. Of course, every case turns on its own circumstances, but there are some common patterns of argument which you need to be familiar with.

10.8.1 Threshold, disposal and standard of proof

You will recall from **9.4.4** that there are two basic stages to the court's decision—the decision on the *threshold criteria*, which determines whether or not the court has the jurisdiction to make a care or supervision order at all, and which depends on the test in CA 1989, s 31; and, if the threshold is established, the decision on *disposal*, where the court decides whether a care order is in the best interests of the child, given the care plan, or whether another order, or no order at all, would best serve the child's welfare.

Whether or not the threshold criteria are established is a *question of fact*, to be proven in the normal way. Suspicion is insufficient, however serious the allegation. The child's welfare has no relevance to this particular decision—it is simply a question of whether the local authority applicant can prove that the facts of the case are such that the child is suffering or likely to suffer significant harm due either to the care being given to him not being what it would be reasonable to expect a parent to give, or to his being beyond parental control. The court has to be 'satisfied' that this is the case. The standard of proof is the ordinary civil standard—the balance of probabilities. *Re H and Others (Minors) (Sexual Abuse: Standard of Proof)* [1996] 1 FLR 80 was approved by the House of Lords in *Re B (Care Proceedings: Standard of Proof)*, see **9.4.6**.

10.8.2 Conceding the threshold

If you are able to undermine the evidence relied upon by the local authority as establishing the threshold, then of course you should seek to persuade the court that the threshold criteria are not met and therefore there is no jurisdiction to make the care or supervision order. However, as indicated in **10.3.7**, the evidence amassed by the local authority regarding the concerns for the child at the outset of proceedings can often be very hard to challenge, and it is often the case that the best line of attack relates to the 'disposal' stage of proceedings, where the argument may be that the parents have now made sufficient progress with parenting skills for rehabilitation, or that there is further assessment required before the court has enough information to decide (see **10.8.3.2**). In other words, frequently more is to be gained by looking at the parents' capacity to change than by trying to defend the (sometimes indefensible) past. If your case falls into this category, you may well need to consider 'conceding the threshold'. This basically means that your client *concedes* (ie, admits) that the threshold criteria are satisfied as a matter of fact, and that the court has jurisdiction to make a care or supervision order. This is not the same as consenting to the care order—it leaves you free to argue the 'disposal' side of the case—whilst you accept that the court has jurisdiction to make a care order if it considers it appropriate, your argument is that it should not make a care order, or that the current care plan is inappropriate, or that a supervision order is more appropriate than a care order, and so on. The benefits of such a course of action are, first, that you *may* be able to limit the findings of fact against your client—although see below—and, secondly, that there could be a significant saving of court time because this will limit the issues.

However, you cannot simply concede the threshold criteria without more. The court has to be 'satisfied' of facts sufficient to meet the threshold criteria. If for a parent, you will need to identify the *factual basis* upon which your client concedes the threshold. Your client will need to admit facts which are sufficient to show that *at the relevant time* (see **9.4.5.2**), the child was suffering or likely to suffer significant harm due to the care he was receiving not being what it would be reasonable for a parent to give. Tactically, you will want to admit sufficient facts for this purpose and no more, and careful discussion with and advice to the client will be required.

These are *admissions of fact*, and they are for the respondent parents to make. They are therefore not something which the local authority is in a position to dictate, although a Schedule of Proposed Findings should be attached to the local authority's application form (see pre-proceedings checklist in the PLO at PD 12A of the FPR 2010). These are likely to form the basis of negotiation. However, if you represent the local authority, you will need to consider the conceded facts with care. First, do they meet the threshold? If not, you will need to prove the facts of the local authority's case further in any event. Secondly, it may be important to the local authority to prove facts beyond what the parents are prepared to concede because of the arguments on the 'disposal' decision. For example, in a case involving serious neglect and emotional abuse, the parents make admissions of fact regarding the neglect which are sufficient to satisfy the threshold criteria. However, the admissions they make are fairly limited—taken at face value, they would support the need for a supervision order, but not for the child to be placed for adoption under a care order. The local authority takes the view that it needs a care order, and proposes to place the child for adoption because the neglect and emotional abuse was far greater than the parents concede, and the child has suffered considerable developmental delay. In these circumstances, the local authority will wish to prove the full extent of the abuse and neglect in order to *justify the need for a care order and the type of care plan that they propose*.

Therefore, if representing the parents you may be able to 'limit the damage' on the findings of fact about the past by conceding threshold on your terms, but be aware that the local authority may want to prove further and more extensive facts which it considers relevant to the next stage of the decision: disposal.

The issue of conceding threshold by admitting facts will also arise on an ICO hearing—however, bear in mind that the threshold is lower, simply being 'reasonable cause to believe' that the CA 1989, s 31 criteria are met. There will also be scope at an ICO hearing for taking a more neutral approach and neither opposing nor consenting to the making of the ICO: see the discussion at **10.2.1**.

Conceding threshold—key authorities

- *Stockport Metropolitan Borough Council v D* [1995] 1 FLR 873
- *Re M (Threshold Criteria: Parental Concessions)* [1999] 2 FLR 728
- *A County Council v DP, RS, BS (by the children's guardian)* [2005] 2 FLR 1031

10.8.3   Final hearing—disposal issues

10.8.3.1   Possible outcomes

There are a number of possible outcomes on the final hearing, and it may be that the parties can agree on one of these courses. First, the court could decide that the threshold criteria were not made out and the local authority's application would fail. This is highly unusual. If the threshold criteria are made out, the court may decide that a final care order is appropriate, and that the care plan is in the child's best interests, in which case a final care order will be made. It may be that the court feels that a care order is disproportionate and that a supervision order is sufficient to protect the child's welfare, with or without requirements (see **9.5**). The court may decide that a care order is appropriate, but does not approve of the care plan—as to which, see **10.7.5** above. The court may decide that neither a care nor supervision order is actually required, in which case it may make no order, or it might make an RO in favour of the parents or some other family member who has been assessed and is willing to care for the child. A common argument, which sometimes succeeds, is that the court has *insufficient information* on which to make a final decision and that further ICOs should be made until that information is available, at which point there should be a further hearing to consider the final decision. This situation is considered in the next section.

10.8.3.2   Final or interim care order?

It is often the case that the parents' representatives argue at a final hearing that the court is not in possession of all the information it requires to make a properly considered final decision. Usually, the argument will be based on the suggestion that there is a further issue or new circumstances that require assessment, for example, the parents have recently separated and there is no assessment of their ability to care for the child alone, as opposed to as a couple (it is sometimes the case that some parents cope better alone, for example because the other parent undermined their parenting ability due to violence). Sometimes, an expert's report produced for the final hearing raises the possibility that the child could be rehabilitated with the family and that this needs to be further assessed. It is also sometimes the case that the care plan is insufficiently clear and specific, although in some cases this is unavoidable and specifics can only be worked out some time after the final hearing.

The lawyer will therefore argue that the court cannot make a final decision on disposal unless this further assessment is available, and so ICOs should be made and the case relisted for final hearing once the report has been completed. Where this course of action is contested, the most obvious argument for the opponents (usually the local authority, often with the guardian's support) will be that the further assessment will cause considerable delay that the child cannot afford. There is likely to be extensive cross-examination of the expert regarding the length of time that such an assessment would require and the likelihood of the parents successfully completing it.

If the court accepts this argument, an ICO will be granted. It is established that whilst delay is normally harmful to the child's welfare, 'planned and purposeful delay' can be in a child's best interests. You must familiarise yourself with the key authorities in the table below before seeking to argue such an application.

Key authorities—interim care orders at a final hearing

- *C v Solihull Metropolitan Borough Council* [1993] 1 FLR 290
- *Re J (Minors) (Care: Care Plan)* [1994] 1 FLR 253
- *Re S (Minors) (Care Order: Implementation of Care Plan), Re W (Minors) (Care Order: Adequacy of Care Plan)* [2002] 1 FLR 815
- *Re K (Care Proceedings: Care Plan)* [2008] 1 FLR 1

10.8.3.3 Care or supervision order?

It may be that it is obvious that the court will not consider that the child's welfare will be properly protected if there is no court order. Whilst the parents may be unable to argue that there should be no order, they may seek to argue that a supervision order will provide sufficient protection to the child. It would give the local authority a statutory basis to remain involved in the family and able to 'keep an eye' on the child's progress, without the draconian step of allowing the local authority to share PR. Whilst a supervision order does have this effect, which can be strengthened by the addition of requirements (see **9.5.2**), it is a much less powerful order than the care order. There is little sanction for its breach (generally, the local authority would have to reapply for a full care order) and the local authority cannot remove the child without further recourse to court (an EPO if the circumstances justify it, and application for an ICO).

When deciding to make a care or a supervision order, the court will need to carefully weigh the level of likely future harm to the child, and the harm which will be caused by removing him from his family. Only if protection of the child demands will the stronger order, the care order, be made rather than a supervision order. Again, the court is considering the issue of proportionality of response to the feared harm.

Key authorities—care or supervision order

- *Re S(J) (A Minor) (Care or Supervision Order)* [1993] 2 FLR 919
- *Re S (Care or Supervision Order)* [1996] 1 FLR 753
- *Re C (Care order or supervision order)* [2001] 2 FLR 753

Mediation in the context of the family

11.1 Defining mediation

Mediation is one of a number of settlement-seeking processes, including negotiation, collaborative law and conciliation, known collectively as Alternative Dispute Resolution (ADR). 'Alternative' in this context is generally understood to mean alternative to court proceedings. However, 'Appropriate Dispute Resolution' is a more accurate term (accepted by the Family Justice Council), because mediation is also used in conjunction with court proceedings, not necessarily as an alternative. In some countries, mediation is the normal means of settling disputes, with the court as the alternative.

11.2 The European Code of Conduct for Mediators

Since the 1970s the use of mediation has developed worldwide. With the rise in international and cross-border disputes, there is need for consistency in mediation practice and procedures. The European Code of Conduct for Mediators was published by the European Commission in July 2004 as a voluntary instrument designed to improve quality and trust in mediation. Mediation is defined in the European Code as '*any process where two or more parties agree to the appointment of a third-party—hereinafter "the mediator"—to help the parties to solve a dispute by reaching an agreement without adjudication*'. The European Code is intended to apply to:

- any type of mediation that falls within the above definition;
- any type of dispute within civil or commercial law; and
- any legal, social or cultural context within the European Union.

11.3 The European Directive on Mediation 2008

Four years after publication of the European Code of Conduct on Mediation, the European Parliament and Council of Ministers issued a Directive on 'Certain Aspects of Mediation in Civil and Commercial Matters', '*to promote the amicable settlement of disputes by encouraging the use of mediation and by ensuring a balanced relationship between mediation and judicial proceedings*' (European Directive on Mediation 2008/52/EC, 21 May 2008, Art 1). Mediation is defined as '*a structured process ... whereby two or more parties to a dispute attempt by themselves, on a voluntary basis, to reach an agreement on the settlement of their dispute with the assistance of a mediator. This process may be initiated by the parties or suggested or ordered by a court or prescribed by the law of a Member State*' (Art 3). A mediator is defined as '*any third person who is asked to conduct a mediation in an effective, impartial and competent way, regardless of the denomination or profession of that third person in the Member State concerned and of the way in which the third person has been appointed or requested to conduct the mediation*' (Art 3b). Although the Directive applies to mediation in cross-border disputes in civil and commercial matters, '*nothing should prevent Member States from applying such provisions also to internal mediation processes*': paragraph (8), of the preamble.

11.4 Family mediation

The development of family mediation as a specialised form of ADR preceded the development of civil and commercial mediation. The Council of Europe's Committee of Experts on Family Law reported in 1998 that '*research in Europe, North America, Australia and New Zealand suggests that family mediation is better suited than more formal legal mechanisms to the settlement of sensitive, emotional issues surrounding family matters. Reaching agreements in mediation has been shown to be a vital component in making and maintaining co-operative relationships between divorcing parents: it reduces conflict and encourages continuing contact between children and both their parents*' (Explanatory Memorandum to Recommendation No R (98)1, 21 January 1998, para 7). The Council of Europe's Recommendation pointed out that family mediation has the potential to:

- improve communications within the family;
- reduce conflict between parties in dispute;
- produce amicable settlements;
- provide continuity of personal contacts between parents and children;
- lower the social and economic costs of separation and divorce for the parties themselves and states;
- reduce the length of time otherwise required to settle conflict (s 7).

In contrast to most (but not all) civil and commercial disputes, family disputes have special characteristics that need to be taken into account:

1. There are usually continuing and interdependent relationships. The dispute settlement process should facilitate constructive relationships for the future, in addition to enabling the resolution of current disputes.

2. Family disputes usually involve emotional and personal relationships in which feelings can exacerbate the difficulties, or disguise the true nature of the conflicts and disagreements. It is usually considered appropriate for these feelings to be acknowledged and understood by the parties and by the mediator.

3. Disputes that arise in the process of separation and divorce have an impact on other family members, notably children, who may not be included directly in

the mediation process, but whose interests may be considered paramount and therefore relevant to the process (Recommendation, s 15).

Family mediation in England and Wales began as a grassroots initiative, following the Finer Report on One-Parent Families (1974) which called for a unified system of family courts in which *conciliation* (distinguished from *reconciliation* and defined in similar terms to *mediation*) would be the preferred means of settling any or all issues arising from separation and divorce. The first family mediation service was started in Bristol in 1978 as a pilot project run by a local interdisciplinary group offering mediation out of court on child-related issues. Independent, out-of-court mediation services developed in parallel with court-directed conciliation schemes in which judges referred disputes over children to the divorce court welfare service (now, the Children and Family Court Advisory and Support Service (Cafcass)). Family mediation services struggled to survive on grants from charitable organisations or support from their local Probation Service. There was no state funding in the early days.

The term *family mediation* is used in Europe in preference to *divorce mediation*, the term used in the United States. Divorce does not apply to cohabiting couples and civil partners. Moreover, divorce mediation implies a process promoting divorce and thus on the side of the partner seeking divorce. The word *family* is important for other reasons. Family mediators encourage parents to consider their children's needs, as well as their own needs. There are many issues involving family members—post adoption contact with birth parents, care of the elderly, inheritance disputes—that can be brought to mediation. In England and Wales, family mediation is defined as '*a process in which those involved in family breakdown, whether or not they are a couple or other family members, appoint an impartial third person to assist them to communicate better with one another and reach their own agreed and informed decisions concerning some, or all, of the issues relating to separation, divorce, children, finance or property by negotiation*' (Family Mediation Council (FMC) Code of Practice 2010, para 1.2).

Although still liable to be confused with counselling and occasionally misunderstood as 'meditation', family mediation is now better known, compared with twenty years ago. Family mediators need to take particular account of the needs of ethnic minorities. Even if the mediator comes from the same ethnic background as the participants, no assumptions should be made, since family values and traditions vary within, as well as between, ethnic groups. Similar problems occur in many families, but each family is unique.

11.5 Mediation and conciliation

The terms 'mediation' and 'conciliation' are sometimes used synonymously, but it is important to distinguish in-court conciliation from out-of-court mediation that takes place mainly prior to the issue of proceedings. The courts may refer cases to independent family mediation services, whereas in-court conciliation is undertaken by Cafcass officers, who undertake risk assessments and provide reports for the court. Normally a different officer would prepare a report from one who has previously acted as conciliator in the same case. Mediation differs from in-court conciliation in a number of ways.

FAMILY MEDIATION	*IN-COURT CONCILIATION*
Mainly prior to court application, many clients referred by legal advisors, courts increasingly encouraged to refer.	Court referral to conciliation following court application on children issues.

Essentially voluntary, but a court applicant is expected to have attended an information and assessment meeting with a recognised family mediator prior to court application. Courts may refer parties to mediation at later stages of proceedings, but cannot order parties to mediate.	Parties in private law disputes over children are expected to take part in conciliation on direction of the judge. Conciliation is thus imbued with the court's authority
Private and independent, mainly out of court. In-court mediation schemes in some courts refer parties to a mediator available in court on the day. Mediation may continue out of court, if both parties willing.	Conciliation often takes place at court in the context of a court hearing.
Participants charged fees, unless qualifying for legally aided mediation.	Free of charge.
All issues—children, family home, finance, etc. Not only separation and divorce—grandparent contact and other proceedings over children.	Children issues only.
Independent, qualified mediators, do not report to the judge.	Family court social workers (Cafcass) are officers of the court.
Impartial and non-directive: parents encouraged to cooperate and take account of children's needs in reaching their own agreements.	Not neutral—welfare of child is paramount and conciliator may be directive in seeking settlement on residence and/or contact.
Confidential, with exceptions (both parties, with legal advice, may give joint written consent for terms of agreement set out in the mediation summary to be made available to the court).	Conciliation by family court social worker is not privileged; outcome reportable to the court.
Facilitates dialogue, often extends over several sessions, seeks sufficiently flexible arrangements for children.	Usually a one-off meeting, 1 hour on average. Tends to produce standardised agreements.
Wide spectrum from cooperative to high conflict.	Difficult disputes over children.
May change attitudes and perceptions and have longer-term effects in improving relationships.	Unlikely to change attitudes or relationships (research by Trinder et al. 2002–7)
Agreements reached through mediation by the parties themselves (with court orders made with consent where needed) are more likely to last over time.	Research by Trinder et al. (2002–7) shows conciliated agreements more liable to break down, but some parents renegotiate contact arrangements.

11.6   What kind of help does family mediation offer?

In coming to mediation, participants are offered the opportunity to:
- consider options and reach terms of agreement in a timescale under their own control, without having decisions imposed on them by the court;

- address issues that are inter-related both in practical and emotional terms, whereas the courts deal with children and financial matters in separate proceedings;
- resolve disputes at an early stage, before positions become entrenched;
- look to the future, rather than focusing on past grievances;
- communicate and cooperate concerning children;
- keep children's needs in the forefront of their discussions;
- clear up or avoid misunderstandings;
- feel less stressed, angry or bitter;
- work out arrangements tailored to their particular circumstances and needs;
- take part in informal discussions that can be arranged quickly, compared with the formality and delays of court proceedings;
- avoid, or reduce, the costs and delays of lengthy correspondence and/or contested court proceedings;
- in some circumstances, recognise a mutual wish for reconciliation, with referral to counselling.

11.7 Suitability of mediation

Mediation is not suitable in all circumstances. Mediators must assess carefully with each party separately, even if they attend a joint information meeting, whether mediation is suitable in all the circumstances. There are particular concerns about the use of mediation in cases involving domestic violence. Verbal and psychological abuse can be even more destructive of morale than physical violence.

In cases involving a history of abuse and/or risks and fears of violence, mediation would normally be found unsuitable. If, however, mediation is suitable and accepted by both parties, safeguards and ground rules may be needed to control threatening or abusive language or behaviour during mediation, or when participants leave the mediation meeting. Mediators must also screen for child protection issues or concerns. If any concern or allegation is raised, the mediator must report it immediately to the appropriate child protection agency. Mediation would not be offered or continue in such circumstances.

11.8 Disadvantages and potential risks in mediation

There could be disadvantages or risks if:

- mediation is used as a delaying tactic, delaying proceedings and increasing costs;
- either party takes part under duress;
- mediation is used in unsuitable circumstances and/or without adequate safeguards;
- face-to-face discussions intensify conflict or distress;
- one party is not acting in good faith;
- power imbalances are not recognised or managed adequately by the mediator;
- the mediator is perceived as showing bias towards one party or acts directively;
- the mediator is not adequately trained or is mediating without proper regulation.

These disadvantages and risks should normally be minimised or avoided by pre-mediation assessments to check and confirm suitability of mediation and each party's motivation and willingness. Mediators' professional training should enable them to intervene and, if necessary, terminate a mediation if discussions become too confrontational or destructive, or if one party seems to be playing for time or withholding information. Mediation should be terminated if a participant refuses to provide information or provides information that appears to be deliberately incomplete or inaccurate. With increased government emphasis on mediation, there are risks of a possible proliferation of individuals setting themselves up as mediators, without nationally recognised training and without adequate regulation of their practice (see **11.21**, Training and regulations for family mediation). Further guidance on the Pre-Application Protocol has been issued to ensure that mediators are recognised by the FMC—see **11.17**).

11.9 Core principles of family mediation

Family mediation embodies core principles that distinguish it from giving legal advice, counselling, arbitrating or adjudicating. The Family Justice Council (FJC) and the FMC published a joint document in 2011 entitled *Independent Mediation—Information for Judges, Magistrates and Legal Advisors*. This paper, endorsed by the President of the Family Division for wide circulation, defines four core principles of mediation:

- It is a voluntary process.
- It is a confidential process.
- The mediator acts in an impartial way.
- Decision making rests with the participants to the mediation.

These principles are central to the delivery of an independent family mediation process and govern the way in which all recognised family mediators work. Mediators cannot dilute these principles which are embedded in Codes of Practice applied by all mediation representatives and regulatory bodies and in documentation provided by mediators to clients.

The FMC Code of Practice 2010 provides guidance on the application of these principles in mediators' practice.

11.9.1 Voluntary participation

The FMC Code of Practice 2010 at para 5.2 states: 'Participation in mediation is voluntary at all times and participants and the mediator are always free to withdraw. Where mediators consider that a participant is unable or unwilling to take part in the process freely and fully, they must raise the issue and possibly suspend or terminate the mediation.' The European Directive on Mediation 2008 upholds the same principle of voluntary participation, stating that 'the mediation provided for in this Directive should be a voluntary process in the sense that the parties are themselves in charge of the process and may organise it as they wish and terminate it at any time' (Art 13).

11.9.2 Confidentiality

The confidentiality of mediation is covered as follows in the FMC Code of Practice:

5.5.1 Subject to paragraphs 5.5.3, 5.5.4 and 5.5.5 below mediators must not disclose any information about, or obtained in the course of, a mediation to anyone, including a court welfare officer or a court, without the express consent of each participant, an order of the court or where the law imposes an overriding obligation of disclosure on mediators.

5.5.2 Mediators must not discuss the mediation or correspond with any participant's legal advisor without the express consent of each participant. Nothing must be said or written to the legal advisor of one party regarding the content of the discussions in mediation which is not also said or written to the legal advisor(s) of the other.

5.5.3 Where it appears necessary so that a specific allegation that a child has suffered significant harm may be properly investigated or where mediators suspect that a child is suffering or is likely to suffer significant harm, mediators must ensure that the relevant Social Services department is notified.

5.5.4 Mediators may notify the appropriate agency if they consider that other public policy considerations prevail, such as an adult suffering or likely to suffer significant harm.

5.5.5 Where mediators suspect that they may be required to make disclosure to the appropriate government authority under the Proceeds of Crime Act 2002 and/or relevant money laundering regulations, they must stop the mediation immediately without informing the clients of the reason.

Participants are asked to sign the Agreement to Mediate confirming that they have understood and accept the confidentiality of mediation and its limits.

11.9.2.1 Confidentiality in relation to the court

The document on *Independent Mediation—Information for Judges, Magistrates and Legal Advisors* (2011) states that:

The confidentiality of any process of family mediation is covered by an existing precedent: *Re D (Minors) (Conciliation: Privilege) Disclosure of Information) [1993] 1 FLR 932*, which states that 'parents would not achieve a compromise unless they approached conciliation openly and were prepared to give and take. They would not make admissions or conciliatory gestures unless they were confident that these could not be used against them. Any attempt at conciliation must be off the record but there were exceptions' and further 'the only exception would be in rare cases where a statement made during conciliation indicates that the maker has caused or is likely to cause serious harm to a child'.

Any client entering a mediation process is asked to sign an Agreement to Mediate which sets out both the scope of and limitations to confidentiality in line with *Re D* (and in regard to legislation relating to abuse and harm and money laundering) and further, participants to a mediation are asked not to call the mediator to provide evidence (either as notes or in person).

This privilege may not be waived by one party unilaterally. Baron J in *Re H (Agreed Joint Residence: Mediation)* [2004] EWHC 2064, [2005] 1FLR 8 commented that it was wholly inappropriate for the mother to invade the privilege of the mediation process by exhibiting the draft parenting agreement. Unless ordered to do so by the court, mediators may not provide information to the court as to the content of discussions in mediation, or reasons why proposals were not reached and/or any view as to whether either party failed to cooperate or declined to accept or continue with a mediated process. If, however, both parties, having taken legal advice, give their written consent to a limited waiving of their privilege to facilitate a court order being made with consent, the Memorandum of Understanding, or some sections of it, may be made available to the court. In the context of First Hearing Dispute Resolution Appointments (FHRDAs), the relevant Practice Direction (PD 12A of the Family Procedure Rules 2010 (FPR 2010)), authorises 'arrangements for the mediator to ask the parties to waive privilege for the purpose of the first hearing where it seems to the mediator appropriate to do so in order to assist the work of the mediator and the outcome of the first hearing: para 4.3(b). 'In all cases it is important that such arrangements are put in place in a way that avoids any pressure being brought to bear in this connection on the parties that is inconsistent with general good mediation practice': para 4.3(c)—see also **8.6.1**.

11.9.2.2 'Open' financial disclosure

Although the content of mediation discussions and correspondence may not be disclosed, the Agreement to Mediate makes it clear that financial and other factual information is provided in mediation on an 'open' basis and can therefore be made available to legal advisors and if necessary to the court, to save duplication of financial disclosure.

11.9.3   Impartiality

The FMC Code of Practice states at para 5.1:

It is the duty of the mediator at all times to ensure that he or she acts with impartiality and that that impartiality is not compromised at any time by any conflict of interest, actual or capable of being perceived as such. Mediators must not have any personal interest in the outcome of the mediation, must not mediate in any case in which they have acquired or may acquire relevant information in any private or other professional capacity and must not act or continue to act if they or a member of their firm has acted for any of the parties in issues not relating to the mediation.

Mediators must decline to mediate if they have any prior knowledge gained in another capacity or through personal contact. Even if participants raise no objection to the appointment of a mediator who has advised or acted previously for one or both of them, or who has a colleague who has done so, they may not realise the potential influence in mediation of knowledge or views stemming from a previous professional relationship.

All information or correspondence provided by either participant should be shared openly and not withheld, except an address or telephone number or as the participants may agree otherwise (FMC Code of Practice, 5.6.3).

Furthermore:

mediators must remain neutral as to the outcome of a mediation at all times. Mediators must not seek to impose their preferred outcome on the participants or to influence them to adopt it, whether by attempting to predict the outcome of court proceedings or otherwise. However, if the participants consent, they may inform them that they consider that the resolutions they are considering might fall outside the parameters which a court might approve or order. They may inform participants of possible courses of action, their legal or other implications, and assist them to explore these, but must make it clear that they are not giving advice (FMC Code of Practice, 5.3).

Mediators should give equal attention to all participants and manage the process in an even-handed way. However, a mediator cannot be neutral in the sense of having no influence in the process. The nature and extent of legal or other information provided by the mediator and the influence, implicit or explicit, of their professional and personal values, are bound to influence the mediation process to some extent.

11.9.4   Party control of decisions

It is a fundamental tenet of mediation that participants retain control over their own decisions. They are assisted to reach informed and considered decisions that are acceptable to them both; they can also choose to disagree. This principle, known as '*empowerment*', has a number of meanings, like neutrality. At one level, there is empowerment through the sharing of information. Mediators explain the need for full financial disclosure and participants undertake to provide full information and relevant documentation. They are encouraged to take legal advice on financial disclosure made in mediation and whether further enquiry is needed. Another aspect of empowerment is protection from pressure. Mediators should prevent pressure being put on one participant by the other and should not give advice or steer participants towards a particular outcome, for example by predicting the outcome in court. The Agreement to Mediate makes it clear that the outcome of mediation is not legally binding on participants. Mediators should discourage participants from any premature agreement that might prejudice one or both of them in a final settlement.

11.10 Mediation and legal aid

From the mid 1970s onwards, successive governments in England and Wales paid lip service to the need for family mediation services but did nothing significant to support them. Eventually, in the 1990s, after pressure from many quarters including senior judges and the All Party Parliamentary Group for Children, a Family Law Bill was introduced that set out a major reform of divorce law, including a requirement for applicants for legal aid for family proceedings to receive information and consider mediation, before they could obtain legal aid (with some categories of exemption). The requirement to consider mediation does not deprive individuals of their right to go to court ('the right to a fair trial'), since mediation itself is voluntary and applicants also have a right to be informed of different routes to settlement and the relative costs and timescales involved. The Family Law Act was passed in 1996. Parts I and II dealing with divorce law reform were not implemented and later withdrawn, whereas Part III, dealing with family mediation, was implemented and re-enacted in the Access to Justice Act 1999. Under this legislation:

a person shall not be granted representation for the purpose of proceedings relating to family matters, unless he has attended a meeting with a mediator—(a) to determine—(i) whether mediation appears to be suitable to the dispute and the parties and all the circumstances, and (ii) in particular, whether mediation could take place without either party being influenced by fear of violence or other harm; and (b) if mediation does appear suitable, to help the person applying for representation to decide whether instead to apply for mediation

Under the subsequently introduced 'Willingness Test', an applicant for legal aid is not required to attend a meeting with a mediator if the respondent declines to attend a meeting to consider mediation, or fails to reply within 10 days. Exemptions from the requirement to consider mediation, including the domestic violence exemption, were reduced in 2007 and reduced further in November 2010.

A client who is referred to mediation by their lawyer, or who self-refers, is offered three options:

1. To attend an information and assessment meeting without the other party being present.

2. To attend an information and assessment meeting jointly with the other party, if both are willing.

3. To state that he or she is willing to accept mediation, if the other party responds to the offer and mediation is found to be suitable.

The mediation service (and/or the applicant) contacts the second party to offer an information and assessment meeting, alone or jointly. As explained above, at this meeting the mediator explores carefully with each party separately, even if they come together, whether either of them has any concerns about domestic abuse and/or child protection issues or other concerns that would make mediation unsuitable. In addition to screening for domestic abuse and child protection issues, a mediator recognised by the Legal Services Commission (LSC) assesses eligibility for public funding. Legally aided mediation is available free of charge or contribution to those who qualify. There is no fixed limit to the number of mediation sessions that clients may attend, but publicly funded mediation is on a fixed rate and most mediations are completed within three sessions. Those who do not qualify for legally aided mediation are charged an hourly or sessional rate and there is also a charge for the Memorandum of Understanding.

Mediation is generally most effective at the pre-court stage, but as Sir Mark Potter, the former President of the Family Division, has pointed out, referral to mediation should also be considered at later stages of proceedings. This principle now forms part of the court's duty to consider the suitability of ADR at every stage of proceedings: FPR 2010, r 3.3. With the consent of both parties and their lawyers, cases may be adjourned so that mediation can take place. Even at Court of Appeal level, it is not too late to consider mediation. In a concluding judgment in the Court of Appeal, Thorpe LJ, who had referred the case to mediation, emphasised the importance of availability of mediation even at an appellate level: 'There was no family case, however conflicted, that was not potentially open to successful mediation, even if mediation had not been attempted or had failed during the trial process': *Al-Khatib v Masry* [2005] 1 FLR 381 [17].

11.11 The main stages of family mediation

The process of mediation normally consists of a series of stages to help participants to define the issues they need to settle, clarify their options and priorities and work towards an agreed outcome that takes account of the immediate and long-term needs of all concerned. Mediation on all issues would normally consist of the following stages.

Stage 1 Signing the Agreement to Mediate
In signing the Agreement to Mediate, participants confirm their acceptance of mediation and undertake to make full disclosure of financial information, with supporting documents as necessary.

Stage 2 Identifying issues for mediation and agreeing the agenda
Each participant is invited to explain what needs to be resolved and to agree an agenda, at least for the first meeting. The agenda needs to be balanced, with priority given to urgent issues. The next stage of the process, such as gathering and sharing information, can then be planned.

Stage 3 Focus on children
Where there are matters concerning children, most parents want these matters to take priority over financial or other issues. Immediate attention can then be given to contact arrangements, possibly on an interim basis. Interim arrangements help to provide reassurance and reduce conflict, increasing willingness to move forwards. Most parents recognise that children need a continuing relationship with them both, although they may disagree over the frequency or length of visits or over the involvement of third parties.

Stage 4 Gathering and sharing information
Gathering and sharing information is central to the process, before options can be explored. Financial forms completed by each party are copied and shared with them

both. Mediators request supporting documents, clarify discrepancies and help participants to gain a full picture of their financial situation, in conjunction with independent
legal and financial advice as necessary. Information is also provided by the mediator.

Stage 5 Exploring options and reality-testing
All available options and their potential benefits and disadvantages need careful consideration. Mediators ask 'reality-testing' questions and ask participants to complete
schedules of current and/or projected average monthly expenditure, to check their bor-
rowing capacity and monthly payments and to take account of child support and other
outgoings.

Stage 6 Negotiating towards settlement
Proposals for settlement may involve short-term and/or long-term arrangements on all
or some issues. These could be confined to contact arrangements or could set out a proposed full and final settlement on all issues, to be used as a basis for a consent order in
divorce proceedings.

Stage 7 Gaining the cooperation of children and others involved
Children, and in some cases new partners, need to understand and cooperate with decisions and arrangements, if they are to work in practice. Parents may need to discuss in
mediation how they are going to explain their arrangements to their children and how
they will give children the reassurances they need.

Stage 8 Drafting the Memorandum of Understanding and Open Financial Statement
The legally privileged Memorandum of Understanding sets out proposals for settlement.
Financial information is summarised in the 'open' statement of financial information,
with supporting documents attached. Participants are invited to confirm the accuracy of
these documents before seeking independent legal advice on them.

Stage 9 Ending mediation
Mediation may end at any stage, with or without agreement. Where there is partial
agreement or even none at all, mediation has not necessarily failed, because the issues
have usually been clarified and often narrowed. Participants may have considered their
options and gained a better understanding of their differences. The dispute may then
settle more quickly if it goes to court.

11.12 Power imbalances in mediation

Mediation on family matters takes place 'in the shadow of the law'. Mnookin and
Kornhauser (1979) observed that separating and divorcing couples do not negotiate in
a vacuum: they 'bargain in the shadow of the law ... The outcome that the law would
impose, should no agreement be reached, gives each parent certain bargaining chips.'
In mediation, one party is often in a stronger position than the other in certain areas.
Mothers often wield more power in disputes over children, whereas men may have
greater knowledge and control of financial assets. In mediation, participants need to
work out how to share or reallocate different areas of control and responsibility, through
recognising their mutual interests and concerns, especially where children are involved.
They are encouraged to take independent legal advice on their proposals, so that they
are fully informed of their legal rights and claims and aware that a mediated agreement
may differ from the outcome they could expect in court.

11.13 Children and mediation

'Mediators should have a special concern for the welfare and best interests of children ... and should remind parents of the need to inform and consult their children about what is happening, and that family disputes and prolonged conflict have a severe negative impact on children' (Council of Europe, Explanatory Memorandum to Recommendation No R (98)1, 21 January 1998, para 45). In England and Wales, regulations for publicly funded family mediation require mediators:

> where there are children of the family, to have arrangements designed to ensure that the parties are encouraged to consider:
>
> (a) the welfare, wishes and feelings of each child; and
> (b) whether and to what extent each child should be given the opportunity to express his or her wishes and feelings in the mediation.

> (CLS Funding Code R9 April 2003, Part D 5.3.)

Family mediators need background knowledge of child development and children's experience of parental separation and divorce. Research studies with children of different ages have compared children's experience in 'intact' families with those who have experienced parental separation. The findings showed that children's feelings were often ignored when parents were caught up in their own conflicts. The level and duration of conflict was found to be a more significant factor in the child's longer-term adjustment to separation than the separation itself. When parents are in dispute, communication often breaks down, not only between the parents but also between parent and child. If children do not receive sufficient explanation, reassurance and support, their distress may result in lack of progress at school, loss of self-esteem, acting-out behaviour and sometimes longer-term depression and difficulty in forming relationships. A study carried out at the Department of Child Health at the University of Exeter (Cockett and Tripp, 1994) found that:

- Fewer than half the children whose parents had separated had regular contact with the parent they no longer lived with. Half these children did not even know where the other parent was living.

- Only 6 per cent of children had been given a joint explanation from both parents of the impending separation or divorce. In over 70 per cent of families, it was left to the mother to tell the children. In some cases the mother told the children only that their father had left, without giving them any explanation or reassurance.

- Most of the children had been very aware of the conflict between their parents. When the children were asked what they thought would have helped them, most said that they needed much more information, explanation and reassurance from their parents than they actually received.

- Many children felt they should have been involved in decisions about contact. This does not mean that they want to be given responsibility for decisions. A significant minority, however, had made their own arrangements to keep in contact with the non-resident parent because their parents were unable to agree, or were not speaking to each other.

- Children were also likely to lose touch with grandparents and other relatives who played an important part in the children's lives, prior to the parents' separation.

Mediators help parents to agree how to explain their decisions and arrangements to their children and reassure them that the separation or divorce is not their fault (as younger children may imagine). Children are reassured to know that their parents are considering their needs, without asking the child to choose between them. Most parents prefer to talk with their children at home, without involving professionals directly with the child. However, children of sufficient age and maturity have a right to be consulted and some parents want their children to have an opportunity to express their views, feelings and needs to someone outside the family. Possible options include meeting with the mediator or with a child counsellor who works alongside the mediation service. In practice, children meet directly with the mediator in a small minority of cases, and only following careful consideration and planning with the parents. There must be agreement between both parents and the mediator that it is appropriate for the child or young person to be invited to take part, clarity about the objectives and agreement about the nature of the involvement. Where both parents and the mediator consider it appropriate and the child is willing to attend, children and young people may meet with the mediator alone and/or with siblings and without their parents being present. Children's acceptance needs to be sought carefully, without any pressure on the child. The confidentiality of child consultation in mediation needs to be explained fully and included in a written agreement signed by the parents and talked through with the child. Mediators are required to have additional training for direct child consultation. Feedback from children has shown that they found it very helpful and that direct child consultation assists parents to reach agreements that meet their children's needs, without children being given responsibility for choices or decisions.

11.14 What evidence is there that mediation works?

The National Audit Office (NAO) examined the effectiveness of public expenditure on mediation in family breakdown and concluded that 'mediation is generally cheaper, quicker and less acrimonious than court proceedings and research shows it secures better outcomes, particularly for children … On average a mediated case takes 100 days and costs £752, compared with 435 days and £1,682 in cases where mediation is not used' (NAO Review, March 2007). 42 per cent of clients who had not been referred to mediation said that they would have been willing to accept it, had they known about it. A large-scale study coordinated by the University of Bristol and funded by the LSC (Davis et al., 2000) examined a sample of 4593 cases in which one or both parties were publicly funded: 70 per cent were referred by lawyers, 12 per cent by the court and the remainder were self-referred. The experience of mediation was generally very positive. 82 per cent of participants considered that the mediator had been impartial and 70 per cent had found mediation very or fairly helpful 71 per cent said that they would recommend mediation to others in a similar situation. Of those who reached some agreement, 59 per cent said they expected to be able to negotiate any further changes between themselves. The researchers concluded that mediation as a process has its own distinctive and positive features and should be supported as a separate system running in parallel to the court system. In contrast, a study by the Centre for Research on the Child and Family (Trinder et al., 2002) found that 'existing legal interventions have limited capacity to facilitate contact or reverse a downward spiral in contact relationships … Resources should be directed towards more creative work to improve parental and parent–child relationships rather than repeated attempts at imposing a solution' (p 4). In a later study, Trinder et al. (2006) found that only half the parents in their study were satisfied with the court process, and even where agreement was reached, only around 60 per cent were completely satisfied with the outcome. Less than half thought it was in their child's best interests. Hunt (2009) found that 'court proceedings may be effective in restoring contact and increasing the extent of contact [but] do not appear … to improve parental relationships and therefore their capacity to manage post-separation parenting' (p 122).

It is not easy to manage the complex power imbalances that couples bring to mediation, while at the same time maintaining balance and impartiality. Questions have been raised as to whether women are put at risk or disadvantaged in mediation. Irving and Benjamin (1995) concluded that mediation does not disadvantage women, since most women said they had found mediation helpful in giving them a voice in decision making that they had previously lacked. Family mediation aims not only to settle disputes but also to encourage cooperation between separated parents and maintain nurturing relationships between parents and children. As two members of Resolution (formerly the Solicitors Family Law Association) put it: 'while mediation provides the chance for parents to repair their relationship sufficiently to be able to co-parent more positively in future, litigation in a real sense teaches couples to argue and to litigate, sometimes rather too well' (Harte and Howard, 2004).

Measuring the 'success' of mediation is notoriously difficult, but according to a government Green Paper, 'the full and partial success rate of publicly funded mediations now stands at 70% (with the full resolution of cases accounting for 66% of this)' (Green Paper on Legal Aid Reform 2010, para 4.71). Settlement rates reported by family mediation services themselves may be rejected as unreliable, on the grounds that mediators are liable to overestimate their own success. However, settlement of some or all issues was reported in 83.9 per cent of mediations completed in 2009/10 by Bristol Family Mediators Association (2011). Other services have reported similarly high settlement rates. Both the Bristol and Stafford services believe that having the facility to provide interdisciplinary co-mediation enables them to handle more complex and higher-conflict mediations.

11.15 Different approaches to family mediation

11.15.1 Co-mediation

The Family Mediators Association (FMA) and its pilot project, 'Solicitors in Mediation', developed a model of co-mediation in which a mediator experienced in family law is teamed with a mediator experienced in work with couples and families, generally from a social work or therapy background. Both must be trained in mediation (Parkinson, 1989). Co-mediation helps to manage high conflict or complex cases and may be arranged to meet special needs. A gender balance is very helpful. The LSC will pay for co-mediation but this must be justified on the case file. Co-mediators offer a wider range of expertise, different perspectives and various techniques and strategies that help to manage the strong emotions and difficulties that arise in mediation.

11.15.2 Shuttle mediation

Although initial information and assessment meetings may be held with each party separately, family mediation normally requires face-to-face meetings with both participants together, unlike civil and commercial mediation where separate meetings (referred to as 'caucusing' or 'shuttle mediation') are the norm. In family mediation, the aim is to help participants to engage in dialogue directly. Parents need to be able to communicate directly over arrangements for their children, after mediation ends. If, in an emergency or for exceptional reasons, participants are seen separately during mediation, this is normally on the basis that all communications between each of them must be capable of being shared with the other. This differs from civil/commercial mediation practice, where information is held in confidence by the mediator, including knowledge of each party's 'bottom line'. The more information the mediator holds from one party without the other's knowledge, the more powerful the mediator becomes. Family mediators seek to 'empower' both parties equally in reaching their own fully informed decisions and in managing direct discussions.

11.15.3   Attendance of legal advisors

It is normal practice in civil and commercial mediation for lawyers to attend mediation sessions with their clients and for the mediator to meet separately with each party and their lawyer in different rooms and 'shuttle' between them. In some American states, lawyers attend family mediation meetings as well. In England and Wales, advising lawyers do not normally attend family mediation meetings. Separated couples, especially parents, need to be able to talk and negotiate directly with each other. They could be inhibited by their lawyers' presence in discussions that are often very personal and emotional. Advising lawyers might try to take control and could gather information from the legally privileged mediation process that they could use in some way in later court proceedings. On the other hand, if participants can take time out from a mediation meeting to consult with their lawyers on the spot, further delay could be avoided. Lawyers, unlike mediators, can advise a client that their position is unrealistic or unreasonable. Advising lawyers can be very helpful in assisting negotiations and in fine-tuning the terms of settlement. If participants want their legal advisors to attend mediation with them, the ground rules covering their lawyers' involvement need to be clarified and the lawyers asked to sign a document recognising the confidentiality of the mediation process. It also needs to be clear that the mediator is not responsible for paying the costs of the lawyers' attendance. These costs are not covered in publicly funded mediation, but private clients may wish to pay their lawyers' charges as well as the mediator's fees. Lawyers who took part in a study in Florida admitted that they attended mediation in order to learn about the mediation process and the mediator's abilities. Once they were satisfied that the mediators were competent and knowledgeable, they felt comfortable about allowing their clients to participate. The survey showed that after gaining first-hand experience of attending mediation, lawyers recognised that the benefits of mediation outweighed any potential disadvantages to their client.

11.16   Some examples of mediation in practice

Case A

A recently separated couple attended three mediation meetings in which they worked out arrangements for their children, the occupation of the family home and proposals for a 'clean break' financial settlement covering division of assets, pension claims and debts. The mediator summarised their proposals in a Memorandum of Understanding and provided a summary of financial information in an 'Open Financial Statement', with copies of key documents. The couple's solicitors advised each of them on these documents and used them as the basis for a Consent Order in divorce proceedings.

Case B

An unmarried couple, Sam and Marie (not their real names), with two sons aged 12 and 14, had cohabited for many years and separated one year previously. Sam continued to live in their jointly owned property, while Marie was living in rented accommodation with the boys. Marie was seeking a sale of the family home and equal division of the net proceeds. There was intense conflict over financial contributions and entitlements. Initially, Sam demanded production of Marie's bank accounts over the past 15 years. Marie was willing for Sam to specify a sample of her bank statements that she would produce for his inspection. Sam did not take up this offer and ceased demanding documentation of all expenditure over 15 years. The co-mediators recognised that both parents were still acutely distressed by the breakdown of their relationship and this acknowledgement of their feelings, combined with a problem-solving approach, helped to shift positions and rebuild cooperation as parents. Sam put forward a proposal for settlement that was accepted by Marie and subsequently formalised through solicitors.

Case C

An elderly couple who were living in separate nursing homes were no longer able to manage their affairs. They each had an adult daughter from a previous marriage. These two adult daughters, each representing their own parent, used mediation to consider the sale of their parents' property and disposal of possessions. These issues were resolved by agreement and the daughters were then able to fund the costs of their parents' nursing-home care.

Case D

Jake, an unmarried father aged 21, who had never lived with Kelly, the mother of his 3-year-old daughter, was referred to mediation by his solicitor. Jake was subject to an anti-harassment order and not allowed to meet face-to-face with Kelly. Although the court might have amended the terms of the order to allow mediation to take place, Jake did not wish to meet with Kelly. Shuttle mediation was offered, because of the particular difficulties. Jake came to mediation with his grandfather (following the death of both Jake's parents, he had been brought up by his grandparents), while Kelly was seen separately. Contact for their daughter, Amy, was arranged to take place at the grandparents' home, with the cooperation of all concerned.

11.17 The Pre-application Protocol, April 2011

Under the coalition government's policy of encouraging mediation and discouraging unnecessary recourse to the courts on matters that could be settled out of court, the Ministry of Justice and Her Majesty's Court Service (HMCS) issued a Pre-application Protocol in April 2011 concerning attendance at mediation information and assessment meetings (MIAMs). This was introduced by the FPR 2010, is referred to in this Manual as the Mediation Protocol and can be found at PD 3A of the FPR 2010; it is different from the litigation pre-action protocol which applies in financial remedies cases—see **5.1**. The Mediation Protocol applies to all potential applicants, including those paying privately, whereas the previous requirement to consider mediation applied only to those seeking legal aid (**11.10** above). With effect from 6 April 2011:

> *all potential applicants for a court order in relevant family proceedings are expected, before making their application, to have followed the steps set out in the Protocol. This requires a potential applicant, except in certain specified circumstances, to consider with a mediator whether the dispute may be capable of being resolved through mediation. The court will expect all applicants to have*

complied with the Protocol before commencing proceedings and (except where exceptional circumstances apply) will expect any respondent to have attended a MIAM, if invited to do so. If court proceedings are taken, the court will wish to know at the first hearing whether mediation has been considered by the parties. In considering the conduct of any relevant family proceedings, the court will take into account any failure to comply with the Protocol and may refer the parties to a meeting with a mediator before the proceedings continue further (PD 3A, para 4.1).

Further guidance was issued in June 2011:

There will be instances where self-funding individuals will attend court and be unaware of the need to have a MIAM. Or they may be referred to a MIAM at the first hearing. It has been agreed by the Justice Minister Jonathan Djanogly MP that mediators ought to be able to charge those that are self-funded for the MIAM or Mediation Sessions within the court precinct. This comes into effect immediately and will help to provide improved access to mediation services and prevent delays. The majority of courts already know their local family mediation services and will have mediators who come into court on a regular basis. However, with this new guidance, courts may be approached by new mediation services. [Lawyers] should make sure that the mediation service is recognised by the Family Mediation Council, who ensure that mediators are trained to an appropriate standards and advise judges of the arrangements [they] have made with the local mediation services (Guidance Note: In-Court Family Mediation Services, June 2011).

Annex B of PD 3A lists 'relevant family proceedings', while Annex C lists circumstances in which a person considering making an application to the court in relevant family proceedings is **not** expected to attend a MIAM:

1. *The mediator is satisfied that mediation is not suitable because another party to the dispute is unwilling to attend a Mediation Information and Assessment Meeting and consider mediation.*
2. *The mediator determines that the case is not suitable for a Mediation Information and Assessment Meeting.*
3. *A mediator has made a determination within the previous four months that the case is not suitable for a Mediation Information and Assessment Meeting or for mediation.*
4. *Domestic abuse*
   Any party has, to the applicant's knowledge, made an allegation of domestic violence against another party and this has resulted in a police investigation or the issuing of civil proceedings for the protection of any party within the last 12 months.
5. *Bankruptcy*
   The dispute concerns financial issues and the applicant or another party is bankrupt.
6. *The parties are in agreement and there is no dispute to mediate.*
7. *The whereabouts of the other party are unknown to the applicant.*
8. *The prospective application is for an order in relevant family proceedings which are already in existence and are continuing.*
9. *The prospective application is to be made without notice to the other party.*
10. *Urgency: the prospective application is urgent, meaning:*
    (a) *there is a risk to the life, liberty or physical safety of the applicant or his or her family or his or her home; or*
    (b) *any delay caused by attending a Mediation Information and Assessment Meeting would cause a risk of significant harm to a child, a significant risk of a miscarriage of justice, unreasonable hardship to the applicant or irretrievable problems in dealing with the dispute (such as an irretrievable loss of significant evidence).*
11. *There is current social services involvement as a result of child protection concerns in respect of any child who would be the subject of the prospective application.*
12. *A child would be a party to the prospective application by virtue of Rule 12.3(1).*
13. *The applicant (or the applicant's solicitor) contacts three mediators within 15 miles of the applicant's home and none is able to conduct a Mediation Information and Assessment Meeting within 15 working days of the date of contact.*

The Family Mediation Information and Assessment Form (FM1) is to be used in connection with family proceedings to which PD 3A applies and should be completed in accordance with the Protocol and filed with the court with any application to which the PD applies. Where either Part 1 or Part 2 applies, the form must be completed and signed by a mediator recognised by the FMC and counter-signed by the applicant or the applicant's solicitor. Where either party may be eligible for legal aid for mediation, the mediator must also have passed the LSC's Competence Assessment in order to assess eligibility and provide legally aided mediation to those who qualify.

It is too early, only a few months after the Protocol's introduction, to assess its effectiveness, but so far there appears to be considerable inconsistency in its application. In some areas, take-up of MIAMs and mediation shows substantial increase, whereas in other areas there is little noticeable difference. 'Expectations' of attendance at a MIAM may be sufficient only where there is strong support for mediation from local judges, lawyers and Cafcass. If the Mediation Protocol is to achieve its stated objectives, attendance at a MIAM will need to be made a requirement, not merely an expectation, and court staff will need to be required to check that Form FM1 is filed correctly with an application. The Final Report of the Family Justice Review may recommend further requirements relating to MIAMs.

11.18 What happens at a MIAM?

At a MIAM the mediator:

(a) receives the applicant or respondent or both parties together and clarifies the issues requiring settlement;

(b) explains ADR options including mediation and collaborative law and their potential benefits; if competent to do so, assesses whether either party qualifies for publicly funded mediation and is eligible to receive mediation free of charge or contribution;

(c) explains the costs of mediation for those paying privately, making some comparison with the estimated average costs of litigation;

(d) considers the degree of urgency from each party's point of view;

(e) considers whether mediation is suitable in the circumstances, screening in particular for any history and/or fear of violence or other harm and/or child protection issues;

(f) ascertains with each party whether, having understood the process, they are both willing to take part in mediation;

(g) provides information about other services if mediation is not suitable, such as further legal advice, counselling, welfare benefits advice or other forms of help.

In assessing whether mediation is suitable, the mediator needs to take account of the level of conflict, any language difficulties or special needs and different kinds of power imbalance. Any indications of fear or intimidation need to be explored and considered carefully. As explained above, mediators must see each party separately, even if they attend the MIAM together, to check for particular concerns or fears that would make mediation unsuitable. Research has shown that a previous incident of domestic violence does not automatically rule out mediation, if there are no risks of continuing violence and both parties wish to address matters jointly. Where there has been an incident in the past and one client is nervous of meeting the other, special arrangements can be offered, including separate waiting areas and different leaving times so that an anxious client can arrive and leave the building safely, without fear of being followed afterwards. These arrangements need to be explained in advance to both parties and have been found to work well.

11.19   The Family Justice Review 2011

Despite the rise in referrals to mediation from 1997 onwards, entrenched disputes over children and financial matters in divorce take up vast amounts of court time and resources. The family courts have become so overloaded that the whole system is close to breaking point, with Cafcass running far behind on welfare enquiries and reports for the court. In June 2010 the Ministry of Justice, together with the Department for Education and the Welsh Assembly Government, set up a Family Justice Review 'to examine the effectiveness of the family justice system and the outcomes it delivers, and to make recommendations for reform'. The terms of reference recognised that 'long and complicated legal processes are emotionally and financially draining for parents and distressing for children'. A system is needed that 'allows families to reach easy, simple and efficient agreements which are in the best interests of the children, whilst protecting children and vulnerable adults from risks of harm. Family mediation and similar support should be used as far as possible to support individuals themselves to reach agreements about arrangements, rather than having an arrangement imposed by the courts' (Family Justice Review, Terms of Reference 2010).

The Interim Report of the Family Justice Review, published in March 2011, noted that:

Every year 500,000 children and adults are involved in the family justice system. They turn to it at times of great stress and conflict. The issues faced by the system are hugely difficult, emotional and important. It deals with the failure of families, of parenting and of relationships. It cannot heal those failures. But it must ensure it promotes the most positive or the least detrimental outcomes possible for all the children and families who need to use it, because the repercussions can have wide-ranging and continuing effects not just for them, but for society more generally (Executive Summary, para 1).

The Interim Report commented that:

Parents can agree arrangements for children following separation with minimal involvement from the court—in fact a study has found the great majority (around 90%) do not go to court. For the other 10% court can become the arena for drawn out intractable disputes over contact and residency of children. Parental conflict damages children. Although courts focus on encouraging parties to reach agreement, parents' perceptions of 'having their day in court' and the adversarial system can exacerbate this conflict. Furthermore, we have heard concerns from both parents and others—such as grandparents—that the length of the case means that existing arrangements become entrenched and they lose all chance of meaningful contact with a child. Using the system is complicated and costly, both emotionally and financially. People enter the system because they are either forced to or are unaware of other ways of finding a resolution (paras 101–102).

In charting the way forward for private family law, the Interim Report recommended an 'online information hub and helpline' to offer information and advice about 'options for supported dispute resolution, which would highlight the benefits of alternative forms of dispute resolution, including mediation, and Separated Parents Information Programmes (PIPs)' (para 114). Widespread consultation was invited. The Final Report of the Family Justice Review was due to be published in the autumn of 2011 but had not been produced at the time of writing.

11.20 Withdrawal of legal aid for most family proceedings

Mediation organisations, in their responses both to the Legal Aid Green Paper and the Family Justice Review, have made it abundantly clear that mediation will not succeed in a climate devoid of proper legal advice and advocacy in its widest sense. There is a real possibility that, instead of increasing, referrals to mediation will drop sharply when legal aid is withdrawn for most family proceedings. Community Legal Service referrals to mediation from solicitors, which form by far the largest source of referrals, will cease altogether. It is impossible to predict with any certainty that would-be litigants will seek mediation of their own volition, if they are no longer referred to mediation under the LSC Funding Code and if attendance at a MIAM remains only an expectation. There are great concerns among mediators, as well as lawyers, that those most affected by legal aid cuts will be the most vulnerable parents and their children. Very limited provision for legal aid is likely to be retained for legal advice from solicitors alongside mediation, to assist in formalising mediated agreements.

11.21 Training and regulations for family mediation

To provide MIAMs and mediation, a family mediator must have completed nationally recognised training and be a member of a national mediation association represented on the FMC (membership must be renewed annually, with requirements that must be fulfilled). Publicly funded family mediation must be provided in an LSC-contracted family mediation centre or service that meets quality-assured standards. There are almost 1000 locations in England and Wales. Publicly funded family mediation is regulated by the LSC and by the mediator's professional body. There are three associations of family mediators represented on the FMC: the Family Mediators Association (FMA), National Family Mediation (NFM) and Resolution. Each association has similar requirements and standards for training and practice, including continuing professional development and professional practice consultancy. Other members of the FMC include representatives of the College of Mediators (formerly the UK College of Family Mediators), the ADR Group and the Law Society. Although the Law Society is not a key mediation provider, it manages the Law Society's Family Mediation Panel for solicitor mediators, providing one of the routes to recognition by the LSC for conducting publicly funded family mediation.

There are approximately 1000 trained family mediators currently in practice, roughly half of whom are qualified and experienced family lawyers with additional training in family mediation, while the other half are mainly qualified social workers, often experienced in family therapy or family court work. Most mediators offer mediation on a part-time basis, either within their legal practice or at a recognised mediation centre. Lawyers and judges who have taken mediation training find that the techniques and skills are valuable in their day-to-day work as lawyers, even if they do not mediate. Understanding and skills include:

- dealing with people in a different way—understanding emotions and feelings;
- taking a non-directive approach in working with both parties jointly;
- helping people in conflict to communicate better;
- responding to non-verbal communication—body language and eye contact;
- developing new skills, eg, balancing, reframing and mutualising;

- gaining greater understanding of children's needs and reactions to parental separation;
- giving information in a balanced and impartial way;
- developing options and reality-testing;
- summarising clearly and constructively, both orally and in writing.

The use of language is particularly important in mediation, to clarify stressful exchanges and to 'reframe' negative statements in terms of needs, rather than as blaming accusations.

11.22 Family mediation in international cases

'The Family Division of the High Court has an increasing number of cases with an international dimension. These cases may arise from the international movement of family members who are the subject of, or parties to, proceedings about children or money' (Family Justice Review, Interim Report, March 2011, para 47). The rise in cross-border marriages and relationships and corresponding risks of family breakdown underline the need for a common approach and international cooperation. Significant steps have been taken towards the harmonisation of legal systems in Europe, to avoid conflicts between different jurisdictions that follow different legal principles and presumptions. The Regulation known as Brussels II Revised (Council Regulation (EC) No 2201/2003 of 27 November 2003 which came into force on 1 March 2005) applies to all EU Member States except Denmark. It takes precedence over the European Convention on Recognition and Enforcement of Decisions concerning Custody of Children and on Restoration of Custody of Children 1980 and over the 1980 Hague Convention on Child Abduction, but preserves the Hague Convention for dealing with applications for the return of a child and gives directions on how the Convention is to be applied as between Member States.

Reunite, the leading UK charity specialising in international parental child abduction, was formed in 1986 to provide advice, information and support to parents, family members and guardians who have had a child abducted or who fear a child being abducted, as well as advice to parents who may have abducted their children and advice on international contact issues. The primary focus is the best interests of the child, with the aim of facilitating the child's return with minimum disturbance and trauma. A research study based on feedback from parents in 30 cases found that 86 per cent were either highly satisfied or satisfied with the outcome of cross-border mediation in child abduction cases, while 95 per cent said they would recommend mediation to others. Key findings showed that international child abduction cases should always be co-mediated in a specially designed model of mediation practice. The key requirements were the expertise, professionalism and impartiality of the mediators.

Child Focus, a Belgian NGO dealing with international child abduction, is currently leading an EU-funded European project on Training in International Mediation (TIM) in partnership with the Katholieke Universiteit Leuven, MiKK in Berlin and the International Child Abduction Centre (Centrum IKO) in the Netherlands. This project is focusing on training mediators for international, cross-border conflicts involving bi-national couples or couples from the same country living abroad. The objectives are:

(1) to develop and pilot training in international family mediation for mediators and trainers from each EU Member State; and

(2) to create a network of international family mediators in Europe.

The first pilot training took place in Brussels in September 2011 and the first training for trainers is being organised for 2012. The focus is on creating an EU network, but many parental child abduction cases involve a child being taken from an EU country to a country outside the EU. As well as trainers from the UK, the training team includes a Muslim trainer linked to a network of Muslim mediators in India, Pakistan and Middle East countries, and a Spanish trainer linked to networks in Spain, Portugal and South America.

11.23 Mediation and future developments

'The state cannot fix fractured relationships or create a balanced, inclusive family life after separation where this was not the case before separation. Court is generally not the best place to resolve these disputes. Where possible, disputes should be resolved independently or using dispute resolution services such as mediation, when it is safe to do so' (Family Justice Review, Interim Report, para 105). Mediation is not a universal panacea and it is not suitable in every case, but it is an essential part of a new system of family justice that 'allows families to reach easy, simple and efficient agreements which are in the best interests of the children, whilst protecting children and vulnerable adults from risks of harm' (Family Justice Review, Terms of Reference 2010).

11.24 Suggested further reading

Brown, H. and Marriott, A., *ADR Principles and Practice* (Sweet & Maxwell, 1993).

Cockett, M. and Tripp, J., *The Exeter Family Study: Family Breakdown and its impact on children* (University of Exeter Press, 1994).

European Code of Conduct on Mediation: ec.europa.eu/civiljustice/adr/adr_ec_code_conduct_en.htm.

European Parliament, *Directive on Certain Aspects of Mediation in Civil and Commercial Matters* 2008/52/EC 21 May 2008.

Family Justice Review, Interim Report, March 2011.

Family Mediation Council, *Code of Practice* (2010).

Hunt, J., *Parental Perspectives on the Family Justice System in England and Wales: a review of research* (Report for the Family Justice Council, December 2009).

Irving, H. and Benjamin, R., *Family Mediation—Contemporary Issues* (Sage Publications, 1995).

Mnookin, R. and Kornhauser, L., 'Bargaining in the Shadow of the Law: The Case of Divorce' [1979] *Yale Law Review*, 88: 950.

Parkinson, L., 'Co-mediation with a Lawyer Mediator' [1989] *Family Law*, 48: 48–9, 135–9.

Parkinson, L., *Family Mediation* (2nd edition, Jordans Publishing, 2011).

Trinder, L. et al., *Making Contact: How Parents and Children Negotiate and Experience Contact after Divorce* (Joseph Rowntree Foundation Research Findings 092, October 2002).

Trinder, L., Connolly, J., Kellett, J., Notley, C., Swift, L., *Making contact happen or making contact work? The process and outcomes of in-court conciliation* (2006) DCA Research Series 3/06.

Trinder, L. and Kellett, J., *The Longer Term Outcomes of In-Court Conciliation* (Ministry of Justice, 2007).

Relevant principles of taxation

12.1 Principles

Those who are going to specialise in family law must be conversant with the tax provisions relevant to divorce. In particular, it is important to be familiar with the way that maintenance is taxed, as many barristers early in practice may be asked to deal with cases requiring such knowledge.

There has been no very coherent policy on the taxation of husband and wife. The historical concept of the husband and wife as one person was used for income tax and capital gains tax (CGT), taxing the married couple as one unit, but inheritance tax applies to each spouse independently. Increasingly, the approach has been to limit special reliefs and allowances available to spouses, and since 1990/91 spouses have been considered separately for income tax and CGT. There are some provisions to prevent tax avoidance within the family. Civil partners are generally in the same position for tax as spouses. Generally, a child is taxed separately from his or her parents, the child being separately taxable on any income he or she receives and having a personal tax allowance from the time of birth, but again there are provisions to stop tax avoidance.

For more information and helpful guides, see the HM Revenue & Customs website (www.hmrc.gov.uk).

12.2 Income tax

12.2.1 Spouses married and living together

Each married person is independently liable for tax on his or her own income with an individual personal allowance, a figure of £7,475 for 2011/12 where total income is below £100,000 in a year. An additional personal allowance is available for someone over 65, depending on the level of their income. The tax rate for 2011/12 is 20 per cent on income up to £35,000, 40 per cent between that figure and £150,000, and 50 per cent on income above £150,000.

The situation as regards tax allowances for children has changed over the years. The current position is that a child is liable for tax on any personal income with an individual tax allowance. A Child Tax Credit is available to any parent who is single, married or living with someone and has at least one child under the age of 16 living with them, or a child up to 20 in full-time education or training. There are also tax credits available to assist with child care costs in some circumstances. If parents are not liable to higher-rate tax, this allowance can go to either of them or be shared. If either of the parents is liable to higher-rate tax, the allowance goes to that parent, and the allowance tapers off to no benefit a little way into the higher-rate tax band. Working Families' Tax Credit is available for families with very low income, and should be researched if appropriate.

12.2.2   Separation and divorce

Provisions for the taxation of maintenance payments are set out in the Finance Act 1988, ss 36–40, see **12.6**.

12.3   CGT

12.3.1   Spouses married and living together

As with income tax, the principle of joint assessment of husband and wife for capital gains tax (CGT) survived for many decades, but (as with income tax) this was abandoned in 1990. Each spouse is separately liable for tax on their own gains, and each has a separate annual allowance of £10,600 for 2011/12.

Married couples have a substantial advantage in that disposals between spouses are treated as being at no gain, no loss, so that no CGT will be payable on such a disposal (Taxation of Chargeable Gains 1992 (TCGA 1992), s 58). This applies provided that spouses are living together 'in' (ie, for the whole or part of) the tax year in question. Note, however, that the original acquisition price of the asset will be retained for calculating gains on a later disposal by the recipient spouse. On the operation of this section, see *Gubay v Kington* [1984] 1 WLR 163.

12.3.2   Separation and divorce

It is important to note that disposals made as part of financial provision on divorce are not necessarily exempt from CGT, and the divorce settlement should be considered carefully to avoid CGT, as it will potentially apply to any gain that is realised—see *M v M (Sale of Property)* [1988] 1 FLR 389. In *Aspden v Hildesley* [1982] 1 WLR 264 a husband agreed to transfer his share in a second home to the wife but it was held that this transaction was not exempt so he would have to pay CGT on the value of his share.

As suggestions for avoiding CGT:

(a) Make disposal or agreement before separation and divorce, so it will be at no gain/ no loss (but remember the original acquisition cost is retained for calculating later gains);

(b) Use exempt assets for provision, eg, a car;

(c) Remember a sterling lump sum will not be liable to CGT (but consider how such a sum could be raised);

(d) Remember that a main private residence is not liable to tax;

(e) After separation and divorce, the spouses will not be 'connected', so it may be possible to argue market value should not be taken.

12.4 Inheritance tax

12.4.1 Spouses married and living together

Spouses are separately liable for inheritance tax on their own estates with their own allowances and own cumulative totals. This can be important in tax planning: assets can be divided between the spouses to ensure that each makes full use of the nil rate band of £325000 each. The nil rate band has remained the same since 2009, but is raised from time to time.

Transfers between spouses are exempt (Inheritance Tax Act 1984 (ITA 1984), s 18); and they can benefit from other exemptions and reliefs, such as provision for maintenance (ITA 1984, s 11) and gifts in consideration of marriage (ITA 1984, s 22).

12.4.2 Separation and divorce

While there is no complete exemption for provision on divorce, it is unlikely that inheritance tax will bite on divorce provision. There will be no tax on the divorce, but only potentially when one spouse later dies. The provision that dispositions for maintenance of the family are not transfers of value applies to maintenance on divorce (ITA 1984, s 11), and if there is provision under a court order it can be argued that there is no intention to confer a gratuitous benefit (ITA 1984, s 10).

12.4.3 Death of one spouse

Tax will be chargeable on the estate of the deceased, including their share of jointly owned property, subject to their cumulative total. Property passing to the surviving spouse will be exempt, but will be chargeable to tax when the survivor dies, so exemptions should be used carefully.

12.5 Cohabitees

12.5.1 Income tax

Couples living together will each be taxed as a single individual, paying tax on their own income with a single personal allowance each.

12.5.2 Capital gains tax

Each cohabitee will be separately taxed and will have their own allowances. Disposals between them will be potentially taxable, which may be a problem if they split up and need to divide assets.

12.5.3 Inheritance tax

Each cohabitee will be separately taxed and will have their own allowances and cumulative total. Transfers between cohabitees will not be exempt, but they may be 'potentially exempt transfers' if they are gifts. A problem can arise if one cohabitee dies, as assets left to the other will not be exempt.

12.6 Taxation of maintenance payments

12.6.1 Generally

The approach of the tax system to maintenance payments has varied over the years. The current system is relatively straightforward, but confusion may be caused if dealing with a variation in a case where an original order was made some years ago. Payments made under obligations entered into before 15 March 1988 were taxed under a complex process by which tax was paid in advance by the payer, but then became a tax credit of which the payee might be able to reclaim all or part depending on his or her own tax position. The current approach is that maintenance payments should have limited and simple tax consequences, because the payer pays tax, but then no further tax is payable by the payee. It is very important to take this into account in looking at appropriate figures for maintenance. The same rules apply to former spouses and former civil partners.

12.6.2 Tax effects for the person paying maintenance

Maintenance payments are not deductible for tax purposes and must be paid in full from taxed income. This applies to payments to or for a former spouse or a child, including assessments under the Child Support Act 1991.

Until 2000/01, an additional personal allowance was available to someone paying maintenance to a former spouse. From 2001/02, maintenance payments relief is only available where the payer or the former spouse is over 75, and it only provides a very limited tax deduction.

12.6.3 Tax effects for the person receiving maintenance

Whether the recipient of the payments is a former spouse or a child, the payments will not be taxable in his or her hands (though obviously he or she will be fully liable to tax on any other income he or she has). The recipient will not be able to set any tax allowance against the maintenance payment, or be able to reclaim any tax paid by the payer in respect of the payment.

12.7 Illustration of tax issues relevant to divorce

Jasper and Fiona married in 2006 and separated in 2010, since when they have not lived together. They have one child, Gemma, currently aged 7.

Fiona has petitioned for divorce and has been granted a decree nisi. Financial provision is currently being negotiated, and Fiona has proposed the following terms:

(a) Jasper should transfer to Fiona his share in the former matrimonial home, which is registered in their joint names and which is currently valued at £250,000. The house was purchased in 2006 for £180,000.

(b) Alternatively, the former matrimonial home should be settled, to be sold when Gemma becomes 18, the proceeds then to be divided with 75 per cent to Fiona and 25 per cent to Jasper.

(c) Fiona should transfer to Jasper a yacht that was purchased in 2000 for £20,000. Although the purchase price was provided by Jasper, the yacht was put into Fiona's name as Jasper at the time had a slight fear that he might go bankrupt. The yacht is now worth £50,000.

(d) Fiona should keep a Volvo car bought for her by Jasper which is currently worth £10,000.

(e) Jasper should pay to Fiona a lump sum of £20,000. To raise this sum he would have to sell shares that he purchased in 1995 for £2,000, which are now worth £30,000.

In the next section, we advise Jasper on any potential tax implications of each term to help him to decide how he should respond.

12.7.1 Advice to Jasper

(a) There will be no inheritance tax consequences as all the transfers would apparently be to meet reasonable claims on divorce and would therefore be 'non-gratuitous' (ITA 1984, s 10).

(b) There is an apparent capital gain of £70,000 on the matrimonial home; however, the gain will be exempt from CGT, as it relates to a main private residence (TCGA 1992, s 222; and see also Extra-Statutory Concession D6, as the couple are already living separately).

(c) If the house is settled, it will become the main private residence of Fiona alone. Therefore, when the home is eventually sold (or if Fiona later buys out Jasper's interest), then the gain that Jasper makes will be subject to CGT (calculated as the gain his 25 per cent has made since the settlement). This must be considered in deciding how attractive this option is.

(d) The yacht has apparently gained £30,000 in value. If Fiona transfers ownership to Jasper, this gain will prima facie be liable to tax at Fiona's marginal rate of income tax, and reduced by Fiona's annual allowance of £10,600 if this has not yet been used for another transaction.

(e) There is no disposal if a spouse keeps an asset, and in any event motor cars are not subject to CGT.

(f) The transfer of money will not in itself attract CGT as sterling is not liable to the tax. However, the gain of £28,000 that will accrue on the sale of the shares will attract CGT at Jasper's marginal rate of tax, reduced by his annual allowance of £10,600 if this has not yet been used on another transaction, and also reduced by the costs of sale. If a capital sum is to be paid, it is always important to consider how it will be raised.

13 Applications for committal orders—checklists

13.1 Introduction

13.1.1 When committal orders may be sought

Committal to prison is a punishment for contempt and is the ultimate means by which a court may enforce an order to do an act within a prescribed time where the individual concerned has failed or refused to obey the order (subject to the Debtors' Act 1869). Similarly, a committal order may be made where a person has done an act which he was ordered not to do. Undertakings given to the court may be enforced in the same way. Punishment for civil contempt is not a remedy in itself, but a way of enforcing a remedy.

There are many different kinds of orders in family proceedings which may be enforced by committal to prison. These include non-molestation and occupation orders (see **Chapter 2**); restraining orders; interlocutory orders concerning the filing of evidence or the disclosure of documents or information; orders requiring the attendance of parties at hearings; and orders made under the Children Act 1989 (CA 1989), ss 8 and 14A, 14B(2)(b), 14C(3)(b) and 14D. Civil Procedure Rules (CPR), which themselves incorporate previous High Court (RSC Ord 52) and County Court Rules (CCR Ord 29), apply, with modification as necessary to committal procedure in family law cases: Family Procedure Rules 2010 (FPR 2010), r 33.1/PD33A, para 1.1.

The party who obtained the original order which may require enforcement by committal to prison is entitled to have a 'penal notice' endorsed on the order drawing the attention of the respondent to the consequences of disobedience. Save in exceptional circumstances no order for committal may be made unless such a warning has been drawn to the attention of the alleged contemnor. A penal notice may not be endorsed on an order made under CA 1989, ss 8 or 14 without the permission of the court: FPR 2010, r 33.7(b).

In any event, in family proceedings, committal orders are viewed as a last resort, when all other reasonable means of enforcement have been tried or are inapt to the occasion.

In proceedings concerning children, although the welfare of the child is not the paramount consideration when considering whether to make an order to commit to prison, it may be a highly relevant consideration. This is well illustrated by *M v M (Breaches of Orders: Committal)* [2006] 1 FLR 1154. A father was found on more than 60 occasions to have breached an order forbidding him from having contact with his children. Nonetheless the court decided not to commit him to prison. The older children were likely to revolt against the idea of their father being sent to prison. This would have made them unmanageable for their mother in whose care they lived, which would have resulted in care proceedings. This would have been detrimental to their welfare. In the circumstances their welfare was the decisive factor in determining that a committal order should not be made.

No order will be enforced by committal unless it is clear and unambiguous in its terms. Thus an order simply requiring a parent to allow the other parent 'staying contact on dates to be arranged' is not enforceable as it did not require the resident parent to do an act by a particular time (*D v D* (*Access; Contempt: Committal* [1991] 2 FLR 34).

The court will not enforce an order to do an act by a particular date unless it is proven that the order was served before that date.

No committal order will be made in respect of a trivial breach of an order. The applicant for such an order is likely to have costs awarded against him (*Adam Phones Ltd v Goldschmidt* [1999] 4 All ER 486).

13.1.2 The importance of abiding by correct procedure

The Court of Appeal has stressed in several cases that, because committal for contempt of court is concerned with offences of a quasi-criminal nature and the liberty of the subject is at stake, the relevant rules of court must be complied with and the prescribed forms must be used. However, 'any procedural defect in the commencement or conduct by the applicant of a committal application may be waived by the court if satisfied that no injustice has been caused to the respondent by the defect' (Practice Direction—Committal Applications, para 10, supplemental to RSC Ord 52 and CCR Ord 29).

In *Nicholls v Nicholls* [1997] 1 FLR 649, Lord Woolf MR gave the following guidance (p 661E):

(1) As committal orders involve the liberty of the subject it is particularly important that the relevant rules are duly complied with. It remains the responsibility of the judge when signing the committal order to ensure that it is properly drawn and that it adequately particularises the breaches which have been proved and for which the sentence has been imposed.

(2) As long as the contemnor has had a fair trial and the order has been made on valid grounds the existence of a defect either in the application to commit or in the committal order served will not result in the order being set aside except insofar as the interests of justice require this to be done.

(3) Interests of justice will not require an order to be set aside where there is no prejudice caused as the result of errors in the application to commit or in the order to commit. When necessary the order can be amended.

(4) When considering whether to set aside the order, the court should have regard to the interests of any other party and the need to uphold the reputation of the justice system.

(5) If there has been a procedural irregularity or some other defect in the conduct of the proceedings which has occasioned injustice, the court will consider exercising its power to order a new trial unless there are circumstances which indicate that it would not be just to do so.

The Human Rights Act 1998 (HRA 1998) has affected the manner in which all committal proceedings must be approached. The President's Direction (Committal Applications and Proceedings in which a Committal Order may be made) [2001] 1 FLR 949 states, at para 2:

In any family proceedings (to which the Civil Procedure Rules Practice Direction Supplemental to RSC Ord 52 and CCR Ord 29 relates) in which a committal order may be made, including proceedings for the enforcement of an existing order by way of judgment summons or other process, full effect will be given to the HRA 1998 and to the rights afforded under that Act. In particular the European Convention for the Protection of Human Rights and Fundamental Freedoms 1950, Art 6 is fully applicable to such proceedings. Those involved must ensure that in the conduct of the proceedings there is due observance of the HRA 1998 in the same manner as if the proceedings fell within the CPR direction.

See also *Mubarak v Mubarak* [2001] 1 FLR 698—although this case related to an application for a judgment summons, it is instructive on the requirement of strict compliance with Art 6.

The checklists which follow are designed to cover the practical points which most often arise, and need to be considered, in preparation for, and in the course of, committal hearings. They are not comprehensive of every point which has reached the Court of Appeal.

13.1.3 Committal procedure: forms, rules and practice direction

Whichever prescribed form of committal application is required, the form 'must set out in full the grounds on which the committal application is made and should identify, separately and numerically, each act of contempt' (Practice Direction—Committal Applications, paras 2.5 and 2.6, and *Harmsworth v Harmsworth* [1987] 3 All ER 816). This requirement and the need to support the application with suitable evidence and give due notice to the respondent are the most important steps to ensure that an application for committal can achieve an effective hearing.

For a summary of the source of the relevant rules (which can get complicated since old rules are being applied and brought through into new procedural rules), see the useful summary in Jordan's *Family Court Practice* (Part I, Ch 36).

Under the President's Direction, the CPR Practice Direction supplemental to the RSC Ord 52 and the CCR Ord 29 applies to all applications in family proceedings for a committal order in the same manner and to the same extent as it applies to proceedings governed by the CPR 1998, subject to:

- the FPR 2010;
- the limited application of the CPR 1998 in family proceedings.

Further important points arising in the CPR Practice Direction and the new FPR 2010:

(a) Where the alleged contempt is in connection with existing family proceedings (other than contempt in the face of the court) or with an order made or an undertaking given in existing proceedings, the committal application shall be made in those proceedings.

(b) Committal applications in the High Court are to be made on notice, using Part 8 claim forms. In the county court, applications are to be made as prescribed by the CCR Ord 29 ('notice to show good reason'). Both should be supported by affidavit.

(c) Where the CPR Practice Direction requires more information to be provided than is required to be provided under the older RSC and the CCR, the court will expect the former to be observed.

(d) The court will ensure that adequate time is afforded to the respondent for the preparation of his or her defence.

(e) The CPR Practice Direction applies to breaches of exclusion requirements made in interim care orders (ICOs) under the CA 1989 and to orders made under the FLA 1996, Part IV.

(f) An application to commit for breach of an undertaking or order must be commenced by the filing of an application notice in the proceedings in which the undertaking was given or order was made. The enforcement rules apply to undertakings as they apply to orders, with necessary modifications: FPR 2010, PD 33A, para 1.3.

County court Forms N78 and N79 were designed to ensure that the procedural requirements of the rules were met, and the requirements for common disposals would be complied with. The forms incorporate the essential requirements in all committal applications and, in the case of Form N79, the menu of common disposal orders. In family proceedings courts, similar Forms FL418 and FL419 apply. Practitioners are strongly recommended to use these forms as a simple inventory to ensure that the essential procedural requirements are followed. Form N78 remains a convenient guide to the contents required for a committal application whether in the High Court, Family Division or the county court. The checklists appearing after this introduction provide a sequential and extended framework for following good practice.

Form N79, the prescribed form for a committal order in county courts, and Form FL419 for family proceedings courts, contain most of the usual orders made on proof of disobedience of an injunctive order or breach of an undertaking. The court—judge or justices and clerk—can delete the orders not required, and enter the precise details of the orders made. Forms N79 and FL419 are supplied to courts with explanatory guidance notes attached and they can be used as a checklist at the time of making an order.

13.1.4 Committal hearings

In general terms, hearings of committal proceedings are in many respects similar to hearings of criminal charges. Thus the burden of proof rests on the person making the allegation of contempt; the standard of proof is the criminal standard; the respondent must be allowed to cross-examine witnesses and to call evidence; the respondent is entitled to submit that there is no case to answer; if a contempt is found proved the contemnor must be allowed to address the court by way of mitigation or seeking to purge his or her contempt; and principles of *autrefois acquit* and *autrefois convict* apply.

The court is entitled to require the respondent to file sworn witness statements or affidavits from himself and his witnesses (*Re B (Contempt of Court: Affidavit Evidence)* [1996] 1 FLR 239). This rule is now subject to the *President's Practice Direction, Committal Applications* which requires the application of the CPR Practice Direction to applications for committal orders in family proceedings. Those rules (backed up by the overriding objective) provide that a respondent may give oral evidence and may call witnesses notwithstanding that he has not filed any written witness statements.

High Court Contempt proceedings are civil proceedings although they incorporate the criminal standard of proof. Thus hearsay evidence is admissible subject to the requirements of the Civil Evidence Act 1995 and the European Convention on Human Rights, Art 6 (*Daltel Europe Ltd (in liquidation) v Makki* The Times, 8 March 2006). The same approach probably applies in the county court.

The European Convention on Human Rights, Art 6(3)(c) provides that 'a defendant is entitled to defend himself in person or through legal assistance of his own choosing or, if he has not sufficient means to pay for legal assistance, to be given it free when the interests of justice so require'.

Note that the court cannot order that an alleged contemnor be given legal aid, but it can invite a solicitor to give 'help at court' (Administration of Justice Act 1970 (AJA 1970), Part 1), or adjourn until similar assistance is available. The power of the court to *grant* public funding in contempt cases applies only to contempt 'in the face of the court' (AJA 1970, s 12(2) and Sch 3). But in *Re K (Contact: Committal Order)* [2003] 1 FLR 277, the Court of Appeal held that a mother's rights under Art 6 had been breached by the making of a committal order at a hearing at which she did not have legal representation. She was entitled (Art 6(3)(c)) to have legal representation at a hearing at which deprivation of her liberty was at stake and the Legal Services Commission (LSC) should have expedited her application for emergency funding for her to be represented. Legal representation might have also made a difference to the outcome which affected her family life by separating her from her children. Thus, her right to respect for family life under Art 8 was also affected by denial of representation. Presumably the grant of funding in such circumstances will survive the current government's proposed cuts.

Under the old law, a judge's failure to inform the respondent of his or her right to legal aid was a material irregularity which would lead to a committal order being quashed (*King v Read and Slack* [1999] 3 FLR 423). In the light of *Re K*, a court would be wise to inform the respondent of his or her right to apply for public funding under the AJA 1999 and the regulations made under that Act.

Judges (including district judges) have broad power to commit for contempt, including under the Family Law Act 1996 (FLA 1996), Parts 4 and 4A. District judges have no power, however, to hear committals under the Protection from Harassment Act 1997 (PHA 1997).

In the case of a contempt in the face of the court, if the facts are not in dispute there is no objection to the judge before whom the contempt took place making findings regarding the contempt. Although the principle that a judge should not be a judge in his own cause does not apply as the purpose of the jurisdiction is to protect the administration of justice, not the judge personally, it is often sensible for the matter to be referred to another judge to forestall any appearance of bias (*R v Murray* [2006] 150 SJ 1191 and see below: *Re G (Contempt Proceedings)* [2003] Fam Law 471).

In any other case where the court has the power to commit a person for contempt of court and no limitation applies to the period of committal, the committal must be for a fixed term. The maximum sentence (for adults) in the High Court and county court is two years' imprisonment; in the magistrates' court one month (Contempt of Court Act 1981, s 14/Magistrates' Courts Act 1980 (MCA 1980), s 63(3)). In addition, or alternatively, these courts may impose a fine. They may also order damages and other methods of enforcement. But only the High Court can sequester the contemnor's assets (see *Hale v Tanner* [2000] 2 FLR 879).

In the High Court and county court the court may make a hospital order, a guardianship order or an interim hospital order under the Mental Health Act 1983, ss 37 or 38 where the person is suffering from mental illness or severe mental impairment (Contempt of Court Act 1981, s 14(4)). A person may be remanded for a report of his mental condition where it is suspected that he is suffering from mental illness or severe mental impairment.

In respect of persons between the ages of 18 and 21 years, any sentence of committal must be served in a Young Offenders' Institution (see Criminal Justice Act 1982, s 9(1), and *Re H (Respondent under 18; Power of Arrest)* [2001] 1 FLR 641).

There is, theoretically, power to sentence a person between the ages of 18 and 21 to an attendance centre order. However before such an order is made, the Minister of Justice must notify the court that such a centre is available. At present no such notification has been given.

A person under the age of 18 may be fined, subject to his means. He may also be made the subject of orders under the Mental Health Act 1983 (see s 14(4) above). In any other circumstances he may not be detained (see Criminal Justice Act 1982, s 9(1); and *Re H (Respondent under 18; Power of Arrest)* [2001] 1 FLR 641).

There is a distinction between a case where a party to proceedings is alleged to have been in breach of an order of the court made in the proceedings, and one where a party has done something that, although not in breach of a specific order is, nevertheless, a contempt of court. In the latter case, there may be more than one way of dealing with it. If the breach is admitted, a warning, together if necessary with a specific undertaking or injunction in terms to prevent a recurrence of the breach, may be sufficient.

A committal order, even if suspended, is a last resort normally reserved for serious, intentional, and in most cases, repeated contempts of court that have been established by due process. If the contempt is not admitted and is sufficiently serious and culpable for a court to contemplate a committal order, due process is obligatory. Nearly all contempt proceedings require adjournment to a separate hearing, often to a different judge. An adjournment would be necessary if the first judge had heard evidence from a party alleged to be in contempt, that he or she would not be obliged to give for risk of self-incrimination if he or she were faced with an allegation of contempt (*Re G (Contempt Proceedings)* [2003] Fam Law 471).

13.1.5 Sentencing powers

Upon finding a contempt has been proved, whether by evidence or admission, the court has a range of powers. For a brief summary, see *Hale v Tanner* [2000] 2 FLR 879, CA. When considering the length of any sentences of imprisonment for contempt due regard must be had to the maximum allowable for the contempt under the provisions mentioned in the previous section. In one case a person who was over 18 but under 21 was found to be in breach of an order which had excluded him from a specified area. The Court of Appeal allowed his appeal against a sentence of two years' detention because the maximum sentence must be reserved for the worst case, and in any event the sentence was excessive (*Turnbull v Middlesbrough Borough Council* [2003] EWCA Civ 1327).

The objective of a judge sentencing for breach of an injunction is to uphold the authority of the court, and not simply to punish the offence itself. Nonetheless, where sentences were passed for breaches of an order under FLA 1996, Part IV, the Court of Appeal held that they should generally be kept in line with penalties imposed for similar misconduct under the PHA 1997, albeit that the latter were charged as criminal offences (*Lomas v Parle* [2004] 1 All ER 1173). It is appropriate that the approach in sentencing for contempt for non-compliance with an order should take into account criminal sentencing cases. Although the maxima are different in contempt proceedings, guidance given for sentencers in criminal proceedings in the Criminal Justice Act 2003, ss 142–144 should be taken into consideration. These, in summary, set out the purposes of sentencing in criminal cases (punishment, reduction of crime, reform and rehabilitation, public protection and reparation); the means of determining the seriousness of the offence (regard being had to the offender's culpability, the degree of harm done by him, his previous record); any acceptance of responsibility and at what stage such acceptance was expressed).

The disposal must be proportionate to the seriousness of the contempt, reflect the courts' disapproval and be designed to secure compliance in future. The principle of proportionality between the seriousness of the contempt and the rigour of the punishment presumes a process of graduated sentences. The court must ask itself whether the contempt is so serious that only a sentence of imprisonment could be justified. If it is not, then imprisonment will be wrong in principle. Thus a suspended sentence should not be imposed unless, but for the special factors justifying suspension, immediate imprisonment would have been appropriate. It should not be imposed merely because the contemnor cannot afford to pay a fine (see *Re M (Contact Order)*, Court of Appeal, The Times 18 April 2005). The court should briefly explains its reasons for the choice of disposal.

Where a first breach of an injunction is serious, an immediate committal to prison may be imposed and there is no principle that a first breach cannot result in a sentence of imprisonment: *Jordan v Jordan* [1993] 1 FLR 533, *Thorpe v Thorpe* [1998] 2 FLR 127. In an extreme case, a mother who prevents contact which is in the interests of a child may be sent to prison: *A v N (Committal: Refusal of Contact)* [1997] 1 FLR 533. However, all other remedies should be tried first: *Re M (Contact Order: Committal)* [1999] 1 FLR 810. In children cases the welfare of the child is not the paramount consideration in deciding whether a contemnor should be committed to prison. The objective is to uphold the authority of the court. If its authority is undermined any orders it makes in the best interest of children will not serve their purpose. Thus where a mother had flouted contact orders, failed to attend the court and had abused the court with obscenities, a sentence of seven days' imprisonment suspended on terms, was fully justified (*Re S (Contact Order: Committal)* [2005] 1 FLR 812).

Where there has been a really substantial error leading to a demonstrable injustice to the victim of a contempt, the Court of Appeal can allow an appeal by the claimant and increase the sentence: *Manchester County Council v Worthington* [2000] 1 FLR 411; *Wilson v Webster* [1998] 1 FLR 1097, CA. A contemnor contemplating an appeal should be warned that the sentence can be increased. There is no jurisdiction to release a contemnor on his or her application to purge his or her contempt by suspending the unserved balance of the prison sentence: *Harris v Harris* [2002] 1 FLR 248. The level of sentencing for contempt of court in connection with domestic violence has increased in recent times to reflect the needs of contemporary society. Sentences should not be manifestly discrepant with those passed in the criminal courts for like offences. Thus where a father had assaulted his children's grandmother and uncle in front of the children leading to a non-molestation order being made, four further incidents of verbal abuse and intimidation, including one of violence where he grabbed the grandmother by the throat and forced her onto the bonnet of a car, merited a sentence of nine months' imprisonment (*H v O (Contempt of Court: Sentencing)* [2005] 2 FLR 329).

Although an attack on a judge in court would be treated as serious contempt in the face of the court, in exceptional circumstances prison may not be justified. The Court of Appeal allowed an appeal against sentence *four days after the contemnor had completed the sentence*. He was understandably upset and frustrated by the way in which he had been treated. He interrupted other proceedings being conducted by the judge who had sentenced him, throwing eggs and shouting out passages from the Court of Appeal's judgment in his case. While his behaviour was a deplorable affront to the dignity of the court, the reality of the situation could not be ignored. His sentence for his contempt in the face of the court was reduced from two months to 28 days (*Hammerton v Mammerton (No 2)* [2007] EWCA Civ 465).

13.1.6 The Domestic Violence, Crime and Victims Act 2004

Hitherto it was possible for there to be parallel criminal proceedings relating to the same facts as were the subject of the contempt proceedings. This led to an unsatisfactory duplication of effort, and was wasteful of resources and time-consuming. It was stressful for the victim to have to go through two sets of proceedings. As sentence in the contempt proceedings needed not to be delayed to await decisions in the concurrent criminal proceedings (*pace: Smith v Smith* [1991] 2 FLR 55), from the respondent's point of view he suffered a double jeopardy. In one case, where the husband had been prosecuted, convicted and sentenced in the criminal courts under the PHA 1997 and in proceedings in the county court for breach of orders under FLA 1996, the sentence for contempt had to be reduced to reflect the criminal sentencing (see *Lomas v Parle*) [2004] 1 FLR 812).

This anomaly has now been remedied by the Domestic Violence, Crime and Victims Act 2004 (DVCVA 2004) which has inserted a new s 42A FLA 1996. This provides that where a person, without reasonable excuse, does anything that he is prohibited from doing by a non-molestation order, he is guilty of an offence (s 42A(1)).

Where a person is convicted of an offence under s 42A in respect of any conduct, that conduct will not be punishable as a contempt of court (s 42A(3)). Equally, where a person has been punished for conduct as a contempt of court, he cannot be convicted for an offence under s 42A in respect of that conduct (s 42A(4)).

The maximum sentence on indictment will be five years' imprisonment; after summary trial, 12 months (s 42A). Breach of a non-molestation order may be disposed of either as a crime under s 42A or as a contempt pursuant to arrest by warrant or the notice to show cause procedure, although the victim may not always have or make the choice (see generally **2.14**).

The non-molestation order may have been made without notice. Where this has occurred, to bring criminal or contempt proceedings, there must be proof that the order was brought to the attention of the respondent.

Under the PHA 1997 duplicated punishments from both contempt of court and an offence under the Act for breach of an injunction granted under s 3(3)(a) in civil proceedings are excluded (s 3(7) and (8)). The principal procedural change brought about by the DVCVA 2004 is that although a breach of an order remains a contempt of court, the court may no longer attach a power of arrest to a non-molestation order made under FLA 1996, s 42. Occupation orders made under ss 33 to 38 will have an existing penal notice endorsed and may have a power of arrest attached. Orders made under s 42 will have endorsed on them a modified penal notice alerting the respondent to the new criminal offence and sanctions, but without any power of arrest.

It is important to remember that separate orders must now be drawn using form FL 404 for occupation orders and FL 404a for non-molestation orders.

A problem arises from the overlap between FLA 1996, ss 33–38 and s 42. The former sections enable the court to make occupation orders which may still be enforced with a power of arrest. These provisions permit a court to exclude a respondent from a defined area in which the dwelling-house occupied by the applicant is included (see generally **Chapter 2**). An order to similar effect can also be made under s 42 to prevent molestation (so-called 'zonal' orders). Thus it is still possible for an individual to be both prosecuted under s 42A and made the subject of contempt proceedings for breach of an occupation order for related infractions. It follows from general principles of natural justice that should such an occasion arise the court must ensure that the wrongdoer is not punished twice over for the same wrong (following May LJ in *H v O* [2005] 2 FLR 329 at 338).

This overlap in the jurisdiction conferred by ss 33–38 and s 42 makes it all the more important to ensure that the order made is drawn up using the correct form. Errors could result in a criminal sanction being imposed for breach when this never intended to be the means of enforcement.

A further problem may result from the contrast between the wording of s 33(1) and (3)(g) of the Act, and that of ss 35–38. Section 33(1) defines the term 'dwelling-house' as used in the section as the place which 'is or at any time has been the home of the person entitled and of another person with whom he is associated' or 'was at any time intended by the person entitled and any other such person to be their home'.

It will be immediately obvious that the phrases 'another person' and 'any other person' are wide enough to include any associated person (as defined by s 62(3) of the Act) and not just the respondent.

It follows that if the applicant has fled the former matrimonial home with her children to escape the respondent's violence, and has obtained a tenancy for them all elsewhere, the new address would appear to be covered by the section as well as the matrimonial home. The applicant would inevitably wish for the respondent to be excluded from an area around the new address. This would be possible, on the literal wording of s 33(1) and (3)(g).

In contrast, s 35 is confined, in cases of former spouses or civil partners, to dwelling-houses which were at any time their matrimonial/civil partnership home. Section 36, in cases of cohabitants and former cohabitants, is confined to dwelling-houses in which they cohabit, have cohabited or intended to cohabit. Sections 37 and 38 relate to a dwelling-house where neither party is entitled to remain in occupation (for example, where they are licensees or squatters) and is confined respectively to the matrimonial/civil partnership home or the home in which the parties cohabited. Thus the area of the possible exclusion zone must be defined geographically around that dwelling-house and nowhere else. Hence the scope of these provisions is narrower than under s 33(3)(g). If a person who cannot bring themselves within s 33 requires an exclusion zone around a dwelling-house which was not the home in which he or she dwells, dwelled or intended to dwell with the respondent, he/she must apply under s 42.

Where the protection of the applicant requires the exclusion of the respondent from a specified area around the family home, it is likely that many applicants will prefer to opt for orders under ss 33–38 rather than s 42 on the grounds that while they require protection from a former partner or spouse, they may have no wish to run the risk of criminalising him. This may be especially so if he is still the main financial provider and has as a continuing relationship with the children of the parties.

13.2 Checklist 1: preparing an application for committal for disobedience of an injunctive order or breach of an undertaking

13.2.1 Form of injunctive order or document recording an undertaking

(1) Was the order one which the court had jurisdiction to make?

If made in proceedings other than family proceedings, does the order support a legal right, eg, forbid a recognised tort or harassment within the PHA 1997, s 1, or protect a legal or equitable interest?

If made in family proceedings (under FLA 1996, Part IV, CA 1989, matrimonial proceedings begun by petition, or under the inherent jurisdiction of the High Court), was the order available as a non-molestation or occupation order? Or was the order available for the protection of family property? Is it an order for the payment of money under FPR 2010, r33.3(2)? The High Court has further injunctive powers under the inherent jurisdiction.

An injunctive order or an undertaking must be obeyed, even if it is irregular, until it is discharged, but lack of jurisdiction may affect the conduct of an application to commit and/or the approach to sentence for a contempt.

(2) Was the instruction to the other party, or the undertaking, precise and explicit as to what the person was required to do or abstain from doing? (See CPR, PD 25 (Interim Injunctions), para 5.3.)

And, if the doing of an act was required, did the injunctive order specify when or by when the act was to be done, as required by RSC Ord 42, r 2(1), CCR Ord 22, r 3; or did the undertaking specify when or by when the act was to be done?

(3)(a) In the case of an injunctive order:

(i)   In the High Court, was there 'prominently displayed on the front' of the copy of the order for service a warning (penal) notice, as required by RSC Ord 45, r 7(4) and CPR, PD 40B, para 9.1?

Note: In the High Court the party wishing to have the penal notice endorsed on the order must do so himself (RSC Ord 45, r 7).

(ii) In a county court, was the injunctive order issued with a penal notice endorsed or incorporated, as required by CCR Ord 29, r 1(3) or FPR 2010, r 10.12 and CPR, PD 40B, para 9.1; was it issued in prescribed form?

Note A: a warning (penal) notice cannot be endorsed on or incorporated in an order under the CA 1989, s 8 unless a judge has so directed: FPR 2010, r 12.33(1)(a).

Note B: in the county court the penal notice is endorsed by an officer of the court. It is a mandatory requirement, but carried out as a purely administrative function (CCR Ord 29, r 1(3) and *R v Wandsworth County Court ex p Munn* (1994) 26 HLR 697).

(iii) In a family proceedings court, was the injunctive order issued in a proper form with a penal notice?

(b) In the case of an undertaking:

(i)   In the High Court or a county court, was the undertaking recorded in an order or form of undertaking in which a penal notice was incorporated or endorsed in accordance with FPR 2010, PD 33A, para 1.4 or para 2.2? Also, was it acknowledged by a signed statement of the giver in accordance with FPR 2010, PD 33A, para 1.5/6? Form N117 is used in the county court and D787 in the Family Division.

(ii) In a family proceedings court, was the undertaking recorded in Form FL422, as required by FPC(MP)R 1991, r 20(14)?

13.2.2 Service of injunctive order or record of undertaking

(1)(a) In the case of an injunctive order:

(i)   Was personal service of the order, with a warning or penal notice prominently displayed on the front **(High Court)** or endorsed on it or incorporated in it **(county or family proceedings court)**, effected?

Personal service is required by RSC Ord 45, r 7(2), CCR Ord 29, r 1(2), FPR 2010, r 10.6 unless (i) the order recites that personal service was dispensed with, or (ii) the terms of the order are only prohibitory, and do not require an act to be done and, pending service, have been communicated to the other party, or (iii) the court effects service (FPR 2010, r 10.6(2)).

> (ii)   If the injunctive order required the other party to do an act, was the injunctive order served personally before the expiration of the time within which he or she was to do the act, as required by RSC Ord 45, r 7(2)(b), CCR Ord 29, r 1(2)(b)?

Note *Davy International Ltd v Tazzyman* [1997] 3 All ER 183 and *Jolly v Hull; Jolly v Jolly* [2000] 2 FLR 69, as to the powers to dispense with service of the order at the hearing of a committal application, under RSC Ord 45, r 7(7) and CCR Ord 29, r 1(7).

> (iii)   If served, is personal service proved?

Proof is usually by affidavit of service in judge courts and by Form FL415 in family proceedings courts.

> **(b)   In the case of an undertaking:**
>
> (i)   If the signed statement of the giver of the undertaking was not given to the court in person, was it either endorsed on a court copy or filed in a separate document (FPR 2010, PD 33A, para 1.6)?

13.2.3   Form of the application to commit and the requirement of an affidavit or statement in support

(1)(a) In civil proceedings in the High Court and county courts, does the Claim Application Notice give the essential information to the respondent and to the court?

There is no separate prescribed form specific to committal applications. The prescribed requirements are in Practice Direction—Committal Applications, paras 2.2, 2.5 and 2.6. County court Form N78 is a useful guide.

(b) In family proceedings, does the part 8 claim form (FPR 2010, r 33.1), or the Form N78 in a county court, or the Form FL418 in a family proceedings court, give the essential information to the respondent and the court?

In particular (all courts: Practice Direction—Committal Applications, paras 2.5–2.6, CCR Ord 29, r 1(4A):

> (i)   Does the application accurately identify the terms of the injunctive order or undertaking of which breach is alleged (CCR Ord 29, r 1(4A))?
>
> (ii)   Does the application 'list' (CCR Ord 29, r 1(4A)) or 'identify', separately and numerically, each alleged act of contempt (Practice Direction—Committal Applications, paras 2.5–2.6)?
>
> (iii)   Does the application clearly inform the respondent when and where he or she must attend to show reason why he or she should not be sent to prison?

The ways in which the party alleged to be in contempt is alleged to have committed the contempt(s) *must* be sufficiently clear to inform him or her what case he or she has to meet.

(2) Is the application supported by an affidavit as required by RSC Ord 52, r 4(1) and Practice Direction—Committal Applications, paras 2.5–2.6 and 3.1 or CCR Ord

29, r–1(4A) or a statement signed and declared to be true as required in the magistrates' court?

13.2.4 Service of the application to commit and the affidavit or statement in support

(1) Is personal service of the application and the affidavit or statement proved (in judge courts usually by an affidavit of service, in family proceedings courts by Form FL415) as required by RSC Ord 52, r 4(2), Practice Direction—Committal Applications, paras 2.5–2.6, CCR Ord 29, r 1(4) unless the court has dispensed with service under RSC Ord 52, r 4(3), CCR Ord 29, r 1(7), or has provided for alternative service under RSC Ord 65, r 4(2), CCR Ord 13, r 4(1) (alternative service is not available in magistrates' courts)?

(2)(a) In family proceedings, was personal service achieved at least two days, not counting Saturdays, Sundays or bank holidays, before the hearing, as required by RSC Ord 8, r 2(2), or at least two court office business days as required by CCR Ord 13, r 1(2) and Ord 1, r 9(4), unless the court has abridged time under RSC Ord 3, r 5(1), CCR Ord 13, r 4(1)?

(b) In civil proceedings, was personal service achieved at least 14 days before the hearing unless the court has directed otherwise (Practice Direction—Committal Applications, para 4.2)?

The Court of Appeal has emphasised the need for the county court to pay particular attention to the requirement that the hearing of the application should not be less than 14 days after service (*Turnbull v N Middlesbrough BC* [2003] EWCA Civ 1327).

13.2.5 Evidence

(1) Is there sufficient evidence to prove, to the criminal standard of proof, the alleged contempt(s)?

(2) Is/are the witness(es) relied on available for cross-examination?

13.3 Checklist 2: preparing for hearing following an arrest under a power or a warrant of arrest granted under s 47 of the FLA 1996 or arrest under a warrant of arrest granted under PHA 1997, s 3

13.3.1 Introduction: summary committal following arrest

Some practitioners and judges consider that upon production in court of an arrested alleged contemnor it is good practice to adjourn, to remand the respondent if the arrest was under the FLA 1996, s 47, and to expect the applicant to issue an application for committal. However, the FPR 2010, r 10.11(2) specifically authorises the established practice that when a person is brought before the court following an arrest under the FLA 1996, s 47, the court 'may (a) determine whether the facts, and the circumstances which led to the arrest, amounted to disobedience of the order, or (b) adjourn the proceedings ...' RSC Ord 94, r 16(5)(a) specifically authorises summary trial in the case of an arrest under the PHA 1997, s 3. Form N79, for recording a finding of contempt, specifically provides for proceeding on the basis of the respondent being before the court upon an arrest without there having been served an application for committal in Form N78, in the case of an arrest under FLA 1996, s 47, or in a claim form, in the case of an arrest on a warrant under the PHA 1997, s 3(5).

Where a person is arrested under either the FLA 1996, s 47 or the PHA 1997, s 3, and is brought before the court within the powers under the Acts, and there is sufficient evidence to proceed with a summary trial, and the arrested person is able to put his case adequately before the court, there clearly is power to proceed forthwith, without requiring preparation or service of a form of committal application. Further, there is no power to remand under the PHA 1997. Where the court does proceed forthwith without a form of committal application being prepared, the arrested person is before the court only for the matter upon which he or she has been arrested, previous alleged contempts are not before the court, and the court must be clear about what the circumstances of the arrest and alleged contempt are. Summary disposal in this way is convenient particularly where the respondent admits the contempt. Where he or she denies the alleged contempt, and he or she may need witnesses to support his or her denial, an adjournment will be appropriate.

13.3.2 Form of injunctive order

(1) Was the order one to which the court had power to attach a power of arrest under the FLA 1996, s 47? (There is no power under the PHA 1997 to attach a power of arrest.)

Section 47(1), FLA 1996, which enabled power of arrest to be conferred for breaches of non-molestation orders made under the FLA 1996 has been repealed (DVCVA 2004, Sch 10, para 38).

A power of arrest remains available in respect of breaches of occupation orders made under the FLA 1996. A copy of the order containing the power of arrest must be delivered to a police station in Form 406 (r 10.10(1) FPR 2010).

Where both a non-molestation order and an occupation order have been made, care must be taken to distinguish between them. Thus if an order prohibited a respondent from harassing the applicant by entering or going within 50 metres of her address then, although it may have been intended to have the same effect as an order simply prohibiting entry or attempted entry into the premises, its *form* is that of a non-molestation order made under FLA 1996, s 42(6) and a power of arrest cannot be attached to it.

In other words, was there evidence on which the court which granted the power could have concluded that the respondent had used or threatened violence against the applicant or a relevant child? If not, the arrest was unlawful and the respondent must be released.

In the case of arrest under a power of arrest, the 'relevant provisions', ie, the arrestable provisions and no other clauses of the injunctive order, should have been delivered to the appropriate police station in prescribed Form FL406: FPR 2010, r 10.10.

A power of arrest cannot be attached to an undertaking: FLA 1996, s 46(2); it must be an order, non-molestation or occupation.

(2) If the arrest was under a warrant of arrest, were there injunctive non-molestation or occupation provisions available as the foundation for a warrant, ie, provisions to which no power of arrest had been attached?

(3) Has the warrant been properly issued?

Warrants of arrest are still available for breaches of non-molestation and occupation orders (FLA 1996, s 47(8), as amended by DVCVA 2004, Sch 10, para 38).

The warrant must be substantiated on oath (FLA 1996, s 47(9)). The application for the warrant must be made in Form FL407. The warrant must be in Form FL408.

(4) If the warrant is sought for breach of an undertaking, was the undertaking properly received by the court?

Undertakings can no longer be accepted without some enquiry by the court. Thus, if a person denies the allegations of the applicant, but offers an undertaking, the court may not be able to accept it without hearing evidence and making a finding of fact against the respondent. This appears to be the effect of an amendment to FLA 1996, s 46 (DVCVA 2004, Sch 10, para 37). Section 3A has been inserted to provide that:

The court shall not accept an undertaking under s 46(1) (which allows undertaking to be given both in respect of non-molestation and occupation of premises) instead of making a non-molestation order in any case where it appears to the court that—

> (a) *the respondent has used or threatened violence against the applicant or a relevant child; and*
> (b) *for the protection of the applicant or child it is necessary to make an order so that any breach may be punishable under s 42A.*

An undertaking is enforceable to the same extent and in the same way as an occupation or non-molestation order (s 46(4)). And see generally **2.13–2.14**.

13.3.3 Service of the injunctive order

(1)(a) Is personal service proved, as required by RSC Ord 45, r (7)2(a), CCR Ord 29, r 1(2)(a) or FPR 2010, r 10.6?

Proof is usually by affidavit of service in judge courts and by Form FL415 in family proceedings courts. Note powers to dispense with service under RSC Ord 45, r 7(7) and CCR Ord 29, r 1(7) and see *Davy International Ltd v Tazzyman* [1997] 3 All ER 183 and *Jolly v Hull; Jolly v Jolly* [2000] 2 FLR 69. Where a respondent has been repeatedly required to comply with an order, it is unreal to argue that waiver of the requirement for service of further orders for compliance is in any sense 'retrospective'. To allow otherwise would be tantamount to encouraging persistent offenders to rely on technicalities to evade liability for contempt (*Benson v Richards* [2002] EWCA Civ 1402).

Or:

(b) Was the arrested person aware of the terms of the injunctive order either by being present when it was granted or by being notified of its terms?

If so, under RSC Ord 45, r 7(6) or CCR Ord 29, r 1(6) he or she may be dealt with for the matter for which he or she was arrested if it was something he or she was forbidden to do. The arrested person cannot be dealt with unless he or she was aware of the terms, because contempt involves disobedience and unless the respondent was aware of the terms he or she cannot be guilty of contempt.

13.3.4 The arrest

(1) In the case of arrest under a power of arrest under the FLA 1996, s 47(6):

(a) Was the operative period of the power of arrest, as recited in the injunction and prescribed Form FL406, still running at the time of the arrest?

(b) Was the arrest by a constable who had 'reasonable cause for suspecting' the arrested person of being in breach of a provision of injunctive order to which the power of arrest was attached (FLA 1996, s 47(6))?

If not, the arrest was unlawful and the arrested person must be released.

(2) **In the case of arrest under a warrant of arrest under the FLA 1996, s 47(8), (9):**

(a) **Were there injunctive non-molestation or occupation provisions available as the foundation for a warrant, ie, provisions to which a power of arrest had not been attached? and**

(b) **Was there evidence on oath before the court which granted the warrant on which it could have had reasonable grounds for believing that the respondent had failed to comply with the injunctive order or the undertaking?**

Note that there is doubt as to whether a warrant can be granted for breach of an undertaking given in proceedings under the FLA 1996, Part IV.

(3) **In the case of a warrant of arrest under the PHA 1997, s 3(3)–(5), was there evidence on oath before the court which granted the warrant on which it could have had reasonable grounds for believing that the defendant had failed to comply with the injunction?**

Note that a warrant cannot be granted for breach of an undertaking in proceedings under the PHA 1997.

13.3.5 The hearing

(1) **In the case of arrest under a power of arrest under the FLA 1996, s 47(6), will the hearing before the judge begin within the period of 24 hours beginning at the time of the arrest (no account being taken of Christmas Day, Good Friday or any Sunday) as required by the FLA 1996, s 47(7)(a)?**

If not, the proceedings are *ultra vires*, there being no power to detain the arrested person beyond the statutory period, and the arrested person must be released.

However, the court may remand the arrested person (FLA 1996, s 47(7)(b)) and adjourn the hearing to be resumed within 14 days of the arrest: FPR 2010, r 10.11(3). If the court does adjourn the hearing, the arrested person may be remanded (s 47(7)(b)) or released (FPR 2010, r 10.11(3)); where the court does adjourn, the arrested person must be dealt with within 14 days of the day on which he or she was arrested, whether by the same or another judge, and the person must be given not less than two days' notice of the adjourned hearing (FPR 2010, r 10.11(3). Personal service of the notice of the adjourned hearing should be effected, unless the arrested person was given notice before being released (see *Chiltern DC v Keane* [1985] 1 WLR 619 at p 622A).

If the arrested person is not dealt with within 14 days, FPR 2010, r 10.11(4) permits the other party to issue an application notice seeking committal for contempt and see: CCR Ord 29. r 1(4).

(2) **Following any arrest, is there sufficient evidence to prove, to the criminal standard of proof, the alleged contempt?**

13.4 Checklist 3: conduct of hearing of application for committal or following arrest under a power or warrant of arrest

13.4.1 Preliminary requirements

(1)(a) **If the application is made** (civil proceedings) **by Claim Form N208 or Application Notice N244 or** (High Court Family Division) **by summons or** issued (county court) in **Form N78 or** (family proceedings court) in **Form FL418, is breach of a specific, explicit (not implied) direction in an injunctive order or a promise in an undertaking alleged? And has the notice of application been served personally on the alleged comtemnor (RSC Ord 52, r 4(2), CCR Ord 29, r 1(4), PD Committal Applications, paras 2.5 and 2.6, two clear or office days before the hearing in family proceedings (RSC Ord 8, r 2(2), CCR Ord 13, r 2(2), CCR Ord 13, r 1(2) and Ord 1, r 9(4), or 14 days before the hearing in proceedings under CPR (PD Committal Applications, para 4.2)?**

(b) **Or, if the respondent has been arrested upon a power of arrest or warrant of arrest and brought before the court, was he or she arrested for an arrestable disobedience and, where arrested under a power of arrest, has the hearing begun within 24 hours of the arrest?**

And: *should the hearing proceed or should an adjournment be allowed to enable the case and evidence to be prepared?* FPR 2010, r 10.11(2), and (under the PHA 1997, CCR Ord 49, r 15A(7)) allow the court to deal forthwith with the matter upon which the respondent was arrested without service on him or her of a Notice to Show Good Reason or dispensation with this under CCR Ord 29, r 1(7). Alternatively, the court may adjourn proceedings for not more than 14 days. In proceedings under the FLA 1996 there is a general power to remand in s 47(7)(b) and (10) and power to remand for a medical report under s 48. There is no power to remand under the PHA 1997.

(2) **Was the respondent a party in the proceedings to whom the injunctive direction was ordered?**

With few exceptions, an injunctive order cannot be made against someone who is not a party. Query whether a non-party can give an undertaking without becoming a party.

(3) **Was the injunctive order (with a warning notice prominently displayed on the front (High Court) or penal notice endorsed or incorporated (county or family proceedings court)) personally served or, if it was prohibitory (not mandatory), was the respondent present when the order was made, or has he or she been notified of it?** (RSC Ord 45, r 7(6), CCR Ord 29, r 1(6), FPR 2010, r10.10.)

Or, was the undertaking recorded in county court Form N117, Principal Registry Form D787 or family proceedings court Form FL422 or, in the Chancery or Queen's Bench Divisions of the High Court, in a document in which the giver signed a statement to the effect that he or she understood the terms of his or her undertaking and the consequences of failure to comply with it in accordance with CPR, PD 40B, paras 9.3 and 9.4? *Was that document delivered to or served on or acknowledged by signature of the respondent?*

(4) **Was the direction or promise either:**

(a) **To do a specified act or specified acts at or before a specified time?**

If so, is the act one which the court has power to enforce by committal proceedings? Committal for contempt is not available, for example, to enforce payment of a money judgment (except where judgment summons is still available; see *Nwogbe v Nwogbe* [2000] 2 FLR 744 (CA)), or a declaratory order such as a defined pattern of contact with a child. *Also, was the order served before the time specified in the order for the act to be done, as required by RSC Ord 42, r 2(1), CCR Ord 22, r 3?* Or

(b) **To abstain from doing a specified act or acts?**

Note the powers to dispense with service under RSC Ord 45, r 7(6) (7) and CCR Ord 29, r 1(6) (7) and see *Davy International Ltd v Tazzyman* [1997] 3 All ER 183 and *Jolly v Hull; Jolly v Jolly* [2000] 2 FLR 69.

(5) **In the case of arrest under a warrant of arrest granted under the PHA 1997, s 3(5), has the person arrested already been convicted of an offence in respect of the alleged contempt?**

If so, he or she cannot be punished in contempt proceedings: s 3(7).

13.4.2 Trial procedure

13.4.2.1 Preliminary procedural points

(1) **Is the court following normal criminal procedure?**

If the court is embarking on a re-hearing after a previous hearing in the absence of the respondent, either because the court dispensed with service of notice on him or her or the court accepts that his absence was not his or her fault, the entire procedure must be followed. No shortcuts. Note that on a review on notice of a committal ordered in the absence of the respondent, the sentence cannot be increased.

(2) **In the case of proceedings under the FLA 1996, should the court remand, before or after deciding whether the contempt(s) is (are) proved, for a medical report under the FLA 1996, s 48?**

(3) **If the respondent is not legally represented, should a solicitor within the precincts of the court be invited to represent the respondent under the duty solicitor's scheme?**

(Regulation 8 of the Legal Advice and Assistance (Scope) Regulations 1989, SI 1989/550; reg 7, ABWOR representation might, by amendment to the Schedule, art 2(b), become available in family proceedings courts.) (Legal aid under the Legal Aid Act 1988, s 29 is **not** available for a person answering an allegation or breach of an injunction or undertaking.) See also *Re K (Contact: Committal Order)* [2003] 1 FLR 277.

13.4.2.2 Conduct of hearing

(1) **In civil proceedings under CPR, Part 8 and Practice Direction—Committal Applications, has the respondent filed affidavits giving any evidence in opposition to the committal application (Practice Direction—Committal Applications, paras 3.1 and 3.2)? But the respondent does not need permission to adduce oral evidence if he or she has not filed affidavits (Practice Direction—Committal Applications, paras 3.3 and 3.4).**

In family proceedings also it is good practice to file affidavits in opposition to a committal application.

(2) **Amendment of the committal application can be permitted by the court (PD Committal Applications, para 2.6.3).**

(3) **Does the respondent admit the allegation(s) and, if so, precisely what does he or she admit?**

The exact finding(s) of contempt will have to be recorded in the committal order (Form A85, High Court; Form N79, county court; Form FL419, family proceedings court). *Are the admissions adequate to enable the court to proceed to consideration of penalty without hearing evidence?*

(4) **Burden of proof on applicant.**

(5) **Normal sequence of evidence.**

Chief, affidavit or statement and/or oral; cross-examination; re-examination. Applicant and his or her witnesses first; respondent and his or her witnesses after. The alleged contemnor is not compellable as a witness at the instance of the applicant or the judge (*Comet Productions UK v Hawkex Plastics Ltd* [1971] 2 QB 67) and cannot be directed to give information (PD–Committal Applications, paras 6 and 7).

The privilege against self-incrimination applies in civil contempt proceedings: *Memory Corp plc and another v Sidhu and another* [2000] 1 All ER 434.

(6) **Respondent entitled to submit 'no case'.**

(7) *Actus reus* **and** *mens rea* **must be proved.**

Mens rea is knowledge of the injunctive direction plus deliberate conduct which in fact is a breach. It is not necessary to prove that the respondent understood the nature of the court's procedures provided he or she knew what was forbidden (*P v P* (*Contempt of Court: Mental Incapacity*) [1999] 2 FLR 897, CA).

(8) **Criminal standard of proof.**

(9) **Contempt(s) found proved must be specified and recorded in committal order.** (Form A85, High Court; Form N79, county court; Form FL419, family proceedings court.)

(10) **A finding of contempt should not be based on hearsay evidence.**

(*R v Shokoya,* The Times, 10 June 1992; *Re B* (*A Minor*) (*Contempt: Evidence*) [1996] 1 WLR 627.)

The defendant is not obliged to give evidence—if he or she has been cross-examined in connected proceedings, he or she may invoke the privilege against self-incrimination to be tried for contempt by a different judge (see *Re G* (*Contempt Proceedings*) [2003] Fam Law 471).

13.4.3 Consideration of penalty

RANGE OF POWERS AND APPROPRIATE APPROACH TO CHOICE OF DISPOSAL

The disposal must be proportionate to the seriousness of the contempt, reflect the disapproval of the court and be designed to secure compliance in the future (*Hale v Tanner* [2000] 2 FLR 879, CA, where the range of powers is summarised).

(1) **Does the contemnor wish to mitigate or attempt to purge his or her contempt?**

(2) **In family cases, does the applicant wish to give his or her views?**

(3) **Is the contemnor eligible for imprisonment being aged 21 or more, or eligible for detention being aged 18 or over and less than 21, or is no custodial sentence available the contemnor being aged less than 18?**

(4) **If available, is an immediate custodial sentence the only appropriate disposal? What alternatives are available?**

Note that there is no principle that 'a first breach [of an injunction] cannot result in a sentence of imprisonment'. Where the disobedience of an injunction or undertaking is serious, an immediate custodial sentence may be imposed (*Jordan v Jordan* [1993] 1 FLR 169; *Thorpe v Thorpe* [1998] 2 FLR 127).

General guidance was given by Hale LJ in *Hale v Tanner* [2000] 2 FLR 879:

(a) Imprisonment was not an automatic response to a breach of an order, although there was no principle that imprisonment was not to be imposed on the first occasion.

(b) Although alternatives to imprisonment were limited, there were a number of things the court could consider—especially where no violence was involved.

(c) If imprisonment was appropriate, the length of the committal should be decided without reference to whether or not it should be suspended.

(d) The seriousness of the contempt had to be judged not only for its intrinsic gravity but also in the light of the court's objectives both to mark its disapproval of the disobedience to the order and to secure compliance in the future.

(e) The length of the committal should relate to the maximum available, ie, two years.

(f) Suspension was possible in a wider range of circumstances than in criminal cases, and was usually the first way of attempting to secure compliance with the order.

(g) The court had to consider whether the context was mitigating or aggravating, in particular where there was a breach of an intimate relationship and/or children were involved.

(h) The court should consider any concurrent proceedings in another court, and should explain to the contemnor the nature of the order and the consequence of breach.

Where a person has been convicted of an offence under FLA 1996, s 42A for any conduct, he cannot be punished for that conduct as a contempt of court; conversely he cannot be convicted of an offence in respect of any conduct which has been punished as a contempt of court (FLA 1996, ss 42A(3) and (4)).

Where the maximum sentence for a contempt is two years' imprisonment, that length of sentence should be reserved for the worst possible case. In determining the length of sentence, two years must therefore be regarded as at the top of the scale of seriousness, and the case in question must be dealt with accordingly.

In cases of serious violence, an immediate custodial sentence is almost inevitable (*Wilson v Webster* [1998] 1 FLR 1097; *Ticehurst v Ticehurst* (1996) 10 CL 204).

5. **What penalty should be imposed for each separate contempt found proved?** *If more than one contempt, should penalties be consecutive or concurrent? Is the total appropriate?* The maximum total imprisonment that can be imposed on one occasion is two years in a judge court, two months in a family proceedings court. Sentences can be consecutive, including an implemented suspended sentence, but the total cannot exceed the maximum of two years or two months.

6. **Should imprisonment (of contemnor aged 21 or more) be suspended or should consideration of penalty be adjourned with liberty to restore? If so:**

   (a) **For how long?**

   (b) **What conditions should be ordered to define the event(s) which would render the contemnor liable to implementation or imposition of a penalty?**

The period of suspension or adjournment should be fixed, but an indefinite suspension can be valid: *Griffin v Griffin* [2000] 2 FLR 44 (CA). The power to remand an arrested person under the FLA 1996, s47(7) (10) is not available where the contemnor appeared in answer to a Notice to Show Good Reason, therefore the case law which established that sentence could not be deferred by remand in custody, after finding contempt proved, should still apply.

13.4.4 Preparation of the order of committal or other disposal

(1) **What should be recorded in the order of committal (Form A85, High Court; Form N79, County court; Form FL419, family proceedings court)? In particular:**

(a) **What precise findings of contempt?**

(b) **What precise terms of disposal have been ordered?**

Form N79 or Form FL419 should be checked and initialled by the judge or the chairman or bench of justices.

(2) **If an immediate custodial sentence is ordered, can the committal order be issued in time to be served when the respondent is detained upon the warrant of committal?**

In a county court, CCR Ord 29, r 1(5)(a) requires that the committal order be served when the warrant is executed, unless the warrant is signed by the judge; if the judge signs the warrant, 36 hours is permitted for preparation and service of the committal order (Ord 29, r 1(5)(b)). FPC(MP)R 1991, r 20(10) permits the committal order to be served within 36 hours after execution of the warrant.

13.4.5 Appeal

Where there has been a really substantial error leading to a demonstrable injustice to the victim of a contempt, the Court of Appeal can allow an appeal by the claimant and increase the sentence: *Manchester County Council v Worthington* [2000] 1 FLR 411, CA; *Wilson v Webster* [1998] 1 FLR 1097, CA. A contemnor contemplating an appeal should be warned that a sentence imposed for contempt can be increased. A sentence for contempt for breach of an order under FLA 1996, s 42 will not be increased on appeal unless it is shown to have been not merely lenient, but unduly lenient. Thus, where a husband subjected his estranged wife to 'an appalling history of intimidation and abuse' despite a series of proceedings taken against him under the PHA 1997 in the criminal courts, and under the FLA 1996 in the county court, the Court of Appeal regarded a sentence of four months' imprisonment as unduly lenient. A sentence of not less than 10 months was merited (*Lomas v Parle* [2004] 1 FLR 812).

The Court of Appeal has recently held that the level of sentencing for contempt associated with domestic violence in the older cases did not fully reflect contemporary requirements and opinion, which now demanded more condign deterrent punishments for such offences. Sentences in committal proceedings for breaches of injunctions under FLA 1996, s 42 should, so far as possible, reflect this range of opinion. The mere fact that a breach of a non-molestation order occurred in the context of a father wishing to have contact with his child was not in any way a mitigating factor; if anything, it was the reverse. As it was essential to have regard to the statutory maximum sentence of two years' imprisonment in Contempt of Court Act 1981, s 14. Subject to that caveat, sentences for breaches of injunction for harassment should not be discrepant with sentences for harassment under the PHA 1997. Similarly sentences for breaches involving violence or threats of violence should be congruent with sentences passed for similar conduct in the Crown Court. For an attack by a father on a grandmother involving verbal abuse, threats of violence, and physical assault by grasping her throat and forcing her onto the bonnet of a car, and three other instances of intimidation and abuse, a sentence of nine months' imprisonment was held to be the right level for a man of previous good character (*H v O* [2005] 2 FLR 329).

Index